A Front Row Seat at the End of History

The untimely essays of David Martin Jones and M.L.R. Smith, 1999-2024

Edited and introduced by M.L.R. Smith

Foreword by Jo Cohen Jones

© Michael Rainsborough

Published in 2025 by The Bruges Group

ISBN: 978-1-7390920-7-8

The Bruges Group Publications Office
246 Linen Hall, 162-168 Regent Street, London W1B 5TB
www.brugesgroup.com

Bruges Group publications are not intended to represent a corporate view of European and international developments. Contributions are chosen on the basis of their intellectual rigour, and their ability to open up new avenues for debate.

Scan me for Bruges Group

Twitter ✕ @brugesgroup, LinkedIn ⓘ @brugesgroup
GETTR ⓖ @brugesgroup, Telegram ⓣ t.me/brugesgroup, Facebook ⓕ @brugesgroup
Instagram ⓘ @brugesgroup,   YouTube ▶ @brugesgroup

'Well, neither did Thomas Hobbes'.

David Martin Jones, responding to a university interview panel on why he hadn't won any Australian Research Council grants.

A Front Row Seat at the End of History analyses comprehensively and rigorously the origins and consequences of the flight from reality that characterises liberal internationalism. In doing so it highlights the wish-fulfilment and hypocrisy of intellectuals and policy makers who it held in its sway. It should come as no surprise to readers that the authors should have paid a high price in reputational terms for their bravely expressed contrarian opinions, having been proved emphatically right by the turn of events.

Gerry Frost, writer and journalist

The End of History is the great lie of our age, its great de-intellectualising dogma; but even more mendacious is that our academics and administrators disassociate themselves from it, if pressed, with sly quips, when it is they who unleash this beast upon us. Someone had to drive a stake into the contemporary Western worldview, and it was Jones and Smith who undertook this quest.

Dr Eric Hendricks, sociologist and essayist

Jones and Smith are the best antidote to these times of universal deceit. This collection of essays is a must-read for all of us concerned for the future of our world.

Andrew T.H. Tan (PhD), Principal Fellow, Institute for Indo-Pacific Affairs, New Zealand.

A wonderful set of essays from two under-appreciated and underestimated voices. They are full of humour and prophetic insight.

Dr Joanna Williams, author and commentator

Contents

Acknowledgements	1
Foreword by Jo Cohen Jones	3
List of abbreviations	5
Glossary of non-English terms	7
Prologue: David, where the lion lay	9

1. Where modernity and tradition collide: The rise of Asia and the new front line of history — 15

Tigers ready to roar?	18
Identity politics in Southeast Asia	23
Islamists defeat the Asian way	27
Still active: *Jemaah Islamiyah* in Southeast Asia	32
The dragon stirs: China's long shadow	35
Can ASEAN ever solve the South China Seas dispute?	38
How Islamic State established a franchise in Southeast Asia	41

2. The war on terror misfires: Western illusions and self-deceptions — 44

The Kentucky Fried Chicken of global jihad	46
Costly delusions	49
Who knows spins	52
The rise of the neo-COINs	56
The strategy of savagery: Explaining the Islamic State	62
The delusions of counter-insurgency	67
A strategy of contradictions	71
Game of drones	74

3. Getting terror wrong: the follies of critical theory and radicalisation studies — 77

We're all terrorists now	79
Carry on empathising: The ISIS-crisis and Western political thought	88
How Western multiculturalism nurtures sacred violence	95
Can you talk to a death cult?	106
Crazy like a fool, wild about jihadi cool	108
Curbing enthusiasm: Radicalisation and fanaticism	110
Why deny? Terror stalks the academy	115

4. Globalist myths: Brexit and British power — 117

Brexit and the myth of European security	119
Orchestrating hooliganism: Russia, Britain and the EU	122
A trade strategy for United Kingdom Inc	125
Brexlit and the decline of the English novel	129
The Chinese Dream: China's challenge to 'Global Britain'	138
The European Union as the new Tower of Babel	142

5. The West's cultural revolution   147

When ideology displaces reason   150
College of fear   154
The West's Maoist moment   159
Terror in the Western mind: Carnage and culture   165
Misreading Mill: On liberty and vaccination   170
We need to talk about trans politics: An oppressed majority   172

6. History re-started:
Geopolitics and the revenge of realism   176

The return of the Machiavellian moment   180
Are we witnessing a return to *realpolitik*?   182
Apocalypse soon?   184
Putin's geopolitics: Making sense of the war in Ukraine   187
How does this end? Europe after Ukraine   192
At the Baal game: The World Cup and the clash of civilisations   195
The return of grand strategy in the Indo-Pacific   199

7. The right state of the union:
Democracy and dystopia   204

Making America miserable again   208
Democracy in the USA: Clarifying acts of violence   210
Democracy and dystopia: Part one – the intangible economy   213
Democracy dystopia: Part two – the revenge of politics   217
Contemplating phenomenology: UFO's, technology and religion   220
From axis of democracy to axis of hypocrisy   226

8. The endnote of history: Britain's terminal decline?   232

A Union without Faith or Law: Part one:
The post-Brexit game of thrones   236
A Union without Faith or Law:
Part two – global Britain or vanishing kingdom?   241
The 1970s weren't all bad   245
The suicide and conquest of Britain revisited   248
Woke Wales: From death to character assassination   251
Was the British Empire evil?   254

Epilogue:
A ballad of disenchanted modernity –
Reading *Woke* in Son Kul   257

Notes on authors   262

Index   263

Acknowledgements

This volume reflects the best part of three decades' worth of endeavour. Sadly, the passage of time and a fading memory as one advances in years means that it is impossible to recollect all of those who positively impacted our lives and who either directly or indirectly facilitated the work that appears in this book. Suffice to say, David and I were always gratified and often pleasantly surprised when our work was accepted for publication. My warm appreciation is extended to all the editors and staffs of the news outlets, journals, periodicals, think tanks and websites, who over the years were receptive to our ideas and who found merit in what we had to say. In that regard, I would like to recognise and thank the following titles that published the essays which feature in this book: *Cieo*, *Daily Sceptic*, *Daily Telegraph*, *European Conservative*, *Hungarian Conservative*, *Jane's Intelligence Review*, *Quadrant*, *Spectator Australia*, *Studies in Conflict and Terrorism*, *War on the Rocks*, *World Defence Systems*, *World Financial Review* and the *World Today*.

Inevitably, one's memory is skewed toward the present when reflecting upon who in one's life has played a central role in bringing this project to fruition. David's widow, Jo Cohen Jones, has shown immense fortitude in times of great anguish, giving genuine meaning to the term personal courage. Her determination to preserve her husband's intellectual legacy is a major reason why this collection of essays makes its appearance. Robert Oulds of the Bruges Group believed in this project from the start. Robert not only saw value in the production of this volume in its own right but following David's death he also felt it a fitting way to honour David's life and work, and for that, along with his patience and professionalism, I am immensely grateful. The support of Joanna Williams has also been invaluable to both Jo and myself. The independent think tank and online publication, *Cieo*, which Joanna founded, provided a forum for many of our essays. David and I appreciated Joanna's unyielding commitment to pluralism, free thinking and creative debate. A kindred spirit, we always felt in tune with her outlook, and I am equally grateful for her continuing efforts to celebrate David's memory.

As much as David and I became estranged from what passes for contemporary Western academia, there were always pockets of scholarly rectitude and sincere friendship that sustained us through our careers. Professor Arthur Aughey, Dr Andrea Benvenuti, Professor David Betz, Professor John Bew, Professor Alan Davison, Dr Ruth Dudley Edwards, Dr Andrew Erhardt, Dr Jules Gaspard, Professor Bruce Hoffman, Jasper Humphries, Dr Nicholas Khoo, Dr Anna Loufti, Dr Shiraz Maher, Dr Niall McCrae, Caroline Soper, Dr A.E. Stahl, Professor Andrew Tan, Dr Celeste Ward Gventer, and her husband Steve, and Dr Jonathan Woodier accompanied us metaphorically, but also sometimes literally, along the ramparts of the end of history. I thank them all for their solidarity and integrity. There are others whom I shall, out of a wish to preserve their good standing inside their institutions, not name so that they remain untainted by Jones and Smith adjacency. I trust they know who they are, and I hope they know how much we valued their support.

For myself, I am grateful to have survived the years with a modicum of dignity and for that I have to thank my wife, Lola and our daughter, Adela as well as my sister, Diane and her family, who provided a welcome relief from academic pursuits as well as being a constant source of love, support, encouragement and good advice.

Finally, and paradoxically, I would like to thank our adversaries. There were a few critics who challenged us openly in debate. No matter how much David and I disagreed and sparred with them, they lived up to their professional vocation and we respected them for doing so. Most however did not. These people I would not call intellectual adversaries because they never to my knowledge deployed any intellectual arguments against our viewpoints. Instead, they hid in the shadows.

We knew who most of them were, of course. Nevertheless, they too are to be thanked. Their relentless manoeuvring, their isolating tactics, their conniving, their secret denunciations, and their attempts at exclusion and intimidation, succeeded only in fortifying our resolve to press on. Genuinely, I am unsure whether we would have produced half our output were it not for their exertions to curtail our freedom to think and express ourselves.

Indeed, the efforts of these people always had a steeling effect, making us even more determined to expose the dark authoritarianism that lurks not very far beneath their machinations. David and I never conceived our writings as part of some moral struggle between darkness and light. We only ever set out to speak the truth as we saw it. But the more we ventured along the terrain of the end of history, the more we sensed that we were traversing an ancient road trodden many times before by people much braver than ourselves. Those courageous souls, from ancient times to the present, were our inspiration, and if this book represents one small paving along that road, then I hope it will encourage others towards an appreciation that the search for truth is not only its own reward but ultimately the only journey in life worth pursuing.

M.L.R. Smith

Foreword by Jo Cohen Jones

'TELLING IT LIKE IT IS' used to be the hallmark of honest, decent men. Today though, not only has the world polarised between what 'it' actually represents, in the halls of academe, on the pages of national newspapers and through the echo chambers of the internet, but the use of the word 'men' can now denote either an oppressive patriarchy or a misappropriation of gender.

My late husband, David Martin Jones, and his long-term friend and collaborator, Mike Smith, happily donned the mantle of manhood and dedicated themselves to the pursuit of what 'it' really is. To use one of David's phrases, this journey meant walking backwards into history, not stumbling blindly forwards into a wishful dream world of biblical towers that crack the sky and the incomprehensible babblings of hubristic elites.

The starting point of this compilation of essays, begun before David's death in April 2024 and completed by Mike, begins with end of history thinking when the world was united in a democratic love fest. No, David and Mike concluded. It's not like that. Informed by decades of observation in Asia and millennia of thinking from Thucydides and Aristotle through the prudential constructions of Machiavelli and Justus Lipsius, to the Asian financial crisis, the rise of jihadism, globalisation and Western self-loathing, they arrived at the gloomy prognostication, another of David's favourite words, of the necessity for multipolarity to achieve any balance of interests, however fragile. A failure to remember Adam Smith's phrase that there is 'much ruin in a union' is, they pointed out, to actualise the thinking of Samuel Huntington, where societies are 'cleft' by unintegrated immigrants and 'torn' by shifts in cultural identity.

I am delighted to write this foreword, because I know instinctively as so many readers also will, that Mike and David were onto something. The problem for them, and for those like me who recognise what 'it' is when we see it, those invested in the emperor and his new clothes cannot afford to give up their admiration. As someone asked David after he had spoken at a conference, 'Realism? Whatever gave you that idea?'

It is only recently, as world events have, tragically, evolved to validate much of Mike and David's work, that their thinking has transcended the excoriations of certain commentators and a 'rhetoric of silence' from the 'Academafia'. To a large degree, the two of them were able to retain their sense of humour. David's play with words, from the 'term "neurocracy" to describe Singapore's ruling class (politics + neuroticism)' and the Welsh 'Costa Geriatrica in the North and a Costa Bureaucratica in the South', to serious understandings of global phenomena including the term 'death cult' to represent the Islamist position that 'You love life, we love death', gives an accessible frame to inconvenient truths.

It is also true that readers will encounter David's predilection for esoteric nomenclature. As a former student pointed out, David insisted he replace the word 'theosophy' in his dissertation with 'soteriology', which he couldn't spell at the time and a publisher subsequently pointed out that he hadn't ever encountered it before. David, of course, enjoyed this. Readers will also encounter 'epigone', 'adumbrated', 'deracinating' and 'recrudescence', legitimised by the 'scholarocracy' whilst befuddling the 'ineptocracy'.

As Mike points out, however, David's passionate nature didn't do well with marginalisation. Whilst he would not kowtow to received wisdom and was consistently ahead of the game, foreseeing the dangers of political religions and the fragmentation that lay inside the wooden horse of progressivism, it was, to use the Chinese analogy, reflective of our current condition, a death by a thousand cuts. Whilst cancellation was not responsible for his actual death, those who protest too much about the exclusion and inequalities in our society would do well to examine their own consciences and avoidances.

To the readers of this volume, I would say, welcome to the uncompromising thought of scholars standing on the shoulders of those you know to be giants. You will recognise the snufflings of your own premonitions, to play with another of David's phrases, and with luck feel validated in your own refusals to succumb to diktats. Vale, David, and thank you, Mike.

List of abbreviations

AfD	Alternative für Deutschland, Alternative for Germany, conservative-nationalist political party
AIIB	Asian Infrastructure Investment Bank
APEC	Asia-Pacific Economic Cooperation
APT	ASEAN Plus Three
ARC	Australian Research Council
ARF	ASEAN Regional Forum
ASEAN	Association of Southeast Asian Nations
AUKUS	Australia, United Kingdom, United States, nuclear technology agreement
BBC	British Broadcasting Corporation, state-licenced UK broadcasting organisation
BLM	Black Lives Matter, American based anti-racist group
BRICS	Brazil, Russia, China, India and South Africa, an international economic cooperation organisation
CCP	Chinese Communist Party
CIA	Central Intelligence Agency
COIN	Counter-insurgency
COVID	Coronavirus Disease
CPTT	Comprehensive and Progressive Agreement for Trans-Pacific Partnership
DEI	Diversity, Equity and Inclusion
EEC	European Economic Community armed forces to preserve internal and external stability
EEZ	Exclusive Economic Zone
ESRC	Economic and Social Research Council, UK
EU	European Union
FBI	Federal Bureau of Investigation
FIFA	Fédération Internationale de Football Association
FTA	Free Trade Agreement
GAM	Gerakanan Aceh Merdeka, Free Aceh Movement, Indonesian separatist movement
GB	Great Britain
GDP	Gross Domestic Product
IMF	International Monetary Fund
IPCC	Intergovernmental Panel on Climate Change
IRA	Irish Republican Army
ISD	Internal Security Department (Singapore)
ISIL	Islamic State of Iraq and the Levant, known also as ISIS or Islamic State
ISIS	Islamic State of Iraq and Syria, known also as ISIL or Islamic State
ITV	Independent Television Network, national British television broadcasting company
MEP	Member of European Parliament
MGM	Metro-Goldwyn-Mayer, American film, television production and distribution company
MI5	Military Intelligence, Section 5, UK Security Service
MILF	Moro Islamic Liberation Front, Philippine separatists
MNLF	Moro National Liberation Front, Philippine separatists
MP	Member of Parliament
NALGO	National and Local Government Officers Association, British trade union organisation

NATO	North Atlantic Treaty Organisation
NGO	Non-governmental Organisation
NHS	National Health Service
NOB	Never Opened Book
NPT	Non-Proliferation Treaty
PAS	Parti Islam Se-Malaysia, Malaysian Islamic Party
PAP	People Action Party
PLAN	People's Liberation Army Navy
PRC	People's Republic of China
QUAD	Quadrilateral Security Dialogue
RAND	Research and Development Corporation, US defence think tank
SCO	Shanghai Cooperation Organisation
SNP	Scottish National Party
THAAD	Terminal High-Altitude Area Defence
UAE	United Arab Emirates
UAV	Unidentified Aerial Vehicle
UFO	Unidentified Flying Object
UMNO	United Malays National Organisation
UK	United Kingdom
UKIP	United Kingdom Independence Party
UN	United Nations
UNESCO	United Nations Educational, Scientific and Cultural Organisation
US	United States
USS	United States Ship
USSR	Union of Soviet Socialist Republics
WMD	Weapons of Mass Destruction

Glossary of non-English terms

Abu Sayyaf	Father of the Sword, Philippine based jihadist group
Al-Ma'unah	Brotherhood of Inner Power, Malaysian based Islamist Group
Al-Muhajiroun	The Migrants, jihadist grouping based in the UK and Saudi Arabia
Al-Nusra	The Victory, known also as the Al-Nusra Front or Front for the Conquest of the Levant, Syrian jihadist organisation
al-Qaeda	The Base, jihadist network founded by Osama bin Laden
Alternative für Deutschland	Alternative for Germany, German conservative-nationalist political party
Assabiya	Arabic term denoting tribal sense of social solidarity
Baal	Hebrew word for owner or lord
Blut und boden	German phrase meaning blood and soil, often associated with Nazi ideology denoting a racially purified realm
Chaebols	South Korea business conglomerates
Cosmion	Greek term meaning little world
Cyngor Gwynedd	Gynwedd Council, governing body for the county of Gwynedd, North Wales
Dabiq	Magazine published by Islamic State/ISIL
Darul Islam	Islamic sphere
Daulah Islamiyah Nusantaraan	Islamic archipelago/Islamic realm
Dwifungsi	Dual function, denotes commitment of the Indonesian armed forces to the country's external security and internal consolidation
Fateha	Malay activist grouping in Singapore
Front Pembela Islam	Islamic Defenders Front
Gerakanan Aceh Merdeka	Free Aceh Movement
Grossraum	German term for great space
Haute bourgeoisie	French term for high bourgeoisie or upper middle-class
Hizb-ut Tahrir	Party of Liberation
Indonesia Raya	Greater Indonesia
Inter alia	Latin phrase for among other things
Jahiliya	Condition of pre-Islamic ignorance
Jemaah Islamiyah	Islamic Congregation, Indonesian based jihadist group
Jus Europaeum Publicum	Latin phrase for European public law
Katechon	Greek word meaning that which holds, used to denote a biblical concept that is developed into a political philosophy
Katibah Nusantara	Katibhah Archipelago, a Malay unit within ISIL
Khilafah	Caliphate, or system of Islamic rule
Kiasu	Singaporean slang denoting a scared to lose mindset
Komando Jihad	Jihad Commando, Indonesian jihadist group
Kuffar	Islamic term for non-Islamic unbeliever
Kumpulan Mujahideen Malaysia	Malaysian Mujahideen Movement, Malaysian jihadist group, known also as Kumpulan Militan Malaysia
Intermarium	Geopolitical plan after World War I to unite Polish and Baltic lands

Mitteleuropa	Middle Europe, German term for Central Europe
Laogai	A Chinese term meaning reform through labour, a term denoting Chinese prison labour camps
Laskar Jihad	Warriors of Jihad, Indonesian Islamist militia
Lega Nord	Northern League, conservative Italian political party
Majlis Permusyawaratan Rakyat	People's Consultative Assembly, legislative branch of the Indonesian government
Meibion Glyndŵr	Sons of Glyndŵr
Mission civilisatrice	French term for civilising mission, a rationalisation for colonial expansion
Muhammadiyah	Followers of Muhammad, reformist Indonesian Organisation
Nahdlatul Ulama	Revival of the Ulama, Indonesian religious organisation, ulama refers to those who are learned in their knowledge of Islam
Nizam	Arabic word for order, arrangement or system
Nomos	Greek word denoting a law or convention of human Conduct
Novus ordo saeclorum	Latin term meaning new order of the ages
Organisasi Papua Merdeka	Free Papua Movement
Parti Islam Se-Malaysia	Malaysian Islamic Party
Périphérie	French word for periphery
Pesantren	Indonesian Islamic boarding schools
Plaid Cymru	Welsh term for Party of Wales, left-wing nationalist party
Pob sais	Welsh term meaning all Englishmen, generic term for English people
Prif Wienidog Cymru	Welsh term for First Minister of Wales
Ragioni	Italian word for reason
Raison	French word for reason, often used in conjunction with *raison d'etat* (reason of state)
Raison d'état	Reason of state, French phrase derived from Italian (*Dello Ragion di Stato*), denoting self-interested actions of the state
Rassemblement National	National Rally, right-wing French political party
Res publica	Latin phrase for public thing or public realm
Res publica Christiana	Latin term for international community of Christian people and states
Ria Novosztyi	Russian news agency
Silat	Set of martial arts originating in Southeast Asia, particularly Malaysia and Indonesia
Sogoshosas	Large Japanese trading companies
Tabula rasa	Latin term for clean slate, denoting absence of preconceived ideas
Thowbs	Traditional Islamic dress for men, also spelt thobes
Volkerrecht	German term for international law
Vox	Latin word for Voice, the name of a national conservative party in Spain
Vox populi	Latin phrase meaning voice of the people, a term used to denote the sampling of public opinion
Y Beibl	Welsh term for The Bible

Prologue: David, where the lion lay

THE OPPOSITE OF ANTHROPOMORPHISM, the assigning of human characteristics to animals, is zoomorphism, the tendency to attribute animal traits to humans. It's funny because I reflect that I always had a zoomorphic idea of my great friend, David. A shaggy, rather tame, but harmless lion was the image I had of him. His unkempt hair was redolent of a mane. He possessed also the slight gait of a lumbering Panthera. This is the picture I hold in my mind every time I recall David lolling towards me to shake my hand in greeting. It is the impression that I have of him as he waited patiently for my appearance at a café, sitting quietly but purposefully in a corner sipping his coffee: like a lion in repose on the savannah, surveying the scene before him. Was it a coincidence, too, that his astrological sign was Leo?

If the analogy continues to hold, David also possessed another characteristic of the metaphorical lion: courage. David exuded kindness and gentleness, but he was also intellectually brave. He was unafraid of going against institutionalised power and orthodoxy, often at some cost to himself. He had no time for the easy, often fake, radicalism inside the universities. A rigid, deeply conformist, progressive ideology began to envelop the Western humanities and social sciences in the 1990s. Later, of course, it was to escape into wider political and public discourse in the second decade of the twenty-first century. Examining the impact of this evolving ideology on Western thinking and policy came to absorb the attention of David and myself, and much of the content that came to shape this book.

The structure of incentives this discourse of ideological compliance promoted was a paradoxical construct. Inside the university it fostered a culture of paranoia and vicious power plays that gradually froze out anyone who was not in alignment, contradicting the very ethos of the university itself. Yet, for all its dark triad Machiavellianism, it also privileged a misguided, if intolerant, idealism that ignored sceptical, but realistic, appreciations of power and politics. Amongst other things, it was this distorted progressivist perspective that contributed to the misidentification of violent non-state threats and increasing authoritarianism at home and for costly failures of military intervention abroad: themes that comprise a substantial number of the essays in this volume.

Throughout our careers, both David and I observed that intellectual consistency and properly grounded scepticism is rewarded with predictive accuracy but not with career advancement. Our prognostications, be they about the shaky underpinnings of the pre-1997 Asian economic miracle, the rise of violent Islamist-inspired groupings, the bad assumptions of the so-called 'war on terrorism', the folly of Western military interventions across the globe, the rise of anti-elitist sentiments in Europe and North America, the re-assertion of geopolitical realities, and the increasingly gloomy prospects for secular societies in the West, all turned out to be more right than wrong.

Despite attaining degrees of predictive accuracy, going against the grain of academic and intellectual orthodoxy has a price. As the phrase has it, it is one thing to be seen as a troublemaker, but the even greater crime is to be proved right. And there were times when we were both viewed as the worst kind of thought criminals within our respective institutions and the broader academic realm in which we mostly functioned. We lost count of the times we had altercations with our self-anointed peers, who vociferously denounced us in the pages of academic journals, or who more usually practiced the 'rhetoric of silence', as David and I came to term our treatment in the pre-woke years before 'DEI' inspired initiatives codified the gaslighting and instituted more formal mechanisms of exclusion and cancellation.

We can't, of course, quantify the number of speaking or conference invitations we did not receive because of our known ideological deviancy, or the times our work was rejected by journals or book publishers, but the rhetoric of silence was undoubtedly practiced. It could be observed in the embarrassed caginess and reticence that would greet our dissident views when they were aired and a general lack of engagement from the rest of academe. But it could rear its ugly head in overt form. David and I enjoyed a spectacular lack of success procuring academic grants to support our work, but in the one case where we did obtain a small award, we had that stripped from us when we refused to toe the line that wanted us to extol Southeast Asia as a region of peace and harmony, which it wasn't, as later events would prove. Several times we were hauled up before our bosses, or in David's case his entire faculty, and implored to denounce ourselves in some absurd struggle session. In other instances, we were variously threatened with termination of employment and removed from positions of departmental authority when colleagues complained that our thought crimes, such as those that appear in this book, damaged their *amour propre*.

Although David and I sought to uphold moderation and civility in our dealings with others, we had no intention of renouncing the positions that we had, through a process of intellectual evaluation, honestly arrived at. We defended ourselves and welcomed robust debate with those who wanted to challenge our views. Candidly, though, we had no respect for people, especially those elevated to positions of undeserved authority in university bureaucracies, who believed they could brow beat us into submission with their vehement but incoherent opinions. If, as a result, a certain lack of professional elevation was our lot in life, we both considered it a price worth paying to retain our self-respect.

David died unexpectedly in London in April 2024, shortly after commencing work on bringing together this collection of our essays. Writing his obituary in *The Spectator Australia*, D.L. Dusenbury captured the essence of David's character, paying tribute to his fundamental integrity and intellectual courage as someone 'Loyal to his Welsh roots, fascinated by China, habituated to Australia, and committed to his inherited traditions of liberty. A realist, but never a cynic. A man of passion and conviction'. Although this volume did not set out to celebrate David's memory, it has inevitably become so and it is hoped that its appearance is a fitting testament to at least some of his life's work and his lasting intellectual legacy.

David and I first encountered each other in 1992 in Singapore – the Lion City, another coincidental twist. We were both lecturers at the National University of Singapore. David was in the Department of Political Science, and I was on the floor above in the Department of History. It would be wrong to claim that we were kindred spirits who immediately hit it off. Although very different in character and temperament, from an early stage we both sensed that we shared similar scholarly sensibilities: scepticism towards power and authority and a suspicion of fashionable convention. Our complementarities derived – I suspect – from our similar lower-middle class backgrounds and relative life experiences: his rough times teaching in the inner-city schools of London before embarking on an academic career, and mine from having recently gone through several years that brought me sharply into contact with the worst aspects of the Northern Ireland conflict. Our mutual experiences, we felt, marked us out from more orthodox academic trajectories.

It was in Singapore that David and I received our first taste of authoritarian duress. In 1994, both of us played a minor – and in my case quite unsuspecting – role in enabling another lecturer, Christopher Lingle, to flee across the causeway to Malaysia. Christopher had fallen afoul of the authorities for openly questioning the impartiality of the Singapore judiciary in the opinion columns of the *International Herald Tribune*. The result was that both David and I attracted the attention of the Internal Security Department (ISD – Singapore's secret police). Identified as part of a subversive liberal plot, David was trailed around the cafés and restaurants in the city, while a couple of goons sat in a white car outside my apartment for three weeks. It was petrifying at the time but all hilariously paranoid in hindsight. David and I developed the term 'neurocracy' to describe Singapore's ruling class (politics + neuroticism). Disconcertingly, David lived long enough to see this neurocratic approach becoming an increasingly observable characteristic of Western governance, especially during the era of COVID-19 between 2020 and 2021.

Our brush with Singaporean autocracy provided us with an amusing 'we have been oppressed' story to tell our friends. It also taught a valuable lesson that there was a cost in upholding a liberal commitment to free expression. Even so, we retained a residual regard for the success of the city-state and its broadly competent and effective governing class. It was in Singapore that our friendship was forged and in time an unbreakable writing partnership flourished that endured for three decades, right up to the time of his death, when we were still planning joint book projects together.

It was in Southeast Asia that both of us became fascinated with how the 'end of history' was playing out in the aftermath of the Cold War. The 'end of history' was Francis Fukuyama's thesis, first proclaimed in 1989, that the world was now in a post-ideological epoch and embarked on an inevitable path that would see the instantiation of a liberal world order. We were intrigued, however, why the depiction of Southeast Asia as a zone of peace and harmony by the region's political elites, and endorsed uncritically by a wide array of Western scholars, seemed at variance with what we saw taking place on the ground in front of our eyes in terms of the doubtful economic foundations of the Asian economic miracle, underlying inter-ethnic tensions and especially the increasing levels of Islamic observance we noticed in countries like Malaysia and Indonesia.

Consequently, from the mid-1990s our attention became focused on the evolving phenomenon of Islamism – political Islam. This kick-started our writing partnership and together we began authoring studies that examined the rise of jihadist activity and the growing influence of *al-Qaeda* (the Base) franchises in the region before the attacks on the United States on 11th September 2001. Much of our work was to appear in academic journals and books, but at an early stage, both David and I wanted to make our work more appealing to a wider audience through shorter essays and editorial pieces. It is these pieces of writing that constitute the bulk of the content of this book.

Since our writing journey sprang from our initial engagement with the East in its Singaporean and wider Southeast Asian manifestation, the first chapter in this collection begins with our assessments of the politics, security and economy of the Asia-Pacific in the aftermath of the 1997 financial crisis. This formative period sets the scene for chapter 2 as we move onto dissect the rise of jihadist violence in Southeast Asia, and the broader failings of the so-called War on Terror after 9/11, as the Western powers became drawn into damaging counter-insurgency operations to uphold an illusory liberal international order.

Our scepticism towards the rationales for the quasi-imperial adventures abroad after 9/11 was matched by our mounting distrust of much of the scholarly writings that purported to analyse the motivations of jihadist activism. This frames the theme for our essays in chapter 3. David and I adopted a strategic approach towards interpreting jihadist actions: that is, examining Islamist texts and determining their strategic intent from what jihadists themselves said they were doing. This set our writings against most mainstream terrorist studies and social science literature that wished to describe – or as we would maintain, explain away – jihadist actions with reference to unfalsifiable second order concerns like psychological problems, economic deprivation, mental illness and especially the self-lacerating assertion that Islamist-inspired violence was really all the West's fault.

As the 2000s wore on, David and I became increasingly interested in the signs pointing towards Western cultural nihilism that we detected in the early manifestations of the scholarly discourse on the question of Islamism. What we saw in the misplaced conformities and delusions that afflicted contemporary social science was the rise of political religions: the idea that the remorseless secularisation of Western societies – a particular trait of the end of history – was leading to the imposition of substitute temporal faiths.

Here a new clerisy, which often included academics, mainstream media commentators, politicians, civil servants and other members of the ruling caste, began to worship non-spiritual gods – regional or global institutions, economic miracles, liberal lifestyles, scientific and technocratic rationalism. It is the critique of these new political religions in the West that informs the essays in the succeeding chapters, 4 and 5. These chapters evaluate the political, economic and cultural questions that arose from Britain's democratic decision to leave the European Union. The ensuing 'revolt of the elites' evidenced in its aftermath, revealed itself in the collapse of integrity inside the universities, the COVID tyranny of 2020-2021 and the elite-driven cult of national and cultural self-negation.

The collective impact of the Western elite's turn towards cultural revolution and new political religion in the aftermath of the end of the Cold War, as well as two decades of the 'War on Terror' that followed, constituted a flight from geopolitical reality. These realities were to return to haunt the West, especially as it became clear that the Western powers were vulnerable to being outplayed on the world stage by the likes of Russia and China in an era that was witnessing the re-emergence of a multipolar world and competing civilisational forces. Most graphically demonstrated by Russia's invasion of Ukraine in February 2022, these forces are capable of further eroding Western power and prestige. These elements are explored in chapter 6.

The consequences of the erosion of Western pre-eminence for both the US and Britain are examined in the essays contained in the final chapters, 7 and 8, which reflect our growing pessimism for the near-term prospects for both countries under their current ruling establishments. However, these essays also hold out the possibilities for the recovery of Western purpose, self-confidence and democratic government through opportunities for political realignment, along with the remnant of scholarship still dedicated to proper standards of objective inquiry.

Selecting the essays for this volume necessitated some difficult choices. With one exception, the essay 'We're all terrorists now', which appears in chapter 3, it was decided not to include our lengthier, more academic, contributions that were published in scholarly journals. Instead, we focused on including our shorter essays that we hope are more accessible to a general audience. Even here, it has been necessary to exclude sixty to seventy percent of our output in order to eliminate areas of repetition and to offer the reader a digestible synopsis of our thoughts and writings over the years.

All the pieces included in this collection are reproduced in their original form with some minor exceptions. Changes have been made to ensure the standardisation of spelling and presentation to produce a uniform text, as well as occasional corrections of syntax to aid clarity. The titles of several essays have been amended to make them more concise, and in cases where essays contained references or endnotes, these have been eliminated, again to assist uniformity of presentation and readability.

In all other respects, the content remains unaltered, even when the passage of time has been less than kind to our original analysis. While our essays do, I would argue, demonstrate a degree of forecasting accuracy, I would not wish to claim that we were always prophetic or without analytical blemishes. Readers can discern for themselves where our assessments were far-sighted, flawed or left wanting. David and I were never swept up in the riptide of the end of history but we could occasionally be pulled by its undercurrents, especially by the 'unipolar' moment in Western foreign policy. In that respect, we were initially too forgiving of Prime Minister Tony Blair's rationale for going to war in Iraq in 2003, believing – naively as it, of course, turned out – that the British government would not intentionally lie about Iraq's possession of weapons of mass destruction and would at least have the competence and sagacity to possess a clear plan for occupying the country.

Disabused of both those assumptions in the aftermath of the invasion of Iraq, David and I came to doubt the entire ideological basis for Western 'forever wars'. We regretted not listening more attentively to wiser heads such as the veteran Australian commentator, Owen Harries, whom we knew tangentially, who prophesied exactly how disastrously such follies would unfold. We were remorseful for any part we might have played, no matter how minor, in contributing to an intellectual milieu that justified these human and political catastrophes. We found the experience of being wrong salutary but formative. We learnt, and imbibed Harries's unflinching foreign policy realism in all our subsequent thinking on geopolitics, and politics in general.

Shortly before he died, David and I discussed what title we should give this volume. We used to joke that we were 'cancelled before it became fashionable to be cancelled' and speculated that this would make a good title. We had long perceived the directions in which the modern arts, humanities and social sciences were heading. From the mid-1990s, we tried to call out the incoherent relativism, moral posturing, Western self-loathing and thinly disguised authoritarianism that lay beneath the veneer of intellectualism in these disciplines. That said, while it could be a lonely road to travel, we were never cancelled in any current understanding of the term. Certainly, we experienced the pre-woke variant of professional isolation and feeble attempts at intimidation. But, in the end, we didn't lose our jobs. We held onto our institutional positions and our voices.

'Always outnumbered but never outgunned' was the next possibility we considered. For sure, we were always swimming against the tide of fashionable opinion, holding our own against those who sought to take us on. The title seemed apposite but while we loved the alliteration, it sounded a touch too melodramatic. And in any case, we discovered it was the name of a 2004 album by the electronic dance band from Essex, The Prodigy. So, that title was abandoned.

Next, we came up with 'Untimely essays: We told you so, but no one listened'. In this, we were riffing off the apocryphal story about Robert Conquest, whose book *The Great Terror* exposed the enormity of death and suffering under Stalin's rule in the Soviet Union. Although much criticised at the time of its publication in the late 1960s by the great and good of Western literature for supposedly exaggerating the scale of the brutality, the opening of Soviet archives after the end of the Cold War fully validated Conquest's thesis. Consequently, when asked by his publisher to suggest a revised title for his monumental study he is said to have responded, 'I told you so, you f**king fools'.

Attractive though this option was, it was a stretch to even imply that we were in the same boat as the great Robert Conquest. No matter how perceptive or correct our writings might have been, we could hardly complain that no one listened to us. If we were siren voices warning of what might lie ahead, the fact is that most people exist in a condition of post-normal lag, dealing with harsh realities only when they arrive on their doorstep. Even then, many people only truly wake up when these unforgiving realities enter through the door, occupy the living room, squat in the kitchen and slap them in the face. Also, we could scarcely be said to have really suffered. We were both comfortably off. Neither of us took a bullet in the throat for our moral principles like our literary hero, George Orwell. Why, we thought, should anyone pay attention to the musings of a couple of wizened academics? After all, we were just spectators at the 'end of history'. Now… there's an idea for a title!

We held onto 'untimely essays' as a subtitle because, whether our writings were seen as oracular or not, we were undoubtedly out of sync constantly with our **academic conféreres**. As Dusenbury remarked in David's obituary, the 'simple realisation', which David had reiterated throughout our writings, that there is no intrinsic congruence between the liberal tradition and democracy, 'put him several disastrous decades ahead of most political commentators – and politicians – in the West'.

The delusion and distorted idealism of secular progressive faith are the fruits of those disastrous decades, and they constitute the main themes that run through the course of this book. Therefore, it is hoped that the reflections contained in these pages will help throw light onto our benighted condition, showing how we got here and where we are going. Sadly, David is no longer here to bring his erudition, curiosity and wit to bear, but perhaps his intellectual legacy can offer some signposts as to how we might be able to extract ourselves from our current predicaments.

Despite his unkempt, shaggy lion demeanour, David was, intellectually speaking, a major force to be reckoned with. As fellow protagonists endeavouring to tell it as it *is* rather than how it *ought* to be, we went through a lot of good and hard times together... Always outnumbered, but never outgunned.

While everyone who knew David is pained that he left us so early while he still had so much to give professionally and personally, I hope these essays bear testament to his intellectual legacy and in some way also convey what an honour it was for me to have been able to share a front row seat with him at the end of history.

M.L.R. Smith, Brindabella Range, Australian Capital Territory, May 2024.

1. Where modernity and tradition collide: The rise of Asia and the new front line of history

SOMETHING AS PORTENTOUS SOUNDING AS THE 'END OF HISTORY' suggests a rather abstract notion, the kind beloved by academics who can be happily left in obscure lecture halls to debate the concept into oblivion. But, for those who lived through the final years of the Cold War and who witnessed the Soviet empire's death throes between 1989 and 1991, the notion did possess tangibility. The sight of protestors tearing down the Berlin Wall with their own hands, or the velvet revolutions in Eastern Europe, was exhilarating to watch. Even the spectacle of Romania's despotic President Nicolae Ceaușescu and his equally repulsive wife, Elena, meeting their demise in front of a chaotic firing squad in January 1990 engendered a certain headiness and sense of expectation for a more optimistic future. The final capitulation of the Soviet Union and the expulsion of Saddam Hussein from Kuwait by a coalition of the willing in 1991 fuelled the sense that aggressors and dictators could be put to flight. US President George H. W. Bush, spoke of the dawn of a 'New World Order'.

American academic and political theorist, Francis Fukuyama, gave specificity to the contours of that New World Order. In *The End of History and the Last Man* (1992), Fukuyama posited the final victory of liberal democratic capitalism. Liberal democracy had vanquished its ideological competitors, fascism and communism. It had shown that freedom and democracy could prevail over dictators and autocrats. It had proved to be the final stage of political evolution. Great ideological struggles were no more. The superior system had won. *History*, in the grand political sense, was over.

What was left of politics in the post-Cold War era, according to this line of thinking, was the necessary effort by enlightened Western progressives to facilitate the transition of the global system into a single harmonious polity that extolled the virtues of free-trade, open markets, universal human rights, individual self-expression and liberal modes of governance. This was the so-called rules-based international order.

In the early 1990s a lack of academic job prospects in Europe, combined with a lingering sense of adventure, meant that David and I found ourselves in the Orient on what was to become one of the paradoxical front lines of the end of history. It was paradoxical because, on the surface, modern Southeast Asia was a flourishing testament to Fukuyama's thesis. The region was a remarkable success story with nearly three decades of unprecedented economic growth based on relatively open economies and presided over by a benign American hegemon. Peace, harmony and cooperation characterised relations among the Southeast Asian nations. Commentators spoke of the Pacific Century, economic miracles, and the rise of the Asian tigers.

Yet, beneath the surface, all was not what it appeared to be. The success of the 'miracle economies' was not entirely a mirage. The skyscrapers and the vitality of the modern cities of Singapore, Kuala Lumpur and Bangkok were proof of a region that had undergone a remarkable transformation. Even so, David and I had an interest in economics, and we were intrigued by what we felt was a great deal of overblown rhetoric about the region's longer-term prospects. Attuned to the idea that economies proceed in cycles, we wondered about the sustainability of the Pacific Century. The more we looked, the more we thought that much of the miracle growth was built on property speculation and opaque government-business dealings. The façade of modernity, to us, seemed to disguise some very traditional practices. This clash of modernity and tradition did not portend well.

Of equal curiosity was how Western commentary viewed the evolving Pacific Century. Much of this commentary tended to read into the Asian economic miracle what it wanted to see, and that was an end of history telos. American pundits, especially, asserted that Southeast Asia vindicated the capital friendly, free-market growth model. These assertions were an extension of 'modernisation theory'. Deriving from the hypotheses of American political science, modernisation theory held that economic development inevitably presaged democratisation. Rising living standards would drive an expanding middle class to demand more openness and accountability from their political masters. David was sceptical of the applicability of this idea to traditional Asiatic understandings of politics and governance. He made his first distinctive imprint on political theory by contesting the democratisation thesis, arguing that Southeast Asian polities were 'illiberal democracies', where the rising middle classes were not a force for change, but a force for the consolidation of the status quo.

It was in the hubristic assumptions that underpinned the democratisation thesis, moreover, that the tensions in the notion of the end of history were to become apparent. And they were to reveal themselves first in Southeast Asia, where David and I had somewhat accidentally materialised.

The belief that nations were embarked on a remorseless liberalising trajectory antagonised the region's political aristocracy. Talk of human rights, freedom overcoming autocracy, and the superiority of liberal democratic values began to sound a lot like Western arrogance and a new informal imperialism. Leaders in the mould of Lee Kuan Yew, the formidable ex-Prime Minister of Singapore, and Mahathir Mohamad in Malaysia, openly contested the universalising claims inherent in the rhetoric of the liberal end of history. Instead, they posited the superiority of 'Asian values', which upheld the virtues of tradition, family and collective solidarity, against the individualising claims of Western cosmopolitanism.

David and I were yet to develop our thoughts fully, but we were later to perceive that the assumptions underlying the modernisation/democratisation thesis intimated less a well-thought-out theory of political development but rather an ideology: a new political religion, which was to become a notable characteristic of secular progressive faith in the post-Cold War epoch. What we did notice at the time was the growth of actual religious observance in the region. Remarkably, the more the countries of Southeast Asia prospered and assumed the outward façade of liberal modernity in their cityscapes and commercial centres, the more it appeared to generate a reaction and a return to tradition amongst a sizeable section of the populace. Most notably, this reaction appeared to be occurring within Islamic communities in particular.

Amongst our students, we detected greater numbers of women taking up the wearing of the hijab and men attending the mosque. To us at least, this presented a puzzle. Modernisation theory promoted the opposite hypothesis: the more societies developed economically, the more secular, materialist, liberal and democratic they would become. Yet, in Southeast Asia, increasing levels of devotion to Islam seemingly represented a response to modernity, an act of resistance against the secularising expectations of the end of history. Although we did not know it then, what we were witnessing were the emerging economic, political and cultural fissures in the New World Order.

In the summer of 1999, David and I embarked on a somewhat anarchic road trip from Singapore to Malaysia. I was still based in Singapore, and we ventured northward through the disconsolate hinterland of the Malay Peninsula in the years and months following the 1997 financial crash that brought the Pacific Century to a juddering halt. Journeying along Malaysia's near deserted highways via its 'Touch n'Go' automated toll roads, we came to think that this was more an ironic allegory for the region's faltering economic prospects. Passing through landscapes dotted with abandoned housing developments and derelict commercial sites, we ventured into Kuala Lumpur where we met with several dejected executives of the Hong Leong bank, an enterprise that was shortly to be folded into a re-structuring that was to bind it into the web of Malaysia's ruling party.

Our assessment of the prospects of Southeast Asia's economic rejuvenation in the wake of the 1997 financial crash thus constitutes the starting point of our investigations into what was to become one of the first ideological battlegrounds of the end of history. In the rupturing of Southeast Asia's growth model, we observed the fragmentary forces that lay not very far from the surface: burgeoning social and economic problems, internal ethno-religious tensions, and hostility and suspicion amongst neighbouring countries, not the least of which was the spread of a sophisticated Islamist terror network across the region. These problems are explored in the essays in this chapter, where we dissected as diligently as we could, the reasons for this fragmentation.

As we progressed into the early years of the twenty-first century, we began to probe the geopolitical implications of an increasingly assertive China, following its admission into the end of history guild. China's entry into the World Trade Organisation in 2002 was regarded by many commentators as a sign of the country's acceptance of the 'rules-based international order'. It seemed evident to David and me, as several of the later essays in this chapter argue, that the only 'rules' that China was willing to observe, were its own. China was a stirring dragon that was intent on bending the states of Asia, and the mechanisms of regional diplomacy like the Association of Southeast Asian Nations (ASEAN), towards its own interests, exerting its power and influence as a rising economic, political and civilisational force in world affairs.

Welcome to the frontline of History.

Tigers ready to roar?

Over the past two years, students of East Asian political economy have been struck by the rapid mood swings in their area. A wander through a Singapore bookshop in 1997 would have offered titles like *Negotiating the Pacific Century*, *The New Rich in Asia: Mobile Phones, McDonald's and Middle-Class Revolution*, or *The New Asian Renaissance*. A year on, these volumes, if not on special offer, have given way to titles like *Asia Falling* or *The Downsizing of Asia*, often by the same authors.

From being miracle economies demonstrating a variety of good practices – long-term technocratic planning, high domestic savings rates, good basic education, low or non-existent welfare costs and close government-business links – they have been transformed into basket cases.

Former virtues have become structural defects. Far-sighted planning became market distortion, hiding cronyism between government and business conglomerates. In the deep recession, even high savings rates look like a drag on consumption, whilst good basic education appeared like initiative stifling rote learning.

Between 1997 and 1998, Asian values turned into Asian vices and the Asian miracle looked about as authentic as the Turin Shroud. Stock exchanges from Seoul to Jakarta took an uninterrupted journey south.

Then something curious happened. In the first quarter of this year, Japan awoke from its decade-long recessive slumber, Asian economies returned to pre-crisis growth rates, trade balances swung back into surplus and the recession if not just a blip, looked like something that could be shrugged off.

What went wrong?
There are two explanations for the crisis, which began in Thailand in June 1997 with what Paul Krugman describes as an outbreak of 'bahtulism'. On the one hand, the less fashionable and market unfriendly school, led by Malaysian Prime Minister Mahathir Mohamad, backed by an otherwise unsympathetic bunch of supporters ranging from George Soros to Gordon Brown and former Indonesian dictator Suharto, believe that it was a product of deregulated global capitalism.

Having opened their markets to global trade in the 1990s, the new boys on the international currency trading block – South Korea, Malaysia, Thailand, Indonesia and even financially streetwise Singapore and Hong Kong – were the innocent victims of a brutal mugging by a gang of spiv hedge funds and futures traders from New York, Chicago and London. From this perspective there was little wrong with Asian development that a few lessons in central banking and sovereign bond floating wouldn't fix.

The alternative, and until recently more popular hypothesis, held that it was the structural features of the Japanese sponsored Asian economic model that caused meltdown. In this view, current account deficits, a speculative property boom, short-term borrowing to fund long-term investment and poor banking and financial regulation, which ran the spectrum from the inept and opaque to the fraudulent and corrupt, were major structural faults.

In 1997, world markets severely punished these defects. By mid-1998, currency contagion had left the region in turmoil with little to show for its vaunted developmental path apart from a profusion of under-patronised high-rise hotels, unfinished office blocks and golf courses.

This academic disagreement has important political and economic ramifications because the cause of the crisis affects how state and international organisations like the International Monetary Fund (IMF) deal with its consequences. If Dr Mahathir's diagnosis is correct, and the medically trained doctor informs us that he is rarely wrong, the prescription is a bit of rest and recuperation behind a wall of currency controls until the market returns to reason.

The cure lies not in the reform of the Asian model but in the building of a new global financial architecture.

The IMF diagnosis, by contrast, requires a rigorous examination of the body politic, the excision of the cancer of corruption inherent in the intimate nature of business-government dealings, and the oxygen of rule-governed transparency supplied through the machinery of public accountability.

Ultimately, this implies a political and economic makeover rendering the rule of strong men and single parties accountable to the constitutional rule of law. Indeed, those most entranced by the prospect of the imminent demise of the Asian model have argued that the economies that successfully weathered the crisis were those that had made some strides along the apparently endless path of democratisation.

Let us briefly examine the apparent easing of the crisis and consider its implications for future economic and political developments.

Scenario 1: Miraculous recovery

Between 1997 and 1998, according to the World Bank, $115 billion fled the Asia-Pacific region. This was equivalent to 28 per cent of the region's Gross Domestic Product (GDP). Significantly, Japan, the pioneer of the Asian model, was both the major creditor of the ailing tiger economies and sent 40 per cent of its exports to Pacific Asia. Moreover, between 15 and 25 per cent of the exports of the meltdown economies went to a deflating Japan.

As regional trade accounted for almost a quarter of the total trade of these export-oriented economies, lower consumer confidence in each receding Asian tiger affected the export performance of its neighbour. After the currency panic of the summer of 1997, what seemed like a virtuous Asian circle of high savings and state engineered growth, turned into a recessionary spiral.

Remarkably, by the second quarter of 1999, currencies had stabilised, and growth had returned. Even the region's weakest economy, Indonesia, was showing some signs of life whilst the most successful Asian bounce back economies have grown by over five percent.

If the overused epithet 'miracle' must be applied to the tiger economies, it should surely refer to this remarkable rise from the dead rather than the unsustainable growth in the 1980s. Regional stock markets have surged ahead, in the case of Singapore and Taiwan, surpassing pre-crisis levels.

Meanwhile, business confidence in Japan has risen sharply after a decade in the doldrums. South Korea's banks have posted $500 million in profits compared with losses of $600 billion the previous year and future growth is forecast at six percent.

From the perspective of Mahathir and his favourite economist, Paul Krugman, the recovery can be attributed to re-imposed monetary stability. Except for the Hong Kong dollar and the Chinese yuan, all the regional currencies were devalued because of hedge fund speculation and capital flight. Once the speculative dust settled and illiquid conglomerates and banks re-hydrated courtesy of the IMF, these economies could revert to the classic growth path.

Consequently, from Japan through South Korea to the Malay peninsula, imports have declined, and exports have grown because of their increasing affordability. Thus, Malaysia, Thailand, South Korea and Indonesia have all seen their ballooning trade deficits for 1993-97 reversed in the fiscal year 1998-99. At the same time, budgets have been balanced and investor confidence restored, foreign investment funds have even returned.

From this monetary perspective, severe alterations to Pacific Asian economic fundamentals are unnecessary. Here, the Malaysian case is salutary. In September 1998, Mahathir sacked his market friendly deputy, Anwar Ibrahim, and imposed both currency controls and restrictions on the movement of foreign investment funds from the Kuala Lumpur Stock Exchange.

To a chorus of international disapproval – including Amnesty International, Presidents Habibie of Indonesia and Estrada of the Philippines, *The Business Times* (Singapore), *The Economist* as well as US Vice-President Al Gore – Malaysia's National Economic Action Council used the state apparatus to impose currency controls to restore financial stability and address foreign debt without recourse to the IMF.

Malaysia 'looked East' for liquidity. Japanese loans, together with judicious raids on the state pension fund, provided the capital necessary to re-float faltering conglomerates linked to UMNO (United Malays National Organisation), Malaysia's ruling party.

Furthermore, in August 1999, the Malaysian Central Bank announced plans to restructure Malaysia's indebted financial sector, combining 58 banks and finance companies into six financial groups. Interestingly, this compulsory restructuring only reinforced the corporatist links between the ruling party and business. For the terms upon which banks were amalgamated depended not upon their bottom line but their ties to politically favoured UMNO patrons.

Fuelled by a cheap currency and external demand for electronics, the Malaysian economy rebounded strongly in the second quarter of 1999. Moreover, when investment restrictions in Malaysia were lifted in September, foreign investors seemed happy to remain.

Malaysia's exceptionalism did not see it reduced to regional pariah. Indeed, Mahathir maintains that those economies that had recourse to the IMF received inappropriate treatment. For alongside a necessary infusion of liquidity, Thailand, South Korea and Indonesia had to accept contradictory and often humiliating strictures on interest rates and debt restructuring. These made the recession and its political consequences far worse than it need have been. If little else, the Malaysian case demonstrates that, structural weakness notwithstanding, the developmental model could survive the challenges of globalisation.

Scenario 2: Rationalise, not reform
Those less enamoured of Asian development argue by contrast that although Asia is certainly recovering from the very deep recession of 1997-98, structural problems continue. In this view, the initial panic was justified because of the undisclosed debt, cronyism, unaccountability and corruption from Japan to Jakarta.

The concern is that the recent 'bounce back' is unsustainable and obscures the urgent need for fundamental financial and political reform such as the restructuring of economies to ensure their long-term viability.

Short-term currency depreciations may give the likes of Thailand and Indonesia a renewed, but brief, lease of life as low-cost manufacturers, but thorough supply side reforms in areas like education, training and financial regulation are absent.

Radical economic restructuring requires the break-up of the crony capitalist relationships between businesses and their political friends in government. In the heady days of rapid economic growth, it was sometimes maintained that the cosy arrangements of informal deal making, preferential loans and *guanxi* (patronage networks) connections were the lubricant of the Asian miracle. A recent survey by Harvard University's Center for International Development challenges this, arguing that the most significant feature of 'Asia's spectacular growth over the past several decades' was that it had been able to hide 'a host of inefficiencies'.

Despite the shock of the meltdown, and the strictures of the IMF, there has been little fundamental change in local business culture and practice. In Thailand, the inadequacy of bankruptcy provisions permits technically insolvent businesses to continue trading. The courts are unable to enforce foreclosure and indebted companies refuse to repay loans.

In Indonesia, the most financially and politically damaged economy in the Asia-Pacific, IMF loans uncannily end up in the accounts of banks linked to the party of incumbent President Habibie.

Even in South Korea, reform minded President Kim Dae Jung has been compelled to investigate the country's five main *chaebols* (business conglomerates) on suspicion that they are extending illegal preferential loans to their subsidiaries.

Meanwhile, the bureaucratic restrictions placed on Western banks or companies taking over ailing South Korean concerns raise continuing doubts about the commitment to reform. The fact that the government permits conglomerates like Hyundai and Daewoo to sustain debt levels exceeding $50 billion and debt/equity ratios over 350 per cent indicates that the latest variant of the South Korean economic model is not driven by market considerations. The Asian model has been rationalised rather than reformed.

Interestingly, then, whether we diagnose the causes of the Asian crisis from the perspective of Mahathir or the IMF, we can show that apart from some judicious financial tinkering, the basic Asian model and its export-oriented character have not changed. Does this lack of structural reform matter?

Clearly, the Asian model was not quite the basket case it seemed in 1997. Problematically, however, the surge in exports from the region, whilst masking structural faults, is also causing new problems.

The pattern of Asia-Pacific trade has always been unbalanced. Japan has always assumed that it can protect its domestic markets while exporting high value-added technology. Since the 1980s, Japanese firms transferred labour intensive manufacturing to countries like Thailand and Malaysia.

The market for all this manufacturing continues to be the United States. Indeed, the strength of the US economy and the openness of its market has been central to Asia's recent recovery. The unexpectedly high demand there has single-handedly revived the flagging electronic industries on which Thai, Malaysian and Indonesian growth depends.

Asian currencies are reviving along with their trade surpluses. Japan achieved a trade surplus of $118 billion to the end of March 1999. To sustain this, the Japanese Central Bank intervenes in the foreign exchange markets to keep down the value of the yen. Other countries, like Singapore, have intervened in money markets. However, the US no longer accepts that 'manipulating currencies' can produce long term prosperity. Given that the American economy has recently incurred record trade deficits, and its growth is likely to slow, this could threaten the basis of Asian recovery and be a precursor to new trade disputes.

Moreover, in the meltdown, Japan lost its regional economic influence. Japanese banks were the first to take fright at the Asian contagion and their *sogoshosha* (large trading companies) are reluctant to return. Mahathir's continuing infatuation with a 'look East' policy notwithstanding, Southeast Asian economies have become increasingly dependent on America and Europe for new foreign investment. This will ultimately alter the economic and political character of Southeast Asia.

In fact, the meltdown and recession have already dramatically altered the international perception of Southeast Asia. Prior to the crisis, it was plausible to speak of common development patterns with export-oriented growth dependent on Japanese investment, technocratic planning, single party rule and a governed labour and domestic market. Since 1997, the strategies adopted to deal with the meltdown have created distinctive differences in the region's political economies.

Thus, whilst Singapore reformed its banks, Thailand and then Indonesia invited the IMF to sort out their finances, Malaysia imposed currency controls and prohibited the repatriation of foreign funds invested on its stock exchange.

Whilst Thailand moved tentatively to open its government as well as its domestic market, Malaysia witnessed acrimonious factionalism in the ruling party, culminating in the trial and imprisonment of Mahathir's erstwhile successor Anwar Ibrahim. Indonesia imploded politically as well as economically.

The fact that the largest country in the region, after China, is politically fragmenting because of its uncertain democratisation has exposed the incoherence of Asia-Pacific regionalism and its much-extolled multilateral security approaches. The Association of Southeast Asia Nations (ASEAN) is notable only by its absence from the anarchy. One of the few areas in which President Bill Clinton and Mahathir seem to agree is the irrelevance of the once heralded Asia-Pacific Economic Cooperation (APEC) forum and its vision of a regional free trade area.

There are signs of East Asian economic rejuvenation. However, with several of its key elements punctured by the crisis, the direction in which the Asian model moves can no longer be as smoothly interdependent and export oriented as it was in the growth era.

Ironically, the failure to develop internal or external rule-governed procedures during the good times, has left Asian states and the regional arrangements they formed weak, unstable, and increasingly vulnerable to the machinations of the global marketplace.

Original version published in *The World Today*, Vol. 55, No. 10, October 1999, by David Martin Jones and M.L.R. Smith.

Identity politics in Southeast Asia

Less than four years ago Southeast Asia epitomised the coming Pacific Century. During the miracle decade of 1985-1995, the booming tiger economies of this ethnically and religiously diverse region seemed to have achieved double-digit growth accompanied by harmonious political balance. Three years after the Asian financial crisis of 1997, this Asian renaissance miracle seems increasingly remote.

Between 1975 and 1997 Asian diplomats and scholar-bureaucrats gave the region's most prominent organisation, the Association of Southeast Asian Nations (ASEAN), the credit for underpinning economic growth and security. Regional analysts maintained that ASEAN's uniquely consensus-oriented diplomatic style, based on non-interference in the internal affairs of member states, had successfully reconciled former adversaries in the region. The financial meltdown and its aftermath, however, cruelly exposed ASEAN's limitations. In practice, the organisation had merely succeeded in using economic growth to ameliorate, rather than solve, problems among its members.

As the region changed from being an economic miracle to a region in need of one, many previously suppressed ethnic and religious tensions bubbled to the surface. For example, on the Malay peninsular the fraught relationship between Muslim Malaysia and the predominately Chinese city-state of Singapore degenerated into bickering over everything from water supplies to the location of customs facilities. This breakdown in relations reflected an emerging pattern of discord across the region that threatens to unravel the already uncertain state boundaries of Southeast Asia.

Inner turmoil
The 1997 crisis revealed the internal fragility of many Southeast Asian states and the relative failure of three decades of nation-building efforts. The rising incidence of low-intensity civil wars in Indonesia, Malaysia, the Philippines and Thailand is evidence of this failure. Two distinctive and in some ways contradictory forces particularly threaten the fabric of the state: rising Islamic fundamentalism; and the impact of globalisation.

The recent activities of the Islamic separatist group, *Abu Sayyaf* (Father of the Sword), exemplify this phenomenon. In April 2000 *Abu Sayyaf* seized 21 tourists from the Malaysian island of Sipadan and held them hostage on the neighbouring Philippine Island of Jolo. Following the payment of ransoms – estimated at US$1 million per hostage – the Malaysian, French and German nationals were freed four months later.

This interaction between international tourism and ethno-nationalism has extorted high political costs. International pressure required the essentially Catholic Philippine Army to abandon, at least provisionally, its crusade against Moro Islamic separatism in southern Mindanao. Also, the large influx of US denominated ransom dollars has distorted the local economy: at one stage the Philippine peso was worth 3 per cent more in Jolo than in Manila. The notoriety of *Abu Sayyaf* and its new-found wealth has swelled rebel ranks and enhanced its capacity to purchase arms on the international black market.

Abu Sayyaf was not an isolated result of post-crisis Southeast Asia. The ASEAN region was never harmonious. Since the late 1960s the Malaysian government has periodically offered tacit support to Muslim separatist organisations in southern Mindanao and Pattani in southern Thailand, aggravating Malaysia's relations with Buddhist Thailand and the Catholic Philippines in the process.

The spread of the new terror
Low-level ethno-religious conflicts in northeastern and southern Thailand, the southern Philippines and across the Indonesian archipelago have proved intractable since decolonisation. Before 1997 ASEAN's political élites assumed that

economic growth would cause communalist sentiment to wither. This assumption has proven unfounded.

The growing influence of Middle Eastern Islamic theory upon the moderate, syncretic, Islam practised in the region also threatens to undermine nation-building. Emergent millenarian Islamic sects, like *Al-Ma'unah* (Brotherhood of Inner Power') in northern Malaysia and *Abu Sayyaf* in southern Mindanao, now disrupt relations along the Thai-Malaysian border and in the Philippine-Malaysian maritime frontier zone.

What is striking about these groups is that they represent a new style of terror, operating globally and locally. American analysts Steven Simon and Daniel Benjamin argue that the new terror 'neither relies on the support of sovereign states nor is constrained by the limits on violence that state sponsors have observed themselves or placed on their proxies'.

The significant feature of this religiously driven terror is its non-negotiable and fundamentalist character. The new radicalism functions through international religious networks rather than through the Cold War mechanism of sponsor states. According to analyst Olivier Roy, the aim of the proponents of the new terror is to wage jihad to reconstitute the Islamic community beyond national or ethnic divides.

Paradoxically, to draw attention to their local plight the 'new terrorists' depend on globalised communication As Roy observes: 'They recruit among uprooted, cosmopolite "deterritorialised" militants, themselves a sociological product of globalisation. In their use of English, computers, satellite phones and other technology, they are an authentic product of the modern globalised world'.

While much attention has been given to the emergence of 'new terror' in the Middle East and the Balkans, perhaps its most significant, neglected, manifestation has been in Southeast Asia since 1997. Raising arms and money for these groups in Thailand, Myanmar (formerly Burma), the Philippines and Malaysia is crucially dependent on a global black market in vice – drug running, money laundering, gambling and prostitution. These groups operate across national boundaries, and communicate and support each other via the internet. Islamist groupings such as *Al-Ma'unah*, led by Mohamad Razali, use the World Wide Web to advertise their belief that 'Jihad is our way'.

Significantly, the area of northern Malaysia has been a fertile ground for Islamic sects since at least the 1960s. In July 2000 *Al-Ma'unah* members raided a military barracks, before being captured after a jungle shoot-out. Two Malaysian intelligence officers were killed during the attack.

The Islamic radicals of north Malaysia share a distinct sense of community with the separatist groups of southern Thailand and the Philippines. Since 1945 the Muslim minorities in the Philippines and southern Thailand have found it increasingly difficult to reconcile the demands of their traditional devotion to Islam with the new nation-building states in which non-Muslims predominate.

The post-Cold War conflict between the forces of globalisation and tradition, along with the importation of Arab and Islamist radicals from Libya, Iran and Pakistan, has heightened the appeal of Islamic separatism. It has also fed the growing Puritanism of the *Parti Islam Se-Malaysia* (PAS) opposition in the north Malaysian states of Kelantan and Terengganu. In Mindanao, despite the signing of a peace accord between the Moro National Liberation Front (MNLF) and the Philippine government in 1997, and recent Philippine Army military successes against the more militant Moro Islamic Liberation Front (MILF), conflict simmers on. Meanwhile, rebel commander Ghalib Andang (alias Commander Robot) of *Abu Sayyaf* – itself a radical splinter of the MILF – has close links with the unremitting 'global fields of jihad' pursued by Osama bin Laden's *al-Qaeda* movement.

Disintegration at the periphery

Most worryingly of all, since the meltdown of 1997 and the uncertain transition to democratic rule, Indonesia, the largest and most significant member state of ASEAN, has been undermined by centrifugal forces. Since the collapse of former President Suharto's 'New Order' regime in May 1998, Indonesia has been plagued by separatist challenges. Across Indonesia's 7,000 inhabited islands, issues of identity and religion, often provoked by dissident elements in the armed forces loyal to Suharto, have beset the unstable civilian coalition that erratically rules the country.

In May 1998, the Chinese districts of Glodok, West Jakarta and Solo in central Java were looted and burned. Later, the decision of President Bacharuddin Jusuf Habibie's short-lived regime to hold a referendum on independence for East Timor was to cause further turmoil. The overwhelming vote for independence provoked the systematic destruction of East Timor by militia groups linked to pro-Suharto elements in the armed forces.

In Aceh, the Free Aceh Movement (*Gerakanan Aceh Merdeka* - GAM) has maintained a secessionist struggle since 1976. Despite the conclusion of a 'humanitarian pause' in the violence in May 2000, this has not led to a moderation of the GAM's demand for independence and the conflict is slowly re-igniting. Elsewhere in Irian Jaya-West Papua, the Free Papua Movement (*Organisasi Papua Merdeka*) has received a considerable boost from the outcome of events in East Timor.

Even more disturbingly, the once peacefully coexistent Christian and Muslim communities of Maluku and North Maluku, which traditionally followed a code of non-violence, dissolved in 1999 into a bloody confrontation that, by June 2000, had accounted for the loss of 3,000 lives.

Since May 2000 Muslim violence has been orchestrated by the *Laskar Jihad* (Warriors of Jihad), a group encouraged by Amien Rais, who is the speaker in the People's Consultative Assembly (*Majelis Permusyawaratan Rakyat*) and leader of the modernising Islamic organisation *Muhammadiyah*. These jihadists, like the leader of the Malaysian *Al-Ma'unah* sect, received military training in Java in preparation for the holy war in Ambon.

The post-New Order regime appears powerless to contain the dissolution of the Indonesian periphery. As Wirabuawa regional military commander Major General Slamet Kirbiantoro observed: 'We are in the process of committing suicide'. Continuing faction fighting within the Indonesian political élite has distracted attention from the problem of regional separatism. Indeed, with the abrogation of the Indonesian military ethic of *dwifungsi* (dual function) – which accorded the armed forces a central role in preserving the internal unity and stability of Indonesia – the central government in Jakarta is left with even fewer resources to sustain the cohesion of a disintegrating Javanese empire.

Regionalism to fragmentation

ASEAN has floundered in both its attempts to manage the regional economic crisis and its legacy of inter-communal violence. This failure is systemic. ASEAN's ineffectiveness ultimately derives from its foundational doctrine of non-interference in the internal affairs of member states. Indonesia, Malaysia and Singapore, the core states of ASEAN, retain an inflexible commitment to this stance even though it is increasingly obvious that ethnic and religiously motivated violence transcends state boundaries.

The murder of a GAM faction leader in Kuala Lumpur by Indonesian agents in June, and the attempted assassination of the Philippine ambassador in Jakarta by suspected Moro secessionists in August graphically illustrates that the new terrorism will interfere in the internal affairs of member states.

The first year of the 'Pacific Century' reveals a Southeast Asia divided in outlook and unable to respond to the anxious demands of an uncompromising identity politics. An assertive Islamic consciousness and its divisive impact upon the multi-ethnic state of the region has replaced the promise of continued growth and harmonious balance.

    The much-vaunted Asian values that, for most of the 1990s seemed to intimate the basis of a new Pacific regional order, have been revealed as a ramshackle edifice put together by ageing gerontocrats to legitimise their fading regimes.

Original version published in *Janes' Intelligence Review*, Vol. 12, No. 11, November 2000, by David Martin Jones and M.L.R. Smith.

Islamists defeat the Asian way

For much of the 1990s, the leaders of Singapore, Indonesia, the Philippines, Thailand and Malaysia – the founding members of the Association of Southeast Asian Nations (ASEAN) – congratulated themselves on their unique development formula. ASEAN's distinctive brand of diplomacy, founded on good interpersonal relations, seemingly generated rapid economic growth whilst sustaining regional harmony and stability. For its many international admirers, from the World Bank to British Prime Minister Tony Blair and Australia's Paul Keating, it was a uniquely Asian attitude to diplomacy and development.

By the late 1990s, the group's rigid non-interference in the internal affairs of its member states appeared a handicap to resolving issues of shared concern, rather than a source of virtue. It seems particularly unwise given the exposure in December 2001 of a sophisticated regional terror network.

Forces at work
ASEAN failed to recognise the forces of jihad at work in its midst when Philippine *al-Qaeda* operatives like Ramzi Yousef and Abdul Hakim Murad helped coordinate the first World Trade Center bombing in 1993. Even when member states reluctantly acknowledged this new phenomenon prior to the 9/11 attacks, they perversely considered it of transient interest. Radical Islam was of far less concern than the purported challenge to regional cohesion posed by the West, and what Malaysian Prime Minister Mahathir Mohamad described as the fanatical advocates of liberal democracy.

The region that once seemed set to exploit the opportunities of a globalised marketplace rapidly mutated after the economic meltdown of 1997, to quote Matthew Arnold, into a darkling plain where ignorant armies clashed by night. One army that emerged was jihadist in nature, fuelled somewhat paradoxically by the very forces of globalisation it sought to deny. A new generation of Malay and Indonesian middle-class radicals, alienated from post-colonial nation building in Indonesia, Singapore and Malaysia, turned instead to a purified Islam, learning it either in Middle Eastern universities or at Western mosques, while ostensibly pursuing the bourgeois qualifications that would contribute to the next growth spurt.

Overlooked
This developing middle class illiberalism has been evident since the early 1990s but was largely overlooked by commentators and the region's security services. Instead, official orthodoxy maintained that Islam in Southeast Asia was capital friendly and well-disposed both to economic modernisation and regional multilateralism. For commentators absorbed by the prospect of Indonesian democratisation after 1998, this benign 'civil' Islam offered the reassuring, if illusory, prospect of a tolerant and pluralist Islamised democracy.

From at least the end of the Gulf War in 1991, it was evident that an all-embracing Islamic programme of social and political change – Islamism – was on the rise. The growing appeal of operating through globalised networks to undermine the 'infidel' notion of the secular nation state, was the critical ideological link between the rise of Southeast Asian Islamism and the franchising terror operations of Osama bin Laden's *al-Qaeda* network.

The idea of a *Dar-al-Islam* – sphere of faith – transcending national boundaries and the call to jihad to achieve it, has long been promoted by radical critics of failed post-colonial arrangements in the Middle East. In Southeast Asia, however, evidence of this has only recently come to the fore.

Total defence – no defence
Whilst ASEAN officially maintained that the regional order had changed little during the 1990s, Southeast Asian regimes encountered political and economic

shifts of huge proportions. Only after 11th September 2002, and the exposure of a previously unsuspected level of Islamist cooperation stretching from Solo in Java to Singapore, Kuala Lumpur, through southern Mindanao and ultimately to Kabul, has a disturbing picture of non-cooperation between ASEAN security services been revealed. This contrasts strikingly with the elaborate mechanisms of global collaboration developed by Islamist organisations dedicated to recasting the infidel states of the region.

Curiously, the illusion of harmony was particularly pervasive in the more densely regulated and economically developed states of Singapore and Malaysia. Despite a long-standing preoccupation with internal security and draconian sentences handed out to internal dissidents, both failed to recognise, let alone counter, the growing presence of revolutionary Islam inspired by fundamentalist Middle Eastern and Afghani clerics. Indeed, the recent arrest of members of *Jemaah Islamiyah* (Islamic Congregation) in Singapore and Kuala Lumpur occurred only because of the lucky discovery of a video application for funding, sent to *al-Qaeda* and found in the Kabul rubble that once housed the jihadist equivalent of the Ford Foundation.

Intelligence failure was particularly acute in Singapore, the rich ethnically Chinese city-state that swam in a region that Singaporean Senior Minister Lee Kuan Yew famously termed 'a sea of Malay people'. Despite its strategy of 'total defence', which requires the continual psychological preparation of the public through state-controlled media and endless campaigns to reinforce the ideal of 'One Nation, One People, One Singapore' – it managed to overlook a well-organised cell with the men and material needed to destroy critical infrastructure.

According to investigators, members of *Jemaah Islamiyah* began infiltrating Singapore as long ago as 1993. The group established sleeper cells to attack Western establishments, including the American, Australian, British and Israeli embassies. One had already taken video footage of the American Embassy and Australian High Commission.

The plan was to pack twenty-one tons of ammonium nitrate, imported through Malaysia, into trucks and explode them either near or inside the diplomatic compounds, which are next to each other. An equally audacious attack, planned since 1997 and ready for activation, was to bomb the Yishun subway station in northern Singapore used by US personnel to reach the recently built Changi naval base. Subsequent revelations suggested that the group also intended to crash a jet onto the main civilian airport.

Scared to lose

This neglect reflects the *kiasu* – scared to lose – mindset nurtured by the ruling People's Action Party (PAP) over three decades of uninterrupted government. Its preoccupation with total administration has produced an uncritical tendency to follow state directives in the media, public sector and academic worlds. The West's liberal blandishments were seen as the main threat to internal cohesiveness. Those denounced and punished with large fines were non-violent social democrats with limited constituencies like Chee Soon Juan or James Gomez, who probably would have thought ammonium nitrate was a designer drug rather than the principal constituent of a bomb.

Likewise, the increasingly alienated Malay-Islamic minority community was dismissed as too indolent to threaten the nation building vision. In fact, the government's single-minded pursuit of development merely exacerbated Malay disadvantage and political marginalisation. Alienation eventually radicalised a younger generation of Malays.

The ruling PAP further compounded the problem by treating young Malay activists, like the *Fateha* (The Opening) group, which seeks to air its grievances through highly regulated public political debate, as indistinguishable from those prepared to advance their cause violently. When *Fateha* leader Zulfikar

Mohamad criticised government policy on Islamic schools and Singapore's links with the US and Israel, he was subject to a campaign of political denunciation. Government ministers and the official leaders of the Singapore Muslim community called his ideas 'dangerous and absurd'. Total defence has only repressed the problem of political alienation, not solved it.

Resentment

In both Singapore and Malaysia, state security agencies ignored the burgeoning problem of Islamist/Malay alienation. This was a direct consequence of the government and ASEAN's insistence that Confucianism and Islam harmoniously blended into 'shared values'. Official Singapore believed its own rhetoric, despite the growing evidence after the 1997 Asian economic crisis that the city-state was the only good house in a rapidly declining neighbourhood. A new generation of radicals resented Singapore's wealth, and its alignment with both Israel, which helped formulate its strategy of total defence, and the United States, whose business – if not its values – it remorselessly cultivates.

Unsurprisingly, the fiercest condemnation of Singapore's infidel connections comes from mosques across the causeway in Johor Baru, a city whose third worldliness contrasts dramatically with the post-modern cybernetic chic of its city-state neighbour.

Networking terror

From this resentment, Islamist groups – coordinated by a nomadic cleric, Sheikh Abu Bakar Bashir, in Solo East Java, and his elusive deputy Nurjuman Riduan (aka Hambali) – constructed an effective terror network after 1992. The 64-year-old Sheikh had spent four years in an Indonesian gaol from 1978 to 1982, courtesy of former President Suharto's New Order government, for his role in the fundamentalist group *Komando Jihad* (Jihad Commando).

He moved to more congenial Malaysia in the mid-1980s before returning to Indonesia after the fall of Suharto in 1998. Then he apparently invited his fellow clerics to prepare for jihad against the US. Significantly, the Sheikh considers Singapore 'anti-Islam... [and] an ally of America', and a legitimate target for Muslim rage.

During Bashir's and Hambali's time in Malaysia, *al-Qaeda* provided finance and training for the militant groups they formed like *Jemmah Islamiyah* and the *Kumpulan Militan Malaysia* (Malaysian Mujahideen Movement) (KMM).

From 1995, charitable and business organisations were used as fronts for increasingly transnational operations. Whilst Hambali coordinated groups in Malaysia and the Philippines, Osama's brother-in-law, Mohammad Khalifa, established a charity and a furniture company through which he channelled funds to the Moro Islamic Liberation Front (MILF), the largest Islamic separatist group, and *Abu Sayyaf*.

Members of groups like the KMM tend to be middle-class professionals, and graduates of regional and Western universities. They include businessmen like Yazid Sufaat, a biochemistry graduate of a US university, whose Green Laboratories allegedly imported ammonium nitrate for the proposed Singapore attack and who, in October 2000, entertained Zacarias Moussaoui and two of the 9/11 Pentagon bombers at his Kuala Lumpur apartment.

Moussaoui, currently on trial for his role in the 11th September attacks, also acted as US agent for Infocus Computers, a company in which Yazid's wife is a major shareholder.

Whilst members of KMM and *Jemmah Islamiyah* are in detention, Bakar and Hambali remain at large and anticipate pardons from the increasingly ineffectual Indonesian government. Significantly, Bashir is both the leading figure in the *Majelis Mujahideen Indonesia* (Islamist Mujahidin Council of Indonesia) (MMI), set up in Jogjakarta in 1998, as well as the brains behind both *Jemmah Islamiyah* and the KMM.

Islamic realism

These groups intend to destroy the precarious work of post-colonial nation building and replace it with an Islamic arrangement stretching from southern Thailand through Malaysia, embracing Mindanao, Singapore and the Indonesian archipelago. This would be governed, not by shared Asian values, but according to a rigid interpretation of Sharia law. Interestingly, the plan revives, under an Islamist guise, the vision initially dreamt up in the 1960s by non-aligned nationalists like former President Sukarno, of a monolithic, non-Chinese, radically anti-capitalist republic. Whilst Sukarno envisaged an *Indonesia Raya* – greater Indonesia – a new generation of revolutionaries visualises a utopian *Daulah Islamiyah Nusantara* – an Islamic realm or archipelago.

Seeds of destruction

ASEAN was formed in 1967 precisely to avoid the threat posed by Sukarno between 1963 and 1966. Ironically, since 1997 it seems that the Association has succeeded only in incubating its potential means of destruction.

Thus, after 1997, Singapore began a myopic attempt to cocoon itself from regional turmoil. In federal Malaysia, the *Parti Islam se-Malaysia* (PAS), the main opposition to Prime Minister Mahathir's ruling United Malay National Organisation (UMNO) coalition, has adopted an increasingly fundamentalist line and imposed Sharia-style discipline in the states of Kelantan and Trengganu that it governs. In late September, the PAS leadership expressed sympathy with the ends, if not the means, of *al-Qaeda*, whilst the son of the Kelantan chief minister is a prominent figure in the KMM.

Meanwhile, in the Philippines, *Abu Sayyaf* (Father of the Sword), a violent Tausug ethnic minority splinter group of the Moro National Liberation Front (MNLF) – has renewed long-standing autonomy claims by Muslim Moro separatists in Mindanao.

Abu Sayyaf not only established links with *al-Qaeda* after 1998, but it also developed a highly profitable line in hostage taking and the kidnapping of unwitting Western tourists. Meanwhile the MILF provided training for *al-Qaeda* at its Camp Abubakar before it fell into Philippine government hands in late 2000.

A notable feature of this increasingly violent separatism is that it ignored the ASEAN injunction to confine political activity within state boundaries. As Colonel Rodolfo Mendoza of the Philippine National Police observes: 'Way back in 1995 we were able to establish the existence of support cells in the region linked to Osama bin Laden. Based on our recent investigations, the *al-Qaeda* set-up was never busted... In fact, it continued and even prospered'.

Most worrying of all, in Indonesia, a younger generation of educated radicals, inspired by events in Afghanistan, challenged the largely apolitical, moderate Islam of Abdurrahman Wahid's *Nahdlatul Ulama* (Revival of the Ulama). Ironically, these Islamist groups, like *Laskar Jihad*, the MMI and the Islamic Defender's Front, only came to prominence during Wahid's inept presidency between 1999 and last year.

Despite the disruption of the terror network in Malaysia and Singapore, and the arrest in the Philippines in January of its alleged chief bomb maker Fathur Rahman al Ghozi – a graduate of Bakar's training school in Solo – the Indonesian government remains unconvinced of Bakar or the MMI's wrongdoing. Disturbingly, since the collapse of the New Order, 'democratising' Indonesia has given comfort to Islamist radicals on the grounds that disrupting their networks would further undermine internal stability. This posture earned an inevitable rebuke from Singapore's venerable former Prime Minister Lee Kuan Yew, which did little to further good relations between the region's political elites.

Just rhetoric

The fundamentalist challenge by the Islamic *internationale* is not the only one that ASEAN faced in the 1990s. So well entrenched was its style of consensus diplomacy that the Association demonstrated little capacity to react to the economic crisis of 1997, maintained a studied indifference to the growing Balkanisation of Indonesia, and conspicuously ignored the plight of East Timor.

Indeed, the mounting levels of regional pain failed to stir any desire to reform its 1976 Treaty of Amity and Cooperation, which holds rigidly, though somewhat incoherently, to the doctrine of non-interference in the internal politics of member states. When confronted, ASEAN's practice has initially been to deny the existence of a threat, followed by an inept and inadequate response.

More effective threat assessment within Southeast Asian states remains unlikely. Indeed, ASEAN has a distinguished history of ignoring intramural disputes, whilst unresolved bilateral tensions tend to produce only periodic diplomatic tantrums. Even the recent discovery of the Islamist regional threat has only provided the opportunity either to condemn the failings of other ASEAN members states or discount them entirely, rather than a chance to devise substantive cooperation.

There are signs that in the face of this serious threat, ASEAN is belatedly acting. A ministerial meeting last month agreed to several low level operational anti-terrorism measures, though significantly couldn't agree on a definition of terrorism itself.

Singapore, and ASEAN more generally, needs less total defence and more critical engagement with the issues that destabilise regional security. If a more realistic sense of purpose does not emerge, *al-Qaeda* and its affiliates will establish a permanent foothold in Southeast Asia, while ASEAN will become an irrelevant rhetorical shell, and the regional economy will make Argentina's look like a growth model.

Original version published in *The World Today*, Vol. 58, No. 6, June 2002, by David Martin Jones and M.L.R. Smith.

Still active: *Jemmah Islamiyah* in Southeast Asia

In the aftermath of the Bali bombing, international pressure belatedly focused regional attention on *Jemaah Islamiyah,* which had been largely untroubled in developing a dangerous regional terror network stretching from the Thai-Malay border, through the southern Philippines and Indonesia, to sleeper cells in Australia. At first glance, it appeared that when the regional states of the Association of Southeast Asian Nations (ASEAN) coordinated their approach, the network could be exposed and disrupted.

Arrests and convictions
Prior to the Bali bombing, the Indonesian government had officially doubted the existence of the group. After the bombing, thirty-four alleged members were arrested, including Abu Bakar Bashir, said to be the organisation's spiritual leader. He was charged with trying to topple Indonesia's secular government, assassinate President Megawati Sukarnoputri and establish an Islamic state. Bashir dismissed all the charges as a Central Intelligence Agency (CIA) plot, and threatened US President George Bush with 'punishment by Allah'.

Amrozi bin Nurhasyim, one of the group's foot soldiers, was found guilty and sentenced to death in August for obtaining the car and explosives for the nightclub bombings. Shortly afterwards, Abdul Aziz, also known as Imam Samudra, received the same sentence after judges decided he was the brains behind the operation.

In September Bashir was convicted of the lesser crime of subversion rather than treason with which he had originally been charged. He was sentenced to four years in prison by a Jakarta court. This relatively lenient sentence raises questions about the regional commitment to get on top of the threat.

Elsewhere, the police and military in the Philippines had been aware for some time of a supranational *al-Qaeda*-linked presence financing and encouraging groups in southern Mindanao, and training recruits at a centre known as Camp Abubakar before its fall to government forces in 2000.

Singapore, too, reacted swiftly to the lucky discovery in Kabul in December 2001 of a plot to blow up a series of Western embassies, military installations and civilian targets, in order, it now seems, to foment war with Malaysia. In Malaysia, which had been a stopping-off point for Zacarias Moussaoui and several participants in the 9/11 attacks on the United States, attacks, security forces have interned sixty-two members of the militant group *Kumpulan Militan Malaysia* (KMM).

Post-Bali, Indonesia even cooperated with Singaporean authorities to pick up the alleged head of the Singapore branch of *Jemaah Islamiyah* and joined an operation with the Australian Federal Police to find the bombers. With all this activity it was assumed it had been made far more difficult to mount terror attacks in the region. With the arrest in Thailand of Hambali, allegedly *Jemaah Islamiyah*'s chief strategist, by US special forces in August the crucial link between the grouping and *al-Qaeda*'s military council was apparently severed, thus damaging its operational effectiveness.

New attacks
However, the group has by no means been rendered redundant. Bombs at Jakarta airport and in the Philippines in May demonstrated a continuing terror capability. The devastating attack on the Marriott hotel on 5th August 2003, in which over a dozen people were killed, only reinforced the threat.

These incidents also indicate a capacity to coordinate action with *al-Qaeda* operations elsewhere, whether in Riyadh, Casablanca, or Nairobi. Southeast Asian and Australian analysts have tended either to ignore or dismiss these global links in *al-Qaeda*'s terror network. Yet, as CIA director George Tenet recently observed, *al-Qaeda* and its affiliates, like *Jemaah Islamiyah*, will remain among the most significant threats to the US and its allies for at least the next five years. Its versatile nature and loose structure, combined with a tendency to act as a global conduit for anti-Western resentment, means that it has become even more elusive and difficult to eliminate.

Nowhere is this amorphous quality more evident than in Southeast Asia. Regional governments find it hard either to acknowledge its presence or to come to grips with its ideological appeal, making attempts to curtail it even harder. It is increasingly clear that *al-Qaeda* seeks to use modern communications such as the internet to globalise Islam. It aims to transcend the nation-state to forge a network with the potential to disrupt, disorganise, paralyse, and terrorise insecure governments. Since allied forces destroyed its Afghanistan base two years ago, the flexible structure has become even more decentralised. It has also proved extremely adept at identifying new missions and forming friendships of convenience.

In Southeast Asia this capacity had grown largely unnoticed since the late 1980s, illustrating the group's long-term, geopolitical planning skills. Observing the intractable ethno-religious conflicts in Mindanao and Islamic resentment in secular states from southern Thailand to Indonesia, *al-Qaeda*'s strategic thinkers have worked diligently to recruit members and exploit local grievances. Indeed, it was in the heady atmosphere of the jihad to remove the Soviet infidel from Afghanistan that the present elite of Southeast Asian extremists received their indoctrination in Islamist principles.

Scepticism remains about the determination of Southeast Asian governments to deal effectively with the evolving regional network. According to Federal Bureau of Investigation section chief, Dennis Lormel, clandestine funds are still finding their way in from the Middle East through Saudi-sponsored 'charity' cover organisations.

Equally disturbing, Indonesian authorities continue to deny any associations between regional Islamism and *al-Qaeda*. Interestingly, the thirty-five-page indictment of Amrozi failed even to mention membership of *Jemaah Islamiyah*, whilst that of Bashir made no reference to links with *al-Qaeda*.

In a similar vein, Thailand threatened to prosecute any foreign journalist who alleged that senior operatives had ever met in the Muslim-populated south of the country to coordinate attacks across the region. In June 2003, however, Prime Minister Thaksin Shinawatra, who had previously derided travel warnings against his country, lost face when Thai police uncovered a *Jemaah Islamiyah* cell planning suicide bomb attacks on Western embassies in Bangkok. Embarrassment was further compounded with Hambali's arrest in the former capital of Ayodhya in August.

Revelations in May that *Jemaah Islamiyah* members ran a school complex in Phnom Penh, along with the discovery of an *al-Qaeda* training camp in southern Mindanao, which hands out diplomas to graduates, indicate the adaptive qualities of the organisation. It seems that there is a constant flow of extremists through the largely unregulated borderlands of Mindanao, the islands in the Sulu Sea, the Malaysian state of Sabah and northern Indonesia.

A recent study by Sidney Jones of the International Crisis Group indicates that *Jemaah Islamiyah* is a much larger organisation than previously suspected, 'with a depth of leadership that gives it a regenerative capacity'. It also depends on a variety of independent Muslim boarding schools. In August, Australian Federal Police Commissioner Mick Keelty maintained that the group would not be defeated whilst the Indonesian government permitted such schools to recruit future generations to the cause. Indonesian Foreign Minister Hasan Wirayuda dismissed Keelty's observations as 'fortune teller's talk' and an intolerable intrusion into Indonesia's domestic politics.

The light sentence handed down to Bashir hardly constitutes a strong signal to discourage further recruitment. Many outside observers had been expecting a fifteen-year sentence. The court found that there was insufficient evidence to prove that he was the leader of *Jemaah Islamiyah* or conspired in the planning of terror operations in Indonesia. This, despite the fact that Bashir's Pondok Ngruki school in Solo produced a number of those accused of being members of *Jemaah Islamiyah*, including Fathur Rahman al-Ghozi, who recently escaped from custody in the Philippines, and several connected with the Bali bombing. Inevitably this increases concern at continuing Indonesian ambivalence towards the prosecution of Islamic terror in the country. Suspicions linger that the decision might have been politically inspired, reflecting a reluctance to confront senior members of the organisation.

Meanwhile, the widespread failure of governments to win hearts and minds in the aftermath of the Asian economic meltdown of 1997 has enabled Islamic radicals to recruit impressionable, if sometimes, ill-informed supporters. This is illustrated by the fact that T-shirts sporting Amrozi's features are fashionable for Javanese youth.

The revelation in June that the Australian Security Intelligence Organisation had disrupted a Sydney based *Jemaah Islamiyah* cell, which had both played host to Bashir and raised over $650,000, indicates the group's evolving reach.

Paradoxically, the threat is likely to be most acute when ASEAN begins claiming triumph over its Islamist problem and downplaying the wider dangers. Although there has been some success in disrupting the Islamist assault on regional targets and links with sympathetic groups in South Asia, the Middle East and beyond, this globalised phenomenon is patient, uncompromising and plans for the long term. The suicide bomber who devastated the Marriott hotel in downtown Jakarta in August also exploded the view that enhanced regional security cooperation had undermined *al-Qaeda*'s network in Southeast Asia.

Original version published in *The World Today*, Vol. 59, No. 10, October 2003, by David Martin Jones and M.L.R. Smith.

The dragon stirs: China's long shadow

Recent events in East Asia have produced much speculation about the region's future: the apparently unstoppable rise of China has cast a long shadow. For when the dragon stirs, it seems the world trembles. As a result of the dragon's growth world power, we are told, will shift inexorably east towards Asia. However, the landscape of the new Asian century appears eerily familiar. During the supercharged East Asian economic growth of the mid-1990s, the vision of a new Pacific Century, and the associated decline of the decadent West, was first conjured by regional statesmen like former Malaysian Prime Minister Mahathir Mohammad, and scholar bureaucrats such as Kishore Mahbubani.

However, the much-anticipated Asian renaissance of the 1990s all ended in tears. Rapid growth coupled with opaque government-business relations and a questionable set of loan portfolios came to a shuddering halt in the Asian financial crisis of 1997. The aftermath revealed a lack of financial and political accountability that saw Southeast Asia mutate from a region of peace, harmony, and growth into one typified by growing ethnic and religious discord and economic instability. The process culminated in this manifestation after 11th September 2001, as the region became the second front in George Bush's 'war' on global terrorism.

Shock absorber
Current commentary about a dynamic and integrated East Asia, therefore, evokes scepticism as well as *déjà vu*. It was in response to the perceived humiliation by global financial markets and Western backed institutions, such as the International Monetary Fund, that the ten Southeast Asian members of the Association of Southeast Asian Nations (ASEAN), together with Japanese and Chinese politicians, began to consider establishing regional structures to avoid, or at least minimise, future financial shocks. Much rhetoric, as well as some financial backing, was given to support this commitment to a new, more integrated, and economically resilient East Asian region.

China, and the role it seeks in the region, is key to this evolving Asian drama. Beijing, unlike its Northeast Asian neighbour and regional rival, Japan, played the economic crisis well by not devaluing its currency, whilst Japanese investment deserted Southeast Asia after 1997.

The momentum of Chinese growth, and its continuing attractiveness to foreign direct investment during and since the financial crisis, has revived the stagnant hi-tech sectors of Northeast Asia and, to a lesser extent, the resource-based economies of Southeast Asia. Japan's partial emergence from economic stagnation and South Korea's recovery from financial crisis, moreover, are entirely the result of the insatiable demand for high technology products from China. Twenty percent of Japan's export trade is with a booming China. The political reflection of Asia's renewed economic dynamism is the grouping of ASEAN Plus Three (APT), comprising China, South Korea and Japan, that has evolved since 1972. In December, Malaysia will host a summit of this APT group, together with other invited countries. Some commentators and regional statesmen envisage this as an embryonic East Asian community, similar in some respects to the European Union or Mercosur in South America.

Signing up
Superficially, and somewhat bizarrely, it appears the economically and politically weaker and less internally resilient ASEAN states have brought this putative community to life. The wider region intends to adopt ASEAN's diplomatic culture of consensus building, peer pressure, and emphasis on proper behaviour, together with its mechanisms of conflict avoidance.

This distinctively 'ASEAN way', rather than the legalistic and rule-based arrangements that characterise Western organisations, will determine the group's approach. Indeed, signing ASEAN's Treaty of Amity and Cooperation (TAC) has become the entry price for summit admission. This has caused a notable difficulty for Australia. Several Asian states, especially Indonesia and Japan, would like Australia to attend the APT's summits, and avoid it looking like a caucus without Caucasians. At the same time Canberra, excluded in the 1990s from some ASEAN meetings, would dearly like a place at the table. However, Prime Minister John Howard had undiplomatically repudiated the treaty the previous year, claiming it represented the tried and failed mindset that had been unable to address the region's various economic, religious, ethnic and boundary differences since its introduction in 1976. Yet when signing the Treaty was made a condition of attendance at the Kuala Lumpur summit, the Australian government performed an embarrassing *volte face*, somewhat reluctantly acknowledging a willingness to accede to its principles. From an ASEAN perspective, this caused Howard a satisfying loss of face. However, the reasons for his misgivings are worth considering.

The Treaty is an unremarkable document requiring all members to 'respect the independence sovereignty equality territorial integrity... of all nations, the settlement of disputes by peaceful means and non-interference in the internal affairs of one another'. Because it relies on internal strength rather than external security, the Treaty has done little to build an economic, political or security community in Southeast Asia. Its promotion of non-interference seems inappropriate in an era of transnational terror and globalisation.

The long view
This approach, however, not only suits the more autocratic members of ASEAN, like next year's chair, Myanmar, and the less democratic states of the region such as Cambodia, Vietnam, and Laos. It suits also other states like, Singapore, and Malaysia, albeit to a lesser extent. It most certainly suits China. And it is China's understanding of what the region should become that gives the forthcoming summit its significance.

This is not without irony. China has always been suspicious of multilateralism and the system of treaties and laws that shape international society. It has a long history and a long memory. In China's view, both now and since 1842, the 'unfair' Western treaty system of the nineteenth century was responsible for a century of Chinese shame and humiliation. China only 'stood up' when the Communist Party, under the revolutionary leadership of Mao Zedong, reasserted national independence and opted for global *realpolitik* to reiterate its national interest, first in alliance with the Soviet Union and then by effectively balancing Soviet and US geopolitical ambitions.

In the post-Cold War era, China initially treated ASEAN with reserve, preferring a bilateral approach to regional issues like the various claims to the Spratly Islands in the South China Sea that first brought the ASEAN designed Regional Forum to Beijing's attention.

Comfortable
More recently, however, China's fourth generation leadership has felt comfortable with the non-binding ASEAN way and its consensus driven approach based on strong interpersonal ties. For Beijing, the emphasis on non-interference and internal strength dovetails nicely with its five principles of peaceful coexistence, first articulated by the late Premier Zhou Enlai, which also emphasise respect for territorial integrity. The People's Republic is also attracted to ASEAN, because the less developed Southeast Asian states like Cambodia, Laos and Myanmar effectively acknowledge a tributary relationship to China, whilst Malaysia, Singapore, Thailand, and increasingly South Korea, are also deferential.

The East Asian summit mechanism allows China to envisage the region reverting to what it sees as the pre-ordained order rudely, but briefly, interrupted by a century and a half of Western colonialism, capitalism, and barbarism. This regards China as the moral, and economic centre of a web of relations embracing the adjacent Confucian countries of Japan, Korea and Indochina, and extending its influence into Southeast Asia.

China's regional vision would comprise the Southeast Asian states of Thailand, Singapore, Malaysia and Indonesia with large Chinese populations. Australia, whose trading relationship with China has blossomed in the last decade, could be included, provided, its statesmen perform the required rites. In this context, the Treaty serves as the contemporary equivalent of the Qing dynasty kowtow. Before this post-modern version of the Confucian peace can establish itself, outstanding issues must be resolved. Japan, which abused the Chinese order between 1895 and 1945, must be brought to heel, apologise, and compensate for the 1930s massacres in Manchuria and Nanjing. The rebellious province of Taiwan must be reintegrated into a unified China – for Beijing, this is an internal matter.

This approach to peace and regional security requires the recognition of China's historic and moral authority in the region. Ultimately, an ASEAN sponsored East Asian community will be pressed to embrace a Sinocentric understanding of the region and the world. Consequently, whilst there is an aspiration to a broader East Asian regional community, if the Chinese view prevails, it will not be particularly egalitarian or democratic.

As China has been attracted to an enhanced ASEAN as a basis of regional order, Japan, the Taiwanese leadership, and Indonesia have become increasingly concerned. Japan has lost out badly in terms of regional soft power and has largely chased events since 1997. Anti-Japanese riots in Chinese cities in April 2005 and the lack of regional support for Japan's claim to a permanent seat on the UN Security Council illustrate its marginalisation. Meanwhile, the ASEAN states are, despite the new arrangements, much weaker economically and more politically divided than in 1997. Regardless of the official consensus, they are drawn increasingly into competing Chinese and Japanese spheres of influence.

Lacking sophistication
While most ASEAN members tacitly or actively acknowledge Chinese influence, others like the Philippines and Indonesia are highly suspicious of its economic and political motives. They, like Japan, seek an Australian presence at the December summit to balance Beijing's growing influence. Australia for a long time 'an odd man in' the region, as former Foreign Minister Gareth Evans once put it, has emerged as a potentially significant player. However, because both the Australian Liberal and Labor parties tend to view Asia as a monolith, regional policy has lacked the sophistication to promote the complex balancing of interests that must occur to avoid East Asia's future becoming Europe's early twentieth century past, as the late Gerry Segal, one of the wisest experts on Asian affairs once presciently argued. Whatever else, the East Asian summit will inaugurate interesting times.

Originally published in *The World Today*, Vol. 61, Nos. 8-9, August/September 2005, by David Martin Jones and M.L.R. Smith.

Can ASEAN ever solve the South China Seas dispute?

The 27th Association of Southeast Asian Nations (ASEAN) summit concluded in Kuala Lumpur at the weekend. The Malaysian host declared the summit 'gruelling' but a success.

The gala dinner celebrating the event witnessed the ten ASEAN leaders, together with delegates from China, South Korea, Japan, Australia, New Zealand, the United States and Russia, dressed in the Malay national costume, which bore a striking resemblance to the Beatles cover for their Sergeant Pepper's Lonely Hearts Club Band album.

Not everybody enjoyed the show. The ASEAN states had to cancel a planned ceremony to sign a common statement on regional security. The difficulty concerned the question of China's claim to the South China Sea. Singapore's Prime Minister Lee Hsien Loong cavalierly dismissed this as merely an issue 'where China and the USA did not see eye to eye', overlooking the fact that for the last two decades, ASEAN has invested enormous time and effort in multilateral forums to promote peace and security in East Asia.

Policymakers continue to voice confidence in ASEAN's inconclusive dialogue mechanisms, even in the wake of the weekend's most recent failure, seeing them as central to resolving disputes in the South China Seas. In June 2014 US Defense Secretary Chuck Hagel declared: 'This regional architecture is helping to develop shared solutions to shared challenges, building a strong and enduring ASEAN security community, and ensuing that collective, multilateral operations are the norm, rather than the exception'.

Australian Foreign Minister, Julie Bishop, in November 2014 called for the 'peaceful resolution' of maritime disputes in accordance with ASEAN principles.

Despite the plaudits given to ASEAN, its role seems increasingly marginal. China claims the South China Seas as a Chinese lake. The US contests this, in November 2015 sending naval destroyers within twelve nautical miles of structures built by the Chinese in the Paracel island group. Tensions rise. Nothing is resolved.

Evaluating ASEAN's role in managing the problem in the South China Seas reveals that far from addressing this evolving conflict over international rights of free passage on the high seas, its weak multilateral approach only further stirs already troubled waters.

On the surface, ASEAN's softly-softly approach seemed to bear fruit with an ASEAN-China Free trade agreement and a Declaration of a Code of Conduct to manage disputes in the South China Sea in 2002. In 1994 ASEAN formed the ASEAN Regional Forum (ARF) to manage China's regional ambitions. China, however, has come to find the ARF a highly convenient vehicle for own ends, ruthlessly exploiting ASEAN's weak state regionalism to advance its national interest in maritime hegemony.

The history of the problem

The source of the South China Seas dispute is traceable to the 1951 San Francisco Treaty, which failed to stipulate possession of the Spratly islands when Japan lost its title to them after its defeat in the Second World War. The chain of 200 islets, coral reefs and sea mounts that constitute the Spratlys, and its northern extension, the Paracel islands, spread across 250,000 square kilometres of the South China Sea, a vast continental shelf that constitutes a potentially rich source of oil and natural gas.

The Spratly's contested ownership developed into an international conflict when, from the mid-1970s, several claimants began extracting resources from the seabed contiguous to their Exclusive Economic Zones (EEZ). China, Taiwan, and four ASEAN states – Brunei, Malaysia, the Philippines and Vietnam – all laid claim and/or occupied part of the islands in the South China Sea.

Together with Indonesia, which also contests maritime zones with China, the parties have failed to resolve their disputes.

The dispute assumed its current form in February 1992, when China laid claim to the entire South China Sea based on its historical right to the area dating from the Xia dynasty (*circa* 2070-*circa* 1600 BC).

ARF workshops involving China and other dialogue partners around the region, including the US, became central to ASEAN's collective diplomacy towards China, adopting a process of open-ended dialogue aimed largely at deferring any formal resolution of intractable disputes.

Despite attending the ARF meetings, China rejected attempts to multilateralise the issue. Before 1997, it had given little indication of a commitment to a peaceful resolution.

In 1995, China occupied Mischief Reef, challenged the Philippine's EEZ claim, furnishing evidence of its willingness to resort to force to recover its purportedly lost territory. From the mid-1990s, China's rising economic power increased the propensity to assert its claims unilaterally.

From frown to smile

After the 1997 Asian financial crisis, however, the Chinese began to tone down their rhetoric and between 1998 and 2008, seemingly, became acquiescent to ASEAN's view that intractable disputes should be peacefully put to one side. Beijing's comfort with the ASEAN process culminated in 2002 in the signing of a non-binding Declaration on the Conduct of Parties in the South China Sea, which eschewed the use of force and sought to build an atmosphere of trust and cooperation.

That Beijing had apparently shifted its stance from confrontation to conciliation suggested to many commentators that, through ARF's good offices, China had moved from unilateralism to multilateralism. China was becoming a responsible regional player. The attribution of this shift to ASEAN's informal dialogue process is wrong. China had switched from 'frown' to 'smile' for entirely cold calculations. The confrontation line China had pursued up to 1998 had raised the possibility of US involvement in the Spratly dispute. Naturally, China preferred to avoid such a possibility.

Thus, by appearing to adopt ASEAN's non-confrontational approach, China could draw ASEAN into its sphere of influence while effectively sidelining the US. Any resolution of the South China Seas dispute remained stuck in the ARF's managerial mode of non-binding consensus. The notional commitment to ASEAN's multilateral dialogue process was therefore a cost-free Chinese investment in good public relations.

The potential to shift from a soft to a hard-line stance always remained an option for China if circumstances appeared propitious. This became evident as China's economy boomed, while the West became distracted by events in Afghanistan, the Middle East, and after the 2007 financial crisis. China's foreign policy grew in assertiveness, particularly in the maritime sphere.

China plays hardball

By 2012, the modernisation of the force projection capacity of the People's Liberation Army Navy (PLAN), enabled the Politburo under Xi Jinping to shift to a more forceful reassertion of claims to the Spratlys.

In April 2012, Chinese navy vessels confronted the Philippine navy in the Scarborough shoals, well within the Philippine EEZ. The growth of China's blue water capacity for controlling the South China Sea exposed ASEAN's diplomatic limitations.

The weakness of ASEAN's multilateral diplomacy was thoroughly exposed, as the Philippines, and remarkably, Vietnam, looked increasingly to the US when confronted by China's renewed assertiveness. The ARF process demonstrated impotence rather than collective strength. Meeting in Phnom Penh in July 2012, ASEAN foreign ministers could not agree the most cosmetic of joint communiques on regional security.

The ASEAN response remains tepid, still officially seeking a code of conduct for the South China Sea, which China refuses. China's naval assertiveness calculates that the weaker states of Southeast Asia will eventually accede to Chinese claims. It seems clear that China intends to salami slice its way to control of the South China Seas, taking it in small increments by making the economic costs of resistance too high, sometimes by restricting Chinese investments and market access on any countries (the Philippines and Vietnam, for example) who contest China's maritime claims.

ASEAN's fragmentation, China's divide and rule

Such assertiveness has led both to the fragmentation of ASEAN and the growing involvement of both Japan and the US in the developing conflict. In June 2014, American Defense Secretary Chuck Hagel remarked, that 'the US policy is clear. We take no position on competing territorial claims. But we firmly oppose any nation's use of intimidation, coercion or the threat of force to assist those claims'. At the same meeting, Japanese Prime Minister Shinzo Abe announced that Japan would provide the Philippines and Vietnam with naval patrol vessels.

Yet, during 2015 China has further escalated tension by its aggressive land reclamation programme in the South China Sea, with the new US Defence Secretary Ashton Carter arguing that China is 'out of step with the international norms that underscore the Asia-Pacific security architecture'.

The ASEAN states, rather than driving regional processes seem increasingly trapped between a rock and a hard place, are trying to avoid making a choice between backing a more assertive US or backing China.

The South China Seas dispute ultimately demonstrates how more powerful actors can manipulate ASEAN's weak multilateral dialogue process to advance grand strategic interests. The strategic manoeuvring brought about by the ARF process, furthermore, has complicated the relationship between the US, Japan and ASEAN. ASEAN processes have allowed its diplomatic rhetoric to be used against it by China in a way that practitioners of *realpolitik* can only admire.

China, in other words, is successfully engaging ASEAN in a policy of divide and rule. For example, in the wake of USS Lassen's steam through the Spratly's, Chinese Foreign Minister Wang Yi, declared that the US must adjust to 'shared' Asian values of the kind that ASEAN often articulates.

Wang stated that Beijing wanted any disputes resolved in negotiations between it and ASEAN on the basis 'of historical facts and in accordance with international law' and that China and ASEAN were working on a code of conduct. All of which is to say, peace on Chinese terms.

Original version published the *Daily Telegraph*, 24th January 2015, by David Martin Jones and M.L.R. Smith.

How Islamic State established a franchise in Southeast Asia

Islamic State activists now pose a threat – not only in Indonesia, the largest Muslim democracy in the world, but also across Southeast Asia.

The bomb attack on 14th January in Jakarta, which killed 7 people – modelled on the Paris attack in November 2015, but without the same impact in terms of creating fear, panic and death – demonstrated the threat that the Islamic State of Iraq and the Levant (ISIL) now poses not only in Indonesia, the largest Muslim democracy in the world, but also to Southeast Asia more generally and even Australia.

How has ISIL evolved a presence in Southeast Asia and can it be dismantled? The attack on the Sarinah shopping centre in the upmarket district of Menteng last week was the first in the Indonesian capital since July 2009 when the surviving remnant of the violent wing of *Jemaah Islamiyah*, *al-Qaeda*'s Southeast Asian franchise, bombed the Marriott and Ritz Carlton hotels a few blocks away from the latest incident.

Islamic State in Southeast Asia

Islamic State has now replaced *Jemaah Islamiyah* as the source of regional violent Islamism. More importantly, ISIL has inherited its regional structure, its ideology, and its strategy from *Jemmah Islamiyah*. Significantly, Abu Bakr Bashir, the 'emir' of *Jemmah Islamiyah*, currently serving a sentence for treason in Cipinang jail, pledged allegiance to ISIL in 2014. Yet until last week, it had seemed that the former *al-Qaeda* linked franchises in Southeast Asia, which included not only *Jemmah Islamiyah*, but *Abu Sayyaf* in the Philippines and the *Kumpulan Mujahideen Malaysia*, had been decapitated and the curtain closed on this theatre of global Salafist jihadism.

However, although the first-generation leadership of *Jemmah Islamiyah*, which had coordinated the Bali bombings in 2002, had either been eliminated or imprisoned by 2009, its ideology and its networks remained in place. It now appears that this previously dormant structure has reawakened.

The evolution of a Southeast Asian terror network

Historically, *Jemmah Islamiyah* evolved as an *al-Qaeda* linked grouping in Southeast Asia during the 1990s. Founded by Indonesian Salafists Bashir and Abu Sangkar in Johor, Malaysia, after they fled the authoritarian but nationalist Indonesian New Order regime, *Jemmah Islamiyah*, like ISIL, drew together former *Mujahideen* who had fought in Afghanistan from across the region.

The evolving jihadist network brought together Indonesian Islamists alienated from the New Order, like Riduan Isamuddin (known also as Hambali) with Malaysian salafists disillusioned with both Malaysia's Islamic party, *Parti Islam Se-Malaysia*, and the ruling United Malay Nationalist Organisation's (UMNO) failure to impose Sharia law in the multiethnic state, along with *Abu Sayyaf*, an organisation founded by returning Moro fighters in Muslim majority southern Philippines.

After the collapse of Indonesia's New Order regime, in 1998, *Jemmah Islamiyah*'s core leadership returned to Solo in Central Java where it continued both recruitment and consciousness raising activities. The Bali bomber Imam Samudra was a graduate of this programme as is the current coordinator of Islamic State in Southeast Asia, Bahrun Naim. By 2000, the network had direct links to al-Qaeda and the September 2001 World Trade Center bombings through Khalid Sheikh Mohammed.

Jemmah Islamiyah's ambition, like that of ISIL, was to coordinate the various Islamist struggles in the region into a coherent movement to create a Southeast Asian caliphate or *darul Islam Nusantara*. The strategy draws essentially localised, separatist struggles in Southeast Asia into a budding, if loose, network of transnational jihadism. *Jemaah Islamiyah* itself evolved as a regional network constituted through kin groups, marital alliances, cliques and radical *pesantren* (Islamic religious schools) between 1985 and 2000.

ISIL takes over the network

ISIL has evidently inherited both the structure and the Salafist theo-political vision strategically conceived in terms of regional and transnational networks.

Southeast Asian recruits to ISIL and returning fighters reinforce these linkages. In its Southeast Asian manifestation, we can trace this ideal, if not the strategy, back to the *Darul Islam* movement in Indonesia that dates from the struggle against Dutch colonial power in the 1940s and subsequently adumbrated by the influence of Muslim Brotherhood ideologists like Sayeed Qutb. In fact, long before the end of the Soviet occupation of Afghanistan, which is often seen as the first intimation of an Islamist *internationale*, pan-Islamist thinkers in Southeast Asia, like those in the Middle East, conceived resistance to *jahiliyia* (the state of ignorance) as a single, unified global struggle that transcended local, state and regional concerns.

The story of *al-Qaeda*, and now ISIL, is essentially how a transnational movement aligns itself with local militant groups with country-specific grievances to increase their global reach and influence. *Jemaah Islamiyah* – and now ISIL – provide a case study of how regional groupings come to share an ideology and a strategy whilst at the same time sustaining their own distinctive character, structure and practice.

ASEAN's ambiguity

After 9/11 and especially after the Bali bombings of 2002, the Indonesian, Malaysian Singaporean and Australian governments, which had previously dismissed a coordinated Islamist threat in Southeast Asia, began taking the *Jemmah Islamiyah* and *Abu Sayyaf* threat seriously. Collaboration with Australian Federal Police and US intelligence agencies enabled the new Indonesian counter-terrorist police, *Densus 88*, to kill or imprison the core leadership of *Jemmah Islamiyah*. Elsewhere, the Malaysian and Singaporean authorities undermined *Jemmah Islamiyah*'s structures in their respective countries.

This notwithstanding, one common factor is that the countries where *Jemmah Islamiyah* and now ISIL have proliferated, all belong to the Association of Southeast Asian Nations (ASEAN). ASEAN has consistently failed to develop a coordinated counter-terrorism policing response to the regional protagonists of transnational Islamism. Consequently, with the rise of the Islamic State and the development of its recruitment and grooming strategies online, it is calculated that ISIL has recruited close to 1000 fighters from Southeast Asia, many of whom have evidently returned to open a new front in the region.

Thus, whilst *Jemmah Islamiyah*'s structure in the 1990s consisted of an 'emir' presiding over a governing council (Markaz), which oversaw four regional spheres of operation or *Mantiqi*, ISIL has by contrast expanded its outreach activities across Southeast Asia and formed a *Katibah Nusantara* (Katibah Archipelago), which operates both across Iraq and Syria and in Southeast Asia.

Consequently, in January 2016, two Malaysian suicide bombers killed 30 people in Syria. Elsewhere, over the past year Malaysian authorities have foiled at least four attempts to bomb public buildings and kidnap politicians and Malay-Chinese businessmen in a country where ethno-religious politics have become increasingly vitriolic since the 2014 election, which the UMNO ruling party won in a campaign riddled with corruption and electoral fraud. At the same time, in the southern Philippines a revived *Abu Sayyaf* has reopened training camps for regional jihadists and pledged allegiance to Islamic State.

Whilst Jakarta was the site of the most recent regional manifestation of global Salafist jihadism, other capitals in the region are by no means immune. Singapore's Prime Minister Lee Hsien Loong observed in 2015 that Southeast Asia had become a 'key recruitment centre for Islamic State'. He also remarked that the terror threat was 'no longer over there it is here'. Somewhat problematically from Lee's perspective, ASEAN, which Singapore, Thailand, Indonesia, Malaysia and the Philippines jointly founded in 1967 to promote regional stability, lacks both a shared understanding of regional security and a coordinated approach to dismantling transnational terrorism. Meanwhile, ISIL exploits the idea of an integrated Islamic region to promote its version of a 'far caliphate' in Southeast Asia.

Original version of article published in the *Daily Telegraph*, 21st January 2016, by David Martin Jones and M.L.R. Smith.

2. The war on terror misfires: Western illusions and self-deceptions

WHERE WERE YOU WHEN 9/11 HAPPENED? This was the inter-generational refrain that replaced 'Where were you when President Kennedy was assassinated?' Sitting in my apartment in Singapore in the early evening of 11th September 2001 watching live on television the events unfold on that bright early morning in New York, it was hard to take in the enormity of the attacks and the ensuing chaos when four airliners were seized by operatives of *al-Qaeda*, two of which were flown into the twin towers of the World Trade Center, with another flown into the Pentagon outside Washington DC, while the fourth crashed into a Pennsylvania field when the passengers courageously tried to re-take the aircraft from the hijackers.

At the time, David and I were afflicted with contradictory feelings. We were in disbelief at the level of destruction. Yet, we were not entirely surprised. Instinctively, we both knew who was behind the assaults on the United States. We had been tracking the trends in Islamist inspired thought and the pattern of mass, indiscriminate attacks they promoted. Like most, we did not anticipate the timing or the scale of 9/11, but it was the culmination – the most graphic expression – of the clash between modernity and tradition which we had been writing about in the years before.

What we explored in our writings both before and after 9/11 was how the grandiloquence of the end of history in Southeast Asia, with all its talk of a 'Pacific Century', and 'Asian Tiger' economies, and the prospective democratisation of illiberal regimes, along with the counter-reaction it produced in terms of the Asian values debate, had obscured the real, underlying, threats to the stability of the region. The rhetoric of both the end of history and Asian values over-promoted the idea of Southeast Asia as a zone of peace and prosperity. Both narratives were attempting to out-compete each other as explanations for the supposed economic success and tranquillity of the region. All this achieved, however, was to conceal a burgeoning Islamist terror network fomenting within. Almost all the region's national elites, including those in Australia, bought into variants of the end of history idea of Southeast Asia as a model of harmony and multilateral cooperation. Each nation severely compromised its security as a result.

It is to these themes that the essays in this chapter primarily attend, as David and I sought to broaden our understandings of the foreign policy dilemmas that 9/11 generated beyond the confines of Southeast Asia. Initially, our concern was to appreciate the genuine challenges that confronted statesmen in the post-9/11 world. It was evident after the attacks on the United States, and other outrages that followed, not least in Southeast Asia itself with the Bali bombings of October 2002, that the extant threat of a violent form of globalised Islamist militancy, needed to be countered.

Our analysis of the decision-making in Western capitals and elsewhere sought to understand the reactions of political leaders to these events. 9/11 had severely disrupted the optimistic assumptions of the post-Cold War 'New World Order', and the era to follow was one of confusion and complication. As much as it is possible to be critical of subsequent Western responses – as David and I were certainly to become – did not mean that policy predicaments about how to adequately address external and internal threats from violent jihadist actors did not exist. We risk simplifying history if we assume that it was all obviously misguided from the start.

The initial thinking of statesmen – from President George Bush in the US to Prime Minister Tony Blair in the UK – were not necessarily wrong in our view about wanting to use degrees of limited force to interdict Islamist conspiracies. Maybe they wanted to do the right thing for the right reasons, at first. However, we began to discern that the distorting ideological prism of end of history thinking regarding the inevitable triumph of liberal-democratic values was twisting military interventions into a series of disastrous 'forever wars' that were draining Western military and economic prestige externally, while contradictorily casting a light hand over the spread of Islamist networks internally within Western nations.

Dissecting the paradoxical effects of Western military intervention to tackle the spread of globalist Islamist violence provides the basis for several articles in this chapter. In particular, David and I began to home in on the elusive concept of 'counter-insurgency', the label under which the long military campaigns in Iraq and Afghanistan were prosecuted. The more we delved into how commentators spoke about these 'counter-insurgency' campaigns, the more we sensed that much of it was a pseudo-industry of bogus expertise, which asserted a universal blueprint for military intervention and the suppression of external challenges. At the same time, we observed that counter-insurgency thinking overwhelming concentrated on matters of operational technique. It ignored far more important first-order questions, such as should Western countries intervene in foreign lands in the first place, and if so, for how long and to achieve what?

Further, the focus on technique and abstruse operational language, along with the side-stepping of the more challenging questions about why Western forces should intervene, we noticed that commentators studiously avoided saying anything about how counter-insurgency principles should be applied to the home-front to tackle Islamist conspiracies within Western states themselves. As much as we were concerned to empathise with policymakers about how to deal with the real threat of jihadist violence, we became disturbed by the superficiality that characterised much Western analysis, especially in understanding the motivating role that Islamist ideology played in the activities of groups like *al-Qaeda* and later the Islamic State.

Much Western discourse, both political and academic, was often lightweight, even frivolous. Often it discounted the brutal realities of Islamist ideology, habitually ignoring jihadist texts that stated directly the intent and meaning of its violence. Instead, Western interpretations invariably focused on unfalsifiable second order concerns such as mental illness, economic deprivation and family problems as the principal drivers of jihadist activity. To us, this was a way of trying to deny the problems that Islamism posed to liberal certitudes in the domestic realm, such as the failure of multiculturalism, the lack of integration of minority communities, excessive levels of immigration and a failing sense of national cohesion.

Such denial was, as the essays in this chapter disclose, yet another manifestation of the quasi-religious assumptions embedded in liberal delusions at the end of history, which held that benighted societies abroad could be fixed with bouts of quasi-imperial intervention, while having nothing to say about how these same delusions were wrecking Western societies at home.

The Kentucky Fried Chicken of global jihad

George Shultz, Ronald Reagan's Secretary of State in the 1980s, observed that terrorism constitutes the 'matrix of different kinds of challenges, varying in scope and scale. If they have a single feature in common it is their ambiguity – they can throw us off balance'. As recent events illustrate all too graphically, a carefully coordinated terrorist act can be extremely effective at doing precisely that – throwing the US, and much of the Western world, off balance.

The threat posed to the US and the West more generally by such acts is asymmetrical. As the US Quadrennial Defense Review noted last year, it can take many forms, including 'the use of chemical, biological and possibly nuclear weapons; attacks against the information systems... as well as insurgency, terrorism, and environmental destruction'. It forecast all too presciently that a future adversary might 'employ asymmetric methods to delay or deny US access to critical facilities; disrupt our command, control, communications and intelligence networks; or inflict higher than expected casualties in an attempt to weaken our national resolve'.

Indiscriminate killing
The application of asymmetrical methods is fast becoming a defining feature of post-Cold War conflict. Between 1968 and 1989, 35,150 acts of international and domestic terrorism were recorded worldwide. That is an incident rate of 1,673 attacks each year. By comparison for the period 1990-96, the RAND-St Andrews chronology of International Terrorism noted 30,725 attacks, giving an average of 4,389 a year – an increase of 162 per cent on the Cold War years. The percentage increase would now be closer to two hundred given the escalating number of conflicts between 1996 and 2001 in Africa, South and Southeast Asia, Southeast Europe and the former Soviet states.

Significantly, this seemingly new form of warfare is often directed at the civilian population rather than at orthodox armed forces. At the turn of the century, the ratio of military to civilian casualties in wars was 8 to 1. Today this has been almost exactly reversed. In the wars of the 1990s, the ratio of military to civilian casualties is approximately 1 to 8.

Consequently, alongside the growth in the number of attacks on civilians, a further characteristic is their increasing lethality. According to RAND, fifty thousand people died in terror attacks between 1990 and 1996. This is double the number of casualties in the previous fourteen years.

Insurgent groups often no longer distinguish between limited and restricted uses of violence. Instead, terrorist acts, following the example of the Real Irish Republican Army, Islamic Jihad and Hezbollah, have become more extreme with indiscriminate killing of civilians the rule rather than the exception. This contrasts strikingly with the terror strategy of the 1970s where hostage taking and hijackings were deemed effective to the extent that they generated publicity for the cause, rather than massive loss of life.

Another by-product of assaults on civilian populations, especially in those states experiencing persistent civil strife, is a heightening of refugee and economic migracy flows towards those states that are either adjacent to conflict zones or seen as desirable destinations – almost exclusively in the developed West. Why, might we wonder, has the asymmetrical threat become the defining feature of post-Cold War security?

Local and global
There are several reasons for the proliferation of low intensity conflicts in the post-Cold War era and the attraction of asymmetric warfare for belligerents. Firstly, the end of the Cold War produced one globally dominant power – the US. Outside an American sphere of influence, yet at the same time often in conflict with it,

international relations between states and sub-state actors are increasingly characterised by civilisational issues of ethnic or religious origin.

These wars are often localised yet rely on a variety of transnational connections to sustain them. Consequently, conventional distinctions between internal and external: between aggression (from abroad) and repression (attacks from inside the country) are difficult to maintain. Commentators often argue that the globalisation of the 1990s is a qualitatively new phenomenon. Its consequences are unstable and contradictory, involving forces that propel both integration and fragmentation, homogenisation and diversification.

These wars are about identity rather than the ideological conflict which shaped many conflicts during the Cold War. They are fought both locally and globally. Often one side or another in these conflicts often relies for support and international pressure on a significant diaspora community and requires for communications the new technologies of the internet and the mobile phone.

Methods and strategies also differ. Unlike the guerrilla warfare techniques promulgated by Mao Zedong and Ernesto 'Che' Guevara during the Cold War, which theoretically at least, aimed to capture the hearts and minds of the population, the new asymmetric strategies explicitly target the civilian population. This is done either through expulsion, forcible resettlement, or by a range of intimidatory methods from systematic rape, through to mass killing, like the World Trade Center attack, or genocide as in Rwanda and the Balkans.

To some extent, such methods merely intensify patterns of resistance to power and authority that have been a feature since at least the American and French revolutions of the late eighteenth century, and arguably long before that. During the nineteenth century European anarchists, Marxists and nationalists justified revolutionary emancipation in terms of blood sacrifice and propaganda of the deed.

By the late 1960s, violent non-state actors had become a notable feature of the international system. The doctrine of the armed struggle flourished from Ireland through Italy and Germany to the Middle East, East Asia and South America. Its protagonists ranged from French thinkers like Regis Debray, to incompetent revolutionaries like Che Guevara and genocidal tyrants like Pol Pot.

New Left ideologies of violence were fuelled by the apparent success of the tactics of the Palestinian resistance – hostage taking, hijacking, assassination – which drew world attention to that struggle after the defeat of the Arab powers by Israel following the Six Day War in 1967.

Islamic radicalism
However, since the end of the Cold War, we have witnessed the intensification of sub-communal rather than ideological conflict and a dramatic rise in the range and extent of militant Islamist assaults on the US and its allies. The recent activities of Osama bin Laden, the renegade, but wealthy Saudi exile, are merely the latest manifestation of an Islamic radicalism that has elsewhere been responsible for bombing the World Trade Center in New York in 1993 and the Luxor tourist massacre of 1997.

The main factors promoting this Islamist terrorism are threefold. Firstly, and of decreasing importance, sponsorship by 'rogue' states like Sudan, Syria, Iran and Libya; secondly the legacy of the Afghan war, and thirdly, the fallout from the stalled Israeli-Palestinian peace process.

Significantly, since coming to power in Khartoum, Tehran and Kabul, Islamist regimes have conducted external and internal relations in terms of the *al-jihad al saghir* – that is, the necessity of transforming internal and external political relations in line with Islamically approved doctrines. They have also facilitated groups like Osama bin Laden's *al-Qaeda*, which functions as a franchising agency for jihadist activity on a global basis – a sort of Kentucky Fried Chicken of global terror.

The significant feature of this often religiously motivated identity politics is its non-negotiable, fundamentalist quality. This new radicalism functions through religious, internationalist and 'nomadic' networks rather than through the Cold War mechanism of sponsor states.

In this respect, Islamist terror poses a major threat to the state system in that it wages jihad (holy war) with the aim of reconstituting the Muslim community beyond national boundaries. Paradoxically, they rely on the globalisation and the products of Western modernity that they profess to despise to achieve their vision of the *darul Islam* (sphere of Islam). Through their use of English, the internet, satellite phones and, indeed as we also know now, sophisticated passenger aircraft, they are paradoxically an authentic product of the modern, globalised world and yet in fundamental conflict with it.

Thus, in Southeast Asia *Al-Ma'unah* – Brotherhood of Inner Power – an Islamist sect in northern Malaysia potentially open to a bin Laden franchise, consists of *silat* (an indigenous martial art) practising warriors who believed their leader, Mohamad Razali, could freeze opponents by the blink of an eye. At the same time, they also used the world wide web to advertise their belief that 'Jihad is our way'.

Other groupings like *Abu Sayyaf* – Father of the Sword – in Mindanao, also sponsored by *al-Qaeda*, which attained its international notoriety by kidnapping tourists, raises funds for its struggle through hostage taking and operates in a hazy area between organised crime and politically motivated violence.

Two worlds
Ultimately, the growth of terrorism in the post-Cold War era represents a complex amalgam of factors. In particular, the end of the Cold War removed the superpower patronage system that held many weaker states together. As a result, many of the post-Cold War successor states are notably unstable.

This has given rise to a sharp cleavage in the international system. At one level, the forces of globalisation have ushered in complex transnational processes that have, to a degree, eroded national boundaries. Many cosmopolitans live and work in relatively stable systems and adopt the 'tolerant' values of multicultural pluralism, communicating in English as a global lingua franca, while their belief in a borderless 'one-worldism' is facilitated by the development of the internet.

However, beyond this cosmopolitanised world, resides another domain where people exist in different 'ages,' with a different sense of time and reality. They inhabit a world of traditional rivalries where national or religious myths flourish and where force rather than persuasion remains the essential arbiter of much political life. It is in this twilight zone of state disintegration, chaos and genocide that new terror is born and which the cosmopolitanised world in terms of both its threat perception and ideology of globalised rights is singularly ill-equipped to address.

Original version published in *The World Today*, Vol. 57, No 10, October 2001, by David Martin Jones and M.L.R. Smith.

Costly delusions

In downtown Jakarta bookstores, for little more than a dollar, it is possible to pick up a slim volume entitled *Saya Teroris? Sebuah Pleidoi* (Am I a Terrorist? A Plea) by Fauzan al-Anshari. It gives an account of the life, times and beliefs of self-styled Sheikh Abu Bakar Bashir, the spiritual guru of the *Jemaah Islamiyah* network, which is allegedly behind the bombing of the Kuta Beach resort in Bali, in October 2002, in which over 200 people lost their lives.

From Bashir's somewhat paranoid perspective, the United States and Zionism have been plotting for decades to destroy Islam to secure global domination. To this end, Bashir maintains, US agencies engineered the World Trade Center attacks to justify a global assault on its enemies, notably the Palestinians and the Taliban. More recently, the Sheikh has argued that 'infidels' perpetrated the outrage at Kuta Beach to discredit the variety of purified Islam that he and his ilk purvey.

The conspiracy that Bashir alleges is that the world is engaged in a war between the forces serving the will of Allah and the 'spider's house' of the US Great Satan and its allies such as Australia. As Allah's will led to the fall of President Suharto and encouraged the revival of a purified Islam on Indonesian soil, that country must, like Afghanistan, now be the target of the great global Satan.

Prepare for jihad
On his return to Solo, Central Java, in 1999 from regional exile in Malaysia, where he established both religious schools and the rudiments of the *Jemaah Islamiyah* network, Bakar immediately invited fellow Muslim clerics to prepare 'for jihad against America'. He formed the *Majelis Mujahideen Indonesia* (Mujahidin Council of Indonesia) to coordinate those Indonesians committed to the purified creed that has gained popularity amongst young Muslim males globally.

This doctrine originated in the Middle East in the 1950s with those radically opposed to post-colonial secular nationalist regimes. It holds that only a pure form of Islam can address the 'hideous schizophrenia' of the modern condition. The Egyptian Muslim Brother Sayyid Qutb maintained that this 'ideological ideal system' alone could 'rescue humanity' from 'the barbarism of technocratic culture', along with the vice of an authoritarian nationalism imposed by a Nasser or a Suharto, as well as 'from the stifling trap of communism'.

This increasingly attractive Islamism, imported into Indonesia since the late 1980s, promotes a traditional and illiberal arrangement in which society is governed by familial and patronage networks of quasi-tribes and alliances forged on kin and services rendered, rather than on formal bureaucratic relations. Mafia activities and terror franchises sustain it. Similarly, *al-Qaeda* operates in this way, be it in Kuala Lumpur, Bali, New York, or London.

Sharia in favour
Since the fall of Suharto in 1998, a bewildering array of Indonesian groups has sprung up sharing the commitment to building an Islamic realm. This includes groups like *Laskar Jihad*, which aim to uphold the integrity of Indonesia and establish Sharia-style discipline across the archipelago.

In Jakarta, *Front Pembela Islam* (Islamic Defenders Front) makes a habit of regularly trashing tourist areas frequented by decadent Westerners. *Hizb-ut Tahrir* (Party of Liberation), a movement begun in Jordan in 1953 but proscribed across the Middle East, seeks to unite the Muslim world as a superpower governed according to Koranic law, while aspiring to recreate the caliphate of the early days of Islam. When US Secretary of State Colin Powell visited Indonesia in August 2002 to strengthen the government's anti-terrorist resolve, one of its leading lights, Rahmat Hassan, pronounced that 'America is the biggest terrorist in the world, they have stomped on Muslims too many times'.

Nor is this increasing fundamentalism a minority matter. In December 2001, a poll conducted by a sociologist at the moderate State University of Islamic Studies found that more than sixty percent of the population supported the implementation of Sharia law in Indonesia.

More recently, in the National Assembly last August, Islamists sought to reinstate a clause, omitted from the original 1945 constitution, that made carrying out the Sharia obligatory for 'all followers of Islam'. Although rejected, the amendment received support from Vice-President Hamzah Haz, speaker of the assembly Amien Rais, and on the streets from increasingly vocal Islamist groups.

Tolerant Islam

It has been evident since 1998 that Indonesia has been transforming itself into another Pakistan on Australia's doorstep. What is surprising is that the official scholar-bureaucratic orthodoxy in both Australia and Southeast Asia studiously maintained that this was not the case. Instead, it was said that, unlike its Middle Eastern equivalent, Indonesian 'civil' Islam was of a distinctly more tolerant hue, both capital friendly and democratic. Any attempt to contest this analysis was to commit the sin of constructing Indonesia as an alien enemy to the north and thus fuel Australia's unwarranted and deep-seated dread of the 'other'.

How did this denial come about? It can be traced to the attempts of successive governments from the 1980s, and particularly during the premiership of Paul Keating between 1993 and 1996, to redefine Australia as an Asian nation. To convince a sceptical public, Indonesia had to be portrayed as a benign, cooperative neighbour within a stable and prosperous Southeast Asian region. Australia's logical and inevitable destiny was to enmesh itself with the attractively diverse and economically booming region to the north.

Tranquillity and order

Maintaining this approach, however, politicised the Australian federal bureaucracy, especially senior advisers working in the Department of Foreign Affairs and Trade and the Office of National Assessments. Consequently, much analytical effort in the official bureaucracy, media and universities was devoted not to the dispassionate analysis of regional affairs, but to lending credibility to a debatable political agenda. The engagement strategy became the dominant view, with little attempt to test its assumptions. Dissenting viewpoints were marginalised or ignored.

As a result, much Australian commentary on Indonesia bore little connection to regional realities. This is revealed most obviously in a record of analytical failure that consistently misread regional prospects stretching from the disastrous Asian economic crisis of 1997, through to the Balkanisation of the Indonesian archipelago, to the Kuta bombings of 2002. Australian observers mirrored the wider, officially sponsored delusion of the Association of Southeast Asian Nations (ASEAN), which, along with its Western adherents, argued during the 1990s that the region was one of increased domestic tranquillity and regional order.

It has been evident to anyone with a semblance of scepticism that ASEAN, together with the regional economy, has been in complete meltdown since the mid-1990s. As analysts were extolling the much vaunted but extremely short 'Pacific Century', *Jemaah Islamiyah* and its regional affiliates like *Abu Sayyaf, Hizb-ut Tahrir* and the *Kumpulan Mujahideen Malaysia* were busily establishing their own networks. ASEAN, meanwhile, was blithely maintaining its doctrine of non-interference in the internal affairs of member states and advertising the utility of shared Asian values.

Analytical opinion towards Southeast Asia was highly 'sensitive' to Indonesian concerns, minimising awareness of internal instability. There was ready credence for commentators in government sponsored institutes of regional affairs like the Centre of Strategic and International Studies (CSIS) in Jakarta, which claimed, just months before the Bali bombing that 'attention to such groups as the *Laskar Jihad* has been overblown. They are rather noisy groups, but small and marginal'. Unsurprisingly, such views were echoed in Australia. Indeed, in early October one analyst observed that 'the tendency is still to overplay the threat'.

Such deference to official regional opinion is even more worrying in the case of the CSIS, long suspected by human rights groups as a front for Indonesian army intelligence. Ironically, according to Human Rights Watch, the Centre was involved in the creation of the fundamentalist group *Komando Jihad* (Jihad Commando) in 1977, where Bashir first plied his fundamentalist trade as part of a military-inspired dirty tricks operation to discredit moderate Islamic political parties.

It is concerning that for the best part of two decades Australian analysts meekly accepted the opinions of official think tanks, which extolled regional harmony and stability, while covertly encouraging the extremism now disturbing the region. Even in the immediate aftermath of the Bali bombing, the Jakarta orthodoxy in Australia doubted whether there was evidence of *al-Qaeda* involvement. More incoherently, received wisdom berated the Canberra government for not acting on US intelligence, whilst simultaneously maintaining that the bombing itself was the result of Australia's excessively close ties to the American-led 'war' on terrorism.

Significantly, in the wake of the Bali bombing the government of Prime Minister John Howard ordered a review of the apparent failure of Australian intelligence agencies to provide warning of the threat. But the Bali bomb was not simply an intelligence failure. It reflects a wider inability to understand the growing instability in Southeast Asia.

Australia needs more accurate threat perception. This requires reassessment of the increasingly vacuous idea of Asian engagement, and stronger bilateral ties with non-Muslim states in Southeast Asia such as Thailand, Singapore and the Philippines, which feel equally threatened by the spread of Islamist extremism. Unfortunately, such a re-evaluation cannot be accommodated in an official climate that disdains the idea that Indonesia might actually be a security problem.

Original version published in *The World Today*, Vol. 59, No. 1, January 2003, by David Martin Jones and M.L.R. Smith.

Who knows spins

'Most reports are false and the contumely of men acts as a multiplier of lies and untruths' wrote Carl von Clausewitz about the use of intelligence in the context of the Napoleonic war. Those who wrote of, or practised, espionage during the Cold War would, no doubt, have endorsed Clausewitz's understanding of the uncertainty and amorality of what we now rather euphemistically refer to as 'intelligence gathering'. The debate over the use and some might say abuse of intelligence to make the case for war in Iraq has highlighted the ambiguous nature of the function of intelligence in the policy process in the post-Cold War era and the post-9/11 world. In the contemporary era, different political priorities and agendas seem to be at work that serve to confuse public perceptions of the goals that intelligence is designed to achieve.

Espionage, noted Graham Greene, who knew the territory well, is not a place for moral judgements. In this Greene was inferring that the shadowy world of spying was one in which ethical behaviour counted for little. The game of nations, of which the world of espionage is a graphic manifestation, is one in which Machiavellian principles rule. Such a view, it seems, now comes as a surprise to many contemporary observers who question, for example, the dressing-up of intelligence reports about Saddam Hussein's WMD programme or are taken aback at the allegation that President's Bush's immediate reaction to the 9/11 attacks was to get his intelligence services to link the atrocities to Iraq.

Meanwhile, the reports that emerged in early March 2004 that British intelligence eavesdropped on the councils of the UN Secretary General induced concern and anger in figures such as former International Development Secretary Clare Short and inspired disaffected members of the intelligence community to leak reports of intelligence gathering operations to the press. Plainly, this underlines how frequently this kind of espionage is perceived as a nefarious and distasteful activity that undermines the pursuit of universal peace, harmony and justice through a UN inspired international regime.

The ambiguity of public perceptions of intelligence

What is going on here appears to be a degree of confusion about how intelligence agencies are expected to conduct their work in the current era. There is a gap between popular images of how intelligence functioned in the days of the Cold War and the different ideas that we now have of the roles that intelligence organisations are expected to perform in the post-Cold War world.

Back in the simpler times of the last few decades of the twentieth century we had some awareness that intelligence was a game of smoke and mirrors. After all, it afforded a whole novel and film genre, the best proponents of which, like John Le Carré's George Smiley, recognised a reality where facts were undecidable, and duplicity constituted the norm. Perhaps nothing illustrates the contradiction in popular imagery about the role of intelligence more than the activities of its most iconic figure in twentieth century cinema, the character of James Bond. On screen, the public preferred to see its spy heroes engage in every known act of 'covert action', including sabotage and assassination on a regular basis. In practice, of course, Western publics were unlikely ever to have been tolerant of such dubious activities (although they did go on in various forms and in varying degrees).

The point is, though, one never saw James Bond doing a humble desk job analysing data about the Warsaw Pact's order of battle, which constituted the staple diet of much intelligence activity during the Cold War. Post-Cold War and particularly in relation to the Iraq War of 2003, we can discern that public expectations assume that entirely different standards must apply. But can they?

Intelligence, as the more sophisticated fictional spy writers knew, was a world of relativities. Those who pursued moral and legal absolutes in international affairs tend to either ignore or discountenance this. Consequently, they overlook the fact that Saddam did have a WMD programme, it is just that the intelligence available could not identify its capacity.

The Coalition that went to war in Iraq in 2003 acted on available but uncertain evidence, being concerned about the potential proliferation of WMD in a globalised environment increasingly characterised by interconnection without integration that has, amongst other things, given rise to challenges from de-territorialised Islamist groups. Thus, the Coalition sought to enforce what might otherwise have been an unenforceable set of UN resolutions.

Ironically, back in the twentieth century those who now condemn how those who currently pursue the policy of weapons non-proliferation, campaigned for a similar end themselves. Those who camped on Greenham Common and called for unilateral disarmament (the official policy of the UK Labour Party in the late 1980s), or an end to French atomic tests in the Pacific because of the potential for the nuclear arsenals of the major powers to reduce the planet to a permanent nuclear winter, seem oblivious to the proliferation of such deadly chemical and biological weapons and for potential leakage of nuclear fissile materials into the hands of unstable non-state actors with a worrying propensity to apocalypse now.

Threat-based versus risk-based intelligence
Intelligence is all about overcoming unknowing. In a dangerous world of 'rogue states', global interconnections and ruthless crime and terror groups, intelligence is by its very nature about trying to find out what you don't know. This presents those in pursuit of the unknowable with a series of paradoxes: How do you know, necessarily, what you want to know? How do you know something you don't know? And when do you know when you have found out what you don't know? The answer in each case is: you don't know. Translated out of Yes-Minister speak, this means that intelligence is, and always has been, a hugely uncertain business. No one can predict the future. Hence intelligence analysis is all about assessing the balance of probabilities, rather than getting everything right.

It is this notion of the balance of probabilities that illustrates the crucial difference between perceptions of the role of intelligence during the Cold War and post-Cold War. During the Cold War, intelligence analysis was threat-based; in the post-Cold War era, it is now risk-based. Threat-based intelligence is much more straightforward. Known threats are recognised and can be acted upon or contained. During the Cold War this was uncomplicated. In an era of superpower competition people generally knew who the other side was. Not only could the threat be easily identified but it could also often just as easily be measured (by counting the missiles, tanks and aircraft of the other side). The probabilities of any given situation were stable and intelligence resources were easily targeted accordingly.

Risk-based intelligence is a much more ambivalent, and therefore politically hazardous enterprise. Unlike threat-based intelligence, risk assessment encompasses the much more problematic weighing up of potential dangers. When the balance of probabilities is seen by decision-makers to favour forms of pre-emptive action, as with the war in Iraq, the scope for political disputation is potentially far larger. This is not because statesmen necessarily want to casually manipulate intelligence material for electoral gain (although that is always a possibility). The dilemma arises because the dangers that are seen to be currently inherent in the international system are felt in some quarters, notably in Washington and London, to have ushered in an entirely different intelligence paradigm. The essence of this new thinking was outlined in a speech by Prime Minister Tony Blair on 5th March 2004 in which he stated:

> The threat we face is not conventional. It is a challenge of a different nature from anything the world has faced before. It is to the world's security, what globalisation is to the world's economy. It was defined not by Iraq but by September 11th. September 11th did not create the threat

Saddam posed. But it altered crucially the balance of risk as to whether to deal with it or simply carry on, however imperfectly, trying to contain it.

If one buys into this line of thinking, then needless to say it is going to dictate a new and unconventional framework in which to conceive the utility of intelligence. The primary role of intelligence is not now the slow accretion of data on enemy force dispositions, as in the Cold War, but rather the precautionary purpose of forestalling potential challenges before they materialise. The idea that 'intelligence' is ostensibly a passive information gathering exercise is overthrown.

The emphasis is now on action-orientated intelligence as Blair noted: 'This is not a time to err on the side of caution; not a time to weigh the risks to an infinite balance; not a time for the cynicism of the worldly wise who favour playing it long. Their worldly-wise cynicism is at best naiveté and at worst dereliction'.

The point is that if one accepts the principle that we are in an ostensibly new security era then the political stakes are high, not just in terms of engaging in pre-emptive action but equally, the dangers of not doing so. It is probably natural that an individual such as Tony Blair, who has made a career out of being highly attuned to public opinion, should be especially sensitive to the political implications involved:

> ...of course intelligence is precisely that: intelligence. It is not fact. It has its limitations. On each occasion the most careful judgement must be made taking account of everything we know and the best assessment and advice available. But in making that judgement, would you prefer us to act, even if it turns out to be wrong? Or not to act and hope it's OK? And suppose we don't act, and the intelligence turns out to be right, how forgiving will people be?

In effect, what we call intelligence has become far more politicised. This contrasts starkly with previous conceptions of intelligence during the Cold War. As the parameters of Cold War espionage were known and fixed, Cold War intelligence was de-politicised; a fact witnessed in that what passes for the discipline of intelligence studies inside universities is often little more than the study of bureaucracies and the examination of politically uncontentious historical case studies. Post-Cold War, we are now having to come to terms with the uncomfortable truth that intelligence is inherently politicised. And this is the cause of much public confusion.

In the current era, investigative journalists, parliamentary committees, and the wider media assume, somewhat idealistically perhaps, that intelligence must reveal some previously unsuspected but unvarnished truth. Therefore, its agencies should act like independent think-tanks purveying objective information about a particular situation to which policy makers then defer. It can never be so. Intelligence is never pure. It needs to be analysed and interpreted, and this means that it is open to spin and manipulation, or more precisely to politics. Like war, intelligence is a tool of politics.

The politicisation of intelligence

Espionage and *raison d'etat* came into the modern world joined at the hip. Intelligence is an inevitable and necessary consequence of the state's pursuit of its national interest. Further, in an age in which direct threats to national security are not always self-evident as they were in the Cold War, intelligence is necessarily more susceptible to political manipulation. The truth is that intelligence and policy are inextricably linked. With hindsight, we can say that those like Tony Blair and his advisors exaggerated the accuracy of uncertain intelligence and politicised it to support a pre-existing desire to invade Iraq. Similarly, we can say that those who opposed the war, invariably in all circumstances, have also sought to manipulate intelligence maintaining that it did not support any invasion of Iraq: an equally contestable political position.

Of course, in any democracy, one can and should be able to dispute the validity of policy priorities and objectives, but the crucial issue is that the intelligence effort will always be governed by political imperatives, howsoever defined. To express surprise at allegations of the monitoring of Kofi Annan's phone conversations or to charge that politicians exploit intelligence material to support pre-existing positions is therefore perhaps to miss the point. That is what intelligence agencies do. That is what they did in the Cold War and that is what they will continue to do so in the future.

Policy and intelligence cannot be separated. To be of any value intelligence must be put at the service of national priorities and will, accordingly, reflect political will, which returns us to Clausewitz, a prime sceptic of the utility of 'intelligence'. He thought intelligence was overrated precisely because it involves the impossible attempt to overcome unknowing. Trying to discern what you do not know thereby renders intelligence open to the 'contumely' – the insolence – of men and that applies most obviously to politicians. Clausewitz, though, was not saying that intelligence is always worthless, merely that intelligence is one of the many variables in war. It can sometimes work for you, or it can work against you. Show it too much deference however and it can impede the proper and swift action of decision makers, for good or ill. War, as Clausewitz stated, is a continuation of politics by other means. So is intelligence.

Original version published in *World Defence Systems*, Vol. 7, No. 2, Autumn 2004, by David Martin Jones and M.L.R. Smith.

The rise of the neo-COINS

Those who follow contemporary military developments in Western armed forces will understand that an important re-orientation has been taking place in the thinking of many Western armed forces. Some commentators have labelled this a military 'cultural revolution'. The sight of this revolution is counter-insurgency (COIN), traditionally regarded as a marginal vocation within most Western armed forces.

In the United States military, the tendency to regard counter-insurgency as anathema to its institutional culture has been particularly pronounced. According to one serving officer, the US Army's traditional focus on the 'big war paradigm' has 'impeded the Army from seriously studying counter-insurgency operations' and, consequently, prevented it from learning the lessons of 'how to fight guerrillas'. Now, all this has changed.

Of course, this shift in military thinking reflects the predominantly American, British and NATO experience of combating civil unrest in Iraq and Afghanistan and has been given expression in the extensive re-evaluation of traditional counter-insurgency theorising, and the re-discovery of the classical thinkers and campaigns from T.E. Lawrence to the Malayan Emergency. For the most part, classical insurgent and counter-insurgency thinking dwelt on conflicts where the colonial metropole sought to defeat uprisings against its rule.

The recrudescence of classic counter-insurgency thinking has found its most formidable expression in the joint US Army and Marines *Counterinsurgency Field Manual*, published in 2007, which leads the reader through an appreciation of the administrative, military, intelligence, legal, and even linguistic aspects, and requirements for modern COIN operations. The flourishing of counter-insurgency studies can be termed neo-COIN, especially as novel insights and operational understandings have been produced in the light of this new era of thinking.

Neo-classicists vs. global counter- insurgents

Despite the innovations in thought generated by neo-COIN thinking, there have been criticisms. One point noted by commentators is that many if not all the underlying premises embodied in the US Army/Marines *Counterinsurgency Field Manual*, and much of the literature surrounding the study of contemporary insurgency, is that insurgencies are things that happen somewhere else: 'over there', but not 'here'.

Critics have observed that to a greater extent neo-COIN encourages the view that insurgencies for the most part are external threats or problems that reside beyond the realm of the 'home' state. This reflects the bulk of classical insurgent and counter-insurgency thinking, which dwelt on conflicts that derived from the colonial era where imperial powers sought to quell violent opposition in their more unruly possessions.

As the experience of insurgency both as a concept and as an existential reality suggests, confining COIN thinking purely to the external realm is untenable when threats, plots, and physical attacks, such as those on the London transport system of July 2005, possess transnational connections and implications that stretch from the Middle East to South Asia, to the inner-city areas of major British cities. This has given rise to a contending subset of neo-COIN.

If the notion of global insurgency has any currency, then it surely means that in theory it is, or has the potential to be, everywhere. Several recent theorists, such as John Mackinlay and David Kilcullen, have drawn attention to this point, arguing that current views of counter-insurgency are still dominated by a concept that sees insurgency – and by implication counter-insurgency – as fundamentally a struggle for control of a population within a given territorial space.

In fact, the thinking encapsulated in publications like the US Army/Marines *Counterinsurgency Field Manual* represents little that is intrinsically new: more a case of neo-classicism than neo-COIN. The neo-classical school of counter-insurgency has certainly reinvented, adapted, elaborated, re-emphasised, and sometimes made more sophisticated, pre-existing ideas.

The true neo-COINS, perhaps, are those who have asserted that the present security environment is one that may have only the loosest correlation between operations and geographical space, because – as events from 9/11 onwards emphasised, we are in a condition of post-territorial insurgency. Such writers have thus extrapolated ideas about the evolution of a 'global insurgency' to suggest that this must logically entail a *global counter-insurgency* response.

In fact, although the neo-classicists and the global counter-insurgency schools exist in degrees of opposition to each other, when examined carefully, both reveal their shortcomings in relation to current concerns about how to combat Islamist terror networks effectively.

The problems with 'global' COIN
Crucially, when scrutinised, global counter-insurgency theory, despite its claim to be a more sophisticated appreciation of the problem of insurgency in the modern world, appears just as constricted in its outlook and solutions as neo-classical understandings. The reason for this arises from the very nature of the counter-insurgency paradigm in which both classical and neo-COIN thinkers located themselves.

The main criticism levelled against the neo-classicist advocates of COIN by the global counter-insurgency theorists is substantially accurate. While the flowering of debate about counter-insurgency has undoubtedly been of great utility for the US armed forces, which has been compelled to re-educate itself in the ways of counter-insurgency practice and away from an obsession with conventional high tech/high tempo war fighting (which only the US is capable of waging, and which any intelligent adversary will therefore be intent on avoiding), the wider applicability of neo-classicist tenets beyond the specific theatres of Iraq and Afghanistan are questionable in an age of transnational threats that emanate from de-territorialized jihadist groups.

That said, global insurgency reveals itself as a hazy idea. What is it exactly? Theorists of global-COIN are often vague in spelling out what they mean in any detail. Critics contend that 'global insurgency is a term akin to the 'war on terrorism': namely, that it is a euphemistic phrase that that seeks to avoid naming – and confronting – the main threat faced by the West from a highly ideological form of Islam.

Thus, global COIN thinkers are little different from the neo-classicists. Whereas neo-classicism may be silent in stating how to handle global insurgency, contenting itself to see counter-insurgency practice as confined to specific geographic theatres in areas external to the home state, neo-COINs are not that far removed, implying that counter-insurgency is about operational technique. The only difference is that global COIN advocates believe that these operational techniques should be applied on a universal scale. In other words, the principles and tactics employed at a local level within a given territorial area, must be adapted and made applicable to work at the transnational level. Hardly a stunning revelation.

What, moreover, do these techniques of global counter-insurgency entail? Again, the global COIN advocates, for all their claims to novelty and greater sophistication, are opaque. It is one thing to re-discover classical counter-insurgency texts and to develop traditional ideas drawn from colonial campaigns like the Malayan Emergency for application in discrete theatres like Iraq and Afghanistan. It is quite another, however, to extract a wider template (drawn off singular campaigns like the Malayan Emergency) to inform the conduct of operations against a worldwide (Islamist) insurgency, which global-COIN thinking implies. The nature of the current Islamist terror threat, that is, global insurgency, is of an entirely different order than merely seeking to apply COIN techniques on a broader transnational canvas.

Classical understandings for 'defusing' an insurgency, require addressing legitimate grievances of the population, the premise of which is that the counter-insurgent has some capacity to deliver tangible benefits to the population. In the case of Malaya, for example, the broadest context of this 'draining the swamp' of discontent was the promise of independence. Global counter-insurgency, however, cannot be simply Malaya writ on a larger scale where one seeks to control and influence the population, provide better administration, improve their socio-economic position, and address their political aspirations.

Yet, the logical extrapolation from the micro (local insurgency) to the macro (global insurgency) level is that wider Western interests could or should be negotiable to undermine support for Islamism. However, this premise rests on the assumption that a) Islamist sentiment is based on a degree of legitimacy b) it can be assuaged and accommodated by concessions and, c) such concessions would be justified and would not imperil key vital interests.

All these assumptions are debatable. For instance, global COIN theorists could potentially view the withdrawal of troops from Iraq and Afghanistan, pressure on Israel to negotiate settlements with the Hamas government in Gaza and the Palestinian Authority in the West Bank, the easing of pressure on Iran's nuclear programme, as legitimate negotiating positions to be traded away.

The problem in extrapolating the micro to the macro level of counter-insurgency is that while the redress of limited grievances may appear feasible in the local sphere, it begins to look dangerously like one-sided concessions at the global level: a willingness to trade or abandon tenets of Western security for the sake of a quiet life, if quiet it does bring, rather than merely re-affirm the self-belief of ideologised Islam, emboldening its quest to score further diplomatic victories over a weak and decadent West. Grievance settlement at the global level thus acts to encourage Islamist assaults rather than defuse the 'causes' of global insurgency.

Current advocates of global-COIN do not necessarily endorse the ideas of one-sided grievance settling explicitly, but they are often ambiguous as to just what a global counter-insurgency programme entails in practice.

Downplaying religion/ideology?

To the extent that neo-COIN thinkers design to clarify their stance, they inadvertently give credence to this idea of counter-insurgency as appeasement. The published works of global COIN theorists, for example, frequently downplay the role of religious motivation in Islamist activism, believing the examination of social networks, psychological profiling, and focusing on patterns of recruitment are the key to dealing with the threat.

David Kilcullen, for instance, dismisses the influence of Islamist ideology as a motivating factor for jihadist violence, arguing instead that the 'sociological characteristics of immigrant populations' is the central factor 'explaining contemporary threats rather than Islamic theology'. He contends, therefore, that Islamic theology per se 'has little functional relationship with violence'.

But this particular emphasis merely reinforces the idea that global counter-insurgency is a matter of technique, intelligence gathering and the fine-tuning of public policy that focuses on discrete, technical issues of recruitment and the role of individual pathology as well as the mollification of a monolithic Islamic community at the expense of looking at the underlying ideological driving forces.

Claiming that religion – Islam – is unimportant is like suggesting that Che Guevara or the Red Brigades had nothing to do with Marxist ideology. It is the ideology that provides the inspiration and the motivation to act. Therefore, any attempt to combat the problem must at least know the ideology behind the threat rather than just concentrate on the surface manifestations of the threat.

The politics of internal security

What this suggests is that contemporary neo-COIN analysts, of both the classic and global COIN persuasions, are committing the mistake of seeing counter-insurgency as an operational technique rather than as a strategy that relates operational means to political ends. The point about our current security condition is that the political ends are often much more pronounced and controversial precisely because they are internal and involve, ultimately, a struggle over political values at home.

The concept of internal security is often a controversial notion, especially in liberal democratic states, involving as it does values like the freedom of the individual, civil liberties, free expression, and protection against any overweening ambitions of the state. The controversial nature of internal security is especially pronounced in societies where multicultural assumptions predominate, which often make it difficult for public discussion to examine the nature and extent of the threat out of a fear of appearing prejudiced or racist. But as some officials, like Peter Clarke, former Head of the Counter-Terrorism Command at the Metropolitan Police has acknowledged, counter-terrorist policing (that is, domestic counter-insurgency), if it is to have any credibility, has become intrinsically more 'political' in its orientation given that it has to pre-empt threats and target resources against a discernible section of the population from which jihadist conspiracies are known to emanate.

The political dimension in the current era thus needs to be confronted. It is this which the global-COIN thinkers seem reluctant to do, finding it easier to focus on less contentious ideas of social networks, prisons, urban deprivation, and family breakdown as sources of jihadist recruitment. Little mention is made of other more controversial and far more significant sources of indoctrination and recruitment such as schools, mosques and universities, which provide much of the ideological motor for Islamism in the West.

Indeed, conspicuously absent in neo-COIN commentary is any mention of the word 'terrorism'. The avoidance of this term is a symptom of the reticence of much contemporary analysis to contemplate the underlying ideological struggle at work, and the necessary strategy with which to oppose jihadism, which all too often challenges the assumptions of Western multiculturalism.

In fact, the idea of a global insurgency is itself something of a misnomer, because it implies that it is a more objective analytical framework that can avoid confronting the awkward political questions of the day. Global insurgency is a fancy way of making the simple sound exotic. Arguably, what is termed 'global insurgency' is a euphemism for something more prosaic, yet more disturbing: namely, a domestic insurgency arising from the forces of Islamism at home.

The ideology may be global in outlook and register a transnational dimension, which demands that elements of the Islamist threat be dealt with at an international level, but at issue is a domestic challenge to the integrity of the state. The nature of the Islamist insurgency may be unique in that it acts both globally and locally, but in essence, the focus of any counter-insurgent operation is going to be within the state itself. Fundamentally, counter-insurgency is about restoring state security, and this requires attention to basic issues of political sovereignty such as securing state borders and the assertion of a strong, inclusive national identity.

In that sense, the solution, contrary to the global COIN thesis, still resides within the state. It is the state that provides the ultimate security for its citizens, and in providing adequate security at home, it thereby contributes to the defeat of Islamism globally.

The problem: whose hearts and whose minds?

In this understanding some interesting questions arise about the application of counter-insurgency principles within the 'home' state. The central precept of classical thought is the control and influence of the people: the battle for hearts and minds. But the notion of a transnational insurgency poses a curious question: who are the people? And whose hearts, and whose minds should be won?

Traditional thinking on the subject would automatically assert that in the current context the focus of hearts and minds operations should be upon minority Muslim communities in the West. Most certainly, any sophisticated counter-insurgency effort would, of course, attend to those communities and their concerns to interdict subversive plots and to wean away elements that might be attracted to the path of violence. But that cannot be the whole story.

In an age of polymorphous violence and clashing ideological/religious values, hearts and minds operations apply with equal, if not more force, to the majority population, which needs to have its sense of identity and national solidarity consolidated. This is necessary to gain their support for limited pre-emptive interventions abroad that may be necessary to counter the threat when it manifests itself externally, as well as to maintain the necessary social cohesion at home to sustain any protracted campaign against internal threats.

What all this means is that the current threat from jihadist groups can indeed be justifiably described as a global insurgency, which uniquely, manifests itself both within the domestic as well as the external sphere. 'Over there' is 'here', and this requires flexible ideas of countering the threat that go beyond the traditional counter-insurgency paradigm.

It suggests that a global counter-insurgency effort involves a global 'hearts and minds campaign', but not necessarily in the sense that global COIN thinking would hold, that of identifying and remedying global grievances. Addressing basic issues of security and socio-economic improvement in the tribal hinterlands of Iraq or Afghanistan is one thing. Tackling issues that lead certain members of the Islamic community towards jihadism within British and European states may be another.

However, the first principle of any war, as the philosopher of war Carl von Clausewitz stated, is to not mistake its essence, and to understand what the fundamental struggle is about. In the case of the struggle against Islamist violence, the struggle is one over political values within the West in general and within the domestic sphere in particular. It is a struggle between the values of political Islam and liberal democracy.

In that struggle, it is not just Islamic communities that are crucial: it is everyone else as well. It is a struggle within Western states involving the whole population, not just minority segments within it. People have to be convinced of the validity of the struggle because to concede in some spheres in, say, the Middle East, such as immediate troop withdrawal from Iraq, or at home, like protecting Islam from criticism by outlawing 'Islamophobia', or conceding the extension of Sharia law, or simply failing to take the internal threat seriously, risks compromising important political values at home, at the expense of liberal tolerance and the sustainability of an open and pluralistic society.

Conclusion: not a long war, but an endless war

The evolution of neo-COIN thinking in many ways represents a remarkable re-discovery of archetypal conflicts and renowned thinkers who have something to tell us about how to approach specific conflicts like those in Iraq and Afghanistan.

The development of a school of global counter-insurgency thinking that considers the transnational complexities that arise when local conflicts connect with multiple external factors, which may help drive those conflicts can enhance our understanding. At the same time, we should not exaggerate and come to believe that we are in an entirely new era, where state responses are marginalised. The state, on the contrary, remains crucial, as it is in the domestic arena where transnational threats will always manifest themselves and where they will necessarily have to be combated.

Moreover, the global COIN tendency can run the risk of distracting concern from important, and inevitably highly political, issues that must be confronted in the domestic realm to defeat the transnational threat from the forces of de-territorialised jihadism. These concerns revolve around contentious notions about how to structure society and what kinds of political values should be asserted to maintain popular resilience in the face of these threat.

In this regard, the rise of the neo-COINS should compel us to recognise that insurgent threats are not things that manifest themselves somewhere else but possess profound implications for individual societies. The key implication involves a constant battle to maintain a liberal and pluralistic society from those forces that would seek to undermine such governing systems.

The most important issue in any global counter-insurgency effort is to comprehend that there is no end of history, and certainly not a pre-ordained liberal end of history. The condition of the global system is one that it has always been: one of conflict and struggle over interests and values. It may be peaceful or violent, but it will always be a struggle. Not a long war, simply an endless one.

Original version published in *World Defence Systems*, Vol. 1, 2009, by M.L.R. Smith.

The strategy of savagery: Explaining the Islamic State

February 2015 saw the Obama Administration playing host to a summit on extremism, held in the wake of the jihadist attacks in Paris and the rise of the brutal theocratic order of the Islamic State of Iraq and the Levant (ISIL) across parts of the Middle and East and North Africa. Speakers at the summit voiced understandable concern at the growing spread of Islamist extremism and revulsion toward the methods it endorses to extend its reach. Whether it be the mass kidnapping of Nigerian school children, the torture and enslavement of Yezidi women, the murder of Jews and journalists trying to carry on their daily lives, or the gruesome executions of hostages, the depth of depravity to which some are prepared to sink is seemingly bottomless.

The rhetoric of politicians and commentators when confronted with such outrages defaults to a few well-worn phrases: barbarity, savagery and medieval brutality. The immolation of Jordanian pilot Moaz al-Kasasbeh in February 2015, captured after his plane was shot down over Syria, according to Roger Boyes of *The Times*, took the 'pinnacle of Islamic State's barbarity' to new heights. Denunciation of what are undoubtedly heinous crimes is only natural, but it also spills over into a less admirable tendency to focus, almost exclusively, on the supposed motivations of individual jihadists.

Boris Johnson, the Mayor of London, and a possible future leader of the British Conservative Party, described those who went off to fight for Islamic State as porn-addicted, sexually frustrated, 'wankers'. 'They are tortured', he told *The Sun* newspaper, 'They will be very badly adjusted in their relations with women, and that is a symptom of their feeling of being failures and that the world is against them'. The most disturbing element was not Johnson's reductionism – he's a grandstanding politician, that's what he does (and in Johnson's case, he often does it very well) – but that his analysis supposedly drew upon an MI5 report into the profiles of Islamist extremists. The MI5 report and Johnson's colourful interpretation of it follow a now-established pattern of writing off jihadists as losers, dunces, and clowns who suffer from a variety of emotional inadequacies, have problems with their fathers, suffer low self-esteem, and can't make it with girls.

Western fallacies and delusions

Attempting to identify what drives young men (and, we should add, women) along the path of jihad and the sanguinary embrace of the Islamic State is hardly the most relevant to understanding the true extent of the current threat. Which average 16–25-year-old male hasn't suffered status anxiety, problems with his father, or worried about his sexuality? The preoccupation with such second-order concerns reflects a Western pathology for rationalising and typologising anything that looks like aberrant behaviour and shows a reluctance to confront the ideology that underpins and motivates those who seek to throw in their lot with revolutionary movements like ISIL.

Moreover, liberal politicians and commentators who do address the ideology, present Islamism merely as a front that masks quasi-legitimate grievances (usually against deprivation, Western foreign policy and/or Islamophobia). Further, even if it were possible to get at the roots of a generic terrorist persona, what would this really entail for any kind of policy practice? Can you screen large parts of the population – Muslim or otherwise – for psychological imbalances? Even if this were possible diagnostically, would it be feasible politically? Surely, this is a route to the totalitarian end of 'pre-crime'.

Not only is such psychologising of personal motivation unprovable, but it is also a distraction that leaves Western states unprepared to confront an implacable enemy. Reducing jihadism to personality traits offers no form of defence. Despite the opprobrium directed towards jihadism, the jihadists don't care because they perpetrate barbaric acts for a reason. They have anticipated, and even welcome, such decadent Western denunciation.

Ultra-violence as political communication

Condemnation is not going to make the threat go away, nor is pseudo-psychology. Instead, an evaluation should begin from the first principle of strategic theory: that all violence is political communication. Or to use Carl von Clausewitz's classic formulation: war is a continuation of politics by other means, where the act of violence is intended to compel the enemy to do our will. Rather than condemnatory rhetoric, analysis should focus on evaluating the intended purpose the acts of savagery are designed to serve. An examination of ISIL's thinking suggests they have thought about the strategy of savagery very carefully.

That ISIL and its jihadist confrères beyond the Middle East adhere to a campaign of ultra-violence, often rotating around graphic displays of killing that shock and disrupt modern sensibilities is itself significant, because it displays how they have deduced what they perceive as the fundamental weakness in Western society: its attachment to life.

Jihadism counter-poses a belief in life with a cult of death. This is not a reversion to medieval cruelty. It has modern origins. Fascism, as Umberto Eco observed, possesses a taste for political necrophilia: elevating slaughter and martyrdom to theatre, symbolism and modus operandi. The Islamist version is similarly obsessed. As the slickly, if somewhat over-produced, video of Lieutenant al-Kasasbeh's killing on the internet demonstrated, adoring, and serving death provides the movement with its fundamental rationale.

Moreover, the Islamists' celebration of death as the dividing line between a pluralist secular world order and their brand of apocalyptic millenarian Caliphism is hardly new. It was announced in the wake of the 9/11 attacks with the formula: 'we love death as you love life'. This slogan has gone through several iterations since 2001, with phrases like 'The Americans love Pepsi Cola, we love death'. In essence, however, this fetishising of death defines itself against secular, Western, Enlightenment assertions of life.

The beatification of violence is as telling as the politically religious commitment. To love death as jihadism does is to say that it is beautiful to receive it, to risk it, and that the most beautiful thing is to distribute it. The intention is not to desensitise youth to the idea of death (as newspaper opinion pages frequently assert) but to sanctify it. Such cruelty and the addictive craving it produces, moreover, serve a broader ideological and strategic purpose that much Western commentary seems unable to comprehend.

The fallacy of lone wolves and stray dogs

Following 9/11, some of the more interesting jihadist theorists like Abu Musab al-Suri and Abu Bakr Naji outlined a blueprint for what a global strategy of Islamist resistance would look like, proposing a more flexible campaign for action than that proffered by *al-Qaeda*'s ostensibly hierarchical and (before the Coalition invasion of Afghanistan) territorially based movement. Al-Suri's and Naji's third generation jihadism required an intensification of violence in the Middle East after the withdrawal of US forces along with a more amorphous, but global, leaderless resistance.

Media commentary often dismisses attacks like those that have taken place in Boston, London, Ottawa, Sydney or Paris as the product of 'lone wolves', or 'stray dogs'. Such terms play into ill-conceived notions that these are the actions of deranged lunatics. For example, writing in *The Guardian*, Yassir Morsi considered the perpetrator of the attack on the Lindt café in Sydney in December 2014, Man Haron Monis, as no more than 'a desperate man with a violent past', while 'terrorist experts' invariably disdain such incidents as 'one-off home grown incidents' or pronounce on little or no evidence that they function in a dislocated manner with no higher direction from entities like Islamic State.

The complacency is not only self-evidently contradictory (for example, there have now been so many attacks that clearly they cannot be said to be 'one-off') but it overlooks another basic precept of strategic theory, as enunciated by Clausewitz, that war is never an isolated act. It is always an act of political will. Therefore, the very notion of a 'lone wolf' functioning in complete isolation is a misnomer. They are not acting in isolation, but within a highly connected, transnational network that is fully plugged into a political agenda and promoted through social media and the wider cybersphere in which a community of like-minded believers operate. This sphere contains all the ideological stimuli to inspire, justify and motivate specific actions.

Therefore, to speak of the actors who carry out these attacks as dislocated loners gives rise to the specious idea that policy prescriptions can be formulated upon the psychologising of Islamist actions down to the personality of the individual. The actions of so-called lone wolves facilitate a wider strategic agenda that fully validates the thinking of the more important jihadist tacticians since 9/11, like al-Suri and Naji.

Fourth generation jihadism

After 9/11, al-Suri recognised that the global Islamist resistance movement required a more sophisticated strategy than the one *al-Qaeda* was pursuing. After 2003, al-Suri's new third generation jihadism, therefore, turned to the concept of 'leaderless' resistance. In 2005, al-Suri published his *Global Call to Islamic Resistance* online.

This document asserted the need for self-radicalised actions 'which will wear down the enemy and prepare the ground for waging war on open fronts... without confrontation in the field and seizing control of the land, we cannot establish an [Islamic] state, the strategic goal of the resistance'. The American born Islamist Anwar al-Awlaki published five articles extracted from the *Global Call* for *Inspire*, the English language online journal that made jihad hip. Al-Suri's thinking now directly influences the transnational online strategy of the Islamic State and the Syrian al-Nusra front.

It is through an examination of al-Suri and Naji's ideas that we can detect how leaderless resistance abroad complements the management of savagery within the protean Islamic State. In this context, it is Naji's thought, as Michael Weiss and Hassan Hassan have argued in their book *ISIS: Inside an Army of Terror*, that has most bearing on ISIL's current strategy.

Of Egyptian background, Naji, like al-Suri, was an *al-Qaeda* insider with links to Abu Musab al-Zarqawi's *al-Qaeda* in Iraq prior to the latter's death in 2008. Ultimately, the purpose of violence, whether in the West or in Raqqa, as Naji explained, is to secure the borders of the Islamic State. As he analysed in *The Management of Savagery: The Most Critical Stage Through Which the Umma Will Pass*, the chaos of savagery represents the intermediate stage of state breakdown, which the revolutionary cadre must manage enroute to the purified Islamic realm. Naji declares: 'If we succeed in the management of savagery, that stage will be a bridge to the Islamic state which has been awaited since the fall of the caliphate'. Here we can discern that in his thinking about how to conduct jihad, Naji has read, and is clearly influenced by, Mao Zedong's thinking on protracted people's war.

In his attachment to a 'stages theory' of revolution, Naji, in the manner of a Marxist dialectician, distinguishes between: a) the stage of state breakdown characterised as one of 'vexation and exhaustion' where the failing state's power, as in the Palestinian Authority or contemporary Afghanistan, for example, remains contested and b) the subsequent stage of 'savage chaos', where the people 'yearn for someone to manage the savagery'.

Managing savagery

The management of the stage of savagery therefore requires securing the region's borders, providing basic food and medical treatment, and establishing Sharia justice, prior to transition to the final historical stage of the reformed caliphate. Stages one and two clearly conform to Mao's understanding of the 'strategic defensive' and 'strategic equilibrium' phases of protracted people's war, as enunciated in *On Guerrilla Warfare* (1936).

As with Mao, so it is with Naji, the control of the people and the support of the masses in achieving both unity and power are secured 'through armed struggle'. The only difference is that Naji's strategy is intended to facilitate not the liberation of the poor and tabula rasa peasantry, but the implementation of Sharia law. To achieve this, Naji points out, 'violence is crucial'. Any backsliding or 'softness' will 'be a major factor in the loss of the element of strength'. Again, this has strong parallels with Maoist thought, which held that demonstrative acts of terror would be necessary to enforce conformity to the goals of the revolution. Even if the caliphate is not achieved in the short-term, it is not the end of the matter. Naji continues chillingly, 'the more abominable the level of savagery is', it is still less abominable than enduring stability under 'the order of unbelief, *nizam al kufir* by several degrees'. Indeed, here one can note a further general tendency in Western commentary to discount – often in its totality – the strategic debate that takes place within the Islamist/jihadist domain.

Islamism is – to adapt another Maoist aphorism – a sea in which many fish swim and there is a continuous and often little remarked-upon self-critique that goes on within its ranks about the best means to attain its goals. One of the better-known examples of this was the 2005 letter sent by Osama bin Laden's deputy, Ayman al-Zawahiri, to Abu Musab al Zarqawi, the leader of *al-Qaeda* in Iraq, censuring the harshness of his methods in leading Iraq down the path of sectarian war. The criticism was not one of morality, it was one of instrumentality: the killing of unbelievers and apostates is not in itself ethically wrong but is a process that needs to be properly managed.

Any actor that seeks to use force, or threat of force, to attain its ends does so by trying to control the escalation process, either upping or lowering the level of violence, to send political messages in a process of violent communication. Without careful thought, it is possible to damage the cause through acts of ill-considered violence, which either alienates important political constituencies or else, more terminally, calls down a massive act of retaliatory counter-escalation that destroys the political movement.

Misunderstanding escalation

In this respect, some commentators argue that the gruesome killing of the Jordanian pilot indicated that the Islamic State might have 'over-reached itself', evincing a 'revolution out of control'. According to Joana Cook, the 'glorification of brutality is further detracting from any suggestion that they provide an attractive state system. Like many terrorist groups before them, they have limited vision for meaningful change. Their long-term goals and present actions are falling out of sync'. The increasing pressures on the group, she added, 'make them more desperate and likely to carry out barbaric acts to keep attention to their message'.

The comforting narrative that ISIL is desperate and has over-escalated lends itself to another distorting lens through which much Western commentary misreads the ideology of Islamism, which is failing to understand the death-cult's post-modern appeal and the considerable attention that Islamists pay to their strategic 'messaging'. Those like Naji are sensitised to the power of the media; and the way the West believes its own media delusions. Naji and his ilk believe that while the *mujahid* and the rightly guided are driven by political religion, the West is vitiated by self-interest.

Naji, in this respect, even quotes Lord Palmerston's maxim that there are no permanent enemies or permanent friends, only permanent interests. The *jahiliya* world (the realm of pagan ignorance) is thus fragile, lacking cohesion, and easily divided. The purpose of the strategy of savagery is to draw the United States and its allies into a real war and not a proxy war. Islamists, according to Naji, therefore have a doctrine of 'paying the price', that is: you bomb us, and we'll bomb you, especially in your heartlands where we know you are weak. In this understanding, they are acutely aware that they are engaged in a 'political game' where 'coarseness' and 'rough violence in times of need' are all part of the policy of 'paying the price'.

Significantly, then, far from being desperate or over-extended, Islamist strategic thinking reveals a rigorous design from first principles that discerns the weaknesses in Western society (which for Islamic State theorists begins with the West's attachment to life) and the way to exploit them to achieve long-term goals. The salutary fact is that these theorists have thought about how to manage the escalation process, thereby controlling the strategy of savagery: doubtlessly, and probably accurately, concluding that the West lacks the collective will to counter-escalate in any coherent way.

Conclusion
What we have learned in this short essay, therefore, is that extending from its political-religious creed, the Islamic State derives its strategy from both anti-democratic Western and non-Western sources. While the Islamist death-cult draws upon twentieth-century totalitarian ideologies for its sanctification of violence, the management of savagery derives its logic from the Maoist theory of protracted people's war.

Those like al-Suri and the Islamic State have considered both their strategic goal and the tactics with which to achieve it: the management of savagery. In their response, Western governments, and large parts of the media all too often merely engage in rhetoric and a discourse of denial. There has in consequence arisen a disjuncture between what Islamists openly say, and have said for years, and what the media and politicians understand motivates Islamists (namely, personality defects and grievances), and what Islamists do. And this brings us back to the 'strange and woolly affair' that constituted the Countering Violent Extremism summit, where such self-delusion appeared on full display with President Obama, interestingly, undercutting the conference when he stated: 'We all know there is no one profile of a violent extremist or terrorist, so there's no way to predict who will become radicalized'. As a few sceptical voices noted, despite all the rhetoric, 'where was the hard-hitting analysis and frank admission regarding the international appeal of Salafist holy warriors?' Nowhere in sight, as usual.

Original article appeared in *War on the Rocks*, 24th February 2015, by David Martin Jones and M.L.R. Smith.

The delusions of counter-insurgency

Western military thinking's fascination with counter-insurgency had its origins in the aftermath of the events of 9/11, in particular, the occupations of Iraq and Afghanistan by Coalition forces. The costs, consequences, and controversies associated with this era preoccupied the thinking of policy makers and security analysts for the better part of two decades. Yet, since 2011, Western forces have drawn down from major theatres of operation, with, at most, advisory missions left behind in low-profile training roles. The likelihood is that these occupations that once loomed so large in the public mind will fade from view, displaced by new and very different crises on the world stage. After the troops have gone, therefore, what we might wonder should we make of counter-insurgency (COIN) and what, if any, lessons emerge from it?

Four broad themes may be identified in COINthink. The first that emerges is the elusive and ambivalent character of the phenomenon that COIN seeks to deter. Somewhat surprisingly, the very idea of an 'insurgency' is difficult to identify with precision. At different times since 1949 practitioners and analysts have deployed a multitude of terms to denote pretty much the same thing. Such terms range from names like small wars, irregular wars, unconventional wars, guerrilla, or revolutionary wars, all of which seek to capture this elusive phenomenon. These assorted terms have rarely succeeded in clarifying what precisely an insurgency is in practice. Accordingly, the notion of counter-insurgency is equally obscure.

Coin as narrative

Even so, when carefully unpacked, the elasticity of the term counter-insurgency connotes not so much a concept, but a narrative. Its actual meaning may be contested, but as an explanatory device through which past events are filtered it becomes a powerful tool. Between 2007 and 2011, the COIN narrative maintained that the confusion and complexity of Iraq's post-invasion civil strife could be reduced to a single practice. In other words, it constituted 'an insurgency', which required those commanders aware of the practice to prepare US forces to 'surge' in the operational theatre and thus achieve enhanced conditions of security. In so doing, COIN applied the recently rediscovered tactics of classic population-centric Cold War counter-insurgency and distilled them into The US Army/Marine Corps *Counterinsurgency Field Manual*. The decline in violence in Iraq after 2007 seemed to vindicate this approach. Irrespective of whether correlation was cause, Western militaries subsequently began extolling the universal virtues of COIN. Indeed, it became something of an intellectual movement that advanced through the corridors of power as well as the halls of academe and policy think tanks.

COIN's narrative power lay, not only in the fact that it offered a simple, if deceptive, explanation for the decrease in violence in Iraq after 2007, but also that it appeared to identify recurrent patterns of conflict that yielded enduring tactical lessons for operational conduct. This claim rested on the analysis of supposedly classic counter-insurgencies, most notably the British conduct of the Malayan Emergency (1948-1960) and French operations during the Algerian War (1954-1962). Other cases also made fleeting appearances in the narrative either as positive or negative examples. These included, *inter alia*, the Mau Mau Rebellion in Kenya (1952-1960), the Northern Ireland conflict (1968-1998) and Vietnam (1965-1975). The somewhat arbitrary categorisation of these distinct conflicts under the rubric of COIN gave historical veracity to the narrative.

COIN as *apolitical* science

Thus, COIN's centrality to armed conflict derived from the apparent proof that past practice yielded lessons for current and future wars. That the theory identified a distinct form of conflict characterised as insurgency led to the further assertion that a series of palliative methods and core operational principles could be implemented that would, if correctly applied, ensure success. These practices invariably included: securing the loyalty of the population; grievance reduction; the integration of civic action plans; democracy and human rights promotion; and the minimum application of military force in 'clear, hold, and build' operations. This emphasis on technique, however, came at the expense of the contingency of political decision making that always gives rise to war and exerts its influence over military interventions.

The methodology of COIN, therefore, reflected an apparently scientific approach to military conduct that rationalised warfare into a series of steps or procedures. However, COIN's over-riding concern for the 'how' of operational conduct pre-empted strategic questions about proportionality such as what crucial political values are at stake in interventions, and what costs are worth incurring to defend them? In other words, it is not just how one fights but *why* one chooses to fight that is important. The 'why' question is political and depends upon contingent circumstances. COIN theory not only had no answer to the question but, rather worryingly, failed even to ask it.

COIN as ideology

This leads to COIN's third characteristic, that although it eschewed overtly political statements, it was, paradoxically, covertly ideological in orientation. Superficially, COIN purports to be an apolitical technique. It offers an all-purpose recipe for action across time and space. The timeless dynamics of insurgency, so it is held, will perpetually respond to the timeless techniques of counter-insurgency. COIN's claim to universal applicability, however, conceals a normative project, namely, modernisation. The goal of counter-insurgency methods, though never explicitly articulated, is to propel backward and conflicted societies mired in customary practice or authoritarian political cultures along the road of socio-economic improvement and democratic development. Rarely asked, however, was the question of whether the non-Western, tribal, and ethno-religiously divided political cultures in the Middle East or South Asia were susceptible to such nation-building blandishments and whether it was worth the long-term costs of Western forces to attempt modernising them. In other words, buried within Western counter-insurgency thinking, as it evolved in the 2000s, was an ideology which believed that successful nation building would facilitate a liberal democratic end of history.

COIN as mythmaking

This brings us to COIN's fourth broad theme. Counter-insurgency assumed an underlying end of history teleology. Consequently, its pretensions to historically nuanced case analysis exhibited instead a capacity to mythologise the past, distort historical understanding, ignore contingency, and obscure complexity.

COIN's promotion of an assumed British expertise in small war and counter-insurgency evinced all these limitations. Analysts repeatedly credited the British armed forces with an almost gnostic counter-insurgency expertise based on their experience with colonial warfare, particularly in winning over the population through techniques of minimum force and hearts and minds. Rarely was this reputation scrutinised. Commentators simply assumed the methods they needed to practice, regardless of the context, or whether such assumptions withstood sceptical analysis when measured against the historical record.

The fact that the British armed forces bought into this myth, constituted one of the more bizarre effects of such historical distortion. By the first decade of the twenty-first century, the British military establishment came to assume that it possessed a distinctive competence in counter-insurgency, even though, until that time, the British Army rarely claimed such expertise, viewing its colonial encounters in terms of orthodox demonstrations of hard power and 'demonstrative force' to curtail rebel activity. As a consequence of buying into this myth, when shortcomings in British military interventions became evident, most notably in southern Iraq in the mid-2000s, commentators expressed dismay at the demise of this non-existent tradition.

Such myth making, moreover, obscured a more prosaic but important reality, namely that Britain had prevailed in its small wars in the past because of the government's commitment to see these campaigns through so that stipulated political objectives were met. Ironically, COIN's cherry picking of the historical record misrepresented the tactical proficiency that the British did possess. This proficiency far from demonstrating a flair for minimum force, exhibited a talent for escalation into the dark arts of intelligence-led Special Forces operations and the penetration of rebel networks. From Malaya to Northern Ireland to the back streets of Baghdad, this is where Britain's military capacities really lay and continue to reside.

Conclusion

Ultimately, what does the identification of these themes mean for our understanding of the theory and practice of those wars grouped under the label of counter-insurgency? Rory Stewart, the British soldier-scholar-politician, traveller, and linguist, reflecting on his time as deputy governor of two southern Iraqi provinces under Coalition Authority, concluded in early 2014 that:

> Our entire conceptual framework was mad. All these theories of counterinsurgency warfare, state building was actually complete abstract madness. They were like very weird religious systems, because they always break down into three principles, 10 functions, seven this or that. So they're reminiscent of Buddhists who say: 'These are the four paths', or of Christians who say: 'These are the seven deadly sins. They're sort of theologies, essentially, made by people like Buddhist monks in the eighth century – people who have a fundamental faith, which is probably, in the end, itself completely delusional.

Stewart's realisation of the quasi-religious underpinnings of COIN theorising illustrates a simple but important truth: COIN is symptomatic of a fallacy at the heart of much contemporary Western social inquiry, which is the attempt to impose structure on contingent conditions of the past that were never present at the time and will never recur in the future. COIN is, as Stewart contends, a delusion. Counter-insurgency 'theory' in this respect is little different from many other systems of thought that attempt to read the past through an understanding of a social or political 'science' as if they identify timeless patterns, lessons and rules. It thus bears comparison with forms of magical or pseudo-scientific thought. In this regard, counter-insurgency is not so much a false analogy but a distorting lens that narrows an appreciation of the past and overdetermines and oversimplifies the present.

COIN is therefore a history distorting narrative and should not be regarded as a formula for comprehending present wars or prescribing the course of future ones. It might be somewhat trite to claim that a study of counter-insurgency reveals yet again that there are no lessons to be learnt from the past. But if one enduring truth may be extracted, it is that COIN-centric readings of history should be treated, like all grand social science theorising, with scepticism. Instead, a sceptical investigation into the incoherence of counter-insurgency suggests that we should return to the more modest, but no less shrewd, claims of realist thinkers such as Niccolò Machiavelli and Carl von Clausewitz.

Clausewitz's dictum that war is more than a true chameleon, always changing its surface manifestation but at heart remaining the same, offers a more stable basis for insight by identifying the one constant about war, namely, that all wars are unique to their time and place. They are conditioned by the unpredictable forces of passion, chance and reason. The analysis of the interplay of these dynamic, volatile, ever-shifting forces gives the study of war its vitality. Ultimately, it is the historical contingency of war that presents itself as much more enduring and valid than any cherry-picking theory of history.

Originally published in *The World Financial Review*, March-April 2015, by David Martin Jones and M.L.R. Smith.

A strategy of contradictions

As the British government considers the possibility of joining in air-strikes on Syria, it is worth reflecting on the paradoxes and contradictions that lie at the centre of Western approaches in tackling the growth of violent jihadism at home and abroad.

Following outrages like those in Paris on 13th November 2015, which resulted in 138 deaths, politicians have developed a curious habit of denying that such attacks have anything to do with religion.

British Home Secretary, Theresa May, asserted that the Paris attacks 'have nothing to do with Islam'. The Australian Prime Minister, Malcolm Turnbull, declared that the attackers were 'godless tyrants' 'completely at odds with the precepts of Islam'. After every attack since 9/11 the secular Western governing classes and other mainstream commentators invariably argue that those attacking in the name of the Prophet wilfully misinterpret his message.

The consequence of official denial results in a strange policy paradox: a domestic policy that treats the homegrown threat as a community relations problem, while foreign policy prosecutes *al-Qaeda*, or its progeny like the Islamic State of Iraq and the Levant (ISIL) by invasion, air strikes and targeted killings. In other words, war abroad and equivocation at home.

Given that those who share the religious ideology and practice of ISIL now move freely between Europe *sans frontiers* and the Middle East, and derive support from Western diaspora communities, this policy appears dangerously incoherent.

The difficulty with the political rhetoric disclaiming a link with Islam is that it clearly denies the connection between these attacks and a literal interpretation of the Koran. This interpretation needs to be understood because without that understanding it is impossible to comprehend ISIL's strategic thinking or devise an effective response.

Salafism on steroids
The Salafist doctrine that informs the thinking of ISIL represents a distinct response to the slow-motion collision between modernity in its globalised form and an Islamic social character.

Islamist ideologue, Sayyid Qutb (1903-66), argued that the political weakness of Muslim society since the nineteenth century could only be redressed by a return to the scriptural certitude practiced by the *salaf al saleh* (the rightly guided seventh century followers of the prophet Mohammad). This reformation further required a revolutionary recourse to apocalyptic violence.

Qutb's key work *Milestones* (1964) distinguished between the properly constituted *darul Islam* (Islamic sphere) and the condition of almost universal ignorance in which the world (both Muslim and non-Muslim) rests. 'Everything around us', Qutb maintained 'is *jahiliya* [ignorance]... even much of what we think of as being Islamic culture, Islamic sources, or Islamic philosophy and thought is the making of this *jahiliya*'.

The way out of this ignorance requires total submission to the sovereignty and rulership of God, that is, the 'wresting of power from the hands of its human usurpers to return it to God alone'. For Qutb and his successors, the 'correct order for the steps of the Islamic method' was first to remove non-Islamic regimes and establish an Islamic society. It is after Qutb that we can refer to Islamism not as a traditional or mainstream Muslim religion but as an ideology, or, more precisely, a political religion.

Like the totalitarian movements of the twentieth century that profoundly influenced this style of Islamist thought, it assumes a specialised knowledge 'of the method of altering being'.

Under the influence of Qutb and contemporaries like Taqiuddin al-Nabhani, who founded *Hizb-ut Tahrir* in 1953, Islamism became a system that critiqued Islam's relationship with modernity and outlined the method of transforming it via jihad if necessary.

The failure of the nation-state in the Middle East, its kleptocratic corruption, its constant military defeats at the hands of Israel and its failure to address the Palestinian problem, has only exacerbated the conflict within Islam.

ISIL's strategy

It is in this politically religious context that ISIL, both in its Sunni heartlands and among its diaspora, functions. Its key achievement, as it evolved from *al-Qaeda* in Iraq after 2009, was a new caliphate declared in Mosul in June 2014. The fact that, unlike *al-Qaeda*, it controls territory means that it can implement an absolutist Sharia order within its domain.

To rebuild the Salafist golden age, however, requires a coherent strategy that adapts salvation to the needs of contemporary jihad. Abu Bakr al-Naji's *The Management of Savagery* (2004) provides ISIL with its playbook. Drawing on al-Naji's analysis, securing territorial borders, establishing authority through total fear, and applying Sharia justice to those who submit are the cornerstones of ISIL's strategy.

Savagery here is the necessary precursor to the final historical stage of the reformed caliphate. Even if the caliphate is not achieved immediately, no matter. Al-Naji continues, 'the more abominable the level of savagery is', it is still less abominable than enduring stability under 'the order of unbelief'.

ISIL, following Naji, also recognises the power of the media, and particularly the West's belief in its own media delusions (about ISIL being increasingly desperate, or that 'lone wolves' in Western cities are deranged lunatics). ISIL's analysis holds that the Western world order is exactly as Qutb believed, *jahaliya*: fragile, decadent, and easily divided. With the division of the world into righteous and infidel, ISIL and its followers now seek a final apocalyptic showdown between the 'forces of Rome' (the West) and that of the righteous on the Syrian plains.

The strategy of savagery thus intends to draw the US and its allies into a real war on the ground and pursues the doctrine of 'paying the price': that is: you bomb us in Raqqa and we'll bomb you in Paris, Sydney, London, where we know you are weak. ISIL thus engages in a political strategy where extreme violence in times of need is a necessary part of the policy of bringing the West into confrontation. Islamist strategic thinking exploits the weakness in Western secularism (beginning with its attachment to life) and plays upon it to achieve utopia.

Western delusions and paradoxes

Paradoxically, after 9/11 it has been multicultural Western cities that have proved highly congenial to ISIL's support network. Over time – and with official government tolerance – a *sui generis* militancy has evolved in diaspora communities whether in the suburbs of Paris, Brussels, London and elsewhere.

Although *Salafism* – a Sunni Islam revival movement based on the literal interpretations of Islamic scripture – remains a minority stream within Islam, globally it appeals to an educated, but deracinated middle-class. In Europe, second and third generation, often tertiary educated, Muslims find solace not in multiculture, but in a re-Islamisation that prefers supranational Islamist organisations.

The nominally peaceful but transnational *Hizb-ut Tahrir* exemplifies this transition from a traditional to a universalist mode of Islamic identity.

The tendency of much official and media commentary either to write off this evolution as having nothing to do with Islam, or to offer its more articulate spokespersons grants or positions on commissions addressing supposed ethnic and religious exclusion in order to build bridges where none exist, merely enhances its domestic profile. Indeed, rather than give up its liberal faith in multiculturalism, Western governments prefer to ignore the distinctly Islamist idiom of expression. Hence, so-called Western de-radicalisation programmes in the UK, Western Europe and Australia all consider the problem of Muslim alienation in terms of 'outreach' programmes to identify those deemed to be at risk of being seduced by the path of jihad.

Tolerating the intolerant?
To address the prevailing, and ultimately self-destructive, paradox that toleration and accommodation must be extended to the intolerant, as current government programmes often assume, it might be worth secular liberal multiculturalists attending to the thinking of a philosopher who understood the necessary conditions for maintaining an open society against its enemies.

Karl Popper, an émigré from the Third Reich, observed that 'unlimited tolerance must lead to the disappearance of tolerance'. In fact, 'if we are not prepared to defend a tolerant society against the onslaught of the intolerant, then the tolerant will be destroyed, and tolerance with them'.

Popper continued that we need not 'suppress the utterance of intolerant philosophies as long as we can counter them by rational argument and keep them in check by public opinion'.

Yet as Popper presciently foresaw, 'it may easily turn out that they are not prepared to meet us on the level of rational argument', but begin as Islamism does, by denouncing all argument, forbidding its followers from listening to rational argument, because it is deceptive, teaching them instead to answer arguments with violence.

Were he alive, Popper would no doubt counsel politicians today that a pluralist democracy must ultimately assert another kind of paradox, claiming that 'in the name of tolerance, the right not to tolerate the intolerant'. A robust democracy that does not comprehend this paradox cannot long endure.

Original article published in the *Daily Telegraph*, 27th November 2015 by David Martin Jones and M.L.R. Smith.

Game of drones

For well over a decade the film and television industry has ranged over the political and moral terrain generated by the 9/11 era and the West's subsequent foreign policy interventions during the 'war on terror'. From the brilliantly satirical (*Team America: World Police*), the conspiratorial (*Syriana*), the trenchantly critical (*Redacted*), the intensely personal (*American Sniper*), to the quasi-factual (*United 93* and *Zero-Dark Thirty*), a whole genre of movies and TV dramas have arisen depicting this most turbulent of eras.

Although ostensibly intended to entertain, which inevitably leads to over-simplification, no one can accuse the contemporary visual arts of shirking any engagement with the zeitgeist. As the overt Western involvements in Iraq and Afghanistan have been scaled back, the 'war' has moved increasingly into the shadows of intelligence-led counter-actions against the forces of transnational jihadism. And this presents further opportunities for creative talents to explore the dramatic space that this facet of the conflict engenders.

The increasing reliance of Western operations on remotely piloted drones to conduct surveillance and targeted kill operations was notably dramatised in the fourth season of *Homeland* (2014) and has also briefly found its way into other series like season three of *House of Cards* (2015). With South African director Gavin Hood's *Eye in the Sky* (US release April 2016) we have the first concentrated cinematic dissection of the acute moral and political dilemmas that drone warfare generates.

Part of the film's novelty is that the action takes place over a few hours in a day. Col. Katherine Powell (Helen Mirren) is coordinating a complex multinational operation from the United Kingdom's Permanent Joint Headquarters (PJHQ) in Northwood, on the outskirts of London. The mission is to arrest Susan Danford, a British convert to Islam and now fanatical jihadist suspected of involvement in the Westgate shopping mall attacks in Kenya. She has been traced to a compound in Eastleigh, a suburb of Nairobi known as 'Little Mogadishu'.

The figure of Danford is an almost exact simulacrum of the real-life persona of Samantha Lewthwaite, the so-called White Widow. She remains one of the world's most wanted fugitives, a suspected member of the Somali based *Al-Shabaab* (the Youth) movement and a culprit behind a series of deadly jihadist attacks in East Africa. The appeal to authenticity in the film, referencing actual places and events, lends an added sense of relevance and plausibility.

The surveillance part of the operation is conducted via a Reaper drone piloted by two US Air Force personnel, Steve Watts (Aaron Paul) and Carrie Gershon (Phoebe Fox). They pilot the drone from their darkened, air-conditioned, lair in Creech Air Force Base, Nevada, while the arrest team led by the Kenyan Army is to be given the go-ahead once Danford and other assorted militants are confirmed in place. Meanwhile, back in London, a small team of the Cabinet Office Briefing Room (COBRA) committee, led by Lt. Gen. Frank Benson (Alan Rickman) and composed of various ministers and legal advisors, is monitoring events. The intention is to witness the final capture of the infamous Danford, who has been on the run for over six years.

The mission intensifies, however, when Kenyan surveillance of the compound reveals that the occupants are unmistakably preparing two operatives for a double-suicide attack. The operational imperative shifts from capture to kill and the Reaper is prepped to fire its Hellfire missiles into the compound. The likelihood of limited collateral damage is accepted, but the ethical stakes clearly dictate that the prospect of allowing the suicide bombers to do their worst outweighs the potential that a few innocents will likely be killed and injured in a precisely targeted missile strike.

The moral calculus changes dramatically when the presence of a young girl selling bread by the side of the compound is detected. Undoubtedly, a drone strike will place her life in mortal danger. This sets in train a tense and suspense-laden dialogue among the participants about how to weigh the life of a young child against the possibility of even more innocents being killed if the suicide bombers are allowed to escape the compound.

Time is of the essence. Military necessity and, indeed, a legitimate utilitarian ethical calculation, demand that the missiles be released. Political expediency and other equally potent moral arguments about not knowingly risking civilian deaths argue against it. The politicians recognise the case for action yet, in contrast to the military, are reluctant to sanction a missile strike. In addition to a pricked conscience, harming young children in the attack could reflect badly on them and undermine the propaganda war against the jihadists.

The legal advisors are torn. The British attorney general, George Matherson (Richard McCabe) accepts, reluctantly, that the rules of engagement do permit an attack. In contrast, the parliamentary advisor, Angela Northman (Monica Dolan), adamantly refuses to countenance any thought that a child should be put in harm's way, even if dozens of others might lose their lives later in suicide attacks. The ministers responsible for giving clearance for the strike therefore feel pressed constantly to request higher authority, leading to the film's lighter moments as the British foreign secretary (Iain Glen) is compelled to offer his less than clear-cut view in the midst of a bout of food poisoning in Singapore, while the US Secretary of State (Michael O'Keefe) is clearly irritated to have his ping pong diplomacy in China interrupted by what he considers to be a trivial non-issue. Is all this an evasion of ministerial responsibility, or an entirely understandable need for political top cover?

The great strength of the film is that no side of the argument is subject to caricature. A complex and absorbing point versus counterpoint exchange ensues with the sympathies of the viewer continually being challenged. The character of Col. Powell, convincingly played by Mirren, is highly driven having been on Danford's tail for years. She is certainly prepared to push and stretch the rules of engagement but never to breach them. Though endlessly frustrated by the political prevarication she now must endure, she nevertheless strives to always maintain a cool head and remains respectful of the chain of command.

Likewise, the roles of the drone pilots, Watts and Gershon, both impressively controlled performances by Paul and Fox, are deeply troubled by what they are being tasked to undertake. Yet, while they properly question aspects of the mission, they never give in to the histrionics of disobeying orders, which would lead other, weaker, plots into the realm of implausibility. Their characters remain professional, and therefore provide a more faithful, and powerful, portrayal of moral complexity.

The cost of moral complexity is that inevitably tragedy will befall someone, somewhere. The film never glosses over the likely human consequences on the ground but neither does it ignore the painful psychological effects inflicted on those who have to make the decisions that result in life or death, be it those whose purpose is to sanction the action, for those who oversee it, or for those who in the end have to squeeze the trigger that releases the Hellfire missiles. The fact that the decisions are undertaken remotely, thousands of miles away from the scene of the action by operatives flying drones from the sanctuary of Creech Air Force Base, at PJHQ in Northwood, or over 'tea and biscuits' in Whitehall, doesn't lessen the trauma.

The psychological price paid by the participants is conveyed in an understated manner, being particularly inscribed on the faces of Watts and Gershon at the end of the mission, whose characters, the film intimates, are likely to suffer a lifetime of pain as their reward for services to their country. Even with the steely character of Col. Powell, it is hinted that her long pursuit of Danford is not without its personal regrets and consequences.

The great German sociologist Max Weber stated in *Politics as a Vocation* that when one enters the political realm one contracts with diabolical powers.

'Anyone who fails to see this,' he memorably declared, 'is, indeed, a political infant'. Above all, this film is about how people engage with these diabolical powers of utilitarian calculation that lead to the weighing up of costs, benefits, and ultimately lives. It invites us not to revile those in positions of power, be it political or military, or to regard their actions primarily as cynical manoeuvring, but asks us to empathise with the acute moral dilemmas they must face.

In fact, if any critical message is contained in the movie, it is that moral posturing is easy, cheap and, perhaps, in some ways just as cynical, or at least self-interested: a point forcefully made by the character of Gen. Benson, a fitting goodbye to the late Alan Rickman in his final role. He reminds the principled, if somewhat pious, Angela Northman that while she may feel offended by an airstrike that kills civilians, she should never tell a soldier that they don't understand the cost of war.

If you like your movies coloured in the moral tones of black and white, with obvious heroes and villains, then this is not the film for you. If, however, you recognise that the best of art imitates, and speaks to, the human condition in all its complexity and ambiguity then you will see in *Eye in the Sky* perhaps the most powerful and intelligent of films of the post-9/11 epoch. Like the very best visual dramas of our times, it does not provide its audience with an easy resolution, but poses the viewer with the question: What would you do?

Original article published in *War on the Rocks*, 22nd April 2016, by M.L.R. Smith.

3. Getting terror wrong: the follies of critical theory and radicalisation studies

SPEND A FEW YEARS IN THE WESTERN UNIVERSITY SYSTEM and you will soon discover that the notion of academia as the honest pursuit of truth is a myth. Most academics, at least in the humanities and social sciences, are not engaged in truth-seeking, they are engaged in career advancement. Having studied terrorist movements – or violent non-state actors, to give the phenomenon its more objective name – for many years, it was a source of amusement to David and myself to witness the sudden proliferation of terrorism experts after 9/11. Having been a distinctly minority vocation within political studies before 11th September 2001, the vast attention generated by the 9/11 attacks, and the huge amounts of government money and academic grants that followed in its wake, spawned a vast terrorism studies industry.

Moral panics. Manufactured expertise. Junk-scholarship. We had seen it all before. When David and I were coming of age in the 1970s, it was the impending ice-age that was the pseudo-scientific *plat du jour*. On the turn of a sixpence this was to give way to 'global warming' in the succeeding decades. And when the data couldn't sustain this contention, the debate 'moved on' to the vacuous and unfalsifiable notion of 'climate change'. In the 1990s we had seen this dynamic play out with respect to Southeast Asia and the cavernous rhetoric about the dawning 'Pacific Century'. Academic grants were shovelled out to the universities to set up research centres on 'regionalism' to promote the kind of multilateral integration supposedly pioneered by bodies like the Association of Southeast Asian Nations (ASEAN) that were – and note the end of history presumption – remoulding the international system towards a harmonious, collaborative, world order. When all that came crashing down after both the Asian financial crisis of 1997 and 9/11, the academic fraternity, yet again, 'moved on'.

As predictably as night follows day, after 9/11 people who had hitherto exhibited no interest in the terrorist phenomenon re-cast themselves as 'experts' on the subject. It was the formation of this pseudo-intellectual complex that attracted our attention as the early 2000s wore on, and to which the essays in this chapter are primarily devoted. From our perspective the growth of this academic industry was fundamentally parasitical as it attracted those who ultimately had no real interest in understanding the underlying factors motivating violent jihadist actions but were out to push their own pet theories about which they had made up their minds long ago.

Sure enough, it didn't take long before the one-trick pony critical theorists sought to get in on the act, bringing the full force of their post-structural obscurantism to bear. For critical theorists 9/11 was not an opportunity to engage in serious scholarly analysis of groups like *al-Qaeda* or the intellectual strands within Islam that were pushing towards violent jihad but a chance to 'deconstruct' Western 'discourses' around terrorism. Deconstructing these discourses, of course, revealed a panorama of Western guilt. Terrorism was, in this rendering, the exclusive fault of capitalism and Western 'othering'. It was, in other words, all our own fault. Well, David and I were interested in deconstructing the deconstructionists. And one thing we noted, is that they always hated it when their own discourse was turned on them.

Our critique of critical theory's discourse alighted in the first instance on those commentators who pretended to know the 'root causes' of Islamist violence. Rarely did such commentary research Islamist groupings, let alone closely dissect their ideology and strategy, but rather asserted that jihadist activism was all simply a matter of resistance to Western neo-imperialist adventurism. In this understanding, Western intervention was everywhere wrong or misguided.

The essays that form this chapter argued against this position. We were not arguing that Western external military involvement was right – on contrary, it was often disastrously self-defeating – but that critical theory's thesis of Western cause-jihadist effect was simplistically one-dimensional. Jihadist violence could not be reduced to a reaction against Western foreign policy. A history of jihadist violence demonstrates that Islamist activism had been embarked on an aggressive confrontation with the forces of secular modernity long before 9/11 and was often directed against non-Western states or Western nations that had not even participated in missions such as the invasions of Iraq or Afghanistan.

Our view was that the world is a complex and messy place. However, critical theory's constituting anti-Western nihilism and liberal end of history's idealism promoted a reductionism that produced damaging policy responses both at home and abroad. Externally, critical theory asserted that Western intervention was always wrong, while neo-liberal interventionism encouraged reckless military involvement in open-ended nation building efforts to 'make the world a better place'. Lost in all this was an understanding of a realistic appreciation of power, prudence and contingency in the international system that might demand military intervention to achieve very limited aims based on a carefully considered case-by-case basis.

Within the domestic realm, critical theory's cynicism and liberal idealism's propensity towards delusion contributed to a refusal to take seriously the ideology of Islamism. Most notably, the inability of secular Western liberal elites to entertain the idea that communities could be motivated by political-religious creeds was reflected in the dull, technocratic, language of 'radicalisation' studies that David and I also discerned as damaging to an accurate appreciation of the threat. Violent Islamist rejectionists are not radicals in any proper understanding of that term. They are ultra-traditionalist fanatics. Implying that they are in any way 'radical' fosters a sense of 'jihadi cool' that merely embellishes Islamism's appeal to second and third generation Muslims in the West, who whilst feeling estranged from liberal multiculturalism find its endless capacity for tolerating the intolerant wonderfully helpful at the same time.

We're all terrorists now

April 2008 witnessed the launch of a new journal devoted to *Critical Studies on Terrorism*. The choice of preposition in the title is not without interest. Why not 'of' is the reader's immediate response? Yet the grammatically challenged recourse to 'on', is, it would seem, tactical. Three articles in the initial offering address issues that might be found in mainstream political science or terrorism research journals. These articles, exploring the relevance of public health models for counter-terrorism practice, namely, an interview with a police officer, and an examination of the state of terror in Pakistan, afford credibility to the journal's claim that it evinces a concern for methodological pluralism and 'inclusivity'.

However, the somewhat ambiguous mission statement introducing the volume, taken in conjunction with the bulk of the articles solicited for publication, subsequently reveals this claim to be disingenuous: for the real – or more precisely surreal – purpose of the journal is to expose the questionable 'ontological, epistemological and ideological commitments of existing terrorism studies'. What this entails becomes increasingly apparent as one wades through the congealed prose, obscure jargon, philosophical posturing, and concentrated anti-Western self-loathing that comprise the core of this journal's first edition. The journal, in other words, is not intended, as one might assume, to evaluate critically those state or non-state actors that might have recourse to terrorism as a strategy. Instead, the journal's ambition is to deconstruct what it views as the ambiguity of the word 'terror', its manipulation by ostensibly liberal democratic state actors, and the complicity of 'orthodox' terrorism studies in this authoritarian enterprise. Exposing the deficiencies in any field of study is, of course, a legitimate scholarly exercise, but what the symposium introducing the new volume announces questions both the research agenda and academic integrity of journals like *Studies in Conflict and Terrorism* and those who contribute to them. Do these claims, one might wonder, have any substance?

Significantly, the original proposal circulated by the publisher Routledge and one of the editors, Richard Jackson, suggested some uncertainty concerning the preferred title of the journal. *Critical Studies on Terrorism* appeared last on a list where the first choice was *Review of Terror Studies*. Evidently, the concision of a review fails to capture the critical perspective the journal promotes. Criticality, then, is central to the new journal's philosophy and the adjective connotes a distinct ideological and, as shall be seen, far from pluralist and inclusive purpose. So, one might ask, what exactly does a critical approach to terrorism involve?

What it means to be critical

In the editorial symposium that introduces the first issue, the editors and contributors explore what it means to be 'critical' in detail, repetition, and opacity, along with an excessive fondness for italics. The editors inform us that the study of terrorism is 'a growth industry', observing with a mixture of envy and disapproval that 'literally thousands of new books and articles on terrorism are published every year'. In adding to this literature, the editors premise the need for yet another journal on their resistance to what currently constitutes scholarship in the field of terrorism studies and its allegedly uncritical acceptance of the Western democratic state's security perspective.

Indeed, to be critical requires a radical reversal of what the journal assumes to be the typical perception of terrorism and the methodology of terrorism research. To focus on the strategies practised by non-state actors that feature under the conventional denotation 'terror' is, for the critical theorist, misplaced. As the symposium explains, 'acts of clandestine non-state terrorism are committed by a tiny number of individuals and result in between a few hundred and a few thousand casualties *per year over the entire world*'. The United States and its allies' preoccupation with terrorism is, therefore, out of proportion to its effects. At the same time, the more pervasive and repressive terror practised by the state has been 'silenced from public and... academic discourse'.

The complicity of terrorism studies with the increasingly authoritarian demands of Western, liberal state and media practice, together with the moral and political blindness of established terrorism analysts to this relationship, forms the journal's overriding assumption and one that its core contributors repeat ad nauseam. Thus, Michael Stohl, in his contribution 'Old myths, new fantasies and the enduring realities of terrorism', not only discovers ten 'myths' informing the understanding of terrorism, but also finds that these myths reflect a 'state centric security focus', where analysts rarely consider 'the violence perpetrated by the state'. He complains that the press has become too close to government over the matter. Somewhat contradictorily, Stohl subsequently asserts that media reporting is 'central to terrorism and counterterrorism as political action', that media reportage provides the oxygen of terrorism, and that politicians consider journalists to be 'the terrorist's best friend'.

Stohl further compounds this incoherence, claiming that 'the media are far more likely to focus on the destructive actions, rather than on... grievances or the social conditions that breed [terrorism] – to present episodic rather than thematic stories'. He argues that terror attacks between 1968 and 1980 were scarcely reported in the United States, and that reporters do not delve deeply into the sources of conflict. All of this is quite contentious, with no direct evidence produced to support such sweeping statements. The 'media' is after all a very broad term, and to assume that it is monolithic is to replace criticism with conspiracy. Moreover, even if it were true that the media always serves government propaganda, then by Stohl's own logic, terrorism as a method of political communication is clearly futile as no rational actor would engage in a campaign doomed to be endlessly misreported by a biased media.

Nevertheless, the notion that an inherent pro-state bias vitiates terrorism studies pervades the critical position. Anthony Burke, in 'The end of terrorism studies', asserts that established analysts like Bruce Hoffman 'specifically exclude states as possible perpetrators' of terror. Consequently, the emergence of 'critical terrorism studies' 'may signal the end of a particular kind of traditionally state-focused and directed "problem-solving" terrorism studies – at least in terms of its ability to assume that its categories and commitments are immune from challenge and correspond to a stable picture of reality'.

Elsewhere, Adrian Guelke, in 'Great whites, paedophiles and terrorists: The need for critical thinking in a new era of terror', considers British government-induced media 'scaremongering' to have legitimated an 'authoritarian approach' to the purported new era of terror. Meanwhile, Joseba Zulaika and William A. Douglass, in 'The terrorist subject: Terrorist studies and the absent subjectivity', find that the 'war on terror' constitutes '*the* single', all-embracing paradigm of analysis where the critical voice is 'not allowed to ask: what is the reality itself?' The construction of this condition, they further reveal, if somewhat abstrusely, reflects an abstract 'desire' that demands terror as 'an ever-present threat'. To sustain this repressed desire: 'Terrorism experts and commentators' function as 'realist policemen'; and not very smart ones at that, who while 'gazing at the evidence' are 'unable to read the paradoxical logic of the desire that fuels it, whereby *lack* turns to *excess*'. Finally, Ken Booth, in 'The human faces of terror: Reflections in a cracked looking glass', reiterates Richard Jackson's contention that state terrorism 'is a much more serious problem than non-state terrorism'.

Yet, one searches in vain in these articles for evidence to support the ubiquitous assertion of state bias: assuming this bias in conventional terrorism analysis as a fact seemingly does not require a corresponding concern with evidence of this fact, merely its continual reiteration by conceptual fiat. A critical perspective dispenses not only with terrorism studies but also with the norms of accepted scholarship. Asserting what needs to be demonstrated commits the elementary logical fallacy *petitio principii*. But critical theory apparently emancipates (to use its favourite verb) its practitioners from the confines of logic, reason and the usual standards of academic inquiry.

Alleging a constitutive weakness in established scholarship without the necessity of providing proof to support it, therefore, appears to define the critical posture. The unproved 'state centricity' of terrorism studies serves as a platform for further unsubstantiated accusations about the state of the discipline. Jackson and his fellow editors, along with later claims by those like Booth, Zulaika and Douglass, again assert that 'orthodox' analysts rarely bother 'to interview or engage' with those involved in 'terrorist activity' or spend any time 'on the ground in the areas most affected by conflict'. Given that Booth and Jackson spend most of their time on the ground in Aberystwyth, Ceredigion, not a notably terror rich environment, if we discount the holiday cottage burning operations of the Welsh nationalist group *Meibion Glyndŵr* (Sons of Glyndŵr), who would as a matter of principle avoid *pob sais* like Jackson and Booth, this seems a bit like the pot calling the kettle black. It also overlooks the fact that journals like *Studies in Conflict and Terrorism* first advertised the problem of 'talking to terrorists' in 2001, which have gone to great lengths to rectify this lacuna, if it is one, regularly publishing articles by analysts with first-hand experience of groups like the Taliban, al-Qaeda and *Jemaah Islamiyah*.

A consequence of avoiding primary research, it is further alleged, leads conventional analysts uncritically to apply psychological and problem-solving approaches to their object of study. This propensity, Booth maintains, occasions another unrecognised weakness in traditional terrorism research, namely, an inability to engage with 'the particular dynamics of the political world'. Analogously, Stohl claims that 'the US and English [sic] media' exhibit a tendency to psychologise terrorist acts, which reduces 'structural and political problems' to issues of individual pathology. Preoccupied with this problem-solving, psychopathologising methodology, terrorism analysts have lost the capacity to reflect on both their practice and their research ethics.

By contrast, the critical approach is not only self-reflective, but also and, for good measure, self-reflexive. In fact, the editors and several of the journal's contributors use these terms interchangeably, treating a reflection and a reflex as synonyms. A cursory encounter with the *Shorter Oxford Dictionary* would reveal that they are not. Despite this linguistically challenged misidentification, 'reflexivity' is made to do a lot of work in the critical idiom. Reflexivity, the editors inform us, requires a capacity 'to challenge dominant knowledge and understandings, is sensitive to the politics of labelling... is transparent about its own values and political standpoints, adheres to a set of responsible research ethics, and is committed to a broadly defined notion of emancipation'. This covers a range of not very obviously related but critically approved virtues. Let us examine what reflexivity involves as Stohl, Guelke, Zulaika and Douglass, Burke and Booth explore, somewhat repetitively, its implications.

Reflexive or defective?
Firstly, challenging dominant knowledge whilst understanding a sensitivity to labels leads inevitably to a fixation with language, discourse, the ambiguity of the noun, terror, and its political use and abuse. Terrorism, Booth enlightens the reader unremarkably, is 'a politically loaded term'. Meanwhile, Zulaika and Douglass consider terror 'the dominant tropic [sic] space in contemporary political and journalistic discourse'. Faced with the 'serious challenge' and pejorative connotation that the noun conveys, critical terrorologists turn to deconstruction and bring the full force of post-modern obscurantism to bear on its use. Thus, the editors proclaim that terrorism is 'one of the most powerful signifiers in contemporary discourse'. There is, moreover, a 'yawning gap between the "terrorism" signifier and the actual acts signified'. '[V]irtually all of this activity', the editors pronounce *ex cathedra*, 'refers to the *response* to acts of political violence, not the violence itself'. Here again, they offer no evidence for this curious

assertion and assume, it would seem, all conventional terrorism studies address every issue and problem solely within the framework of homeland security.

In keeping with this critical orthodoxy that he has done much to define, Anthony Burke also asserts the 'instability (and thoroughly politicised nature) of the unifying master-terms of our field: "terror' and "terrorism"'. To address this 'instability', he contends that a critical stance requires us to 'keep this radical instability and inherent politicization of the concept of terrorism at the forefront of its analysis'. Indeed, 'without a conscious reflexivity about the most basic definition of the object, our discourse will not be critical at all'. More particularly, drawing on a jargon-infused amalgam of Michel Foucault's identification of the relationship between power and knowledge, the neo-Marxist Frankfurt School's critique of democratic false consciousness, mixed with the existentialism of the Third Reich's favourite philosopher, Martin Heidegger, Burke '*questions the question*'. This intellectual *potpourri* apparently enables the critical theorist to 'question the ontological status of a "problem" before any attempt to map out, study or resolve it'.

Questioning the question is, at one level, fair enough from an academic point of view, provided one is approaching a 'problem' from an attempted position of disinterested inquiry. Interestingly, however, Burke, Booth, and the rest of the symposistahood deny that there might be objective data about violence or that a properly focused strategic study of terrorism would not include any prescriptive goodness or rightness of action. While a strategic theorist or a sceptical social scientist might claim to consider only the complex relational situation that involves as well as the actions, the attitude of human beings to them, the critical theorist's radical questioning of language denies this possibility.

The critical approach to language and its deconstruction of an otherwise useful, if imperfect, political vocabulary has been the source of much confusion and inconsequentiality in the practice of the social sciences. It dates from the relativist pall those French radical post-structural philosophers like Gilles Deleuze and Felix Guattari, Foucault, and Jacques Derrida, cast over the study of history and the social sciences. The post-structuralists sought to demonstrate how social and political knowledge depended on, and underpinned, power relations that permeated the landscape of the social and reinforced the repressive practices of the liberal democratic state. This radical assault on the possibility of either neutral fact or value is ultimately unfalsifiable and functions as a substitute for a proper philosophy of social science or a real theory of language.

The problem with the critical approach is, as the Australian philosopher John Anderson argued, that to achieve a genuine study one must either investigate the facts that are talked about or the fact that they are talked about in a certain way. More precisely, as J.L. Mackie explains, 'if we concentrate on the uses of language we fall between these two stools, and we are in danger of taking our discoveries about manners of speaking as answers to questions about what is there'. Indeed, in so far as an account of the use of language spills over into ontology, it is liable to be a confused mixture of what should be two distinct investigations: the study of the facts about which the language is used, and the study of the linguistic phenomena themselves.

It is precisely, however, this confused mixture of fact and discourse that critical thinking seeks to impose on the study of terrorism and infuses the practice of critical theory more generally. From this confused seed no coherent method grows.

What is to be done?

This ontological confusion notwithstanding, Ken Booth sees critical theory as a means to expose the dubious links between power and knowledge in established terrorism studies. He also sees it offering an ideological agenda that transforms the face of global politics. '[C]*ritical knowledge*', Booth declares, '*involves understandings of the social world that attempt to stand outside prevailing structures, processes, ideologies and orthodoxies while recognizing that all conceptualizations within the ambit of sociality derive from particular social/historical conditions'*. Helpfully, Booth – assuming the manner of an Old Testament prophet – provides his critical disciples with '*big-picture* navigation aids' to achieve this higher knowledge. Booth promulgates fifteen commandments (as Clemenceau remarked of Woodrow Wilson's fourteen points for peace, in a somewhat different context, 'God Almighty only gave us ten'). When not stating the staggeringly obvious, the Ken Commandments are hopelessly contradictory. Critical theorists thus should 'avoid exceptionalising the study of terrorism', 'recognize that states can be agents of terrorism', and 'keep the long term in sight'. Unexceptional advice to be sure and long recognised by more traditional students of terrorism. The critical student, if not fully conversant with critical doublethink, however, might find the fact that she or he lives within 'Powerful theories' that are 'constitutive of political, social, and economic life' (6th Commandment), sits uneasily with Booth's concluding injunction to 'stand outside' prevailing ideologies.

In his preferred idiom, Booth further contends that terrorism is best studied in the context of an 'academic international relations' the role of which 'is not only to interpret the world but to change it'. Significantly, academic – or more precisely – *critical* international relations, holds no place for a realist appreciation of the status quo but approves instead a Marxist ideology of praxis. It is within this transformative praxis that critical theory situates terrorism and terrorists.

The political goals of those non-state entities that choose to practice the tactics of terrorism invariably seek a similar transformative praxis and this leads critical global theorising into a curiously confused empathy with the motives of those engaged in such acts, as well as a disturbing relativism. Thus, Booth again decrees that the gap between 'those who hate terrorism and those who carry it out, those who seek to delegitimize the acts of terrorists and those who incite them, and those who abjure terror and those who glorify it – is not as great as is implied or asserted by orthodox terrorism experts, the discourse of governments, or the popular press'. The gap 'between us/them is a slippery slope, not an unbridgeable political and ethical chasm'. So, while 'terrorist actions are always – without exception – wrong, they nevertheless might be contingently excusable'. From this ultimately relativist perspective gang raping a defenceless woman, an act of terror on any critical or uncritical scale of evaluation, is, it would seem, wrong but potentially excusable.

Based on this worrying relativism a further Ken Commandment requires the abolition of the discourse of evil on the somewhat questionable grounds that evil releases agents from responsibility. This not only reveals a profound ignorance of theology, but it also underestimates what Eric Voegelin identified as a central feature of the appeal of modern political religions from the Third Reich to *al-Qaeda*. As Voegelin observed in 1938, the Nazis represented an 'attractive force'. To understand that force requires not the abolition of evil, which is necessary for the relativist, but an effort that seeks to comprehend its attractiveness. Significantly, as Barry Cooper argues, 'its attractiveness, [like that of *al Qaeda*'s for its followers] cannot fully be understood apart from its evilness'.

The line of relativist inquiry that critical theorists like Booth evince toward terrorism leads in fact not to moral clarity but to an inspissated moral confusion. This is paradoxical given that the editors make much in the journal's introductory symposium of their 'responsible research ethics'. The paradox is resolved when one realises that critical moralising demands the 'ethics of responsibility to the terrorist other'. For Ken Booth it involves empathising 'with the ethic of responsibility' faced by those who, 'in extremis' 'have some explosives'. Anthony Burke contends that a critically self-conscious normativism requires the analyst, not only to 'critique' the 'strategic languages' of the West, but also to 'take in' the 'side of the Other', or more particularly, 'engage' 'with the highly developed forms of thinking' that provides groups like *al-Qaeda* 'with legitimizing foundations and a world view of some profundity'. This additionally demands a capacity not only to empathise with the 'other', but also to recognise that both Osama bin Laden in his *Messages to the West* and Sayyid Qutb in his Muslim Brotherhood manifesto *Milestones* not only offer 'well observed' criticisms of Western decadence, but also 'converges with elements of critical theory'. This is unsurprising given that both Islamist and critical theorists share an analogous contempt for Western democracy, the market, and the international order which these structures inhabit and have done much to shape.

Histrionically speaking

Critical theory, then, embraces relativism not only toward language but also toward social action. Relativism and the bizarre ethicism it engenders in its attempt to empathise with the terrorist other are, furthermore, histrionic. As Leo Strauss classically inquired of this relativist tendency in the social sciences, 'is such an understanding dependent upon our own commitment or independent of it?' Strauss explains, if it is independent, I am committed as an actor and I am uncommitted in another compartment of myself in my capacity as a social scientist. 'In that latter capacity I am completely empty and therefore completely open to the perception and appreciation of all commitments or value systems'. I go through the process of empathic understanding to reach clarity about my commitment for only a part of me is engaged in my empathetic understanding. This means, however, that 'such understanding is not serious or genuine but histrionic'. It is also profoundly dependent on Western liberalism. For it is only in an open society that questions the values it promotes that the issue of empathy with the non-Western other could arise. The critical theorist's explicit loathing of the openness that affords her histrionic posturing obscures this constituting fact.

Given this histrionic empathy with the 'other', critical theory concludes that democratic states 'do not always abjure acts of terror whether to advance their foreign policy objectives... or to buttress order at home'. Consequently, Ken Booth asserts: 'If terror can be part of the menu of choice for the relatively strong, it is hardly surprising it becomes a weapon of the relatively weak'. Zulaika and Douglass similarly assert that terrorism is 'always' a weapon of the weak.

At the core of this critical, ethicist, relativism therefore lies a syllogism that holds all violence is terror: Western states use violence; therefore, Western states are terrorist. Further, the greater terrorist uses the greater violence: Western governments exercise the greater violence. Therefore, it is Western liberal democratic states rather than *al-Qaeda* that are the greater terrorists.

In its desire to empathise with the transformative ends, if not the means of terrorism generally, and Islamist terror in particular, critical theory reveals itself as a form of Marxist unmasking. Thus, for Booth '*terror has multiple forms*' and the real terror is economic, the product of 'global capitalism'. Only the *engagée* academic finding in deconstructive criticism the philosophical weapons that reveal the violent, capitalistic purpose informing the conventional study of terrorism and the democratic state's prosecution of counter-terrorism can identify the real terror lurking behind the 'manipulation of the politics of fear'.

Moreover, the resolution of this condition of escalating violence requires not any strategic solution that creates security as the basis for development, be it in London or Kabul. Instead, Booth, Burke, and the editors of the journal contend that the only solution to 'the world-historical crisis that is facing human society globally' is universal human 'emancipation'. This, according to Burke, is 'the normative end' that critical theory pursues. Following Jürgen Habermas, the godfather of critical theory, terrorism is really a form of distorted communication. The solution to this problem of failed communication resides not only in the improvement of living conditions, and 'the political taming of unbounded capitalism', but also in 'the telos of mutual understanding'.

Only through this telos with its 'strong normative bias towards non-violence' can a universal condition of peace and justice transform the globe. In other words, the only ethical solution to terrorism is conversation. Sitting around an un-coerced table presided over by the likes of Kofi Annan, along with Ken Booth, Osama bin Laden, President Obama, and some European Union pacifist sandalista, will allow a transcendental communicative reason to emerge, which will be able to promulgate norms of transformative justice. As Burke enunciates, the panacea of un-coerced communication would establish 'a secularism that might create an enduring architecture of basic shared values'.

In the end, un-coerced norm projection is not concerned with the world as it is, but how it ought to be. This not only compounds the logical errors that permeate critical theory, but it also advances an ultimately utopian agenda under the guise of *soi-disant* cosmopolitanism where one somewhat vaguely recognises the 'human interconnection and mutual vulnerability to nature, the cosmos and each other'. And no doubt we all burst into a spontaneous chanting of Kumbaya.

In similar visionary terms, Booth defines real security as emancipation in a way that denies any definitional rigour to either term. The struggle against terrorism is, then, a struggle for emancipation from the oppression of political violence everywhere. Consequently, in this Manichean struggle for global emancipation against the real terror of Western democracy, Booth further maintains that universities have a crucial role to play. This is something of a concern for those who do not share the critical vision. For those like Booth university international relations departments are not apparently in business to pursue dispassionate analysis but instead are to serve as cheerleaders for this critically inspired vision.

Overall, the journal's fallacious commitment to emancipation undermines any ostensible claim to pluralism and diversity. Over determined by this transformative approach to world politics, it necessarily denies the possibility of a realist or prudential appreciation of politics and the promotion, not of universal solutions, but pragmatic ones that accept the best that may be achieved in the circumstances. In the end, presenting the world in terms of how it *ought* to be rather than as it *is* conceals a deep intolerance notable in the contempt with which many of the contributors to the journal appear to hold Western politicians and the Western media.

It is the exploitation of this oughtistic style of thinking that leads critical theorising into a Humpty Dumpty world where words mean exactly what the critical theorist 'chooses them to mean – neither more nor less'. To justify their disciplinary niche, however, they must insist on the failure of established modes of terrorism study. Having identified a source of government grants and academic prerequisites, critical studies in fact does not deal with the notion of terrorism as such, but instead the way the Western liberal democratic state has supposedly manipulated the use of violence by non-state actors to 'other' minority communities and create a politics of fear.

A missed opportunity
Of course, the doubtful contribution of critical theory by no means implies that all is well with what one might call conventional terrorism studies. The subject area has in the past produced superficial assessments that have done little to contribute to an informed understanding of conflict. This is a point readily conceded by John Horgan and Michael Boyle who put 'A case against "critical terrorism studies"'. Although they do not seek to challenge the agenda, assumptions and contradictions in the critical approach, their contribution to the new journal distinguishes itself by having a well-organised and well-supported argument. The authors' willingness to acknowledge deficiencies in some terrorism research shows that critical self-reflection is already present in existing terrorism studies. It is ironic, in fact, that the most clearly reflective, original, and *critical*, contribution in the first edition of the journal should come from established terrorism researchers.

Interestingly, the spectre haunting both conventional and critical terrorism studies is that both assume that terrorism is an existential phenomenon, which possesses causes and solutions. Burke makes this explicit: 'The inauguration of this journal', he declares, 'indeed suggests broad agreement that there is a phenomenon called terrorism'. Yet this is not the only way of looking at terrorism. For a strategic theorist the notion of terrorism does not exist as an independent phenomenon. It is an abstract noun. More precisely, it is merely a tactic — the creation of fear for political ends — that can be employed by any social actor, be it state or non-state, in any context, without any necessary moral value being involved.

Ironically, then, strategic theory offers a far more 'critical perspective on terrorism' than do the perspectives advanced in this journal. Guelke, for example, propounds a curiously orthodox standpoint when he asserts: 'to describe an act as one of terrorism, without the qualification of quotation marks to indicate the author's distance from such a judgement, is to condemn it as absolutely illegitimate'. If you are a strategic theorist this is an invalid claim. Terrorism is simply a method to achieve an end. Any moral judgement of the act itself is entirely separate. To fuse the two is a category mistake. In strategic theory, which Guelke ignores, terrorism does not, *ipso facto*, denote 'absolutely illegitimate violence'.

Intriguingly, Stohl, Booth and Burke also imply that a strategic understanding forms part of their critical viewpoint. Booth, for instance, argues in one of his commandments that terrorism should be seen as a conscious human choice. Few strategic theorists would disagree. Similarly, Burke feels that there does 'appear to be a consensus' that terrorism is a 'form of instrumental political violence'. The problem for the contributors to this volume is that they cannot emancipate themselves from the very orthodox assumption that the word terrorism is pejorative. That may be the popular understanding of the term, but inherently terrorism conveys no necessary connotation of moral condemnation. 'Is terrorism a form of warfare, insurgency, struggle, resistance, coercion, atrocity, or great political crime', Burke asks rhetorically. But once more he misses the point. All violence is instrumental. Grading it according to whether it is insurgency, resistance, or atrocity is irrelevant. Any strategic actor may practice any tactic or form of warfare if it suits their purpose. For this reason, Burke's contention that current definitions of terrorism have 'specifically excluded states as possible perpetrators and privilege them as targets', is wholly inaccurate. Strategic theory has never excluded state-directed terrorism as an object of study, and neither for that matter, as Horgan and Boyle point out, have more conventional studies of terrorism.

Yet, Burke offers – as a critical revelation – that 'the strategic intent behind the US bombing of North Vietnam and Cambodia, Israel's bombing of Lebanon, or the sanctions against Iraq' are also terroristic. He continues: 'My point is not to remind us that states practise terror, but to show how mainstream *strategic doctrines* are terrorist in these terms and undermine any prospect of achieving normative consensus if such terrorism is to be reduced and eventually eliminated'. This is confused, not least because strategic theory does recognise that actions on the part of state or non-state actors that aim to create fear (such as the Allied aerial bombing of Germany in World War II or the nuclear deterrent posture of Mutually Assured Destruction) can be terroristic in nature. The problem for critical theorists like Burke is that they impute their own moral valuations to the term terror.

Consequently, those interested in a truly 'critical' approach to the subject should perhaps turn to strategic theory for some relief from the strictures that have traditionally governed the study of terrorism, not to self-proclaimed critical theorists who only replicate the flawed understandings of those whom they criticise. Horgan and Boyle conclude their thoughtful article by claiming that critical terrorism studies has more in common with traditional terrorism research than critical theorists would possibly like to admit. We agree: they are two sides of the same coin.

Conclusion

In the looking glass world of critical terror studies, the conventional analysis of terrorism is ontologically challenged, lacks self-reflexivity and is excessively policy oriented. By contrast, critical theory's ethicist, yet relativist, and deconstructive gaze reveals that we are all terrorists now and must empathise with those sub-state actors who have recourse to violence for whatever motive. Despite their intolerable othering by the media and by Western governments, terrorists are no different from us. In fact, there is terror as the weapon of the weak and the far worse economic and coercive terror of the liberal state. Terrorists therefore deserve empathy and should be discursively engaged.

At the core of this understanding sits a radical pacifism and an idealism that requires not the application of active counter-measures but communication and 'human emancipation'. Until this radical post-national utopia arrives both force and the discourse of evil must be abandoned. Instead, therapy and un-coerced conversation must be practiced. In the popular ABC drama *Boston Legal*, Judge Brown perennially refers to the vague, irrelevant, jargon-ridden statements of lawyers as 'jibber jabber'. The Aberystwyth-based school of critical internationalist utopianism that increasingly dominates the study of international relations in Britain and Australia has refined a higher order of incoherence that may be termed Aber jabber. The pages of the journal of *Critical Studies on Terrorism* are its natural home.

Original article published in *Studies and Conflict and Terrorism*, Vol. 32, No. 4 (2009), by David Martin Jones and M.L.R. Smith, reproduced by kind permission of Taylor & Francis.

Carry on empathising:
The ISIS-crisis and Western political thought

Malcolm Caldwell may not be a name that is readily remembered today. A Marxist academic at the School of Oriental and African Studies in London, a virulent critic of American foreign policy and ardent apologist for the genocidal Khmer Rouge in Cambodia, he was murdered in mysterious circumstances the night after an apparently congenial meeting with the object of his veneration, Pol Pot. Shot dead in his guesthouse by unknown assailants in December 1978, connected possibly to the factionalism then consuming the disintegrating regime in Phnom Penh, the faintly ridiculous tragi-comedy figure of Caldwell gained brief notoriety in the world beyond.

Deluded though he may have been in his sympathy with the mad autarchy of the Khmer Rouge, the point about Caldwell – the only point in his defence – was that at least he was prepared to follow through on his empathic preferences, travelling into the heart of Indochina to sample the delights of the Kampuchean utopia, where he met his untimely demise. Caldwell, the socialist-Maoist, anti-American, true believer, exhibited a degree of warped intellectual consistency. Though now residing in a degree of, probably deserved, obscurity, few could accuse him of not living – and dying – according to his principles.

We shall return to the memory of Malcolm Caldwell later. For the moment, his example demonstrates, as we shall indicate below, that moral and intellectual consistency, albeit sometimes of a hopelessly misguided character, is rare in what passes for the social and political sciences in contemporary Western universities. Fast forward thirty years later and the point brings us, in a roundabout way, to the mid-noughties and the current dilemmas confronting the foreign and defence policies of Western governments in working out how to deal with the persistent threat posed by the activities of violent, politicised Islam.

Back to the future
In 2007 a lively exchange took place in the pages of the journal, *International Affairs*, when several outraged scholars denounced us for various offenses against academia that we had supposedly committed in an article that appeared in the journal in November 2006. The article critiqued public policy in the United Kingdom in the aftermath of the attacks on the London transport system on 7th July 2005 – the so-called 7/7 bombings – in which 52 people lost their lives (56 if you include the bombers themselves). Our thought crime was to draw attention to the fact that much public commentary – journalistic, academic, legal and political – had consistently underplayed the threat posed by jihadist activism in the years before 2005. Indeed, this ignorance had contributed to the evolving threat by disregarding the appeal to jihad among deracinated second-generation Muslims in British cities, who had, among other things, been encouraged in their ideological evolution by a blinkered official faith in multiculturalism to despise mainstream British society and revel in a separate identity.

Our advocacy was for a modest return in British policy to prudent realism both at home and abroad: to develop a shared, inclusive, public morality at home that provided a sense of something worth defending and did not foster soft forms of apartheid that encouraged minority grievance and separate development in ethno-religious ghettoes. From a set of commonly accepted and openly articulated values would, we argued, extend a clearer sense of the national interest upon which a coherent long-term foreign policy could be constructed.

In that regard, we offered a critical appraisal of the Blair government's incoherent foreign policy that, inconsistently, was willing to prosecute wars against Islamist militancy abroad in conjunction with the United States in Afghanistan and Iraq, while indulging jihadist activities at home. This meant turning a blind eye to the rantings of hate preachers in mosques and the behaviour of Islamist groups such as *Al-Muhajiroun* (The Migrants) and *Hizb-ut Tahrir* (Party of Liberation) which garnered converts within the UK and spread subversion abroad. It also meant inadvertently facilitating the growth of radical Islamist ideology through the award of grants and privileged access to policy formation to its more eloquent, but still relativist, spokesmen in the belief that overcoming the jihadist phenomenon resided in dealing with the repulsive forms of minority exclusion, alienation and social deprivation.

It was not a surprise – at least not to us – that the result of the quasi-official view that ethnic and religious minorities were victims of prejudice, Islamophobia and discrimination at the hands of the majority culture, was to produce a steady stream of British-schooled jihadis and suicide bombers: something that since 2005 has entrenched itself as one of the UK's few remaining export industries.

To a range of critics who excoriated us in *International Affairs*, our views were abhorrent. Ignoring the central claims in our thesis about the existence of an edifice of denial about the extent of the building threat prior to 2005, we were, it seems, instigators of a new McCarthyist witch hunt that sought to impose an illiberal order based on conservative 'British values', while closing down the space for debate across the media and college campuses. We were, apparently, unconcealed haters of multiculturalism, open admirers of US foreign policy, and advocates of even greater militarisation of British responses to terrorism.

To read these fulminations by academics from such venerable halls of learning as Oxford, Manchester and Cambridge, one might have been forgiven for thinking we had been responsible for 7/7. And in a way, that was the allegation: for our offence had been to question the ruling orthodoxy that believed that violent jihadist diehards were no more than a few dunces and losers who posed little threat, except possibly to themselves. Raising the prospect of a more serious danger to society was to be guilty of promoting the 'politics of fear'. This belief held that to draw attention to the new political religion of ideologised Islam was no more than an Orientalist trope used by racists and conservatives to crack down on dissent, discriminate against minorities and curb civil liberties through draconian laws. In this view, an overreaction to a fringe minority merely fuelled Muslim grievance and – somewhat unfalsifiably – either created or exaggerated the threat.

The fallacy of 'root causes'
For our critics, the solution lay not in ascertaining the appeal of a doctrine of militant Islamism, but in the identification of 'root causes'. Predictably, they claimed the possession of a higher knowledge that enabled them to divine what these 'root causes' comprised. This capacity for Olympian insight was, needless to say, denied to other mortals. The key to obtaining this higher knowledge was a position of fully-fledged empathy. According to one of our protagonists, Tarak Barkawi, writing in 2004: 'Should it not just be accepted that suicide bombers are fighters in a cause', which 'can be recognised, with just a small dose of empathy, as a response to historic injustice?' He went on: 'Only by granting one's enemies a full and unqualified humanity can one ever hope to understand them'.

Through the policy of empathy its adherents were granted the unique capacity to uncover the 'root causes' of Islamist violence, which did not reside, they discerned, in the growth of an insidious death-worshipping cult. Instead, they believed the problem could be found in the long-term grievances arising out of the suffering at the hands of decades of Western imperialism and prejudice. Unbearable Islamophobia endured by Muslim communities within the domestic realm created injustices that demanded redress. Armed with this special insight, Barkawi asserted that through empathy it was possible to learn to 'live in peace with people different from ourselves, people who may not choose to live as we do or to organise their societies along Western lines'.

For us, the problem with this thesis was that the homegrown bombers responsible for 7/7 were not the product of a different society: they were the product of British society, a society that routinely extended tolerance, asylum and empathy to its many faiths and minority communities. Yet, despite this, British society was still attacked from within. The difficulty was that the suicidal ideologues that Barkawi and others felt were deserving of 'full and unqualified humanity' did not appear especially willing to grant much in the way of humanity in return.

In the aftermath of July 2005, much media and academic commentary shifted its focus, refusing to look inward into the policies that might have contributed to the extremism of activists in Britain itself, but instead looked outward, externalising responsibility for the attacks. Homegrown radicals of Western liberal democracies were, it was implied, the product not of the failed policies of multiculturalism at home but as a reaction to the insensitivity of a Western foreign policy abroad that invaded Muslim lands, foisted unacceptable regimes on its populations, and supported Israel.

Enraged by the occupations of Iraq and Afghanistan and the treatment of the Palestinians in the Occupied Territories, it was a logical consequence that a few lone wolves would take matters into their own hands to avenge the injustices and humiliations being visited upon their religious brethren abroad. This was blowback in its purest form. Indeed, this was the very justification given by one of the perpetrators of 7/7, Mohammad Siddique Khan, in his videoed statement before he proceeded to immolate himself and six others on the London Tube:

> Your democratically elected governments continuously perpetuate atrocities against my people all over the world. And your support of them makes you directly responsible, just as I am directly responsible for protecting and avenging my Muslim brothers and sisters. Until we feel security, you will be our targets. And until you stop the bombing, gassing, imprisonment and torture of my people we will not stop this fight.

The West: Keep out
The lesson for the empathisers was clear: the West should give up on its neo-imperialist battlefields and resist the temptation for further interventions. Muslim lands should be left to govern themselves free from malign interference from abroad in order that they could discover their own distinctive, and attractively non-Western, identity and developmental path. Moreover, in this path of self-discovery, according to another of our critics, Richard Jackson, Islamism was not the enemy of democracy. '*Jihadist* texts', he maintained, 'reveal a nuanced political analysis of the situation in the Middle East and a clear set of goals'. Islamist parties, he argued, were committed to multiparty democracy, accepted the legitimacy of elections, and where they gained political influence, they 'evolved in strikingly moderate and pragmatic directions'.

Since 2007, Western nations have largely followed the advice of this critical orthodoxy: withdrawing from Iraq in 2008, drawing down in Afghanistan, and eschewing intervention in Syria in 2013. Now, with formation of a putative Islamic State over large swaths of Iraq and Syria, the public decapitation of American journalists, the taking of aid workers as hostages, the mass execution of Iraqi Army prisoners, and the widespread persecution of Shi'ites and Yazidis, along with other examples of Islamist governance, such as the Muslim Brotherhood's brief rule in Egypt, which resulted in the ramping up of extremist rhetoric and the exclusion of moderate voices, the moment would seem propitious to consider the sagacity of the empathisers' prescriptions for non-intervention, and to review the character of Islamism's commitment to democratic principles and its evidently 'strikingly moderate and pragmatic directions'.

The paradox of disengagement: An increased threat
Of course, what a cursory consideration reveals are the strikingly erroneous positions of those neo-Caldwellians who perceive 'political nuance' in jihadist

ideology and would extend unqualified empathy, which has now seen the mutation of an Islamist dream into a temporal reality. The consequences of non-intervention have revealed themselves, not in a reduced threat to the West, but in the creation of a jihadist beacon on the hill that has drawn in recruits from across the Sunni Muslim world, from Pakistan to Indonesia, as well as from an alienated diaspora of Muslims located in the West.

Thus, an estimated 350-500 jihadist fighters exported from Britain have been joined by Americans, French, Dutch, Swedes, German and Australian nationals. The result is an increased threat arising from the migration of displaced peoples, the potential for further terror assaults by returning jihadis trained in the arts of bomb making and beheading, along with the unpredictable consequences of regional instability. Ironically, as a result of following the exact formulas for reducing the threat offered by the critical theory orthodoxy, the prospect of direct military intervention in Iraq and Syria is now back on the table.

In terms of what these events portend for Western self-understandings, they disclose, in the first instance, the folly of relying on simplistic cause and effect reasoning that holds that Western intervention necessarily provokes the very threat it is intended to counter. The dissolution of any prospect for enduring stability in the Middle East occurred only after 2011, at a time when Western involvement in the region was notable for its decline. Western forces had departed Iraq by the end of that year.

Support for anti-Gaddafi forces in Libya, delivered via air power at a distance by Western powers in 2011, only taught the West to be wary of any further Middle Eastern interventions, humanitarian or otherwise. Libya descended into tribal and religious factionalism despite, or perhaps because of, the ousting of the Gaddafi regime, which received UN authorisation under the Responsibility to Protect mandate. Subsequently, European national parliaments explicitly rejected intervention in the far more strategically important Syrian civil war.

The West's post-2008 disengagement from the turbulent politics of the Middle East and the wider Islamic world, together with the popular rejection of any further exercises in re-building failing states or engaging in large-scale counter-insurgency operations therefore radically questions the 'correlation as cause' argument of the anti-interventionist commentariat. Recent events thus demonstrate a further level of incoherence embedded in the empathic orthodoxy, which is that 'keeping out' equates to the fostering of stability.

Staying uninvolved is not as easy as it appears, or at least comes with costs attached. We might justifiably slate naïve ideas of nation-building, evident in misguided counter-insurgency efforts in Afghanistan or Iraq, which held that invasion and forced modernisation would produce stable democratic states. But that doesn't mean the converse is true: that keeping out and leaving regions of concern to their own devices is necessarily a precursor to stability either. As ever, the reality is contingent and messy.

Empirical refutations
Furthermore, the other level of inconsistency in the Western cause/jihadist effect thesis offered by the critical empathisers is that it routinely overlooks ample evidence that contradicts their thesis. In the first instance, of course, it fails to observe the inconvenient fact that Islamist attacks upon Western targets pre-dated the invasions of Afghanistan and Iraq, and indeed, 9/11. Bombings in Lebanon in the 1980s, the attacks upon US bases in Saudi Arabia in 1996, the US embassies in East Africa (1998), and the attack on the USS Cole (2000) early on signalled a wider assault on what Ayman al-Zawahiri, the Lenin of Islamist thought, identified as 'the infidel invaders'.

Secondly, the advocates of empathy ignored the fact that the citizens of nations that were critical of, or unaligned with, the United States either before or after 2001 were afforded no more protection from the visitations of jihadist violence. This was clear in the first wave of jihadist attacks on tourist venues in

Egypt and Casablanca from the late 1990s onwards. Moreover, murderous assaults against other non-Islamist Muslims occurred with growing frequency, again from the 1990s, from Pakistan to Nigeria. Paradoxically, the rising pre-9/11 incidences of jihadist attacks reflected the belief of *al-Qaeda* and its affiliates that the West was decadent, weak and lacked moral or political purpose. Contrastingly, after the Iraq invasion, *al-Qaeda* attacked countries that, whilst European and secular, had played no part in the coalition of the willing.

The Western culpability thesis also expediently neglected to mention examples where NATO or US led coalition forces intervened to defend Muslim populations in Kuwait, Kosovo and Bosnia. If the cause-effect thesis had any validity, then one would expect some acknowledgement from the supposedly politically nuanced Islamists that the West's actions were not all bad, or badly motivated. Instead, both the jihadists and the critical empaths insist on the collectivisation of ethics that defines Western actions as intrinsically malignant.

Finally, and posing even more of an inconsistency for the critical orthodoxy, if there were any correlation between Western behaviour and Islamist retaliation, it was more often based on the accusation of Western *non-intervention* that energised the call for a radical and violent reaction. Accordingly, the initial reluctance of European states and the international community to interdict the Bosnian genocide after 1993 fuelled Euro-Islamic resentment and drew recruits to groups like *Al-Muhajiroun* operating from radical mosques in London's Finsbury Park. Analogously, today's jihadists criticise the West's failure to intervene in Syria and assert that Western indifference legitimates the Islamic State's turn towards a hard-line, chiliastic millenarian alternative.

Three inconvenient truths

In other words, a cursory examination of the politics of intervention and non-intervention since 1990 fails to demonstrate a simple process of Western cause and jihadist effect. What it demonstrates are three profound realities, utterly ignored by the critical commentariat:

1) The West is damned if it does intervene, and damned if it doesn't.
2) The West, and indeed, all non-Islamist inclined polities, are rendered culpable not for what they do, or do not do, but for what existentially they represent for the ideology of jihadism: infidel, *kuffar* (unbeliever) states, lost in a condition of secular and pagan ignorance.
3) The mere fact of their *jahaliya* (pre-Islamic ignorance) status confers a duty upon the jihadist to seek a violent, non-negotiable showdown. In the words of one *al-Qaeda* training manual: 'The confrontation we are calling for... does not know Socratic debates... Platonic ideals... nor Aristotelian diplomacy. But it knows the dialogue of bullets, the ideas of assassination, bombing and destruction and the diplomacy of the cannon and machine gun'.

Finally, then, what do these three realities portend for a more effective analysis and strategic response beyond the crude anti-interventionist Western cause and jihadist effect thesis? Five general points suggest themselves.

Five points for a more effective strategy

First, the prosaic, but necessary, starting point is to accept that the world is complex and throws up challenges that are rarely reducible to simplistic mono-causal explanations. Consequently, the conceit that claims empathy as a method to discern 'root causes' should be rejected because it is misleading and counterproductive. Causality in social relations, as philosophers from classical times have known, is endlessly debatable. 'Causes' don't exist in any objective sense. They are a contingent construction of the intellect that may have an infinite number of variations depending on the individual stance of the onlooker. The problem the 'root cause' thesis poses in terms of the current strategic dilemma confronting Western nations in the Middle East is that it erects, on little empirical evidence, a monolithic Islamist identity and attempts to impose a single ideological answer to the monolithic problem it has erroneously identified.

Secondly, then, similarly, false inferences should be rejected that assert singular solutions (which are often built upon mono-causal explanations) as universal norms of conduct. Such grand theoretical claims might proclaim that Western intervention in foreign lands is always iniquitous, or that negotiating with intractable enemies is the only way, or that only the unanimous approval of the United Nations can possibly legitimise any basis for action. The international system is one of risk and exigency, where threats arise within a complex, ever changing, milieu. Thus, even a superficial examination of the intense sectarian and tribal divisions and rivalries affecting the diverse societies of the Middle East or across the wider and more diffuse 'Muslim world' renders grand, rationalist, claims both abstract and spurious. Indeed, the diversity of Islam both in its heartlands and its diaspora illustrates the absurdity of trying to assert a set of timeless practices that will somehow supply a universal remedy for very different issues and conflicts.

Therefore, thirdly, contingency rules. A prudent Western strategy needs to be guided by a case-by-case evaluation of the merits of intervention together with a careful assessment of its practical and moral limitations. To achieve this requires a strategic appreciation of what constitutes the national interest and how it should be maintained, which is ultimately premised on the state's right to self-defence. It may contradict the critical orthodoxy in international relations, but in this pragmatic state-determined world, political diplomacy requires a sophisticated appreciation of history, culture and past precedent, not an abstract commitment to a historicist teleology or an Olympian cosmopolitanism.

Fourthly, selective involvement can work, as examples of Western state intervention attest from Bosnia, Kosovo, to Sierra Leone. In other words, a legitimate state, based on the political consent of a plural society within a given territory, asserts its interests via a well-considered foreign policy. This may in certain circumstances demand the strategically necessary, but not always morally virtuous, intervention overseas. Such a position is not to maintain that external involvement, howsoever conceived, should be the default position of Western policy. Far from it. As many commentators and scholars have articulated, there are often principled, ethical and strategically compelling reasons for keeping well away from conflicts that promise only to stir a hornet's nest: the Syrian civil war, perhaps, being a potent example.

Our argument is against those who are ideologically opposed to Western intervention merely because it is undertaken by the United States and other Western powers, a stance that is perhaps more commonly asserted in pacifist and utopian European thought, rather than in more sceptical and pragmatic appreciations of foreign policy that tend to characterise the more realistic debates in the United States. The point is that an argument against ideological anti-interventionism cannot be answered by asserting an opposing ideology of pro-interventionism. Pragmatism is the name of the game, and that can only be a matter of good judgement. Good judgement can only be informed by a principled examination of what is practical, attainable and politically feasible in each separate circumstance.

Finally, the liberal democratic state has the right to demand a minimal standard of civil association from its citizens. Minorities, and indeed, any member of the electing public, who reject such strategic calculations have the right to dissent, but not the right to blow up fellow citizens in the name of a transnational ideocracy. Moreover, if citizens of a democracy commit themselves to an enemy entity like the Islamic State by joining the jihad, they necessarily forfeit the rights of political citizenship that assume consent to government authority as a condition for enjoying those legal rights and the security they afford.

Conclusion: where are they now?
Taking a step back, what the assessment here ultimately divulges is that the argument against all forms of Western intervention is no solution to the hard security dilemmas posed by the absolutist claims of militant Islamism, which does not seek any form of accommodation with its self-proclaimed enemies. To that extent, the arguments of the critical empaths have, naively, facilitated the end of jihadist extremism. As Shiraz Maher has observed, the West's reluctance to intervene is 'precisely what Bin Laden always envisioned'. 'His main thesis', Maher noted, was that 'Western interference in the Middle East prevented the rise of Islamic governments. Weaken the West's sphere of influence, he argued, and a caliphate would emerge'. And so it has.

Consequently, now that the world faces the black flag-waving reality of an Islamic State in the Middle East, we might plausibly ask: where are the representatives of the critically empathic orthodoxy, now that their arguments lie in ruins? They are, for the moment at least, little seen or heard. This is not, one suspects, because they are taking a leaf out of Malcolm Caldwell's book and are being drawn to the region to extend the hand of unqualified humanity. Far more likely, they are continuing to pontificate upon their utopian schemes at a distance from the safety of their comfortable university sinecures funded of course by hideously Orientalist, neo-imperialist, Western governments. Far preferable to carry on empathising when, unlike Caldwell, one never has to experience the consequences of one's empathy.

Original version published in *War on the Rocks*, 11th September 2014, by David Martin Jones and M.L.R. Smith.

How Western multiculturalism nurtures sacred violence

Western governments and their security agencies appear not only shocked by the ultra-violence of the new Islamic State, but also surprised that jihadist recruits from Britain, Australia and Europe celebrate the killings they commit. Significantly, British and Australian jihadis promulgate most of the English-language posts and internet videos that glorify violent extremism.

They justify their methods on the grounds of their allegiance to a radical, anti-democratic, non-negotiable, modern form of Islam committed to world purification and the violent restoration of the caliphate. In 1924, the Turkish modernising autocrat, Kemal Atatürk, dissolved the Ottoman caliphate, a lineal descendant of the Umayyad and Abbasid caliphates that dated back to the first centuries of Islam. In Mosul, in June 2014, Abu Bakr al-Baghdadi, the nominal head of the Islamic State, declared its re-establishment and styled himself the new caliph, Ibrahim.

On the eve of the NATO summit in South Wales last month, the US President and UK Prime Minister declared that the way to contain the problem of global jihadism and its aspiration to re-create the caliphate was to 'invest in the building blocks of free and open societies, including creating a new and genuinely inclusive government in Iraq'. Not only does such a response seem naive, but it also notably fails to address the problem of home-grown radicalism and how the ideology that legitimates and ultimately sanctifies violence emanated less from the Middle East and more from the radical Islamist charities and organisations that have proliferated across Europe and to a lesser extent Australia since the last decade of the Cold War.

In other words, it was the 'free and open societies' of the West that tolerated and afforded state funding to the leading advocates of jihadism. In so doing, they incubated this distinctively illiberal, ideological mutation. European and Australian political elites acted in this curiously self-destructive manner because at the end of the Cold War they came to share a commitment to multiculturalism and diversity as the basis for greater political inclusivity and enhanced global and social justice.

It was, however, in the UK that the political elites, their media and leading academics (together with their Australian offshoots, in a perverse post-modern version of the cultural cringe), most fervently embraced this post-imperial multicultural commitment. And it was in its capital, Londonistan, that the new political religion found its most congenial home.

Before committing more soldiers and materiel overseas, it would seem prudent to examine the character of this home-grown jihadist phenomenon, and why the media, academe, the political elites and, most disturbingly, the police and security agencies, either discount its political appeal or attribute its 'root causes' to social deprivation, marginalisation, or anything other than the ideology that renders it seductive. How did this costly misunderstanding evolve, and what precisely is the basis of Islamism's appeal to wealthy, often university-educated, second- and third-generation migrants from Asian or Middle Eastern provenance in Britain and Australia?

Third way multiculturalism and war

To understand how jihadism achieved its current status we need first to examine how British, and to a lesser extent Australian, elites prosecuted the war on terror abroad after 2001, whilst allowing elements of Islamism's command-and-control to obtain sanctuary and state handouts in multicultural cities like London, Birmingham, Sydney and Melbourne. Multiculturalism's incoherent manifestation as a security doctrine exhibited itself in 'Tony Blair's way' post-1997, 'Kevin Rudd's way' in Australia after 2007, and latterly in 'David Cameron's way' since 2011.

These doctrines required Anglospheric democracies to prosecute the war forcefully against those who resort to jihad (holy war) abroad, actively participating in military coalitions whether in Afghanistan or Iraq, whilst, at the same time, affording some of Islamism's key ideologists and strategists a high degree of latitude at home. According to Blair, speaking in 2001, this reflects the fact that, whilst recognising that 'today, conflicts rarely stay within national boundaries' and 'interdependence defines the new world we live in', Blairism and its watered-down Ruddite equivalent also wished to 'celebrate the diversity in our country' and gain strength 'from the cultures and races' in their midst, some of whose adherents drew upon the interdependent and transnational character of conflict to render British or Australian infrastructure a soft civilian target.

Although, after February 2011, David Cameron sought to distance his government from a policy of 'state-led multiculturalism', which he argued had facilitated Islamist militancy, official policy nevertheless remained, at best, ambivalent. Meanwhile, academic bodies like the Economic and Social Research Council (ESRC), like the Australian Research Council (ARC), continued to disperse large grants to teams of sociologists, educationalists and psychologists to demonstrate that, despite some 'concern' over the London bombings of July 2005, the model of successful multiculturalism remained intact.

In the UK and Australia, this quasi-official doctrine of multiculturalism masked an incoherent policy oscillation between prosecution and celebration, complacency and arbitrariness. Thus, while Tony Blair remained steadfast in his commitment to the war on terror abroad, until 2004 the British Home Office permitted self-styled sheikhs Abu Hamza al-Masri and Omar Bakri Mohamed to recruit for *al-Qaeda* from their state-subsidised mosque in Finsbury Park, North London, whilst Abu Qatada operated as *al-Qaeda*'s emir in Europe.

These leading figures in the protoplasmic *al-Qaeda* network sought the achievement – by jihad, if necessary – of a unified Islamic world. Groups like Omar Bakri Mohammed's *Al-Muhajiroun* (the Migrants) and its breakaway front organisations like the Saviour Sect and *Hizb ut-Tahrir* (Party of Liberation), which, after 2002, extended its outreach activities to Sydney and Melbourne, dismissed the more moderate voices of diasporic Islam, who dissented from their promotion of a de-territorialised Salafist utopia, as 'chocolate Muslims'. The proselytising missionary work of groups like *Hizb-ut Tahrir* preached to a generation of alienated Muslim youth the inevitable confrontation of their creed with liberal democracy's decadent secularism.

Deracinated second- and third-generation migrants thus found solace not in the polymorphous joys of secularism and multiculturalism, but in a re-Islamisation that favoured supranational Islamist organisations instead of nation-state Islamic movements. *Hizb ut-Tahrir* exemplified this transition to a universalist mode of Islamic identity. As Olivier Roy explains:

> ...this fundamentalist party based in London... was originally set up as a Palestinian Islamic movement in 1953. Officially non-violent, its ideas are nevertheless very radical. It advocates the immediate re-establishment of the caliphate... and the ultimate conversion of the entire world to Islam. *Hizb ut-Tahrir* is now a genuinely international movement.

Ed Husain, a former member of *Hizb-ut Tahrir*, observed that the party 'borrowed' its organisational structure and confrontational tactics from 'radical socialists'. It functions as an elite vanguard party, recruiting from university campuses, which it finds particularly congenial. As Husain again observes:

> At many universities the tactics of confrontation and consolidation of Muslim feeling under the leadership of Hizb activists were being adopted... What dumbfounded us was the fact that the authorities on campuses never stopped us.

Prior to the London bombings of July 2005, the UK government, as with university campuses, did little to discourage Islamist activism or to encourage a sustained criticism of its questionable premises. The same was perhaps even truer of Australia where media and academic elites railed against Australia's commitment to a US-inspired 'violent peace' at the expense of a misunderstood and non-Western 'other'.

In other words, a bizarre combination of political correctness and a complacent indifference to the Islamist call enabled groups like *Hizb-ut Tahrir* to get a head start in the battle for hearts and minds amongst second- and third-generation migrants of Muslim background. This fatal misunderstanding was dramatically illustrated as early as August 2002 at a little-advertised, but Metropolitan Police-approved, rally of Islamist radicals held in Trafalgar Square, London. Clad in a variety of colourful *thowbs*, the crowd, on first impression, resembled something left over from a hippie counter-culture festival of the late 1960s. Instead of love and peace, however, they chanted 'Osama, Osama, Osama'.

Uncompromising certitude accompanied the flowing robes and beards. Peddling their ideological wares from four green tents marked 'Islam', 'Capitalism', 'Democracy', and 'Globalisation' – located just behind the backs of the statues of two heroes of empire, Sir Henry Havelock and Sir Charles Napier, whilst Admiral Nelson turned a blind eye from atop his pedestal – the militant disciples of the Islamic *internationale*, stylishly accoutred in black headscarves and matching Ray-Bans, projected an image of radical Islamist chic. Their handouts, such as 'A Call to Boycott America and Israel', excoriated the 'hyenas and vultures which operate under the guise of the coalition against terrorism'.

This heady mixture of posturing and utopian activism increasingly appealed to a younger generation of Muslim youth, recruited to the ranks of Islamic radicalism and its affiliates in growing numbers. Reinforced in the decade after 2005 by the new social media of Twitter, Facebook and YouTube, the blandishments of a post-modernised call to Islam, adumbrated with gangsta-rap-style narcissism and amplified by the intoxicating appeal of a sacralised violence, proved irresistible to a younger, educated, but deracinated generation of diasporic Muslims. Why? And, one might ask, why in multicultural cities like London and Sydney?

First, and ironically, because many Muslims in places like London are lured away from community and Islamic tradition by the attractions and opportunities of Western life. The radical championing of the transnational *ummah* (Islamic nation) addresses the universalist and apocalyptic yearning of young European Muslims 'who cannot identify with any specific place or nation'. And second, because states like Algeria, Egypt, Jordan, China, Russia, Singapore and Malaysia exercise a far greater degree of control over radical Islamist activity than occurs in Europe generally, and London and Sydney in particular. These non-Western states can control the press, limit internet access, and overcome their concerns – if they have any – about civil liberties violations with consummate ease. Not so in the Anglosphere, where liberal guilt about colonial sins trumps common sense.

Political religion, sacred violence and the cult of death
Given post-Cold War secular Western democracy's failure to take the ideology seriously, it is necessary to identify the way an Islamist ideology, or more precisely, following Eric Voegelin's classic identification of the phenomenon, *a political religion* based on Islam, came over the course of the twentieth century to serve a gnostic and violent purpose.

Voegelin identified the ersatz religious purpose that informed the European totalitarian movements of the 1930s. Like his Weimar contemporaries Hannah Arendt and Leo Strauss, Voegelin contended that the secularisation of the world – the significant achievement of Western modernity – had failed to silence the quest for meaning or the urge to find alternative ways of satisfying this existential human need. What interested Voegelin was the satanic seduction involved in the Nazis' political appeal, which replaced the transcendent God with a social collective:

> They build the corpus mysticum of the collectivity and bind the members to form the oneness of the body... The formation of the myth and its propaganda by means of newspapers and radio, the speeches and celebrations, the assemblies and parades, the planning and the death in battle, make up the inner world forms of the unio mystica.

As one of Voegelin's disciples, Barry Cooper, observed, 'to put it bluntly, it was a question of comprehending the attractiveness of evil'. The seductive appeal of political movements that seek to transform modernity and 'immanentise' (that is, to bring utopian ideals into reality) the revealed truth of the ideology, via the internet rather than newspapers, provides insight into how contemporary apocalyptic movements are prepared to countenance catastrophic violence to advance their cause. Indeed, it is impossible to understand contemporary jihadist violence without paying close attention to the deformed spirituality that these activists experience.

Ironically, the desire to build a state along supposedly rational Islamically-planned lines reflects the impact of Western cultural life and particularly of Western ideological thinking of a totalitarian character upon a generation of Western-trained Islamic thinkers. It was after the Muslim Brotherhood's Sayyid Qutb defined its essential character in several works written between 1955 and his execution by the Nasser's regime in Egypt in 1966, that we can refer to Islamism not as a traditional religious form but as an ideology, or more precisely, a political religion.

Like the totalitarian movements of the twentieth century, which profoundly influenced this style of thought, Islamism assumes an activist mysticism and a specialised knowledge or gnosis 'of the method of altering being'. As Voegelin explains, in 'the Gnostic attitude' we recognise the 'construction of a formula for self and world salvation, as well as the Gnostic's readiness to come forward as a prophet who will proclaim his knowledge about the salvation of mankind'. Under the influence of Qutb and subsequently Taqiuddin al-Nabhani, the founder of *Hizb ut-Tahrir*, Islamism became both a system (*nizam*) and an ideology that critiqued the contradictions in modernity, Islam's relationship with modernity, and the means of radically transforming it via jihad.

As Nabhani explained, 'the Islamist does not flatter the people, is not courteous to the authorities, or care for the people's customs and traditions... Rather he must adhere to the ideology alone'. Consequently, Nabhani argued for a complete destruction of the existing political order, particularly in Muslim countries, and its replacement by the '*khalifah* [caliphate] system'.

Unlike the pluralist secularism it confronts, then, Islamism offers a non-negotiable, politically religious alternative. Consequently, it rejects Muslims who practise a traditional faith and instead reinforces the gnostic character of European Islamism. Following Voegelin, we can see the Islamist, like the 1930s fascist, drawing a distinction between the experience of mundane reality and the second or transformed reality that the imaginative projection of the political religion intimates. This second reality, as Voegelin explains, 'screens the First Reality of common experience'.

From this perspective, violence is both necessary and justifiable to immanentise the apocalyptic dreamer's truth. As Voegelin explained in *The New Science of Politics*:

> Gnosticism as a counter-existential dream world can perhaps be made intelligible as the extreme expression of an experience which is

universally human, that is of horror of existence and a desire to escape from it.

Translated into a political religion in the context of modernity, the gnostic impulse is inherently polarising, and violent. Immanentising the transformational end justifies the violent means.

Moreover, the end state to which the ideologist aspires has natural enemies, notably those who accept the world as it is with all its messy secularism and pluralism. From the Islamist's perspective, to use Voegelin's words, violence or other 'types of actions which in the real world would be considered as morally insane, because of the real effects which they have, will be considered moral in the dream world because they intend an entirely different effect'.

Combining the sociology of Muslim reformism, as it evolved amongst the diaspora over the twentieth century that came to associate, as Ernest Gellner observed, greater piety with upward mobility and a shift from the mimetic folk Islam of the *assabiya* (tribal sense of social solidarity) to standards learned through the printed page, with Voegelin's understanding of gnosticism, reveals Islamism as a distinctive but comprehensible ideological formation.

If this account of the evolution and character of European Islamism is correct, it also sheds a disturbing light upon the conduct of Western governments in general and the 'third way' vision of New Labour in its British and Australian manifestations in their dealings with this implacable political religion and its cult of death.

Sacred violence and the idea of politics

Eric Voegelin argued that the ideological fanaticism of the Nazis was not only a moral and political mistake but also a spiritual perversion. More precisely, so far as the political religions of the twentieth century, like fascism, Stalinism, Maoism, and Islamism are concerned, the meaning or substance of religious phenomena moved from a spiritual concern with transcending the mundane world towards the realisation of imaginary fantasies of immanent apocalypse and the fashioning of this-worldly utopias.

At the same time, as Leo Strauss presciently remarked, the first half of the troubled twentieth century had also undermined faith in the secular, liberal, democratic Enlightenment project. 'The crisis of the West', he wrote:

> ... consists in the West having become uncertain of its purpose. The West was once certain of its purpose – of a purpose in which all men could be united and hence it had a clear vision of its future... We do no longer have that certainty and that clarity. Some among us even despair of the future, and this despair explains many forms of Western degradation.

After a brief end of history moment after 1989, this crisis of the West has become more acute. A society accustomed to understanding itself in terms of a liberal, universal and progressive purpose cannot lose faith in that purpose without becoming utterly bewildered. This bewilderment and its implications for the liberal democratic or political appreciation of the threat of political violence from non-state actors has only further crystallised this sense of bewilderment.

It is evident that, since the end of the Cold War, the pursuit of political and spiritual purification and an apocalyptic transformation of a corrupt world order is by no means confined to Islamist jihadis. *Al-Qaeda* and now the Islamic State only present the most evident manifestation of this activist style. The challenge it poses is the latest in a line of revolutionary assaults on the political systems of modern liberal democratic states since the late nineteenth century.

Those attracted to this style of thinking and the utopian and apocalyptic solutions they provide to local and global problems pose a complex challenge for political rule and the Western secular order. At the core of the West's difficulty is a need to take utopian ideologies seriously, whatever their provenance, whilst reaffirming the idea of politics as a distinct form of activity practised within a territorial unit of rule.

Western governments, their militaries, their media, and their educational and philanthropic institutions have underestimated the role that political religion of an Islamist complexion plays in both recruiting adherents and the passage to the violent act, which its dogmatic teaching sacralises. Instead, a progressive commentariat, itself a product of Western self-loathing, discountenances the rhetoric of Islamist purity, re-describing it as a response to social and economic exclusion, which in its more radical academic iterations, legitimatises resistance to Western capitalism and global injustice.

Thus, one leading 'critical' terror analyst asserted in 2008 that 'terror has multiple forms and the real terror is economic', the product of 'global capitalism'. When not searching for these opaque 'root causes' of terror, the progressive media, transnational NGOs and their academic fellow travellers, condemn any attempt to sanction radical Islamism as playing on 'the politics of fear'. From this perspective, governments in the UK, Australia and the US exaggerate the threat to persuade a gullible citizenry to accept an illegitimate extension of state power.

Yet, in what used to be standard introductions to politics written during the Cold War by, *inter alia*, Bernard Crick, Robert Dahl, Kenneth Minogue, Hannah Arendt and Leo Strauss, the Western European and North American experience of political democracy sustained, with difficulty, what Minogue termed a 'common world in which we may talk to each other'. Central to political democracy properly understood but now largely neglected by academe, the media, and the mainstream political parties, therefore, is a limited government that accepts the separation of the public from the private realm.

It is the recognition of such a separation that, according to Minogue, 'distinguishes politics, which we may loosely identify with freedom and democracy, from despotism'. Indeed, he argued, 'the Western political tradition rested on the rejection of despotism'. The over-arching public world of the state further maintains a structure of law appropriate to a self-determining association to sustain this civil life. Against this, the despot considers everything in society his private property. The politically religious and the modern politically correct versions of despotism see everything in society, and on the planet for that matter, as material for intervention and regulation.

Post-modern ideological despotism further assumes, as we have seen, the achievement of a post-democratic state of perfection via resistance, regulation and purification. By contrast, politics accepts the human condition for what it is, and this condition is never perfect. As Bernard Crick perceived, politics is 'not religion, ethics, law, science history, or economics. It neither solves everything nor is present everywhere'. Crucially, as Aristotle first recognised, it is about the acceptance of difference rather than the despotic imposition of unity.

Ultimately, politics can only occur in organised units of rule or states whose members or citizens, recognising a condition of mutual equality, nevertheless accept themselves to be an aggregate of many members and not a single tribe, religion, interest or tradition. Consequently, politics in the West became a plausible response to the problem of governing a complex modern state. Political freedom, rather than an abstract liberation, is a further result of this recognition because political democracy tolerates the articulation of different interests and does not propose an ideal, utopian or transnational solution to the problem of rule.

A particular order sustains the practice of political freedom and political rights. The authority to make a common law through representative institutions and apply it equally to all citizens requires, as Thomas Hobbes discerned, a Leviathan state. Indeed, one of the tasks of political science, as opposed to political religion, is to explain the processes by which political society evolved from tribe and clan 'to the power-units whose rise and decline constitute the drama of history'. Along with elucidating this process, 'we can also trace', Voegelin contended, 'the attempts to rationalize the shelter-function of the *cosmion*, the little world of order, by what are commonly called political ideas'.

In other words, political thinking from Aristotle to Hannah Arendt sought to rationalise the territorially bounded shelter that gives meaning to human life against the external forces of 'disintegration and chaos, a shelter in the end that is maintained by force'.

Ultimately, the order that enables political activity, commerce and cosmopolitanism itself to thrive is state defined. It is not transnational, multilateral, regional or international. Although a sovereign political democracy may participate in such arrangements, it cannot share sovereignty or have its lawful authority subject to supranational guidance or international or regional courts of law and human rights, without losing its integrity. Accordingly, how a politically democratic state conducts foreign relations will be very different from its internal ordering.

Politics, then, requires the constitutionally limited authority of the state for its practice. Maintaining its borders and the terms of membership is a matter of necessity and prudence rather than abstract justice. As early modern theorists of the state from Machiavelli to Milton acknowledged, the *res publica* (the public thing) has the right to maintain itself. This right, moreover, may be expressed in terms of both the right of the state's survival as well as the conditions for preserving and developing civilisation or, in the language of Miltonic republicanism, maintaining liberty and virtue. Tragically, our political elites, constitutional lawyers, progressive media and academics seem to have forgotten this political fact, with the disastrous consequences we are now observing in the Islamic State.

The Western strategic response to Islamic State jihadism

At the start of Ramadan, 28th June 2014, Abu Bakr al-Bagdadi ('Caliph Ibrahim') announced the resurrection of the Sunni caliphate in the recently formed Islamic State that runs from southern Syria through the Sunni provinces of Iraq almost to Baghdad. An unintended consequence of the internal war against the Assad regime in Syria, the Islamic State emerged from the chrysalis of the even more nebulous para-state of Iraq and al-Sham via a merger of Iraqi Islamists with the Syrian *Al-Nusra* (The Victory) jihadist brigades.

The new entity controls key cities like Mosul and the oil plains stretching from Mosul to the fields of Syria's Euphrates Oil Company. In fact, for the first time since the dawn of the so-called war on terror in late 2001, jihadists directly control territory and resources (the oil fields contribute more than $1 million a day to the Islamic State's coffers). Rather than relying on the tolerance of friendly regimes like the Taliban in Afghanistan before 2001, or weak ones, like Yemen or Somalia, to afford them a base, the jihadists now meet the Weberian definition of a state by exercising the monopoly of violence in a territorial unit of rule.

This dramatic and little-understood development has serious implications for the foreign policies and strategic thinking of Western democracies as well as for the Middle East itself. The caliphate, long an Islamist dream since its dissolution by the modernising Atatürk regime in Turkey in 1924, presents itself as a transnational ideological alternative to the secular nation-state. As the Islamic State's official journal, *Dabiq*, observes, Sunni (and Shiite) militancy since 2013 has effectively dissolved the post-Ottoman world defined by the secret Anglo-French Sykes-Picot Agreement of 1916.

Moreover, because of its territorial unity and its promulgation of a political religion with a global reach, the Islamic State draws recruits from the Sunni Muslim world, from Pakistan to Indonesia, as well as from an alienated diaspora of Muslims located in the West. Thus, Americans, Britons, French, Dutch, Swedes, German and Australian nationals, as well as Indonesians, Filipinos and Malays, swell the ranks of the Islamist equivalent of the Spanish Civil War international brigades.

The curious mutation of an Islamist dream into a temporal reality undermines the ruling academic and media assumptions that governed post-Cold War Western thinking about the evolving new world order and a liberal democratic end of history. In the Middle East, Western thinking assumed, amongst other things, that the US-orchestrated coalition had, by 2011, decapitated both the core leadership of *al-Qaeda* as well as *al-Qaeda* in Iraq, It believed, in other words, that it had significantly degraded both the threat and organisational structure of transnational Islamism. It assumed also that the Arab Spring movements, which after 2011 challenged authoritarian rule in Tunisia, Libya, Iran and Egypt, had set the Middle East on a path towards greater openness, regular elections, and a long-anticipated democratic transformation. Finally, it assumed following the 2006 Surge of US forces, that Iraq had been returned to a degree of post-Saddam stability. The exit of Western forces in 2011 had, so the narrative went, bequeathed Iraq a functioning, if ethno-religiously partisan, democracy comprising an elected government and a Western-trained state security force.

Somewhat problematically for this historicist teleology, recent events across the Middle East portend something far more unpredictable. Along with the developing power politics in Eastern Europe and the South China Sea, this intimates an era of instability marked by internal and potentially external or inter-state war. In its Middle Eastern manifestation, the Syrian civil war that began in 2012, the slow-motion disintegration of 'liberated' Libya since 2013, the Israeli intervention in Gaza in August 2014, and the fragmentation of Iraq since 2011, announce significant challenges not only to the wider region but also to European and Anglosphere states not directly involved in the crisis.

These threats arise from the migration of displaced peoples, the terror threat posed by returning jihadis trained in the arts of bomb making and decapitation, the problem of energy security and the unpredictable consequences of potential major power conflict.

Everything solid dissolves into air
Significantly, the dissolution of any prospect for enduring stability in the Middle East occurred only after 2011. In other words, it occurred at a time when Western involvement in the region was notable for its absence. Western forces had largely departed Iraq by 2008. Support for anti-Gaddafi forces in Libya, delivered at a distance by France and the United Kingdom in 2011, only taught the West to be wary of any further Middle Eastern interventions, humanitarian or otherwise. Libya descended into tribal and religious factionalism after the ousting of the Gaddafi regime, which was, somewhat ironically, endorsed by the UN under the post-2005 Responsibility to Protect mandate.

Subsequently, national parliaments in Europe explicitly rejected intervention in the far more strategically significant Syrian civil war. Meanwhile, US foreign policy after 2008 appeared increasingly indifferent to shaping the international order in general and the Middle East in particular. The fracking revolution, which gave the US resource independence and facilitated Obama's somewhat uncertain pivot to Asia after 2010, permitted the US to downgrade the Middle East from an existential threat to a perennial nuisance.

The cost in both troops and materiel of Western interventions in Iraq and Afghanistan further rendered it unlikely that the US, let alone the British or other European governments, would embark again on costly and largely futile state-building exercises. As the US military prepared to leave an uncertainly pacified Afghanistan, the cost to the US taxpayer of this long war in terms of military operations and reconstruction exercises exceeded £350 billion and had cost the UK taxpayer more than £22 billion.

The West's post-2008 disengagement from the turbulent politics of the Middle East and the wider Islamic world, together with the popular rejection of any further exercises in re-building failing states or engaging in large-scale counter-insurgency operations, affords the opportunity, therefore, to assess one of the long-standing claims of anti-interventionist critics of the post-2003 Iraq stabilisation effort. In the post-9/11 decade a powerful academic and public media commentariat came to assert that the West would induce conditions of greater regional stability and harmony, and reduce the jihadist threat both at home and abroad, if it desisted from waging wars in 'neo-colonial battlefields'.

The incoherence of non-intervention

After the Iraq invasion in 2003 this non-interventionist lobby influenced the study of terrorism and insurgency at international relations departments from Cornell to Queensland and informed the coverage of public broadcasters like the BBC and Australian Broadcasting Corporation. It also dominated the opinion pages of newspapers and journals as various as the *Guardian*, *New Statesman*, *New York Times*, *Washington Post*, *American Interest*, and in Australia *The Monthly* and the publications of the Fairfax Media group.

Stripped of its fashionable, if somewhat opaque, constructivist and critical theoretical architecture, the orthodoxy promulgated the view that Western foreign policies and the doctrine of pre-emption had, as if by an invisible hand, created the home-grown and external jihadist threat. Indeed, this policy constituted the 'root cause' of instability across the Muslim world, as well as the principal factor in alienating European and American Muslims, leading a minority to jihad against the West and its secular democratic 'idols' and its ignorant state of *jahiliya*.

This academic and media orthodoxy maintained, for all intents and purposes, that Western statecraft after the Cold War had engineered the cause and the effects of the Islamist threat both domestically and from overseas. From this perspective, an Orientalist fear of the Muslim 'other', which pre-dated the Cold War, fuelled an interventionist foreign policy that during the 1990s had the countervailing consequence of inspiring jihadist activism.

Moreover, the critical orthodoxy also held that Western state recourse to new anti-terror laws after 2001 responded to no clear and present danger but instead induced a home-grown politics of fear that only further alienated minority communities. It further contended that Western interests, as well as those of the Muslim world, would be far better served by empathising with the sources of Muslim alienation and leaving the Middle East to discover its own distinctive and attractively non-Western identity.

However, with the black flag flying over the new Islamic caliphate, as well as in London's Blackwall Tunnel, this conclusion, and the narrative that sustained it, appears increasingly delusional. In fact, the causal link between an Islamophobic West, governed by a politics of fear, and jihadist activism rested on a series of now falsified assumptions. Thus, this critical theory perspective overlooked the inconvenient fact that violent Islamist activism pre-dated Western intervention in Afghanistan, Iraq or Africa.

Attacks such as the bombing of the US and French embassies in Lebanon in 1983 or the raid on the *USS Cole* in 2000, represented the beginnings of a wider assault on what *al-Qaeda*'s chief ideologist, Ayman al-Zawahiri, argued was 'the infidel without'. This first wave of jihadist strikes was by no means limited to US targets, as attacks on tourist venues in Egypt and Casablanca and against other non-Islamist Muslims illustrated. These occurred with growing frequency from the 1980s. Paradoxically, the rising pre-9/11 incidences of jihadist assaults reflected the belief of *al-Qaeda* and its affiliates that the West was decadent and weak, lacking the moral and political purpose to resist. Contrastingly, after the Iraq invasion, *al-Qaeda* attacked countries that, whilst European and secular, had played no part in Western-led military operations.

The Western-responsibility thesis also conveniently overlooked examples, notably in post-Cold War Europe, where NATO or international forces intervened to defend Muslim populations in Kuwait, Kosovo and Bosnia. Paradoxically, even if there was any correlation, rather than direct causality, between Western behaviour and Islamist retaliation, it was more often Western procrastination or a refusal to intervene that animated the call for a drastically violent reaction.

Accordingly, the initial reluctance of European states and the international community to intervene to prevent the Bosnian genocide after 1993 fuelled Islamist resentment and drew recruits to groups like *Al-Muhajiroun* operating from radical mosques in London's Finsbury Park and Sydney's Lakemba district. Not dissimilarly, today's jihadist online critics of the West's failure to intervene in Syria assert that Western indifference justifies the Islamic State's turn towards a hardline, violent, alternative.

In other words, a cursory examination of the politics of intervention and non-intervention since 1990 fails to demonstrate a simple process of Western cause and jihadist effect. Instead, it reveals a condition of complexity. What does this complexity disclose, not only about Islamist strategic thinking but more importantly about how the West might respond?

Abandoning grand narratives – returning to prudential realism
First, it discloses that the search for 'root-causes' is misleading and counter-productive. The problem here is one of stretching concepts and erecting, on little empirical evidence, a monolithic Islamist identity. The root-cause approach further attempts to impose a single ideological answer to the monolithic problem it has erroneously identified. This solution comes in a variety of forms, ranging from pacifist utopianism to internationalist transformational idealism to cynical conservative pessimism (which is also non-interventionist).

Yet a cursory examination of the intense sectarian and tribal divisions and rivalries affecting very different societies in the Middle East or across the wider and more diffuse 'Muslim world' more generally, exposes the practical limitations of such rationalist abstract solutions. Indeed, the diversity of Islam in its heartlands and its diaspora illustrates the absurdity of trying to impose a mono-causal explanation that will somehow reveal the hidden interconnection between very different issues and conflicts.

Instead, a prudent foreign policy requires the case-by-case analysis of the merits of intervention. This requires a strategic appreciation of what constitutes the national interest and how it ought to be maintained. This is ultimately premised on the state's right to self-defence. The premise informed classic French sixteenth-century reason-of-state theorists, who conceived the idea of state *raison*. In this pragmatic state-determined world, policies based on the hypothetical notion of an 'international community' that promotes supposedly universal norms of conduct cannot achieve coherence, let alone order. Inter-state political diplomacy requires a sophisticated appreciation of history, culture and past precedent, not an abstract commitment to a historicist teleology or an Olympian cosmopolitanism. In the context of the Middle East, a careful reading of post-Ottoman history would counsel against intervention to advance Western ideological preferences.

In other words, a legitimately constituted state based on the political consent of a plural society within a given territory, asserts its interests via a well-considered foreign policy. This may in certain circumstances demand the strategically necessary, but not necessarily virtuous, intervention overseas. Unfortunately, Western governments along with their security agencies, most of the mainstream media and publicly funded academic analysts of terrorism largely reject this prudent, strategically contingent, understanding of foreign policy conduct and prefer to promote the view that to take Islamic rhetoric seriously overreacts to a problem associated with an excluded and misunderstood minority. Somewhat disturbingly, most government-funded academic research into jihadism largely accepts the view of the transnational Islamist organisation *Hizb ut-Tahrir* that 'ISIS is but the new *al-Qaeda* used as a bogeyman by western states to justify intervention'.

Such a complaisant perspective fails to address the world-wide appeal of what is essentially a death cult. As early as 2004, in the wake of Madrid train bombings, Islamists defined their absolute repudiation of a pluralist secular worldview and their commitment to an apocalyptic alternative with their formula: 'You love life, we love death'.

This privileging of death rejects absolutely any secular political commitment to the good life. As the Italian philosopher Umberto Eco explained in relation to the rise of totalitarianism in the 1930s, in *Setti Anni di Desiderio* (1983), a taste for killing and martyrs represents fascism's purest form. In its Islamist mutation, as numerous slickly produced videos on the internet demonstrates, it adores and serves death, whether it be as the slayer or the slain.

In fact, the beatification of terrorist violence, or the management of savagery, which Islamic State's journal *Dabiq* continually proclaims, is more telling than its professed religious dimension. Indeed, to love death, as jihadism does, is to say that it is beautiful to receive it and to risk it and, even more perversely, that the most beautiful and saintly love is to distribute it. This aspect of jihadism and a version of Islam that sustains it, does not, as some security analysts pronounce, 'desensitise' youth to death. Rather, it sacralises it.

Before throwing more money at the problem of domestic 'extremism' and creating even more sweeping government powers, the elected representatives of Western secular democracies should consider more effective policies to defend a political way of life and resist, via a campaign of hearts and minds, a home-grown but essentially fascist death cult.

Ultimately, in an anxiety-prone disorder where global interconnectedness by no means presages integration, a secular democratic market state minimally requires a shared public morality to sustain the national interest expressed through domestic legislation. This civil association applies equally to all citizens and requires an active foreign policy to secure its interests and values over time, both at home and abroad.

Neither a mentality of studied indifference, nor a cosmopolitan idealism that, while theoretically open to intervention, sets impossible standards of moral consistency, addresses the complexity of the Western democracies' besetting dilemmas. Both attitudes foster an outlook of apathetic passivity. And passivity in the face of threats of an illiberal and apocalyptic character does not constitute a foreign or domestic policy worthy of the name.

Original article published in *Quadrant*, Vol. 58, No 10, October 2014, by David Martin Jones and M.L.R. Smith.

Can you talk to a death cult?

The immolation of Jordanian pilot Moaz al-Kasasbeh at the hands of the Islamic State of Iraq and the Levant (ISIL) took the Islamist cult of death to 'a new pinnacle of barbarity'.

In *The Times*, Roger Boyes argued that in undertaking such ruthless action ISIL may have 'overreached itself', evincing a 'revolution out of control'. An out-of-control revolution is presumably doomed.

However, if ISIL is not doomed, the only long-term alternative strategy, if we read former Tony Blair adviser Jonathan Powell correctly, is to engage with its leaders and 'treat them as statesmen'.

In *Talking to Terrorists*, Powell contends 'governments proclaim they will never negotiate with evil, yet they always have and will'.

The tendency in much commentary either to write off groups like the Islamic State or, after a convenient lapse of time, consider negotiating with them, indicates a profound failure to understand the nature of the death cult's post-modern appeal both in the Muslim world and amongst its diaspora.

Beheading fatigue or Thanatos unchained?

Before we too quickly assume the inevitable implosion of ISIL or establish terms for opening negotiations, we need to know more precisely what ISIL seeks to achieve via its ultra-violent strategy.

As early as 2004, in the wake of the Madrid train bombings, Islamists defined the divide between a pluralist secular world order and their brand of apocalyptic millenarian caliphs with the formula: 'you love life we love death'. This slogan went through several mutations after 2004, with phrases like 'The Americans love Pepsi, we love death'. In essence, however this celebration of death defines itself against a secular Western Enlightenment belief in life.

As the Italian philosopher Umberto Eco observed, in a different ideological context, fascism is political necrophilia. A taste for killing and martyrs is its purest form. Islamo-Fascism is similarly obsessed. It means, as the slickly produced video of Lieutenant Kasasbeh's death on the internet demonstrated, adoring and serving death.

In fact, this beatification of violence is as telling as the professed politically religious commitment.

Indeed, to love death as jihadism does is to say that it is beautiful to receive it and to risk it and that the most beautiful and saintly thing is to distribute it. This putrid need of death is evident today across the Middle East. If that is what jihadism at its fundamentalist core wants, it has certainly got it. It is a form of political nihilism made possible by the sacralisation of violence.

This aspect of jihadism and the capacity of its version of Islam to play into the cult of death is not to desensitise youth to death (as opinion columns frequently assert) but to make it sacred. Hence the recent tactical shift from somewhat passé decapitation to something even more transgressive and therefore stimulating to those suffering the ennui of beheading fatigue. Such cruelty and the addictive craving it elicits, moreover, serves a broader ideological and strategic purpose.

Managing savagery

After 9/11 more thoughtful jihadists like Abu Musab al Suri and Abu Bakr Naji recognised that the global Islamic resistance movement required a more flexible strategy than that offered by *al-Qaeda*.

Al Suri's and Naji's third generation jihadism required both an intensification of violence and a more amorphous, but global, leaderless resistance like that practised in Paris last month, when jihadist gunmen killed 17 people, including 11 journalists of the satirical *Charlie Hebdo* magazine.

In 2005, al-Suri's *Global Call to Islamic Resistance* called for spontaneous, self-radicalised actions, 'which will wear down the enemy and prepare the ground for waging war on open fronts... without confrontation in the field and seizing control of the land, we cannot establish a[n Islamic] state, the strategic goal of the resistance'.

The American-born Islamist, Anwar al-Awlaki, published five articles extracted from the *Global Call for Inspire*, the English language online journal that made jihad hip for a diasporic audience. However, leaderless resistance abroad complements the management of savagery within the protean Islamic State. Ultimately, the purpose of violence whether in the West or in Raqqa is to secure the borders of the Islamic State.

As Naji argued in *The Management of Savagery: The Most Critical Stage Through Which the Umma Will Pass* (2006), the savage condition represents the stage of state breakdown, which the revolutionary cadre must manage enroute to the purified Islamic State. As he explains, 'if we succeed in the management of savagery, that stage will be a bridge to the Islamic state which has been awaited since the fall of the caliphate'.

Moreover, even if this is not achieved immediately, it is not the end of the matter. Naji continues chillingly, 'the more abominable the level of savagery is', it is still less abominable than enduring stability under 'the order of unbelief, *nizam al kufir* by several degrees'.

Engaging death cults

Before assuming death cults will wither on the vine or at some point adopt a more moderate and negotiable position where the Islamic State's self-styled caliph Ibrahim mutates into a version of Gerry Adams but with a better beard, the elected representatives of any secular democracy should to do far more to defend a political way of life and target the promulgation and appeal of this potent and ultimately fascist death cult.

Original article published in the *Daily Telegraph*, 7th February 2015, by David Martin Jones and M.L.R. Smith.

Crazy like a fool, wild about jihadi cool

Much of the condemnation following the attacks in Paris against the office of *Charlie Hebdo* reflects the shock and disbelief that Western governments have in understanding the cultic appeal of the Islamic State of Iraq and the Levant (ISIL). US President Barack Obama spoke of the 'outrageous attempt to terrorise innocent civilians', while German Chancellor Angela Merkel expressed her solidarity with the French people, proclaiming that 'we will fight against those who have carried out such an unfathomable act against you'.

But there is a problem here. Understandable though such declarations are, the acts perpetrated by ISIL are not, in themselves, unfathomable. It is the manner of official rhetoric, media analysis, and much academic commentary that often obscures an understanding of the threat. And the most misleading word in public commentary is the term radicalisation.

The stream of young Muslims who reject their host nations and travel to Syria to throw in their lot with the Islamic State in all its manifest brutality vexes Western nations. Much of the concern about what is happening within certain Muslim communities is expressed as a problem of 'radicalisation'.

In the wake of the atrocities in Paris, radicalisation is again cast as the central issue. A report in the *Guardian* following the attacks highlighted France's 'struggles to tackle radicalisation among its Muslim community'. The report noted that nearly half of the estimated 3,000 Muslims from Europe have travelled to the Middle East to participate in jihad are French.

Meanwhile, it was reported in Britain that counter-terrorism sources fear some 450 'radicalised' Britons have returned from Syria and could perpetrate similar attacks to those witnessed in France. The Director of the Office for Security and Counterterrorism, Charles Farr, states in this respect that ISIL's radical dogma is 'a form of ideological grooming'. Yet, what does this term radicalisation mean? Is this term an accurate description of the process that leads a young Western Muslim to jihad? Words matter. An adequate response needs accurate diagnosis.

George Orwell observed that 'the slovenliness of our language makes it easier to have foolish thoughts'. If the threat is to be countered effectively then at the very least one must be sure that the political terminology one uses truthfully describes the actual nature of the problem. Orwell noted that 'political chaos' results from the 'decay of language' and ends up in prevailing orthodoxies that 'conceal and prevent thought'.

This is precisely what has happened with the misuse of the term radicalisation. Radicalism, in fact, has precise origins. The word entered modern usage in the nineteenth century in the context of political and economic reform and social progress. It was those secular, liberal, utilitarian reformers associated with Jeremy Bentham and James Mill (John Stuart's father) who devised the modern understanding of radical. It stood for a programme of rational, constitutional, social and economic reform. Radicalism as an ideology dismissed religion as irrational superstition and sought political reform along secular, capitalist and progressive democratic lines. The one thing we can easily discern about Islamic State and its message is that it is does not do democracy or secular modernity. Therefore, it is not radical, and it does not engage in radicalisation. Thus, fulfilling Orwell's prophecy, distorted meaning ends up obscuring and preventing thought.

Rather than being radicalised, young Western Muslims are attracted to what a more religious age than our own recognised as enthusiasm, zealotry or fanaticism. Any analysis of jihadism's self-confirming zealotry suggests that those who are labelled as radicalised are not radicals at all. Ideological radicalism, properly understood, requires a clear break from traditional religion of whatever form to achieve a pluralist secular modernity.

Modern day jihadists are, then, the antithesis of radical. Their worldview is fashioned by a scriptural literalism based on the message of the Prophet Mohammed and the hadith of his rightly guided successors from the Seventh Century. It is this that inspires the thought and practice of Islamic State and its followers who look to the past to build tomorrow's religious utopia purified by ultra-violence. They are ultra-traditionalists, not radicals.

This ultra-traditionalism guides every action in the present. Today's jihadi is an enthusiast (not a radical) as defined by the *Oxford English Dictionary* as one who is 'possessed by a god', or in 'receipt of divine communication'. No matter how deluded their actions seem to modern attitudes, through their enthusiasm they engage directly in a divine mission to re-create the caliphate. This renders them immune to community sensitive 'de-radicalisation' programmes promoted by Western governments because there is nothing radical in jihadist self-understanding.

The distorted rhetoric of radicalisation is, though, far more damaging than merely offending semantic sensibilities because associating such atrocities as those committed in Paris with radicalisation reinforces the idea of 'jihadi cool'. For to be radical means in some sense to be 'street smart'. Contemporary Islamists are adept social entrepreneurs who understand this only too well. Islamic State and its media outlets release over 90,000 social media posts a day. That's nearly 33 million a year. The appeal of social media is clear. There are no gatekeepers. Messages posted from one remote or hidden location are immediately transmitted to the hip pocket of anyone with a smart phone. An audience counted in millions.

Social media is the command-and-control network of fanatical Islamism. It is used to brand the ISIL product, literally, to promulgate the message and recruit online. Segueing off the L'Oreal advert, for instance, a recent Islamist recruitment message targeting young Western women runs 'Cover Girl, No. Covered Girl, yes. Because you're worth it'.

Western radicalisation rhetoric further distorts the threat because it implies that those Muslim youngsters inclined to join the jihad are merely deluded naïfs who don't really mean what they say and do, when of course they only too clearly do as their willingness to kill and be killed for the cause demonstrates. In effect, much public commentary about 'radicalisation' removes human agency from those who seek participation in the jihad because they have 'unfathomably' been pumped full of ideological steroids and brainwashed by unscrupulous preachers of hate who groom their prey.

The simpler but harsher truth is that they have been attracted by a message of jihadi cool in which Western governments have been indirectly responsible for fostering. While ISIL offers jihadi cool messaging, governments merely respond with insipid pieties about cohesion achieved through culturally sensitive and misdirected 'de-radicalisation' initiatives that have proved expensive and ineffective. In this context, it is worth asking, before engaging any more academics and bureaucratic agencies in taxpayer funded programmes, what precisely does the counter-terrorism community understand by 'radicalism' and 'radicalisation'? An answer to this question may reveal that we in the West have been only too successful in brainwashing ourselves.

Original article published in the *Daily Telegraph*, 16th November 2016, by David Martin Jones and M.L.R. Smith.

Curbing enthusiasm: Radicalisation and fanaticism

It was only after the 7/7 bombings in London that 'radicalisation' established itself firmly in the Western lexicon of criminology and counter-terror policing to describe the process that leads teenagers down the path of violent extremism. Yet before Western taxpayers pour yet more money into countering home-grown violent extremism, it might be worth asking what the problem is that de-radicalisation supposedly solves. Simply put, jihadist groups — or more precisely, the Islamic State — do not seek to 'radicalise'. They want to achieve something else, and far more apocalyptic, and this fact eludes the official gaze along with much media and academic commentary.

After the attacks in Paris on 13th November 2015 and the palpable fear of further home-grown mass-casualty assaults in other European capitals, it might be worth pausing to assess the political benefit of government programmes devoted to de-radicalisation. In this context, the New York Police Department (NYPD) was the first police force to commission a report into 'Radicalization in the West' in 2007. The report defined radicalisation as a four-stage process involving 'pre-radicalization', 'intensification', 'indoctrination', and eventually 'jihadization', and on this basis outlined a programme of intervention. After 2002, the British government's formal strategy for countering the call to jihad among alienated second-generation Muslim youth germinated a policy called *Prevent*, which modified the American approach. According to *Prevent*, 'radicalisation is a social process particularly prevalent in small groups'. It is about 'who you know... Group bonding, peer pressure and indoctrination are necessary to encourage the view that violence is a legitimate response to perceived injustice'.

It may seem a matter of semantics, but unpacking 'de-radicalisation' reveals a misleading neologism that obscures more than it elucidates. Somewhat paradoxically, the notion of 'radicalisation' itself nurtures a sense of 'group bonding' that encourages some Muslims down the path of violence. Moreover, by treating the problem as one for community workers and therapists, official de-radicalisation policies discountenance the utopian appeal of religious enthusiasms that offers meaning to otherwise meaningless lives.

What does it mean to be jihadi cool?
Islamist propaganda posts thousands of messages a day on social media, reaching a receptive audience of millions. After 9/11 a new wave of tech-savvy global Salafist jihadists turned to the internet. Abu Musab al-Suri developed the strategy of leaderless resistance online via his *Global Call to Islamic Resistance*. The American born and educated Anwar al-Awlaki re-packaged the message for Western youth and made jihad cooler than hip-hop. Awlaki was killed in Yemen in 2011, but by then he had created the 'Jihadi John' phenomenon in the West.

Awlaki and his successors, like the former west Sydney male stripper and boxer turned zealot Feiz Mohammad, or failed Melbourne rapper Neil Prakash (aka Abu Khalid al Cambodi), use social media to brand the Islamic State product. Jihadist activists consider this aspect of their movement so important that in August they formed the Anwar al-Awlaki Brigade to promulgate the message and recruit online.

The flow of young second-generation Muslim men and women — brought up in secular, Western, multicultural societies — to the Islamic State demonstrates the success of the messaging. Western governments seem as shocked by the cultic appeal of the Islamic State as they were surprised by the rapidity and lethality with which it achieved de facto authority over vast swathes of Syria and Iraq.

In February 2015 Barak Obama, the US President, convened a summit of like-minded democracies to counter violent extremism to discuss ways to 'prevent violent extremists and their supporters from radicalizing, recruiting, or inspiring individuals or groups in the United States and abroad to commit acts of violence'. Yet the default governmental response is to introduce more tranches of counter-terrorism legislation and throw even more money into security agency budgets and counter-radicalisation strategies. After more than a decade of activist intervention, however, they have singularly failed to curb the enthusiasm for jihad.

In the United Kingdom, the government's *Prevent* strategy is widely disparaged as ineffective. Despite an annual budget of £40 million (approximately US$60 million), the number of British Muslims leaving for Syria to throw in their lot with the Islamic State has risen substantially. Between June and August 2015, 796 people were referred for de-radicalisation in England and Wales, double the number of referrals for intervention in the first three months of 2015. It might be the case that the strategy has stopped people from travelling a violent path. However, it is difficult to prove a negative and the effectiveness of *Prevent* may be impossible to measure with accuracy. Clearly, though, the rising figures suggest that de-radicalisation policies fail in curtailing the appeal of jihad.

Elsewhere in Western Europe, Denmark's de-radicalisation programme has been criticised for being soft and trusting, focusing only on the reintegration of returnees from Syria rather than challenging their ideology. Denmark was the command-and-control centre for the Islamic State's attack on Paris.

The United States has engaged less with formal counter-radicalisation policies and has a relatively low level of foreign fighter recruitment. Nevertheless, the NYPD, according to its 2007 report into radicalisation, addressed the phenomenon 'as a self-driven process' that led to clusters of violently inclined individuals, but who required 'certain archetypes to evolve from just being a "bunch of guys" to an operational cell'. Notably they required a 'spiritual sanctioner' and operational leader. 'Terrorism is the ultimate consequence of the radicalisation approach', the report found. Yet, the report offered no definition of radicalisation and no obvious reference points for intervention to inhibit individuals moving from Islamist thought to jihadist action. This notwithstanding, in recent years, the US Justice Department has funded de-radicalisation initiatives aimed at understanding the motives of those who might be attracted to violence.

Analogously, down under, the Australian federal government has allocated over AU$40 million (US$29 million) to counter violent extremism since 2013. The government devotes AU$13.4 million specifically to counter radicalisation through programmes like 'Living Safe Together'. After Neil Prakash groomed 15-year-old Farhad Jabhar online to carry out a gun attack on a Paramatta police station resulting in the death of police accountant Curtis Cheng in October 2015, the government of Prime Minister Malcolm Turnbull announced it would devote more funding to social programmes aimed at 'preventing youth radicalisation'.

The latest approach will stress the need for 'social cohesion'. 'Early intervention and community-based solutions work best', counter-terrorism coordinator Greg Moriarty averred. Yet in the same week that state and federal governments announced new de-radicalisation initiatives, *Hizb-ut Tahrir*, the transnational Islamist party, which only established a presence in Australia after 2001, denounced both the Australian oath of allegiance and the 'forced assimilation' implied in singing the national anthem at its Sydney conference.

It comes as no great surprise then that, despite a decade of de-radicalisation efforts, a recent worldwide study in the journal *Behavioural Science of Terrorism and Political Aggression* found that only one of 87 programmes 'dealing with countering violent extremism deals with those who have been radicalised... Efforts have instead been spent on diffuse programmes promoting multiculturalism rather than targeting individuals'. The authors of the study concluded that 'There is little independent evaluation or evidence-based research to suggest that social cohesion or prevention initiatives have led to an actual reduction in extremism anywhere in the Western world'.

In other words, while the Islamic State and its followers offer jihadi cool messaging, public authorities respond with insipid pieties about cohesion and community bonding achieved through culturally sensitive de-radicalisation programmes that in the United States, Europe and Australia have proved ineffective. It might be worth asking, therefore, before engaging more academics, counsellors, community groups and bureaucratic agencies in taxpayer-funded programmes, what precisely does the counter-terrorism community mean by 'radicalism' and 'radicalisation?'

What's in a name: radical or fanatic?

Seemingly, no government agency or counter-terrorism organisation has paused to consider whether the term 'radicalisation' in fact describes the process that converts a young Western Muslim to the Salafist cause. Neither Western governments and academics, nor police and security agencies used the term very much before the London bombings of 7th July 2005. After 2005, it became the fashionable catch-all term to capture various aspects of the internal security, integration, and foreign policy debate about Islamism. It also served, at the same time, both an analytic and public policy function.

However, its attempted social scientific objectivity played into the notion of jihadi cool, because to be 'radical' in youth argot means to be street smart. The political vocabulary matters. An adequate response needs an accurate diagnosis. And here language needs to be understood accurately lest it obscure and mislead.

Obscurity is precisely what we find with the misuse of the term radicalisation. 'Radicalism', in fact, has a precise etymology. It entered modern usage in the nineteenth century in the context of political and economic reform and social progress. It was the eighteenth and nineteenth-century secular, liberal, utilitarian reformers such as Jeremy Bentham and James Mill who devised the modern understanding of radicalism. Radicalism, in its original understanding, stood for a programme of constitutional, social and economic reform. Radicalism as a political ideology dismissed religion as irrational superstition and sought reform along secular, capitalist and progressive democratic lines.

If we know anything about Islamist thought, it is that it refutes secularism and modernity. Rather than being radicalised, young Western Muslims are attracted to what a more religious age than our own recognised as enthusiasm, zealotry, or fanaticism. This phenomenon has a long and troubled history in the Jewish, Christian and Islamic religious faiths. Seventeenth-century Europe knew well the revived post-Reformation penchant for religious sectarianism and enthusiastic zealotry, and its deracinating social consequences. Ben Jonson satirised the phenomenon of the religious enthusiast on the Renaissance stage in plays like *Bartholomew Fair* (1614) where characters like Zeal-of-the-Land Busy, somewhat hypocritically, imposed their puritanical views on the wider populace.

Fanatical millenarian sects like the Ranters or the Fifth Monarchists violated social and political norms during the Commonwealth of England (1649–1660) to establish what they thought would be the chiliastic millennium leading to the rule of Jesus Christ in England. Ranters like Abiezer Cope claimed that to 'the pure all things are pure', including, of course, murder and rape. In the aftermath of the political chaos caused by religious sectaries, eighteenth century social commentators, wits and philosophers like David Hume, Jonathan Swift, Alexander Pope and Joseph Addison identified the limited character of the zealot. Writing in *The Spectator* in 1711, Addison noted that:

> Zeal is... a great ease to a malicious man, by making him believe he does God service while he is gratifying the bent of a perverse revengeful temper. For this reason we find that most massacres and devastations which have been in the world have taken their rise from a furious pretended zeal.

Hume, meanwhile, thought fanaticism and enthusiasm had produced 'the most cruel disorders in human society'. Hume, Pope and Addison would recognise in the activity of today's jihadi zealots' fanaticism, not an anachronistic radicalism.

Salafism and zealotry
Therefore, any analysis of jihadism's self-confirming zealotry suggests that those labelled 'radicalised' are not really radicals at all. Ideological radicalism, properly understood, requires a clean break from traditional religion, of whatever form, to achieve a pluralist, disenchanted, secular modernity.

By contrast, a scriptural literalism based on the message of the Prophet Mohammad ensures that Islamist thought looks to the past and that through purificatory violence today seeks to build tomorrow's religious utopia. Like the seventeenth century puritanical sectaries, they are fanatics who adapt the tenets of an ultra-traditional literalism to guide present action, being 'possessed by a god' or in 'receipt of divine communication'. No matter how deluded their actions appear to modern secular sensibilities, they consider themselves directly engaged in an apocalyptic and divinely ordained mission to re-create the caliphate.

Therefore, they are not radical in any meaningful sense of the word, because prior to the Enlightenment most of the world – and certainly most of Europe – subscribed to non-negotiable religious precepts with a fanaticism similar to that which motivates present day jihadism.

Both medieval Christendom and, in its aftermath, the early modern confessional state saw battle as an instrument of divine will, a providential means to deliver God's judgement. Even after the Enlightenment and with the decline of religious enthusiasm in Europe, the rise of political religions that replaced divine ordinance with ideologically determined nations, races or proletariats remained enamoured with purifying violence. These ideas reached their apocalyptic apogee in Nazi Germany and in World War II.

Radicalism and modernity
By contrast, the progressive emergence of cosmopolitan and representative liberal-democratic modes of rule in the nineteenth century constituted the 'radical' structural break with the past. Consequently, modern democratic pluralism in the West embraced secularism and, with it, as Max Weber observed, a condition of disenchantment. Soteriological order receded before a world increasingly governed by scientific reasoning. This secular-rationalist worldview achieved spectacular and revolutionary change, but also narrowed the horizon of the good life, rendering citizenship modular and promising fulfilment through consumption and the joys of shopping for physical and material rewards.

But modernity also had a downside. From the late nineteenth century, sociologists, psychologists and philosophers like Sigmund Freud, Émile Durkheim and Friedrich Nietzsche recognised in modernity not only democratic opportunities for self-discovery and the revision of life choices, but also the anomie, anxiety and alienation associated with a complex mass society. By the late twentieth century writers as various as Herbert Marcuse, Tom Wolfe and Christopher Lasch identified a modern culture of narcissism and anxiety where altruism disappears in an increasingly atomised, relativistic and techno-managerialist world.

Thus, secular modernity offers a radical form of life against which the jihadists rage, considering it a hideously schizophrenic condition, as the Muslim Brother ideologue, Sayyid Qutb argued in the 1950s. Indeed, from the fanatic's perspective, the *kufr* world order is inherently weak, and ready for the taking because it lacks the capacity to submit to a politically religious truth. Our refusal to recognise this point exposes the scale of the problem facing Western governments. It also creates the stage upon which the modern zealot can disport his oppression, proselytise and strategise.

The global Salafist jihad's appeal resides, then, in its ability to *re-enchant* the world with a Manichean worldview and a millenarian vision. Its style is not so dissimilar to the way the seventeenth-century religious sects promised a new heaven and a new earth, or the Nazis offered a racially pure future as a means of overcoming the failings of Depression-era Germany. Contemporary Salafist fanatics transform the fears and anxieties of disaffected sections of the diasporic Muslim youth in the West into a non-negotiable enthusiasm via the use of social media.

What is to be done?
To curb jihadi enthusiasm, Western societies need to recuperate their foundational understanding of what political activity entails and the basis of a tolerant and pluralist pursuit of the good life. This will not be straightforward as there are no quick fixes to the problems of urban disenchantment.

It is possible, however, to make a start by abandoning the language of radicalisation that perversely misreads the problem. De-radicalisation reflects and reinforces a progressive secular rationalism that dismisses religious worldviews rather than seeing them as coherent within their own politico-theological terms of reference. It persists in perceiving disaffected Muslims inclined to travel to Syria or diss the national anthem as 'clowns' and 'numbskulls', rather than zealots that in some cases are willing to die and behead for the realisation of the total vision.

The result is that public policy in the West ignores fanatic agency and responds instead in self-consciously depoliticised ways. In effect, this criminological, therapeutic, approach treats the converted zealot not as a danger to the wider society but as a victim pumped full of ideological steroids by unscrupulous online recruiters who, like predatory paedophiles, groom their otherwise innocent prey. The approach becomes even more suspect when extended to the case of the young women who happily trip off to Islamic State-controlled territories to offer themselves as jihadi brides. De-radicalisation paints these young women as the deluded subjects of brainwashing. The simple but harsh truth is that like the men they embrace, they too have found meaning in an enthusiasm, which the wider society finds rebarbative, but which inspires fanatical action.

Neither 'radicals' nor victims, they are largely immune to community sensitive de-radicalisation programmes promoted by Western governments because there is not much that is particularly radical in jihadist self-understanding. Arguably, it is we in the West who are deluded, and we should make a start by 'de-radicalising' our own thinking.

Original article published in *War on the Rocks*, 8th December 2015, by David Martin Jones and M.L.R. Smith.

Why deny? Terror stalks the academy

Henry Kissinger observed that academic politics are so vicious because the stakes are so small. The politics remain vicious, but as continuing revelations of the campus activity of Islamists in the UK and elsewhere suggest, the stakes are now considerably higher than the good Doctor opined.

As campuses gear up for a new term, it might be worth asking why is it that university administrators and the academic study of terrorism has, too often, denied the importance of religion – or more accurately religious ideology – in the recruitment to transnational networks like *al-Qaeda* and Islamic State and even welcomes former Guantanamo internees like Moazzam Begg to lecture students in 'safe spaces'?

As several ex-Islamist followers like Shiraz Maher and Ed Husain have pointed out, the second and third generation migrants brought up in secular, multicultural liberal democracies but not attached to them, face a dilemma. Unimpressed by Western secularism, they are also alienated from the kinship ties and traditions of their Asian roots that they find lacking in style and sophistication.

Consequently, they discover in a *sui generis* Islamism that promotes a transnational caliphate a solution to their alienation that resolves the tension between tradition and secularism. From this perspective a Koranic absolutism meets the requirements of an Islamic lifestyle and serves as an antidote to turmoil in the *jahiliya* (age of pre-Islamic ignorance) world attached to life, sensuality and spiritual ignorance. However, the ideological glue cementing the British jihadi movement draws as much from Antonio Gramsci as it does Mohammad and insists on a strategy of capturing educational institutions for consciousness raising purposes.

In its most recent evolution, it is not only Gramsci, but also Frankfurt School and post-colonial discourse theories that seek emancipation from the global capitalist order that the transnational Islamist mind finds highly congenial.

Rejecting religious explanation

Yet many academic theorists and commentators often reject this interpretation of campus extremism. Why? The answer is not hard to find. Ever since 9/11 liberal political elites, academe and state broadcasters have consistently denied any connection between political religion, in its Islamist form, and religiously inspired violence.

After the bombings of London's transport system in July 2005 or more recently the attacks in Paris a predictable chorus of experts appear in the media to claim that the latest outrage has nothing to do with religion. Well might they. For over a decade research grants and chairs in terror or peace and conflict studies have been dedicated not only to showing that modern terrorism has no Islamic association but even if it does that it is part of a wider anti-capitalist 'resistance' on the part of 'the Rest' against the West. Thus, although mainstream analysts since 9/11 recognise that Islamist plots discovered or carried out successfully, begin in Europe, they quickly move on to deny these actions have anything to do with Islam. David Kilcullen, known for his role in the promotion of the post-2006 Iraq 'Surge', confidently pronounces that 'Islamic theology has nothing to do with violence'.

Islamism as anti-capitalism

More disturbingly still, critical theory, a fashionable academic orthodoxy that has established a grip over many UK and Australian departments of political science and international studies since 9/11, contends not only has post-9/11 terror and insurgency no relation to religion, but it is also in fact an anti-capitalist response and constitutes part of a global 'resistance' movement.

The last decade has witnessed a proliferation of peer reviewed academic articles and books that reinforce this message. Tracing this critical posture reveals how deeply imbued contemporary academe has become with a distinctive species of anti-Western self-loathing.

From these works we learn for example that 'the rhetoric of freedom and the democratic way of life it upholds inflames the Muslim community'. The antidote is not to condemn this viewpoint, but to enter 'force free dialogue' with the forces of resistance.

Such fashionably relativist theorising shares an elective affinity with Muslim 'resistance'. From this perspective, the free market and the West perpetuate the real global violence, not terrorists, who merely resist the capitalist behemoth.

Reading Islamism as a form of revolutionary Marxism with a religious façade enables the empathic Western theorist to present the Islamist in more attractive academic garb as a fellow critic 'representing a distinctive combination of Islamic and enlightenment thought'.

Not surprisingly Islamism's most effective online journals like *Inspire* or *Dabiq* embrace this unmasking of the 'true' sources of terrorism. They also consider the war on terror 'a narrative' and a distorted Western 'construct' that Islamism 'deconstructs' and accepts that orientalism and colonialism are the real causes of their 'radical' reaction.

Rejecting realism
Such a discourse is made possible because in many Western campuses the study of international relations has, since the end of the Cold War, rejected the realist attempt to depict the world as it is in order to pursue an idealist and emancipatory agenda that promotes global justice and uncoerced communication. In this realism free zone, there are no material threats only negative discourses. Indeed, in this understanding the West discursively engendered the Islamist threat to curtail civil liberty and create the surveillance state. Yet as Moazzam Begg has interestingly pointed out 'blaming the government for our actions... did our propaganda work for us. More important, they also drew away any critical examination from the real engine of our violence, Islamist theology'. The relativist approaches that now dominate the academic study of terrorism reflect the political confusion that has overtaken the West since 9/11.

Academic delusions
The global jihadism that confronts Western society in the particularly virulent form of the Islamic State is, like all wars, informed by political will and ideology. Critical theory and campus administrators deny this, preferring to address second order phenomenon that demand empathy with a misunderstood 'other'. But this misreads the nature of the threat. Ultimately, to empathise with Islamism and provide it with a justification for its hyper-megalomaniacal violence is delusional. Such a delusion, ironically, depends on the liberal pluralist tolerance that both Islamic State and critical theory otherwise abhor. Because of this histrionic attempt at understanding the 'root' of Islamist inspired violence there has arisen a curious disjuncture between what Islamists say and have said for a while, and what the critical academic says they mean and what Islamists actually do.

Original article published in the *Daily Telegraph*, 12th January 2016, by David Martin Jones and M.L.R. Smith.

4. Globalist myths: Brexit and British power

'YOU ARE ALL LITTLE ENGLANDERS', so spluttered an irate academic colleague to my face on learning that I had voted Leave in the EU referendum in June 2016. This individual, who cast themselves as an 'international ethicist', was never to forgive me. Factually, their claim that everyone who voted leave was a 'little Englander' was itself ludicrous and easily falsifiable with basic data (a majority in Wales, 44 percent in Northern Ireland, 37 per cent in Scotland, as well as substantial numbers of people from ethnic and religious minority backgrounds – one of whom was my wife – also voted Leave).

And, in any case, so what? This was a democratically constituted election. People were given a choice. They made up their mind one way or the other. This is how democracy works; do I need to point out? Most of my immediate family, including my sister and mother, voted Remain for reasons that made sense to them. I didn't love or respect them any less for it. It never occurred to me to dismiss people on the other side of the argument with bovine insults. Really, what was the big deal? As it happened, I had worked for the European Parliament back in the 1980s and knew far more about the workings of the European Union than my splenetic colleague and had concluded as far back as 1988 that membership of the EU – or the European Community as it was known back then – was incompatible with British historical sensibilities and democratic traditions.

Crass and ignorant though such insults against leave voters were, David and I long ago ceased being angry about these kinds of attitudes. For years we had come across people in the academic world who possessed moral stances rather than an intellect. They were capable only of talking in platitudes and found it inordinately difficult framing cogent arguments or engaging in anything that resembled robust debate without parroting cliches or resorting to denunciations. We saw the humorous irony in how people such as this 'international ethicist' advanced through the academic firmament, speaking solely in banalities, yet being fawned over by gullible co-workers. A latter-day Svengali, he played everyone in the university like a fiddle.

Rather than anger, we treated these people as they should be, like scientific specimens to be examined, probed and investigated. They were, after all, microcosms of the current parlous state of British universities and of the moral and intellectual degeneracy of the calcified British establishment more generally. Their superficial mantras of Leave voters as bad and bigoted, and everything about the EU as good and virtuous, provided an insight into the ideological fixations of this stratum that made up so much of the ruling class. In our view, the people who comprised this species of being deserved dissevering and analysing.

The essays in this chapter therefore partly focus on dissecting the *classa politica* before and after Brexit. They deconstruct several myths and assumptions that underpinned the claims of the pro-EU side of the referendum and the wider belief system of which it was a part. Prior to the referendum we detected in the British elite's emotional attachment to the 'European project' impulses that were neither progressive nor democratic. Rather, these impulses were dangerously authoritarian, being symptomatic of a post-national cynicism that ultimately despised its own population.

David and I had an abiding interest in football, and the political and cultural symbolism that often underlay it. It was possible to observe the chattering classes' post-national reflexes in their reaction to the European football championships held in France in the weeks before the referendum. The commentariat automatically blamed English fans for the violence and disruption during the competition, when in fact there was little to no evidence. On the contrary, it was often state-licensed Russian hooliganism that instigated the violence, celebrating, as it saw it, getting the better of the English supporters. To us, this was a classic example of the elite's blinkered prejudice and innate strategic incompetence: blame your own nationals first while being outmanoeuvred by everyone else.

Elite reflexes were also in evidence in the communal hissy fit that characterised the literary community's response to Brexit, which David's essay on '*Brexlit*' entertainingly, but methodically, explores. The progressive left cannot help but project and the novels that his essay examines reveals the hysterical and often comically paranoid fever-dream of bile and intolerance that constitutes the worldview of the 'liberal' intelligentsia. *Brexlit* writers are exemplars of an accelerated Godwin's Law, namely, that as soon as a discussion of Brexit is initiated, the Third Reich analogies come raining down. The *Brexlit* novels, as David's article relays, provides a window into the soul of those who accuse others of being Little Englanders.

David sent me a poignant message the day after the result of the referendum: 'I went to bed Thursday night to grey skies and the prospect of endless euro tyranny and woke up to blue skies and the sweet zephyrs of liberty'. For those of us on the Leave side, the days afterwards were ones of optimism and excitement as we breathed a little freer. Our broad interest in geopolitics and economics meant that the potential opportunities that could be grasped by becoming a properly sovereign nation once again should be surveyed. Our ideas in this domain encompassed the possibilities for expanding trade and global influence and the challenge that a rising China would pose for post-Brexit Britain's security.

It did not take long for us to glimpse the British political establishment's instinctive reluctance to seize the chance to re-build Britain's stature on the world stage. The collective nervous breakdown of the political class in the wake of the Leave vote confirmed how far it had become wedded to the construction of the EU as a new Tower of Babel, which the final essay in this chapter clarifies. In the months and years after the vote, the promising noises initially emanating from Prime Minister Theresa May's post-referendum government gave way to an establishment determined to thwart the democratic result. The corrosive effect of these years was to whittle away trust in the institutions of the state and the confidence of the government, exposing the underlying timidity of May's administration, where Brexit came to be seen as an extended damage limitation exercise rather than an opportunity to renew Britain's politics and economy.

The problem, in the end, was the myopic Little Europeanism of the political classes who ran Britain, not the supposed Little Englanderism of the masses.

Brexit and the myth of European security

As the campaign for the United Kingdom to leave or stay the European Union gathers steam, Remain supporters, along with an expanding assembly of the global commentariat, have voiced increasingly alarmist claims about the economic and political consequences of Brexit both for Europe and the UK. Prime Minister David Cameron contends that Brexit is 'a threat not only to British economic and national security' but will potentially 'divide the West'.

In a similar vein, former Conservative MP and journalist Matthew Parris believes 'there is such a thing as the West', and Britain's exit 'would wreck it' and seriously 'wound' the 'clout that the continent of Europe carries'. And former Australian foreign minister Gareth Evans predicts that 'if Britain steps away from Europe... it will find itself very lonely indeed'.

The view from the Beltway
American commentators have also weighed in. Eight former US treasury secretaries thought Brexit could open a Pandora's Box of repressed nationalism. Strobe Talbott, former deputy secretary of state, cautioned Brexit could be 'contagious for the European project as a whole', whilst Harvard University's Joseph Nye claimed that the United States would need to 'double down on its own big bet on European unity as a vital national interest'.

Channelling this Beltway orthodoxy, President Barack Obama, in a visit reminiscent of a Roman Emperor attending to a recalcitrant province, warned the United Kingdom of its irrelevance to the US vision of Western security if the Brexiteers get their way. But what exactly has ever closer union added either to European or global security since the end of the Cold War?

The myths of European security
The logic of those who assume the European project is a force for security, democratic values and economic and political stability rests on a number of myths that have little relationship to contemporary political reality.

Myth 1 assumes the EU to be an effective basis for delivering collective and progressive democratic goods along regional rather than discredited national lines.

Myth 2 assumes ever-closer union and the integration of a 28-member bloc contributes to peace and security generally and, in particular, helps deter an expansionary Russia that gleefully awaits its imminent demise.

Myth 3 assumes Brexit will leave the EU intact while the UK is reduced to the margins of European as well as world politics.

Examining recent European history reveals a very different story.

The EEC as a peace process
To begin at the beginning, the Cold War formation of a six state European Economic Community (EEC) in 1957 did not bring peace to Europe.

The EEC was the conclusion of a peace process, not the cause of peace itself. Peace after a half century of total war on the dark continent was achieved through force. On the Western side of the continent this was largely the product of American arms, with some British help.

The US proceeded to function as the guarantor of security after 1945 and has continued to do so since the fall of the Berlin Wall in 1989.

Peace in Europe has nothing to do with Brussels, but everything to do with NATO, of which the UK remains a core contributor.

Illiberal utopianism
By the late 1980s, the Common Market had evolved into a community of thirteen West European democracies. Yet those who first contemplated a union of like-minded European states in the early 1950s never conceived of it as part of a uniform 'West'.

Winston Churchill, mistakenly cited by American advocates as a proponent of the current European project, wanted no such thing. Churchill hoped the American special relationship with the UK would facilitate a united states of open democracies not the incremental evolution of a European superstate.

A European superstate, by contrast, was precisely the illiberal utopian vision of those like Jean Monnet and the Russian-born, French philosopher-turned-eurocrat, Alexander Kojève. They envisaged a monolithic union administered from Brussels but running along a Franco-German axis. This would constitute the basis of a third force in global politics situated between the Soviet and American blocs and not an appendage of an American-led West. The fall of the Berlin Wall offered Monnet's successors, European Commission presidents like Jacques Delors and Jorge Manuel Barroso, the opportunity to realise the illiberal vision.

It required the rapid widening of Europe into the former Soviet bloc at the same time deepening the community into the lineaments of a European superstate run along increasingly centralised lines by an unelected commission of commissars, some of them, like Mr Barroso, former Maoist revolutionaries.

Europe *sans frontiers* = no security
A heady mixture of supranationalism, subsidiarity and Olympian elitism, thus fuelled the post-Cold War dream of ever closer union and ignored the historical, religious and constitutional differences that divided even the more developed Western European states.

Rather than contributing to stability or facilitating democratic accountability, the Schengen Agreement (1985) and the Maastricht Treaty (1991), which created a *Europe sans frontiers* founded on the pillars of a common foreign and defence policy and currency union and the abolition of inter-state border controls, have heightened insecurity and economic instability. The EU has, in this regard, struggled to incorporate the economically fragile states of Eastern Europe, who enjoy less than democratic heritages, into the rapidly expanded bloc.

Indeed, widening Europe has only contributed to further division and disagreement given that the new members have been net financial receivers rather than contributors to the project.

What you get when idealism replaces prudence
Euro-idealism replaces prudence with predictably catastrophic consequences. Subsidiarity notably increased the power of Brussels and the European Commission along with other supranational bodies like the European Court of Human Rights.

A burgeoning but increasingly sclerotic bureaucracy implementing deeper union has paradoxically undermined regional stability. Europe without frontiers comes at a massive and unsustainable security cost exploited most graphically by people smuggling gangs and those like Islamic State of Iraq and the Levant.

These are the factors leading to fragmentation of which the British referendum is a symptom, not a cause. The common defence and foreign policy pillars of the EU have thus proved less than solid. The European Union was founded in 1993, and from the Bosnia crisis at its inception, to its most recent attempts to sanction Vladimir Putin, the Russian president, and address the Syrian refugee crisis, through to the buying-off of Turkish autocracy, EU policy has looked a bizarre mixture of incoherence and appeasement.

A big Germany does what big Germany wants
An unintended consequence of the failure to achieve a coherent defence and foreign policy, an integrated market, or an effective currency union means that under the illusion of a shared European destiny, a big Germany, formed after the fall of the Berlin Wall, now dominates the EU, pulling its centre of gravity inexorably eastward.

The direction of EU policy inevitably follows Germany's supervening interests. The failure to consult long standing members of the EU over the refugee crisis, or funding Turkey to contain the problem, sees smaller European countries, like Greece and Italy, looking towards Moscow rather than Berlin.

Taken together, it can come as little surprise that some states in Eastern Europe like Hungary, and mainstream political voices in its Western member states, are beginning to exhibit profound disillusion with the EU, with even a figure like George Soros declaring the European project to be on the 'verge of collapse'.

World orders come and go
There is, to adapt Adam Smith's phrase, much ruin in a union. Ironically, the Obama presidency and the Washington Beltway more generally has bought into the idea that the European Union is a force for democratic progress rather than a bureaucracy, which as its current president recently admitted, interferes 'too much in the lives of its citizens'.

The problem is that regional unions, associations, currency and trading blocs come and go, not only in Europe but also in Asia and everywhere else. What remains permanent in Europe and the world are nation states that ultimately have no permanent friends and no permanent enemies, only permanent interests.

In the UK, a minimal permanent interest, as those countries like Australia or the US, and indeed as other European states are beginning to notice, requires border security and a sovereign authority vested in a national parliament not in an unelected transnational judiciary in the Hague or a commission in Brussels.

'Good fences', as the great American poet Robert Frost observed, 'make good neighbours'. In this he was echoing the words of Benjamin Franklin, 'Love thy neighbour, yet don't pull down your hedge'.

Given that this understanding is the spirit of 1776, it seems bizarre that American Democrats prefer mythology to a prudent appreciation of modern history.

Original article published in the *Daily Telegraph*, 27th April 2016, by David Martin Jones and M.L.R. Smith.

Orchestrating hooliganism: Russia, Britain, and the EU

In the aftermath of the violence in the old port of Marseilles last weekend, much of the British media – together with the Football Association – lamented the latest outbreak of the English disease. Geoff Pearson observed in the *Times* that 'England fans have form in Marseilles'. Zoe Williams in the *Guardian* thought English officialdom had 'infantilised' football crowds, thus creating conditions for 'a comical menu of grievance' concerning 'the other'.

Less originally, the FA considered that 'while the vast majority of England fans behaved impeccably', a small but 'aggressive hard core' engaged in violence and 'score settling'.

Threatened with expulsion from the competition, the England Manager, Roy Hodgson, publicly appealed to supporters to 'stay out of trouble', while Wayne Rooney called for fans to 'be safe [and] be sensible'.

State-endorsed hooliganism

All this English self-flagellation seems not a little bizarre given that at the end of the game in Marseilles on 11th June, organised groups of Russian 'ultras', launched a premeditated attack on inadequately protected English supporters. The British government condemned the violence and called for 'calm on all sides'.

The measured response of the government and Football Association, along with balanced British media reporting, contrasted dramatically with that of the Russian government's football federation and the state-licensed Russian media. Reports on Russian state TV about the violence bordered on the triumphant, claiming: 'English fans started the fight... but 250 Russians from different corners of our motherland... repulsed the attack by the heavily drunken islanders'. The spokesman for Russia's top investigative agency, Vladimir Markin, mocked French efforts to contain violence in the stadium, claiming that they could not handle 'real men' because they were used to policing gay pride marches.

Igor Lebedev, deputy chairman of the Russian football federation and deputy chairman of the Duma (Russian Parliament) saw 'nothing wrong with fans fighting' and called for 'the lads' to 'keep it up'. He also noted that were Russian Sports Minister Vitaly Mutko not inconveniently situated in the stands he 'would have got into the fight' himself.

Meanwhile, blogs on Russian fan sites like Okolofutbol and Fanstyle.ru have posted videos showing the Russian supporters acting in a coordinated manner, organised in squads and going equipped to attack English fans in the old port.

The Moscow correspondent of *Le Monde* translated the blog of one fan, Alex Molodoi. It described how a dozen Moscow Dynamo fans singing *Katioucha* descended upon the English, whose 'nerves cracked and they fled'. Molodoi's blog remarked on the importance his 'Dynamo mates' attached to 'evaluating the opposition forces and coordinating their actions'.

Russian football ultra-violence

This degree of tactical awareness is not entirely surprising. The French authorities noted the speed and ruthlessness of the small groups of ultras who came equipped with martial arts gloves, gumshields and kagoules to commit 'ultra' violence. They also noticed that the 'Hard core hooligans from Russia were hard to identify, ultra rapid and ultra violent'. No Russians were detained after Marseilles.

This level of organisation reflects the fact that those who conducted the violence belonged to the Moscow clubs, Dynamo, Spartak and Lokomtif with close links to the state police, the FSB and the military. As the *Daily Mail* commented, not only are the Russian ultras 'the most vicious species of hooligan around, but also the best organised, partly because many have daytime jobs that involve wearing uniforms'.

Yuri, another Russian ultra, posted on Facebook in February, 'We are hard men, many from the army and police... not soft Englishmen in their Lacoste clothes and girl's shoes'.

In other words, far from yet another outbreak of the decadent English disease, Russian ultra-violence is not only broadly approved by the Russian state but also possesses a degree of state license.

Discerning the purpose: the politics of Putinism
So, what is going on? Why is it that the British authorities deplore soccer related violence, even to the extent of guiltily assuming the culpability of English fans, while the Russian state is semi-complicit? As any strategic analyst will tell you, there is no such thing as random or meaningless violence. Any violent act – from a punch on the nose to all-out war – always contains a purpose. The task is to figure out what that purpose is all about.

President Vladimir Putin, not himself averse to machismo, has often empathised with the Moscow clubs' ultra-behaviour, deliberately cultivating virility as a feature of an assertive nationalist identity designed to save Russia from dissolution and democracy. Indeed, Putinism finds its justification in the political thought of the white Russian exile, Ivan Ilyin (1883-1954) who foresaw the Soviet collapse and argued that a post-Soviet state must adopt an inclusionary corporatist ideology informed by a leadership principle to unite the motherland. 'Soft power' Putin style thus projects a populist neo-fascist message to unite those Europeans alienated from liberal-Western multiculturalism, diversity and democratisation.

Football fascism
This association of football violence with masculinity and national identity, moreover, is by no means something uniquely Russian. Football and fascism have long cohabited. The beautiful game has a dark underbelly, falling prey to right-wing extremism and violence that extends far back before the heyday of English hooliganism in the 1970s and 1980s.

International football and fascism emerged symbiotically in the 1930s. Hitler, Mussolini and Franco considered all mass sport as a form of ideological indoctrination. Mussolini, especially, saw football as a vehicle for popular unity and an instrument of government.

The fascist regime directly controlled Italian football, built the stadiums, and introduced Serie A. Vittorio Pozzo, the dictatorial national team manager (no surprise there) coached Italy to the 1934 and 1938 World Cups, known locally as the 'Coppa del Duce'.

Football enhanced the Italian regime's international prestige, shaped opinion, infiltrated daily life and reinforced ideological conformity. After the Second World War, ultra-fanatical fans with extreme right associations and a penchant for flares and fireworks were particularly associated with Serie A teams Roma and Lazio.

Hooliganism, Balkan style
From the late 1980s, ultra-violence and ultra-nationalism found a congenial home at clubs in Eastern Europe as the Soviet bloc imploded. In Yugoslavia violent confrontations between Dynamo Zagreb and Red Star Belgrade supporters in 1990 announced the Serbo-Croat war and the dissolution of Yugoslavia.

Zeljko Raznotovic (aka Arkan) subsequently formed his 'Tigers' from the Red Star Belgrade supporters club, a notoriously brutal Serbian paramilitary grouping, and engaged in ethnically cleansing Bosnians from lands claimed by Greater Serbia after 1992. Meanwhile, Zagreb's Bad Blue Boys form the backbone of Croatia's ultras who chant Ustasha slogans and in a qualifier for the European championships against Italy earlier this year daubed a Swastika on the pitch.

On Friday, Croatian ultras launched flares and fireworks, interrupting the game between Croatia and the Czech Republic. The intent, it seems, was to get the national team evicted from the championship in order to embarrass the allegedly corrupt national football association.

The international politics of soccer violence
In this context of ultra-violence linked to nationalist and neo-Nazi political agendas, the overweight and over-the-limit English hooligan looks a forlorn figure. Why, one might wonder, did the Russian ultras treat them to a version of Kremlin-inspired hybrid warfare?

Two reasons stand out. First, in Russian ultra-think, the English hooligan has an undeserved reputation for aggro that collapses when confronted by the disciplined cadres of Dynamo Moscow.

Second, and more strategically, Kremlin-orchestrated hooliganism isolates England and could lead to the national team's expulsion from the championship, adding symbolic fuel to the Brexit campaign.

The day after further outbreaks of fan violence in Lille on Wednesday, Putin hosted a Davos style economic forum in St Petersburg. Guests included European Commission President Jean-Claude Juncker, Italian President Matteo Renzi and former French President Nikolas Sarkozy; European statesmen Putin considers well-disposed to ending European sanctions imposed on Russia after it violated the sovereignty of Ukraine following the take-over of Crimea in 2014. The sanctions are due for renewal on 24th June.

Whilst Renzi, Juncker and others look favourably on a relaxation of sanctions, Putin knows that the British Government is strongly opposed. Thus, Putin's strategic hooliganism suits his vision for fragmenting the European Union and ending Russian isolation. Football and fascism have an interesting historical lineage that Putin has drawn upon for political effect.

Unfortunately, the British press still think the game is beautiful and beyond crude national calculation. And in all this international strategic gamesmanship we should, for once, perhaps have some sympathy for the poor, put upon, stereotyped, English fan.

Original article published in the *Daily Telegraph*, 21st June 2016, by David Martin Jones and M.L.R. Smith.

A trade strategy for United Kingdom Inc

In *Memoirs of Extraordinary Popular Delusions and the Madness of Crowds*, Charles Mackay wrote:

> [I]n reading the history of nations, we find that, like individuals, they have their whims and their peculiarities; their seasons of excitement and recklessness, when they care not what they do. We find that whole communities suddenly fix their minds upon one object and go mad in its pursuit; that millions of people become simultaneously impressed with one delusion, and run after it, till their attention is caught by some new folly more captivating than the first.

He continued: 'At an early age in the annals of Europe its population lost their wits about the sepulchre of Jesus and crowded in frenzied multitudes to the Holy Land'.

We might update Mackay's memoir by noting that at a later age in the annals of Europe, its population lost their wits, fiscal credibility and economic sense over the delusion of an ever-closer European Union.

Recovering from transnationalism

The regulatory behemoth of the European Union (EU), with its five presidents, high representatives, 28 commissioners, serried ranks of bureaucrats and courts of counsellors, legal representatives and other functionaries has inhibited growth and consigned a generation of youth in Southern Europe to unemployment (56 percent in Spain, 62.5 percent in Greece). It has committed poorer member states to debt, austerity and destitution in its futile pursuit of a currency union leading to a federated European imperium.

Curiously, this fiscally challenged *ancien régime*, whose banking sector post-Brexit appears on the brink of collapse, continues to attract plaudits from commentators who arguably should know better. Mackay's study of the madness of crowds discerned that a reckless mixture of greed, panic, fear and delusion drives the pursuit of implausible financial schemes (and, indeed, financial markets generally). Such delusion has an interesting universal transcendence and is capable of gripping the popular mind across time and space, whether it be Dutch Tulipomania in the seventeenth century, the illusion of never-ending growth before the 2008 banking crash, numerous hailed – but now failed – economic 'miracles' (Mexico, BRICS, Celtic Tigers, the Pacific Century, etc.), or the faltering euro project.

Were he alive today, Mackay might find in the response of those in the United Kingdom and elsewhere currently clamouring for a re-run of the European referendum or for the democratic vote to somehow be ignored, confirmation of his dictum that, 'Many persons grow insensibly attached to that which gives them a great deal of trouble'.

The immediate fevered aftermath of the Brexit vote witnessed runs on banks and property stocks and the vertiginous drop in the value of the pound. Yet it becomes important that in predicting the apocalypse and the end of Western civilisation as we know it, we don't talk ourselves into a recession we don't have to have. 'Men [and women]... go mad in herds,' Mackay concluded, 'while they only recover their senses slowly, and one by one'.

Economic pragmatism is the place to start

Politics is often about perception and momentum. Instead of debating when to trigger Article 50 of the European Union that sets a two-year timetable for withdrawal, the British government should be examining how it realistically responds to Brexit and the opportunity it creates for a newly independent, flexible, and sovereign market state. In this context, the former Chancellor, George

Osborne's proposal to cut the corporate tax rate offers the United Kingdom the basis of a pragmatic new start.

Freed from the endless commitocracy of the European Union, however, the United Kingdom should be looking more closely at the practices of successful market states. Often founded in the era of Empire that once put the Great in Great Britain, these entities comprise Special Administrative Regions like Hong Kong and sovereign Commonwealth states like Canada, Singapore, Malaysia, India, Australia and New Zealand. All these states have followed constitutional and economic practices bequeathed by the former colonial power often with unparalleled economic and political success.

Learning from others

Unlike Britain, these states did not abandon sovereignty and a version of the Westminster parliamentary system for a utopian delusion. Instead, they focused on adapting institutions and practices to the challenges and opportunities offered by later twentieth century globalisation.

By last year, Asian city-states like Singapore had a per capita GDP (US$51,855), well above that of Britain and most West European states with the exception of Norway, Luxembourg and Switzerland.

Singapore, like Hong Kong, is a regional trading hub, which facilitates foreign direct investment through a business-friendly climate and excellent infrastructure. While Britain has endlessly deliberated over a third runway at Heathrow, Singapore has built a third runway and fifth terminal at Changi Airport and two Mass Rapid Transport train lines connecting the island's five million people.

Notably, despite the recent downturn in China since 2015, East Asia has maintained growth rates across the region in excess of 5 percent over the last decade. Openness to global production networks and free trade agreements have been central to this growth. The pattern of development and the opportunities it offers are worth exploring and, where possible, adopting.

The benefits of FTAs

The most significant factor in twenty first century Asian growth has been the evolution of free trade agreements (FTA) among states across East Asia and with the United States. The pattern of agreements, which evolved in the aftermath of the 1997 Asian financial crisis, increasingly links the economies of Pacific-Asia with the United States and India.

Significantly, FTAs entail no loss of sovereignty, and they do not require the adoption of a single currency or regulatory regime. They do, though, facilitate mutually beneficial investment and enhance agricultural, services and manufacturing interests and practices.

Since 2003, the more dynamic and export-oriented economies of the Asia-Pacific have negotiated a range of bilateral and trilateral agreements covering goods, services, manufacturing, agriculture and economic collaboration. South Korea, for example, has 24 FTAs with, among others, Chile, Singapore, Peru, the United States and India. Singapore has 32 FTAs, Japan has 24, China has 23, while Thailand and Malaysia both have 22 each.

Australia, which has 19 FTAs, concluded three in the course of 2014 alone with China, South Korea and Malaysia. It had earlier reached deals with Singapore and the United States. The Canberra based Centre for International Economics notes:

> Free trade agreements that include Australia led to an increase in Australian exports, production, and GDP relative to what would have been the case without the FTA.

Meanwhile, a 2014 study by the Australian government's Rural Industries Research and Development Corporation concluded:

> Agreements excluding Australia result in small declines in Australian exports (relative to the baseline) as products from the FTA partners become more competitive relative to Australian products.

The Australia–US FTA alone has accounted for a substantial increase in the volume of trade and investment since the agreement entered into force in 2005. Interestingly, it is in this context of rapid growth in trade and regional development that the US pivot to Asia after 2011 must be situated. Defense Secretary Ashton Carter, as recently as May 2016, described the Asia-Pacific – not Europe – 'as the single region of the world of most consequence for America'.

As evidence of this, the United States sees the promotion of a free trading Trans-Pacific Partnership as far more important than the glacially slow progress it has made on the Trans-Atlantic Trade and Investment Partnership with the European Union.

Canzukus?
During the EU referendum campaign, in April 2016, President Barak Obama warned the United Kingdom that if it voted to leave it would have to go to the 'back of the queue' on any free trade negotiations with the United States. However, despite Obama's ill-judged remarks (which saw the leave vote rise in opinion polls after his intervention), the likelihood that a newly elected administration would recognise the complementary nature of these two market-oriented states and move to affect an FTA is high. Such a move would have both political and geopolitical implications. It could ultimately facilitate a more elaborate version of what James C. Bennett termed Canzuk, Canzukus perhaps, which adds military co-operation, liberalised migration rules, and other co-operative measures to free trade with Canada, Australia, New Zealand, the United States and, in time, Singapore and India. This would afford the basis, in conjunction with Commonwealth countries, not only for evolving economic linkages but geopolitical ones as well, in terms of a shared language and a shared political culture based on sovereign institutions and the rule of law.

Look East?
Somewhat differently, China considers the Association of Southeast Asian Nations (ASEAN) led Regional Comprehensive Economic Partnership (RCEP) a core part of its bold 'Belt and Road' development initiative. This seeks to improve connectivity by building land transportation corridors that link China to Europe, and South Asia as well as with Southeast Asia, whilst its Maritime Silk Road promotes port development to enhance trade with Southeast Asia.

Reflecting and informing this partnership is China's Asian Infrastructure Investment Bank (AIIB). The partnership involves 50, primarily Asian, members but includes the United Kingdom. With assets of more than US$1 billion to invest in regional infrastructure, the AIIB could prove a significant boon to the integration of Southeast Asia as a single market facilitating a free flow of goods. The initiative could, thereby, see the United Kingdom participating in China's regional growth strategy. The developing Asian model offers Britain an environment to embrace the global market and develop an industrial strategy rather than subject itself to the regulatory intense environment of Europe with its protected manufacturing and agriculture. The fact that English is the language of international trade and business, and that Britain can draw upon its historic Anglospheric connections with India, Hong Kong, Singapore and Australia means that it already enjoys a comparative advantage in dealing with Asia.

Like the United States, Asian states find doing trade deals with the European Union an enervating experience and are looking for alternatives.

Pointedly, within days of Brexit, South Korea's top diplomat, Yun-Byung-se, announced he wanted a bilateral trade deal with London Similarly, on 1st July, the *China Daily* reported that China was frustrated by its attempts to make trade deals with the European Union. A spokesman for the Chinese Ministry of Commerce noted that, post-Brexit, China had a strategy to develop its business links with the United Kingdom and, like South Korea, would seek trade talks.

Clearly, an entrepreneurially orientated United Kingdom, liberated from the constraints of negotiating through the European Union's single regulatory mechanism, has an opportunity to seize the growth prospects that trade agreements with the Asia-Pacific offer.

A return to liberal reform?
In the aftermath of the European referendum, politics in the United Kingdom has undergone an administrative revolution. In July 2016, Prime Minister Theresa May, fresh to the job, appointed not only a new Chancellor but a special minister for Brexit, David Davis. In addition, for the first time in two generations, May is explicitly seeking to develop an industrial strategy for the United Kingdom Inc.

The immediate shift in tone and doctrine of the new administration reflects not only May's thinking but that of her advisory team who wish to resurrect a particular understanding of trade and industry policy. It is associated with the influential Birmingham based industrialist-turned politician and social reformer, Joseph Chamberlain, and the late nineteenth century liberal-unionist movement for tariff reform for which he campaigned.

Channelling an understanding of Chamberlain, the new government envisages not only negotiating a new relationship with the European Union. It has also signalled its intention to move from a free-market philosophy that restrains government to one of government activism, economically as well as socially. This perspective assumes there is insufficient dynamism in the British economy, marked as it has been by consistently low productivity and weakening growth. The new government wants to see lower prices and a more reliable supply of energy. It wants to keep a watch on foreign takeovers if they threaten job losses, and to create new treasury mechanisms to raise more funds for infrastructure investment. A further ambition of the late nineteenth century Birmingham school of social and municipal reform was the transformation of the agglomeration of disparate British colonies into a coherent military and trading imperial federation – what Chamberlain came to call 'Greater Britain'.

A 'Greater Britain' is not necessarily what May had in mind when she stated: 'Brexit means Brexit'. However, there have emerged over the last weeks various 'alternatives to Europe'. Few considered such alternatives while Britain was trapped in the European Union, which set the economic and fiscal rules both for its single regulatory mechanism governing trade and labour movement within the Union, and free trade negotiations with external partners outside it.

Conclusion
The post-referendum British government, therefore, must carefully evaluate these options if it is to fashion Brexit as a positive movement towards global change rather than an extended damage limitation exercise. With this aim, the government led by May has an opportunity to improve on Chamberlain's vision. Although the municipal reforms he pioneered in his home city of Birmingham remain widely regarded as a model of intelligently thought through social design, his broader ideas of imperial preference and liberal trade were killed by the stroke that disabled him in 1903. Revitalising his vision might also provide the new government with just the 'Big Idea' it needs.

Original article published in *War on the Rocks*, 21st July 2016, by David Martin Jones and M.L.R. Smith.

Brexlit and the decline of the English novel

After the June 2016 referendum, novels about what had happened began to appear on best-seller lists and the shelves of British bookshops. Brexlit addressed 'the mind-bending horror of Brexit'. It explored not only the polarising political cleavage between Remain and Leave voters, but 'deep cultural and attitudinal divisions' that will, the *Guardian* argued, 'animate British politics for decades to come'.

The horror of the long-drawn-out crisis comes with a political health warning. Fintan O'Toole thinks the Brexit vote was informed by 'a strange sense of imaginary oppression'. Voting leave on a ballot paper, he says, was the white racist equivalent 'of scratching the name of England on their arms to prove their love'. James Graham, discussing his Brexit docudrama, *The Uncivil War*, thought that David Cameron called the 2016 referendum believing he inhabited one reality only to find the electorate lived in a different one, 'dominated by anger, populism and anti-establishment sentiment that had been bubbling away under the surface. It just erupted and the volcano has not stopped spewing'. Given the British preference for social analysis in novel form, how might *Brexlit* help us negotiate what Graham considers the current 'national trauma'?

English fiction, from Charles Dickens to George Orwell, has frequently provided a more compelling insight into the 'condition of England' question than the polysyllabic howl of sociologists. In a recent edited volume, *Brexit and Literature: Critical and Cultural Responses* (2018), Robert Eaglestone, Professor of Contemporary Literature at the University of London, observes that literature broadens our ability 'to think, feel and argue'. Consequently, fiction might afford 'an especially useful and appropriate way to address political arguments about national identity which lie at the heart of Brexit'.

So far so good. When, however, the professor says that Brexit 'is no friend to creative cosmopolitan literature or to attentive and responsive literary scholarship' things take a distinctly Orwellian turn. It has 'stirred up a terrifying political discourse' where 'opponents of Brexit are described as saboteurs or enemies of the people', Eaglestone tells us. His fellow professors of contemporary literature and European thought at the universities, *inter alia*, of East Anglia, Kent, Dublin, Warwick and the LSE agree. Thomas Docherty considers Brexit 'an assault upon the intellect'. Michael Gardiner asserts that Brexiteers use 'anachronism as a weapon' to disrupt our 'neo-liberal present'. More specifically, Lyndsey Stonebridge, considers Brexit stupid: 'Men too stupid to think about the consequences of their action tricked the British into making a fatally stupid decision'. In Stonebridge's judicious assessment, Boris Johnson and Nigel Farage 'took evident pleasure in performing their twitfuckery' upon the unsuspecting British people.

Summing up the views of the professoriate, Baroness Young of Hornsey finds Brexit an 'existential mire' that the 'creative mind' must work through via 'the insightful and valiant efforts' of novelists like Ali Smith, Andrew Cartwright, Jonathan Coe, Rachel Cusk, Olivia Laing, Sam Byers and Douglas Board, all of whom discuss the consequences of Brexit in a variety of genres, ranging from auto fiction to social novels and political satire.

Ali Smith's *Autumn* (2016) was 'the first significant post Brexit novel'. Long listed for the Booker Prize, it opens in sub-Dickensian mode: 'It was the worst of times. It was the worst of times'. Through the not very compelling relationship between Elisabeth, a young lecturer in Art History and her dementia-ridden ageing mentor, Daniel, Smith reflects upon the recent past and the disturbing present condition of England. A week after the 2016 referendum, Elisabeth finds her mother's village in 'a sullen state' – 'Go Home' in black capitals adorns the local bus shelter. Her mother is tired of 'the vitriol, the anger, the meanness', as well as the 'violence', which somewhat inconveniently, 'hasn't happened yet'.

Since Brexit, the UK has disintegrated:

All across the country people felt it was the wrong thing. All across the country, people felt it was the right thing... All across the country people looked up Google: what is EU? All across the country people looked up Google: move to Scotland. All across the country people looked up Google: Irish passport applications. All across the country people felt unsafe... All across the country people drew swastika graffiti... All across the country racist bile was general... All across the country, everything changed overnight.

A few months later, 'a bunch of thugs' in the street outside Elisabeth's London flat chant:

Britannia rules the waves. First, we'll get the Poles. And then we'll get the Muslims. Then we'll get the gyppos, then the gays. You lot are on the run and we're coming after you, a right-wing spokesman had shouted at a female MP on a panel on Radio 4 earlier that same Saturday. The chair of the panel didn't... even acknowledge the threat.

Such an unlikely response from the national broadcaster suggests the author herself might inhabit a parallel reality. It is one all the Brexit novelists share. Anger at the 'Leave' vote and the threat it presents to their borderless worldview pervades *Brexlit*. Indignation comes naturally to the self-indulgent contemporary genre of auto fiction practiced by Olivia Laing and Rachel Cusk. Thus, *Times* best-selling author and *Guardian* columnist Olivia Laing's *Crudo* introduces the reader to her alter ego, Kathy, engaging in an apocalyptic rant about the state of the post-Brexit world. Laing's Kathy is a fictionalised, Anglicised version of the 1980s New York punk author Kathy Acker, who lived fast and died youngish. Acker wrote largely forgotten paeans to *Blood and Guts in High School* (1984), masturbation, body piercing and sado-masochism. Even the *New York Times* considered that she 'raised literary masturbation to an anti-art form'. Laing's expurgated version of a re-born Kathy offers her millennial readership sanitised, snowflake-sensitive, literary masturbation.

Laing's Kathy is 'avant-garde, middle-class-in-flight', but she 'did not like the bourgeoisie'. Now a forty-something successful but impeccably progressive writer, she commutes between London, Rome and New York, attending literary conferences.

Although living the literary high life, Kathy hates 'living at the end of the world'. Anticipating the coming apocalypse: 'she was fairly certain that by the time she was an old lady they'd be eating out of rubbish dumps, sheltering from a broiling impossible sun. It was all done, it was over, there wasn't any hope'. Like liberals everywhere, 'she missed Obama. Everyone missed Obama. She missed the sense of time as something serious and diminishing. She didn't like living in the permanent present of the id', even though Kathy serves up nothing but the angry id of liberal narcissism.

Analysing the referendum, she finds that: 'People were told Brexit would be good, so they voted for Brexit and now all the EU citizens would be sent home, according to a leaked document'. She assumes that 'Jacob Rees-Mogg would be the next Prime Minister, he went on *Good Morning Britain* and explained pleasantly that he thought abortion should be illegal even for rape and that he would like to ban gay marriage'. Consequently, Kathy:

hated everything... it was all so tawdry, the endless malice of the polite right... At the weekend she was going to a party with people who had openly praised Enoch Powell, at the weekend she was going to a party with people who had said of refugees crossing to Greece, it's ridiculous, they should just bomb the boats.

In alt-paranoid style, Kathy contemplates a bleak future:

> run by strongmen, she saw the poorer nations of the world obliterated by climate change, she saw the liberal democracy in which she had grown up revealed as fragile beyond measure, a brief experiment in the bloody history of man... she knew she shouldn't read the paper, but she snuck looks from the minute she woke up... How's the car-crash of Brexit proceeding, how are they getting along with changing all the country's laws in secret, how much do we hate foreigners today, who's winning? Kathy... was riven by despair.

Whilst Olivia Laing's Kathy surfs a wave of liberal dread, Rachel Cusk's *Kudos* explores her fictional alter ego, Faye, a successful feminist writer's encounters with fellow writers at an expenses-paid conference in an unnamed European country. Cusk thinks that 'character' doesn't 'exist anymore'. Instead, Faye passively records random conversations. One is with a 'Welsh writer', who observes patronisingly that: 'the people who lived in the most helpless poverty and ugliness were those who had voted most overwhelmingly for Brexit, and nowhere was that truer than his own small country'. It was, he states, 'an act of collective self-harm', 'a case of turkeys voting for Christmas'.

The Welsh proles are stupid. The writer knows of:

> housing estates down south in the post-industrial wastelands, where the men still rode ponies and shot at one another with guns and the women brewed up cauldrons of magic mushrooms in their kitchens: he didn't imagine they spent much of their time discussing their membership of the EU even if they knew what it was.

Visiting his parents after the referendum, the writer stops for coffee at a motorway service station, and 'a great pockmarked tattooed creature' sits near him 'tucking into a huge plate of fried food and announcing to the whole room that at least he could be an Englishman eating a full English breakfast in his own country'. It makes you think, the writer concludes, that 'democracy wasn't such a good idea after all'.

The Brexit novelists want to elect a new people. The current white male population – racist, homophobic, dumb and illiberal – is not fit for purpose. White middle-class liberals Sam Byers, Jonathan Coe and Douglas Board, who satirise Brexit's dystopic aftermath, exemplify this tendency. In Douglas Board's *Time of Lies* the leave vote presages the rise of an English fascist movement. It is set in the near future when the financial crisis that follows Brexit sees the 'wreckage' of Corbyn's leadership split Labour in two. The Conservative government clings to power, while the Supreme Court rules that the way it negotiated Brexit was so stupid, it 'was null and void'.

Facing new elections, a populist party, 'Britain's Great', with its paramilitary youth wing, 'The Vigilance', overtakes both the Conservatives and Labour in the polls. Bob Grant, a more attractive, but unstable, version of Donald Trump, leads Britain's Great (BG). He's 'a piece of off-white trash. Someone who left school with a knife more times than with homework'. The right-wing media, of course, love him, and sluttish journalists like *Shock News* reporter Annabel Deil promote his Britain-first nationalism. A self-made millionaire, Grant expresses himself in a limited, but comminatory, South London patois: 'Britain's Great', he intones, 'cos we are. You want to know why? Need to be told. Then Fuck off'. 'Britain's Great. End of'. BG's preferred rallying ground is the Den, home to Millwall, an unfashionable championship league football club known only for its London dockland fans' past links to the National Front. BG adopts the club supporter's chant: 'No one likes us. We don't care'. The heady cocktail of British identity politics combined with an assault on financial capital proves irresistible. Elected to government in the May 2020 general election, BG requires all bankers and former bankers to wear a large letter 'B' on their clothes in a laboured Third Reich analogy. Zack, Grant's liberal brother, finds it 'scary how hope has been sucked out of our national life. It's never been more important to read about how the world should be rather than how it is', he opines. He finds solace in the *Guardian*'s 'refreshing' wit and reason. English politics has descended to the 'kindergarten'. BG's controversial manifesto commitment to 'strong borders, controlled migration and safe streets', had unleashed a 'mindless politics which had weakened every democracy in the world' whilst unravelling the 'rule of law tweet by tweet'. Within weeks, the new populist government is at odds with the European Commission and threatening to explode a nuclear bomb over its Brussels headquarters. A Civil Service-engineered coup, however, ends BG's brief populist experiment.

A similar populist contempt informs Sam Byers's *Perfidious Albion* (2018). Edmundsbury, a small town on the outskirts of London that serves as a microcosm for post-Brexit Britain, hosts the anonymous multinational Green, a company that follows 'the disruptive logic of the Silicon Valley'. Moving fast and breaking things, Green harvests personal information and runs social experiments to build an algorithmically-ordered digital dystopia. The plot involves Downton, a private housing trust, with close links to Green, 'decanting' residents from a decaying 1960s public housing estate it now runs, in order to transform it into an upmarket, high-tech, gated community. One of the estate's old white residents, Alfred Darkin, stubbornly refuses to move. Darkin, who lives in state-pensioned squalor on a diet of cigarettes, fast food and lager, becomes the focus for the populist post-Brexit party 'England Always' and Ronnie Child's 'Brute Force', a white fascist 'militia', while the novel's feminist heroines, Jess, Deepa and Trina, seek to discover Green's sinister social plans.

Progressive or reactionary, gay or straight, the white English male cast of *Perfidious Albion* are either hypocrites or racists. Darkin is bitter and broken: 'You want to get something out of this country?' he asks rhetorically; 'Change your country'. Ronnie Childs is hard and stupid, while Hugo Bennington, a sleazy right-wing journalist with political ambitions, influences Darkin and the England Always worldview.

Bennington, and the conservative media generally, offer only a bleak portrait of England. 'The country was overrun, under threat, increasingly incapable. Hordes of immigrants massed at its borders. Its infrastructure frayed at the seams'. Meanwhile, 'British television had... given itself over to a comforting nostalgia', perpetuating 'a faded and frequently offensive ideal', a 'tsunami of whitewashed and chocolate box history' distasteful to multicultural millennials like Trina and Deepa.

England Always embraces the faded ideal and seeks to turn back the tide of 'political correctness gone mad'. 'Chests puffed with post-exit pride', the party transformed itself from one 'concerned with redefining England's place in the world to a party preoccupied with people's place in England and had moved from shaping England's post-Europe future to capturing its pre-contemporary pomp'. Byers's satire reduces populism to a mixture of mindless thuggery, racism and cynical manipulation. The *Guardian* found the novel, 'furiously smart... and madly funny'.

The *Observer*, similarly, welcomed Jonathan Coe's *Middle England* (2018), a novel that 'tells us something about the temper of our times'. The temper, of course, is bad. The country is 'in a wretched state... fractured, groaning under the pressure of an austerity programme'. Coe's social satire traces the period from the electoral defeat of Gordon Brown in 2010 through to 2017 through the experience of three generations of an English family, the Trotters, from Birmingham, their friends, and relations. Brexit exposes the fault lines that emerged after 2010 between town and country, young and old, contrasting the mindful cosmopolitanism of tertiary-educated young Londoners with the mindlessness of old, provincial racists.

The novel's main character, Benjamin Trotter, is a fifty-something divorcee who sells up in London so he can write a novel in a converted mill house on the Welsh border. Benjamin is a working-class product of an independent boys' school and a scholarship to Oxford. His father, Colin, worked at the now defunct Longbridge motor plant that once provided employment for much of the post-war Midlands working class, like the father of Doug Anderton, Benjamin's old school friend. Doug, now a successful left-wing journalist, lived, before they split, with his wealthy ex-catwalk wife and their snowflake daughter, Coriander, in a six-million-pound Chelsea house. Benjamin's niece, Sophie, teaches art history at the University of London. She completed her doctoral thesis on 'Contemporary Portraits of Black European Writers'. The thesis leads to a book contract, a permanent lectureship, and a series on the television channel Sky Arts. Sophie marries Ian, surprisingly a heterosexual white middle-class male, blissfully indifferent to academic politics. Ian, however, is frustrated by his failure to get promoted in the diversity-sensitive public sector where he works. His wife's impeccably liberal standards don't help. On a lecturing cruise, Sophie is told, 'you'd better decide… which is more important… your husband or being politically correct'. Ian's mother, Helena, and Sophie's grandfather, Colin, agree. Helena thinks England suffers under a tyranny of political correctness. Colin thinks Britain has 'gone soft' and the rest of the world 'is laughing at us'. Ian feels 'like a victim in his own country'.

Any reply to this viewpoint, Sophie decides, would 'mean confronting the unspeakable truth: that Sophie (and everyone like her) and Helena (and everyone like her) might be living cheek-by-jowl in the same country, but they also lived in different universes, and these universes were separated by a wall, infinitely high, impermeable, a wall built out of fear and suspicion'.

Several years later, Coriander, now an LGBT-aware student union rep, condemns Sophie's art history tutorial for 'transphobia'. Sophie is briefly suspended from her post. Her gay friend and fellow lecturer Sohan, who is writing a book on 'Deep England', suggests she takes her story to the *Daily Mail*. Sophie, however, like her persecutor, Coriander, supports Jeremy Corbyn, the 'wise avuncular socialist' leading the much-needed return to traditional Labour values.

It is the referendum and its aftermath, however, that cements the differences bubbling beneath the surface of not-so-cool Britannia. Benjamin is horrified to read Boris Johnson comparing the European Union to Nazi Germany because both strove to create 'a German-dominated European super state'. He considers the referendum 'duplicitous'. Doug thinks it showed David Cameron to be 'a weak, cowardly, malignant, narcissistic fool'. Meanwhile Sophie's mother, Lois, who has never recovered from the IRA bombing of a Birmingham pub in 1974, finds her trauma rudely revived when she hears the news of Remainer MP Jo Cox's murder by a man shouting 'Britain First'. She has a fit, beats the wall with her fists and screams, in terms Professor Stonebridge would approve, 'You stupid people – letting this happen'. Curiously, the Islamic State-inspired murder of Lee Rigby (2013), the attacks on *Charlie Hebdo*'s offices and the Bataclan in Paris (2015), and in Nice and Brussels (2016) evoke no such traumatic response in Lois or disturb the progressive verities of *Brexlit* more generally.

Lois's father, Colin, has a stroke and dies after voting Leave, while Sophie splits from her Leaver husband. They reconcile only when Ian awakens to his mother's racism and the error of his ways. Sophie feels that Brexit has stripped her of 'a small but important part of her own identity – her modern, layered, multiple identity'.

Doug, in investigative journalist mode, shows that the ignorant masses who voted Leave have been duped by dark forces. The emergence of a no-deal agenda in 2017, stoked by 'a disparate, amorphous coalition of vested interests', organised by the sinister Sir Ronald Culpepper and his free-market Imperium

Foundation think-tank, compounds the fears of Doug and the Trotter family. Brexit had been 'the wet dream' of conservatives like Culpepper 'for years'. Charlie, another old school friend, reinforces the point. The post-war social contract, 'has been unravelling since 1979... that's the real story... the process is pretty much complete now'. Ultimately, the social divisions Brexit crystallised are Margaret Thatcher's legacy.

Disillusioned by Brexit, Lois and Benjamin sell their respective properties and open a creative writing school in Provence. Sophie, a cosmopolitan anywhere, joins them. She now feels more at home 'on the Boulevard Saint-Michel' than in northern England. An old friend, Claire, visiting Benjamin, asks, 'What the hell is going on in Britain at the moment? All the Italians think the Brits have gone completely crazy'. Claire and her wealthy Italian husband evidently hadn't heard of the *Lega Nord*.

No *Brexlit* character pauses to consider that the conduct of the European Commission might explain Brexit's popular appeal. Instead, *Brexlit* saves its self-righteous indignation for the old, the white and the working class who spoilt their cosmopolitan dream. In Brexitland all Europeans and migrants receive bouquets, the brickbats are reserved for the dull, racist, nostalgia-obsessed, provincial Brits. In fact, *Brexlit* nowhere tackles the impact of mass migration, facilitated by a Europe *sans frontieres*, on wages and public services or how this might induce popular resentment. At the 2011 census the UK's second city, Birmingham, the setting for several Brexit novels, approached majority-minority population status. Nearly 40 per cent of the population identified as South Asian; more than 20 per cent practised Islam. This remarkable urban transformation and its cultural impact pass unseen. The only intimation that Birmingham now hosts a Muslim population that has altered the city's character occurs when Benjamin Trotter remarks that his old school now had a prayer centre to cater for the school's 30 percent of boys 'who practised the Islamic faith'.

The viewpoint of a cosmopolitan Remainer elite is thus *Brexlit*'s default mode. Brexit is an unmitigated disaster. It exemplifies 'the English disease' – nostalgia. The English are 'obsessed with their bloody past... and look where that's got us'. Anthony Cartwright's *The Cut* is the only Brexit novel to express any sympathy for the white working-class predicament. Meike Ziervogel, Cartwright's German publisher, was 'shocked' to find herself living in a 'divided country' and commissioned him 'to build a fictional bridge between the two Britains'. Cartwright represents this division through the contrasting characters of Cairo Jukes, an ageing ex-boxer, also from Birmingham, working as a contract labourer cleaning up industrial sites, and Grace, a worldly, cosmopolitan, Hampstead-based, documentary filmmaker.

Grace arrives in Birmingham to canvass opinion on the referendum. She finds an 'invisible veil between her and these people... This is how it began, she supposed, prejudice on the scale of a whole country'. Cairo is the only local who speaks to her. He tells her, 'We've had enough'. The short interview is a social media sensation, even though Cairo's speech requires subtitles. Cairo's odd dialect reveals that 'all you people want to say is that it's about immigration. That we'm all racist. You doh wanna hear that its more complicated than that'.

The interview with Grace leads to a documentary film commission and their unlikely relationship blossoms. Grace discovers that the white working class have lost 'jobs, houses, security'. 'There is a culture that has been neglected here', she opines fatuously. Cairo's father tells her there used to be 'man's work' at the furnaces, 'not like now'. The town of Dudley is 'a hole' worse than the 'border camps, Serbia ... Syria'. A drunken brawl in a local curry house run by Cairo's friend, Jamie Iqbal, where UKIP activists hold regular Friday meetings, symbolises Leave voters' hypocrisy about immigration. Cartwright demonstrates how 'this carrying on about foreigners', as Cairo's daughter puts it, and a working-class aversion to a metropolitan elite, obscured debate. The novel ends when metropolitan Grace tells Cairo she is having his child. Cairo finds the situation intolerable and immolates himself outside a local mosque. This melodramatic conclusion leaves fictional bridges burnt rather than built. Analysing social divisions in these simplistic terms fails to explain why so many voted for Leave, which was neither just a provincial nor a working-class phenomenon. Consequently, no novel makes a serious effort to explore the wider cultural dimensions of Brexit. *Brexlit* ignores the Islamically-inspired terror attacks across Europe after 2014, and the impact they may have had on the popular perception of immigration, especially in the wake of Angela Merkel's arbitrary decision to open Europe's borders to refugees in 2015.

Middle England's clumsy attempt to integrate recent history into the lives of its fictional characters never considers the impact the terror attacks between 2016 and 2018 on Westminster Bridge, Borough Market or Manchester Arena might have had on social attitudes. The auto fiction of Cusk and Laing, the predictable satires of Board and Byers, and Cartwright's laboured attempt at kitchen-sink realism, studiously avoid the cultural issues raised by religious terror, mass migration, the financial crisis and globalisation.

Brexlit instead reinforces the smug, self-referential worldview found in English literature departments, literary reviews and progressive publishing houses. Characters are one-dimensional, the plots soap operatic. It's hard to think of a time when the English novel would not have made more of the ironic possibilities that the chaos of Brexit affords. Post-war English writers as various as Evelyn Waugh, Anthony Powell, George Orwell and John Braine would surely have dealt with Brexit in a more controversial and provocative manner. They would certainly have done some research, as Orwell did when he took *The Road to Wigan Pier* and would never have expressed such contempt for the working classes or shown the unqualified respect for Labour politicians, liberal journalists, the progressive European establishment or Remainer civil servants as *Brexlit* does. Anthony Powell would have found in Olly Robbins a fine example of the civil service's Widmerpool tendency. Waugh's Lord Copper would have enjoyed the Conservative and Labour parties' shambolic reaction to the 'Leave' vote. John Braine's Joe Lampton would have shown far more resilience than Cairo Jukes as well as contempt for the patronising, progressive views of women like Grace or Sophie Trotter. But we need only consider briefly how the modern condition-of-England genre first emerged to see the depths to which it has now fallen.

Literature and the condition of England question revisited

The first condition-of-England novels of the 1840s responded to the acute political crisis the 1832 Electoral Reform Act, which rationalised, but did not extend, the franchise, generated. The progressive reform ministry's subsequent passage of the Poor Law Amendment Act (1834) that curtailed outdoor poor relief, its failure to repeal the Corn Laws, which kept the price of grain artificially high, and draconian restrictions on freedom of assembly, association and the press, fuelled working-class resentment. The rise of the Chartist and trade union movements campaigning for reasonable wages and the right to vote stirred riot and rebellion. These premonitory snufflings of popular democracy coincided with revolution on the continent and famine in Ireland. European society then, as now, endured 'struggling, convulsive unrest'.

In November 1839, George Maule, Treasury Solicitor to the Attorney-General, wrote to Thomas Jones Phillips, the Mayor of Newport, concerning a Chartist 'uprising' that left twenty-two dead. His letter ends, 'We live in dreadful times'. The leaders of the 'insurgency', which demanded universal manhood suffrage and secret ballots, were sentenced to death for high treason. The Crown subsequently commuted the sentence to transportation for life to Van Diemen's Land. A similar fate awaited trade unionists and strikers protesting against their poverty, and demanding the Charter, in the factory towns of Manchester and Birmingham between 1842 and 1848. Then as now the liberal establishment had little time for the ignorant masses and their duplicitous leaders.

However, the nineteenth-century novelist, rather than caricaturing the stupidity of the industrial working class, tried to understand the motivation that drove them to violence. Writing shortly after the Newport Uprising, Thomas Carlyle asked, 'What means this bitter discontent of the Working Classes? Whence comes it? Whither goes it?' Charles Dickens, Elizabeth Gaskell, Emily Bronte and Charles Kingsley all tried to answer Carlyle's question. His tract on *Chartism* (1840) provided a useful starting point. Carlyle considered Chartism a natural reaction to the insouciant liberal progressivism of the day. After 1832, Robert Peel's reform ministry demonstrated indifference bordering on contempt for the economic plight of the industrial working classes during the recession of 1838 to 1844. In these complicated times, Carlyle wrote, 'with cash payment as the sole nexus, the lower classes declare in their confused and emphatic way that they must be governed'. Instead, a 'paralytic' radicalism, committed to an abstract *laissez faire* ideology, believed government could do nothing. Absent a welfare state, public education or social insurance, stagnation of trade leads to wage cuts, immiseration, strikes and demands for democratic accountability. Migration and the corn laws exacerbated the pressure, making food dear and the price of labour cheap. The natural consequence was physical force, Chartism and trades unionism. Condition-of-England novelists like Elizabeth Gaskell made this point explicit in novels like *Mary Barton* (1848) and *North and South* (1855). Gaskell, like Dickens in *Hard Times*, did not consider working-class characters like Nicholas Higgins, John Barton or Stephen Blackpool as mindless thugs. Instead, they sought to expose the wilful ignorance of the propertied class, their preoccupation with 'facts', and their lack of inquiry into the condition of the poor. The condition-of-England novel, in profound contrast to *Brexlit*, sought to correct that lacuna.

In *North and South*, set in Milton (Manchester), Gaskell's chapter 'What is a Strike?' opens with an Anti-Corn Law League hymn: 'But work grows scarce / while bread grows dear / and wages lessened too / for Irish hordes were bidden here / our half-paid work to do'. Nicholas Higgins, the independent-minded handloom weaver and trade union organiser, takes up the cause of justice. 'Why are we to have less wage now', he asks reasonably, 'than two years ago?' When Henry Thornton, the inflexible mill owner, imported 'hands' from Ireland, it 'irritated the Milton people excessively... and the stupid wretches wouldn't work for him'. Higgins, who wants a fair day's pay for his work, particularly resents the decision to import 'Paddies' who 'did na know weft fro warp'. The problem of the industrial classes, as Carlyle and Gaskell observed, was not the responsible, abstemious English workers, but the wretched, feckless Irish who drove the price of labour down. Gaskell is not unsympathetic to 'Paddy work' as 'a navvy', but Carlyle and the Manchester mill-owner and Karl Marx collaborator Friedrich Engels see the Irish undermining solid Saxon working-class values.

'The uncivilised Irishman', Carlyle wrote, 'not by his strength, but by the opposite of strength, drives the Saxon native out, takes possession in his room. There abides he, in his squalor and unreason, in his falsity and drunken violence, as the ready-made nucleus of degradation and disorder'. Engels, writing in 1845, thought Carlyle 'perfectly right'. The Irish:

> insinuate themselves everywhere... With such a competitor the English working-man has to struggle, with a competitor upon the lowest plane possible in a civilised country, who for this very reason requires less wages than any other. Nothing else is therefore possible than that... the wages of English working-man should be forced down further and further in every branch in which the Irish compete with him.

The vicious Irish drunk of the mid-nineteenth century and the later nineteenth century 'hooligan' gang share an interesting affinity with the tattooed English oafs of *Brexlit*. By an interesting metonymy, *Brexlit* has transformed the English working classes into the equivalent of Irish savages and transferred their nineteenth-century virtues to the virtuous migrant. Moreover, while *Brexlit* novelists present their progressive liberal cosmopolitan peers in positive terms, novelists like Dickens found their nineteenth-century equivalents risible. Dickens had little time for the workings of Chancery in *Bleak House* or for Gradgrind in *Hard Times*. He reserved particular scorn for those like Mrs Jellyby, who ignored the poverty of outcast London to devote herself to educating the natives of Boorioboola-Gha on the left bank of the Niger. What Dickens satirised as Jellyby and her government admirers' 'telescopic philanthropy', the *Brexlit* novelist would consider uncritically as virtuous cosmopolitanism. The progressive London literary establishment, its academic book reviewers and Remainer publishing houses like Faber & Faber and Penguin have turned the English novel, not into a mirror to investigate the condition of England, but into a form of ideological groupthink that Soviet-era dissidents like Czesław Miłosz would have well-recognised.

Original article published in *Quadrant*, 3rd September 2019, by David Martin Jones.

The Chinese dream: China's challenge to 'global' Britain

The Central Committee of the Chinese Communist Party (CCP), the Party's highest decision-making body, met for the sixth plenum of its current cycle earlier this month. Although little remarked upon in the West, the plenum passed an historic resolution, only the third such in its hundred-year history. The resolution attributes the People's Republic of China's (PRC) resurgence, power and wealth to actions taken by Xi Jinping and the CCP. The resolution paves the way for the next party congress in 2022 to confirm Xi Jinping as the Party's General Secretary and leader of the country 'forever'. The Central Committee's decision represents a significant concentration of power in the leader of this one-party state.

The UK government and the mainstream media's failure to recognise the implications of this latest stage in China's development as a totalitarian despotism is disquieting. The CCP, and its dictatorial leader, represent a serious threat to a United Kingdom struggling to recover from the social and economic devastation wrought by COVID-19 and successive lockdowns. Unlike other threats to national security that emerge from outside or within the UK, China directly challenges both the UK's internal security and its interest in securing a rule-governed, international post-pandemic order. The UK thus needs a far more coherent defence and foreign policy posture to address the threat from China.

Foreign policy
In foreign policy terms, the challenge China poses to the UK starts in Taiwan and moves South. The UK's commitment to the Indo-Pacific and the negotiation of the Australia, UK and US nuclear technology agreement (AUKUS) is a promissory note that must take account of the potential for conflict both in the South China Sea and over the status of Taiwan. Since 1949, China has considered Taiwan to be a rebellious province. It is increasingly considered ripe for forcible reunification with the mainland.

The UK has traditionally been an open society and, prior to its baleful period of EU membership, committed to free trade with the world. However, a revitalised UK foreign policy must now confront what the Chinese Communist Party intends, by the centenary of its foundation in 2049, to be a world system that functions on its own terms. This is a world order that will not be moving towards liberalism. As Xi Jinping made clear in his speech to the twelfth Party Congress in 2013: 'To accomplish the Chinese Dream we have to take a Chinese path. This is the path of socialism with Chinese characteristics. This is not a path that opens up by itself'.

In order to retard the Chinese Dream, the UK will need to balance its growing commercial interests in the Indo-Pacific with deterring Chinese adventurism. It is in its post-Brexit shift to the Indo-Pacific where the vital importance of the UK's special relationship with the US will need careful calibration to ensure neither increased dependency on an unreliable President Biden, nor kowtowing to China.

In this context, the UK needs to attend carefully to what other like-minded democracies are saying and doing. Significantly, Australia declared in its most recent strategic defence review that the prospect of high intensity conflict is now less remote than it was, but also noted that more 'grey zone' incidents are already occurring. The Japanese also recognise the growing threat from China. For the first time, Japan has removed Taiwan from its map of China and has dedicated separate chapters of its latest defence review to Taiwan and the communist-ruled mainland. The review notes the growing CCP threat to the island and states that, 'it is necessary that we pay close attention to the situation… more than ever before'.

The tone and relative precision of Britain's allies in the Asia-Pacific stands in marked contrast to the contradictory and languid prose of the UK's most recent *Integrated Review* which vaguely proposes to 'do more to adapt to China's growing impact on our lives'. Tellingly, the Australian, Japanese and US responses to China's regional adventurism offer a more pragmatic guide and a better insight into dealing with China's global ambitions. We should therefore recognise, as Australia, Japan and the US already do, that the unveiling of Communist China's hostility to the free World has been a key geo-political development in the post-COVID world.

Illiberal Sino-centrism

China deploys its soft and hard power to advance an allegedly harmonious, but notably hierarchical, illiberal, Sino-centric alternative to a rule-governed world order. The CCP's United Front for Cultural Work has a well-established track record for producing internal and external propaganda to advance this hegemonic agenda. As Miles Yu of the Hoover Institution has argued, the United Front has sought and always found willing accomplices among Western elites, notably in academe, business and politics. The United Front now assumes physical shape in the form of Confucius Institutes proliferating across European, Australian and North American campuses. Their purpose is to raise awareness of China whilst at the same time dismissing or censoring any inconvenient truths about human rights abuses in Xinjiang, Tibet or Hong Kong.

The Party's soft power, elite capture, and growing social media presence has in recent decades enabled China to undermine the conventional practices of political democracy and advance the understanding of China as 'a justly aggrieved nation' led by enlightened leaders toward a world historic comeback after a century of 'Western humiliation'. China understands and plays the West all too well. By contrast, the *Integrated Review* intimates that the British government barely understands Xi Jinping's 'China Dream' at all.

One of the policy imperatives for Britain is to undo the CCP's United Front work that has succeeded in capturing elite interests and opinion, not least inside its universities. Confucius Institutes require urgent regulation, if not rolling back, as too does the CCP's acquisition of UK infrastructure and high-tech companies. In the short time since its publication, the *Integrated Review*'s failure to follow through on the Prime Minister's geo-strategically pivotal decision to exclude Huawei from any role in the development to the UK's 5G networks is one of its major defects. Critical national infrastructure and technology need to be secured to allow Britain to trade intelligently with China. This notwithstanding, the new National Security and Investment Act (2021), designed to interdict China's technology and infrastructural acquisitions, proved powerless to stop China's state linked WingTech electronics company snapping up Newport based Wafer Fab, the UK's leading semi-conductor plant for a knockdown price of £65 million in July.

However, Xi Jinping's belligerence, like several sons of heaven before him, might be a sign of an acute case of imperial overreach. Despite buying global influence through its Belt and Road Initiative and its leadership of the Shanghai Cooperation Organisation of fellow despotisms, China is 'a lonely power'. Xi Jinping's aggressive foreign policy posture, which, Mao apart, contrasts starkly with all his predecessors, has increased international opposition, undoing years of effort by Chinese officials to assure regional governments that a stronger China will be a peaceful and accommodating good neighbour rather than a domineering one.

China's self-defeating foreign policy

Xi's foreign policy has been self-defeating in a number of important respects. Xi's conversion of the CCP's diplomatic corps into 'wolf warriors' who 'dare to show the sword' (gǎn chū jiàn) has witnessed Chinese diplomats insulting and threatening not just Western democracies but, *inter alia*, Brazil, Kazakhstan, Venezuela, Thailand and South Korea. The result is not surprising. Public opinion surveys in Australia, South America and the US show a marked decrease in positive feelings towards China over the last two years. Former Singaporean senior foreign ministry official Bilahari Kausikan thinks that 'China's 'wolf warriors' are doing a better job than any American diplomat in arousing anti-Chinese feelings around the world'.

Equally damaging to China's international status was the June 2020 skirmish in the Galwan Valley. The clash along the disputed Sino-Indian border began when Chinese troops ambushed and killed an Indian colonel. This incident pushed India into closer alignment with its QUAD (Quadrilateral Security Dialogue) partners – Japan, India, US and Australia. The Indian government cancelled infrastructure construction deals, halted the purchase of Huawei information technology equipment, and sought to de-couple China economically from other important sectors. Apart from a deepening commitment to the QUAD, India was quick to express support for the AUKUS agreement and now sends warships into the South China Sea – acts that Beijing finds threatening.

It is in the South China Sea, where Beijing began building sizable artificial islands in 2013, that Xi's policy has spectacularly backfired. China has installed military facilities, including runways, docks, barracks and missile batteries, on at least three reefs in the Spratly group. Beijing's South China Sea policy attempts to impose its will upon weaker neighbours rather than negotiating a mutually acceptable compromise through the Association of South East Asian Nations' (ASEAN) code of conduct for regional maritime disputes, which China signed up to in 2012. It also demonstrates the Chinese government's willingness to disregard international agreements like the UN Convention on the Law of the Seas to which China is also a signatory. Ironically, the strategic utility of these islands, located far from mainland China, is uncertain. They might prove more of a liability than an asset in a time of conflict. More than any other single policy, the new bases convinced international observers that the PRC under Xi had taken a distinctly confrontational turn that emphasises winning rather than managing strategic disputes.

Meanwhile, in the geopolitically fraught case of Taiwan, Xi has essentially doubled down on his predecessors' demonstrably failed policies. Xi maintains that unification is essential to China's rejuvenation, although the PRC is both prosperous and secure without controlling Taiwan. He has continued to insist that Taiwan's destiny is 'one country-two systems'. However, since its democratic opening in 2000, Taiwan has never supported the idea of one country-two systems, and the destruction of Hong Kong's liberties has completely discredited the concept. That Xi would still speak of one country-two systems in a message to Taiwan as recently as October 2021 indicates a wilful intellectual and political blindness.

Xi's increased military pressure on Taiwan has only deepened resentment towards China and bolstered support for the pro-independence Democratic Progressive Party. The heightened sense of danger has also persuaded Taiwan to implement an asymmetric defence strategy, which will make it more capable of resisting any attempted PRC invasion. The Biden administration has reaffirmed US support for Taiwan as 'rock solid'. Australian Defence Minister, Peter Dutton announced in November that Australia would support Taiwan in the event of an attack, and Japanese leaders are now openly discussing the increasing likelihood that Japan would help defend Taiwan. Xi's tone-deaf policy towards Taiwan eliminates all possible solutions other than war. Even in the best-case scenario, war would be disastrous for China.

Elsewhere, China's recent strategy of economic coercion against Australia has similarly failed. In April 2020, Canberra displeased Beijing by calling for an inquiry into the origins of the COVID-19 pandemic. The PRC retaliated by cutting the imports of ten Australian products. Canberra refused to accommodate the political demands made by the Chinese embassy in November 2020 and the consequences of the sanctions were worse for China than for Australia. Australia suffered little from the import ban, finding other buyers for most of the resources China turned away. Australian Treasurer Josh Frydenberg described the damage done to Australia's economy as 'relatively modest'. In addition to the reputational cost to Beijing, the Chinese government's campaign against Australia drew greater international attention to the dangers of doing business with the PRC. Power outages in China during autumn 2021 are partly due to coal shortages, worsened by the sanctions against Australian coal imports.

The unilateral attempt to punish Australia has further increased international momentum to address China's systematic violation of both the spirit and the letter of its World Trade Organisation obligations. Canberra's refusal to capitulate may serve as an inspiration for other governments facing Chinese economic pressure over a political disagreement and diminish the utility of this tactic. It also ought to serve as a model for the UK in its evolving ties with both Australia and with China. Despite the sixth plenum's resolution, the Xi Jinping leadership group is far from achieving the 'great rejuvenation of the Chinese nation'. Xi's personality cult combined with the concentration of decision-making powers in himself and prioritising loyalty over pragmatic analysis is not conducive to advisors warning him against his more egregious mistakes. The Mandate of Heaven could well pass from him.

A PRC that other states perceive as aggressive and capricious has engendered, as if by an invisible hand, an increasingly coordinated regional resistance. This will make it harder for China to become a regional or a global leader. If other governments believe China is expansionist, they will believe every strategic gain by China emboldens Beijing to strive for more. In other words, China can best be checked by a containment and deterrence strategy. In this, the UK can play a major role if the Foreign Office can be persuaded to get its somewhat lacklustre act together. Evidently, the UK can best help resist continuing Chinese expansionism through building robust alliances. In this context, the UK must reassess its free world commitments and build alliances with those where trust is most complete, namely within the Anglosphere, the Commonwealth and with the 'Five Eyes' intelligence nations (US, UK Australia, Canada and New Zealand) at its core. AUKUS (the recent defence agreement to provide nuclear submarines to the Australian navy) therefore represents a welcome recognition of the need to engage more fully with key Anglospheric allies.

In sum, there are several signs that British foreign policy is moving towards a greater appreciation for the need to engage with allies and partner countries in the Indo-Pacific region to balance the China threat. At the same time, this realisation needs to be accompanied by a firmer resolve by Britain's policy establishment to confront the spread of CCP influence at home: in business, the technology sector and in higher education. The key lesson to observe is that when it comes to China, foreign policy is not something that exists merely as a discrete external enterprise but is intimately connected with domestic concerns as much as international ones.

Originally published in *Cieo*, 24th November 2021, by David Martin Jones and M.L.R. Smith.

The European Union as the new Tower of Babel

As the conservative historian Niall Ferguson observed in 2017, the EU richly deserved Brexit. Warnings about the problem of currency union in the 1990s have come to fruition. The dire debt situation of the weaker member states has been exacerbated by the Europan Central Bank's response to COVID and the inflation and shortages that now beset Europe, amplified of course by the current Ukraine crisis, itself a product of European inertia.

Like its fiscal policy, Europe's foreign policy has been an exercise in managerialism rather than realism and the consequences have been failure in both Eastern Europe and the Middle East. Over the last decade, responses to migration and Islamism have merely exacerbated both problems, whilst in Ukraine, EU policy, with US help, overreached without making the sustained commitment to deter Russia and the slow-motion revenge of Putin's revisionist power.

Brexit and the disorder of Europe
The West, if it is not to enter the decline that Oswald Spengler anticipated at the end of the First World War, needs a foreign policy geared to long-term interests in a rapidly changing world no longer *en route* to a liberal-democratic end of history. This has become a more urgent task since the UK left the European Union in 2020 and US foreign and economic policy since Trump has demonstrated a disturbing propensity for capricious unilateral behaviour.

European policy must not only consider the economic dimension of Brexit and the war in Ukraine, but also how economics and geopolitics are linked in an interconnected but by no means integrated world. In this context, a common European defence force, proposed as its 'compass' for security at its most recent EU summit in May, without the UK or an enhanced commitment to NATO seems wishful. With a proposed rapid-response force of only 5000 troops in the next decade the EU will conduct diplomacy without a serious military capacity, resembling, as Frederick the Great wrote during the partition of Poland, an orchestra without instruments.

This has evident consequences for Russia's near abroad and why one suspects the Eastern European and Baltic states will need to function more coherently as a bloc in the future. This will become even more crucial as the European Union under its own centrifugal pressure begins to fragment. Populists in France and Italy see no need for the current regime of sanctions against Russia.

Meanwhile, the constant incantation of a return of the Cold War rhetoric regarding Russian irredentism offers only a lazy anachronism and demonstrates the fallacy of conducting current conflict according to the last, albeit colder, war. As the British historian J.M. Roberts wrote, 'it is always disappointing when intelligent people seriously talk nonsense... The hardest thing to understand about much of the past is its errors and delusions'.

Errors and delusions, as recent Russian actions in Ukraine demonstrate, have implications. In this troubled context of the apparent fraying of the European body politic it is perhaps the task of sceptical conservatives to identify what has occurred rather than propose specific remedies.

Rationalism and the body politic
The current wave of geopolitical and economic uncertainty troubling Europe and its political institutions at both the state and the regional level is nothing new. The British historian Norman Davies has shown in several books and articles how European principalities, republics and monarchies often collapse or mutate into new forms. In *Vanished Kingdoms*, Davies traced the rise and fall of various European political forms from the end of the Roman empire in the West, to the 'ultimate vanishing act' the Soviet Union performed in 1991. Davies's history of half-forgotten Europe concludes with a chapter examining 'How States Die' and assesses whether 'discernible patterns of causation' can account for this demise.

Davies's historical analysis coincides with a developing field in political science research analysing the manner in which state systems and, more particularly liberal democracies, fail, break down, wither, disintegrate, end, or die.

This current enthusiasm for comparing and categorising failing states and their political breakdown draws without acknowledgment on a long-standing European tradition of political thought which, since Plato and Aristotle first identified the phenomenon, has evaluated the factors that explain state dissolution, stasis or disintegration. Greek reflection on the failure of Athens during the Peloponnesian War influenced a large and varied literature in the Greco-Roman and Medieval Christian periods, as well as the Abbasid and Ottoman Muslim traditions of statecraft. The great Muslim thinkers Ibn Khaldun and Kateb Celebi devoted treatises to the relationship between the various organs in the body and the means of correcting their defects. Civilisations, these writers discerned, proceed inexorably through stages of growth, maturity and luxury and once corrupted decline into increasing senility and inevitable death.

Similarly, during the disintegration of Christendom over the long sixteenth century and the emergence of a European state system after 1648, the idea of the political body, the stages of its growth and development and the reasons for its death offered writers and thinkers a potent analogy for capturing their experience.

Seventeenth-century English political philosophers, like Thomas Hobbes and John Locke, attempting to understand the course of the English Civil War and its aftermath, sought to disclose, from different perspectives, the internal 'diseases that tend to the dissolution of a commonwealth'. The most common intestinal problem they identified was internal and external war, leading to the disintegration of a political commonwealth, whether in England or Europe. In referring to the decay of commonwealths, Hobbes particularly drew upon, and revised, the enduring metaphor of the body politic. States and unions, Hobbes wrote, could dissolve from a number of 'distempers' or diseases.

If we consider our current predicament from this analogical perspective, it is evident that body politics like the European Union come and go with far more frequency than we like to admit. From his careful examination of vanished kingdoms, Davies contends that apart from the internal and external factors affecting state development and decay, involuntary and voluntary factors also play their part. In Europe's modern history five mechanisms may be identified: implosion, conquest, merger, liquidation, and infant mortality.

Thus, the Polish Lithuanian commonwealth that vanished in the course of the eighteenth century, as a result of a series of partitions enforced by its stronger neighbours, died from unnatural causes. By contrast, other political arrangements start life through an amalgamation of pre-existing units. The degree of amalgamation differs widely. Spain and the UK offer obvious contemporary examples – best described in the corporate language of merger and demerger. A recent example of demerger would be Czechoslovakia, which split into the Czech Republic and Slovakia in 1993. Meanwhile other mergers like those leading to the evolution of the Soviet Union after 1917 were essentially coercive.

Given their own difficult histories, the states of Eastern Europe with their variable geographies should be aware of this, far more perhaps than the Western European community of states they joined at the end of the Cold War. The terms of membership by which one more successful body incorporates others is always a source of tension. It is no wonder perhaps that the remarkable document signed at Horodlo that created a Polish Lithuanian estate was more successful than the Treaty of Lisbon (2007). The preamble to the Act of Horodlo (1413) noted that 'whoever is unsupported by the mystery of love shall not achieve the grace of salvation... For by love laws are made, kingdoms governed, cities ordered, and the state is brought to its proper goal. Whoever casts love aside shall lose everything'. Compare this with the bureaucratese of the Lisbon Treaty and the current absence of love displayed, whether between Brussels and the UK or Brussels and Hungary.

In this brief history of political bodies merging and demerging, it is evident that the USSR imploded. The party state had the equivalent of a heart attack and died from natural causes. A similar fate after Brexit could be reserved for the European Union unless some radical surgery takes place.

Mythology and statecraft

Despite its current weakness and potential for implosion, demerger, or death from natural causes, it is nevertheless worth bearing in mind Europe's promethean capacity to reinvent itself. The Old Testament myth of the Tower of Babel which expressed an unchanging, human, yet peculiarly Western disposition might in these troubled times shed an interesting if neglected light upon the all-too-human yearning for integration and unanimity.

In its Old Testament version, after the Flood, God, man and nature were reconciled in a covenant made between God and Abraham. Abraham's grand-nephew Nimrod, however, found the terms unacceptable and launched his followers on a project to conquer heaven, building a tower to reach it. Rather than let loose another flood, Abraham persuaded God to solve the threat by 'confounding the tongues' of Nimrod and his fellows. Thus, not by a flood, but in a deluge of meaningless words, was the empire of Nimrod destroyed. Babel, which originally meant the city of liberation, acquired its mythic significance as the city of confusion.

Two major thinkers and writers of the twentieth century – the Austro-Hungarian liberal novelist Stefan Zweig and the English conservative philosopher Michael Oakeshott – both adapted the Babel legend to the historical evolution of the modern European political project. They address the myth in very different but, from the perspective of ever-closer union and the potential for catastrophic fragmentation, equally prescient ways.

Zweig wrote that the symbols found in origin myths harbour a 'wonderful poetic force', suggesting 'great moments of a later history in which peoples renew themselves' and the most significant epochs have their roots. For Zweig the Babel myth intimates a desire for unity – humans find themselves in a foreign place with no means of escape, a place that seems uncertain and filled with danger, but high above them they see the sky and pool their resources in an attempt to reach it. This 'communal work brings them together'.

Their endeavours are remarkably successful, but a cruel and fearful God, concerned by this human drive for a unity only the Godhead achieves, sows dissension through the Babel of different languages, ensuring they do not understand each other. God's 'dark resolution' smote 'the spirit of unity and dedication'. The project collapsed, 'centuries... passed and men lived in the isolation of their languages', but the dream did not die. After millennia the abandoned project of community and the longing to come together again reasserts itself.

As a result, the Tower of Babel once more 'began to rise gradually from the soil of Europe, the monument... to mankind's solidarity. But it was no longer raw materials that went into this tower's construction... The new tower was built with a more delicate and yet more indestructible substance which they discovered on earth' in the long era of division and separation, 'that of spirituality and experience, the most sublime material of the soul'.

However, a cruel God, horrified at their endeavour, caused confusion to break out amongst them. 'This is the monstrous moment we are living through today', Zweig wrote in 1916. He returned to the theme again in 1930 and 1932, observing, 'The new Tower of Babel, the great monument to the spiritual unity of Europe, lies in decay, its workers have lost their way'. Zweig would no doubt see contemporary Europe's predicament as the response of a vengeful God who has sown dissension amongst Europeans who, indifferent to the union's collapse, 'believe their contribution can be withdrawn from the magnificent construction'.

Nevertheless, Zweig would maintain that Babel's 'battlements stand, still its invisible blocks loom over a world in disarray'. Moreover, some exist who believe that never can a single people, a single nation achieves what a collective of European nations could, which 'must be brought to completion in our Europe'.

Zweig's optimistic paean to the 'heroic' European 'endeavour' to overcome national attachments contrasts with Oakeshott's pessimism towards what he understood as an exercise in rationalism. Oakeshott tells the tale somewhat differently. The modern-day Nimrod inspires his Babelian subjects with a vision of 'forcing open the gates of heaven', dislodging the 'miserly deity from his estate and appropriating for the enjoyment of all Babelians the limitless profusion of paradise'. Ultimately, the motivation for such an endeavour stemmed from greed and a 'profound feeling of being alike deprived: allowed to have wishes but denied their immediate satisfaction'. Because of the joint endeavour the city of freedom acquired over time 'a new communal identity in place of their former distinct individualities'. All conduct was recognised only in relation to the enterprise. Proverbial gaiety gave way to a spurious gravity.

Moreover, as the endeavour proceeded with no apparent end in sight, supported only by a precarious vision of limitless satisfaction, and marked by no interim satisfactions to break the monotony, it took its toll in emotional stress. Suspicion and distrust concerning Nimrod and his managerial elite's intentions led to the alienated masses launching a catastrophic assault on the tower, precipitating its collapse. 'What had been designed as a stairway to paradise' became 'the tomb of an entire people, not perished in a confusion of tongues, but the victims of a delusion and confounded by the distrust which dogs those who engage in titanic exploits'. Ultimately, as Oakeshott noted, 'those who in Elysian fields would dwell, do but extend the boundaries of hell'.

The conscious endeavour to instrumentalise a morality of ideals, in this case a European ideal, is ultimately hubristic. The attempt to build a European Union represents the antithesis of a creative moral or, we also might add, a political project. Properly understood, as Oakeshott wrote:

> the situations of a normal life are met, not by consciously applying to ourselves a rule of behaviour, nor by conduct recognised as the expression of a moral ideal, but by acting in accordance with a certain habit of behaviour. The moral life, or for that matter a political condition, in this form does not spring from the consciousness of possible alternative ways of behaving and a choice, determined by an opinion, a rule or an ideal, from among these alternatives.

Conduct, instead, is as nearly as possible without reflection. And consequently, most of the current situations of life do not appear as occasions calling for judgement, or as problems requiring solution. There is, on the occasion, nothing more than the unreflective following of a tradition of conduct in which we have been educated or more precisely habituated.

This is evidently not our current condition. Indeed, this form of moral or political behaviour constituted in terms of the pursuit of a moral ideal or an abstract set of moral rules might, for an individual, be 'a gamble which may have its rewards'. However, as Oakeshott concluded, 'when undertaken in a society not itself engaged in the gamble, it is mere folly'.

Conclusion

The project of finding a short cut to heaven is as old as the human race and conduct that orients itself by ideology or rules is precisely an attempt at this kind of short cut. As with the attempt to build a tower to heaven, people mistakenly believe that they may avoid the difficulties of life by engaging in a project in which the ends have been determined for them.

In our current European predicament, these rules are set by a Commission pursuing ever-closer union. It explicitly pursues a future state of perfection, all the while neglecting the joys and sorrows of our present temporality. It substitutes the illusions of affairs for self-understanding. The truth is that a morality and a political project in this form, whatever the quality of its ideals, breeds nothing but distraction and moral and ultimately political instability.

Chagrin ultimately awaits all those who embark upon such an endeavour.

Original article published in *Quadrant*, 4th November 2022, by David Martin Jones.

5. The West's cultural revolution

LONG BEFORE WE WASHED UP IN SINGAPORE, David and I, fortunately perhaps, had already studied Asian politics and history. Throughout our careers we joked that we were 'Old Asia Hands', evoking the idea that we were heir to a tradition extending back to the era of nineteenth century merchants who acquired a knowledge of the Orient, especially of Chinese culture and language.

David's schooling in classical political theory endowed him with a familiarity with the distinctive traditions and practices of Asian modes of governance and the way they contrasted with the liberal philosophies of the West. David's expertise informed several of his early academic books, such as *Towards Illiberal Democracy in Pacific* Asia (1995), as well as his single authored volumes, *Political Development in Pacific Asia* (1997) and his masterful, and to my mind underrated, *The Image of China in Western Social and Political Thought* (2001). For my part, I had spent my early childhood in the near region and had concentrated a large component of my undergraduate studies on courses such as 'A History of Chinese of Communism', 'Chinese Foreign Policy' and 'The Origins of the Pacific War'.

It is easy to assume that Asian forms of politics, with their emphases on the collective over the individual and autocratic rule by a hierarchy guided by the Mandate of Heaven, are radically different from those in the West. By the early 2000s, this was an assumption that David and I began to question. People in the West might think they are too individualistic and therefore immune to the cult-like ideological conformism that characterise authoritarian approaches to rule in Asia. But the more we looked, the less sure we were. We detected the growing presence of Maoist inflected styles of thought in public discourse, especially inside the universities. Supposedly bastions of free thought, Western universities were steadily mutating into institutions with an ethos that ultimately contradicted the ideas of academic integrity and liberal pluralism. The first essay in this chapter, written by David in 2010, pursues this theme.

The second essay details my own travails as I experienced the impact of this inversion of core academic values. In 2018/19 I established a speaker series entitled 'Endangered speeches: Debating the culture wars'. I was Head of the Department of War Studies at King's College London at the time, and the series was set up in response to student interest. The speaker series was intended only to stimulate civil discourse on the topic. The university management, however, hated the very idea of such a programme, and I was subject to a bizarre succession of harangues by the management. The executive dean of my faculty declared that I was bringing my department into disrepute. He couldn't articulate why. The speaker series, he also proclaimed, had nothing to do with war. The invincible ignorance of this statement (clashing understandings of social and cultural norms is the very foundation of war) was such that I told him he was speaking nonsense. He was furious at being contradicted, and never forgave me. The university's reaction was visceral rather than intellectual. A perfect metaphor, in fact, for what was going on inside these once venerable institutions.

Yet again, these kinds of run-ins that David and I had with authority left us curious rather than angry. Why was there this level of resistance to the concept of free expression, which should have been the core mission of the university to test ideas and extend the boundaries of knowledge? Unhappily, the answer was that academia had become infected by a secular religious intolerance of a kind that wouldn't look much out of place in Mao's China. The university wasn't a liberal project anymore because many people who staffed them weren't committed to the principles of liberal discourse. Inflexible, dull-witted, risk-averse managers occupied one end of the staffing spectrum. Then there were the shallow careerists who would go along with any outlandish doctrine so long as they might prosper. Of course, there were the 'quietists', the hope-the-crocodile-will-eat-me-last types, who constituted the majority. At the other, far end of the spectrum were the progressive ideologues, usually upper or middle class and privately educated, who formed a loud, activist minority. The latter group was always able to browbeat the three former groups into submission.

It intrigued us that this latter group of progressivists and their ciphers in the media often sought to deny the existence of a 'culture war', arguing that the very thought was a figment of the frenzied imagination of the 'far right'. This ignored the fact that *kulturkampf* (cultural struggle) was thoroughly embedded in European, particularly Germanic, ideas of politics from the nineteenth century onwards. Such ideas also connected with a much longer tradition of iconoclasm going back hundreds if not thousands of years. The critical theory of the so-called Frankfurt School of Marxism was, moreover, explicitly focused on cultural critique from the 1930s onwards. Anyone with even the most fleeting of contact with the Western arts and humanities subjects could scarcely avoid having to wade through a mass of obscure Marxist influenced aesthetic, educational, philosophical and literary theory: from Walter Benjamin and György Lukács, to Berthold Brecht and Michel Foucault.

In other words, the entire construct of European Marxist thought was premised on cultural struggle. This is why European intellectuals were so enamoured with the ideology of Mao Zedong, who elevated culture war to an explicit practice during the Great Proletarian Cultural Revolution from 1966 to 1976. Maoist thinking began permeating Western discourse from the late 1960s through a generation of French, or French based, Marxist thinkers who were inspired by the Cultural Revolution. Many of them travelled to China in the late 1960s and early 1970s to experience the joyous spectacle of culture war in action. Their epigone gradually made their way through the halls of academe, introducing two generations of graduates to fundamentally Maoist ideas of thought reform, from which modern notions of political correctness and culture war spring.

The fruits of their labours were to manifest in the summer of 2020, which demonstrated a distinct lineage in thinking and action between the image breaking of the Chinese Cultural Revolution and the violence perpetrated during the so-called Black Lives Matter (BLM) riots across the United States, Britain and elsewhere. More insidiously, the spirit of Maoism revealed itself in a species of cultural nihilism that overwhelmed the institutions of the West, spreading out from the universities to museums and schools, to health providers and the civil service. The corrupting influence of this ideology even began infecting the police and armed forces. None of this, if one understands anything about the Maoist inflected radical left, was intended to make the world better or improve the life-chances of anyone in society. It is what it was *always* intended to be: a way to gain power. It is a power play to divide people, often along racial lines. The aim is precisely to create a 'land of hatred' over which a new political elite is only too happy to preside.

As the essays in this chapter reveal, Western self-negation of the kind exhibited in 2020 did not arise out of nowhere but had been festering away for decades. For those who cared to look, it was evident for years before in many manifestations of Western cultural life. David and I were interested in how the arts had reacted to the events of 9/11 and its extended aftermath of the 'war on terror'. Our explorations in this area found much that was disturbing. In novels, films, television dramas and museum exhibitions the full panoply of Western self-loathing was on display from the early 2000s onwards. Aside from some valid critique of the post-9/11 surveillance state, much else was critical theory inspired relativism that seemed to relish the prospect of Western cultural suicide.

The authoritarianism inherent in this elite guided collective self-destruction came into plain sight during the so-called COVID-19 era. We were immediately sceptical of the need for (middle-class) lockdowns, vaccine mandates, the parade of incoherent rules, the imposition on the public of a bullying health despotism, the vast wastage of financial resources, and the numerous other social harms inflicted upon the population. These were assaults upon the very concept of a free society and the attempts to twist the principles of liberalism to serve an authoritarian agenda were, in our view, especially worrisome.

If the following essays, which examine these cultural straws in the wind, exhibit a more pessimistic vision of the West, David and I saw the possibilities for the recuperation of democratic traditions and Western self-belief in an evolving idea of 'transpolitics'. We were not talking gender here, but of the prospects for a political realignment that transcended notions of 'left' and 'right', in favour of the 'people' against the 'elites'. The final essay in this chapter surveys this evolving phenomenon, as the one hope for escaping the fate of all those who have had the misfortune to experience the doubtful joys of a Maoist inspired cultural revolution.

When ideology displaces reason

Anyone who has endured a university seminar series devoted to exposing the failings of the West, its racist and sexist 'othering' of non-Western cultures and its complicity with the evils of capitalism, will open Melanie Phillips's new book, *The World Turned Upside Down*, with a mixture of relief and foreboding. Relief that an award-winning London-based journalist like Phillips understands the extent of what she terms 'the intelligentsia's' betrayal of the core Western values of freedom and reason. Foreboding at the implications of this betrayal for the survival of the Western, secular, democratic project.

Phillips came to prominence with her exposure of how radical Islamism had permeated the United Kingdom and transformed 'Londonistan' into the epicentre of Islamic militancy in Europe. She now turns her attention to the larger question of whether Western civilisation actually wants to defend reason and modernity any more or 'whether it has reached a point where it has stopped trying to survive'.

The prognosis is not good. As Phillips explains, her growing perplexity and cultural disorientation arose from the fact that 'public discourse has departed sharply from reality'. Thus, over a range of contemporary issues from the war on terror to manmade global warming as well 'as the phobias and isms' like homophobia, racism and sexism, the intelligentsia, aided and abetted by a compliant media, has radically circumscribed public debate. Increasingly, as anyone teaching in an Australian university knows, there can be no dissent from a ruling, grant-supported orthodoxy that is incontrovertibly true and right.

Except of course that it is not. How is it, Phillips rightly asks, that the academy that ostensibly stands for freedom and reason has perverted its constituting understanding? Modern universities, after all, developed as 'crucibles of reason and the supreme guardians of free inquiry and debate'. When universities persecute those who dissent from what Hannah Arendt termed the 'tyranny of the single truth', a shocking betrayal of academic integrity and the values of a free society has taken place. Phillips traces – with a classic journalistic regard for the facts rather than fashionable academic and media shibboleths – how systemic distortion, antithetical to both reason and truth, has prevailed in the academy.

Using a series of well-researched case studies upon subjects as diverse as global warming, the war in Iraq, the treatment of Israel, and the science informing a neo-Darwinian atheism, she uncovers a disturbing intellectual practice that perverts reason, logic and evidence in favour of irrationality, prejudice and ideology. So much is this the case that on these issues 'the Western mind has been closed tightly shut'.

Beginning with anthropogenic global warming, Phillips discloses a pattern of denial and distortion that renders the case for the human contribution to global warming at best questionable and at worst unsustainable. Yet, troublingly, revelations of the systematic distortion of evidence perpetrated, *inter alia*, by the Climatic Research Unit of the University of East Anglia and the United Nations International Panel on Climate Change do not lead to a properly scientific conclusion that new facts have falsified and rendered obsolete a once-plausible thesis. Instead, a consensus of grant-supported climate scientists resort to hysterical claims concerning the planet's imminent demise adumbrated by increasingly shrill denunciations of those who deny their incontrovertible truth. Myth posturing as science has prevailed.

Phillips detects an analogous pattern of denial in those who, like Richard Dawkins, promote an atheistic materialism as the only proper basis of scientific inquiry. For Phillips, this attempt to prove the non-existence of God leads paradoxically to the province of unfounded assertions and the promotion of scientism rather than science. In their refusal to accept the scientific limits of materialism, neo-Darwinists share with global warmists a propensity to Soviet-era

Lysenkoism (after the Soviet geneticist Trofim Lysenko), where a forcibly instilled illusion takes on an existence of its own in people's minds, despite all evidence to the contrary. Doubting Darwinian materialism or climate change invokes penalties for deviationism not dissimilar to those enforced in the old Soviet academy: denunciation, loss of tenure and ostracism.

Distortion and mythmaking characterised the media treatment of the war in Iraq. Here Phillips contends that selective reporting created an orthodoxy that the coalition went to war on a lie. Not only claiming that Saddam had presented no threat, the intelligentsia, in the face of widespread evidence to the contrary, further maintained that the West confronted 'no systemic terrorist threat at all'.

The process of misrepresentation extended after the demise of Saddam to the misrepresentation of Israel and the treatment of Palestine. Here the intelligentsia bought the Arab-Muslim narrative about Palestine and presented a conflict, subjected to an unprecedented level of scrutiny, in a way that drives out inconvenient facts. Thus, the media downplays the fact of a Jewish presence in Palestine since 1300 BC, and ignores the fact that Israel is the only functioning democracy in the Middle East, whilst tired myths about the Israeli occupation and the treatment of the Palestinians are endlessly recycled. The media holds Israel, uniquely amongst states created since 1945, accountable to a different standard of public morality despite being engaged in an existential struggle for its survival.

The intelligentsia, Phillips contends, has swung behind an anti-Israel, pro-Third World ideology. In the process it has come to empathise with an Islamist view of Israel which, following the paranoid vision of the central Islamist thinker Sayyid Qutb, presents the Jew as the virus that incubated the 'hideous schizophrenia' of Western modernity. This Islamist view, as Phillips shows, obviously shares an elective affinity with Nazism. Equally, she contends, anti-Israeli sentiment in the West disguises an anti-Semitism 'incubated in the supposed citadel of reason: the university'. Here, the work of the Palestinian-American theorist Edward Said exercises an extraordinary hold over the academic mind. Said held that an orientalist agenda to colonise the non-Western 'other' informed all ostensibly objective Western scholarship of Eastern society. This conspiracy theory posturing as critical theory now dominates the academic treatment of the Middle East and feeds the 'frenzy of falsification, selective reporting, moral inversion, historical fabrication, and bad faith' that characterises it.

Phillips concludes from her case studies that the consistent misrepresentation of Israel crystallises a wider Western self-loathing which permeates the intelligentsia's worldview. This ideology, masquerading as cutting-edge research and facilitated by large grants, is in fact unstitching the fabric of Western society as it undermines the pursuit of objective knowledge.

Phillips's answer to her initial perplexity therefore is that ideology has replaced reason and the disinterested pursuit of truth and has corrupted the Western project of modernity. This process, she further contends, has evolved since the Enlightenment first launched its radical assault on traditional modes of understanding and experience. Indeed, it was the enlightenment that gave birth to the intelligentsia in the shape of the *philosophes* who initially proposed to recast society along abstract, rationalist lines. The rationalist style ruthlessly subordinated evidence to an unchallengeable idea. This style influenced both the Jacobins and the post-Hegelian thinkers that gave philosophic substance to nineteenth-century historicism, romanticism and Marxism. From these ideological seeds the totalitarian movements of the twentieth century germinated.

In the pursuit of this worldly utopia, fascism, Stalinism and Maoism not only consigned those deemed unworthy to the gulag or the death camp, but they also inculcated a millenarian fervour in their adherents. By a curious irony, the rational ideological project required a distorted form of faith to sustain it. The totalitarian form in fact constituted a political religion, and the new faith had to be rigidly policed. As with contemporary Islamism, the European totalitarians of the twentieth century proposed a Manichean division of humanity into the saved and the damned. This soteriology, which informs contemporary Islamism, scientism, and environmentalism, has no place for alternative views. It also induces a narcissistic self-regard in those who share the utopian vision. As Phillips relays:

> this agenda of self-regard is the key to unlocking the mystery that has dogged us from the beginning... how people who profess to be so rational they will have no truck with religion have nevertheless embraced beliefs and attitudes that defy reason

Despite the conspicuous failure of the twentieth-century totalitarian projects, the cast of thought that brooks no dissent continues in the new red-green-Islamic axis that pervades Western academe. Central to its success has been its assault upon the Judeo-Christian order that sustained the conditions for political pluralism and the disinterested pursuit of reason from the Middle Ages to the Enlightenment.

The crux of Phillips's argument, then, is that the new, post-modern, political religions have fatally eroded the Judeo-Christian order that provided the moral foundation for the success of Western modernity. This order constituted the crucible that forged the capacity for reason and freedom. The post-Enlightenment attack upon this framework, adumbrated by the philosophically relativist assault on Western values, has not in fact created a more rational, pluralist, or critical awareness. Rather, the relativising nihilism of post-modernism created the conditions for new ideologies of a cultist or utopian dispensation to flourish. Islamism, multiculturalism and environmentalism informed by a chiliastic millenarian purpose seek to transform the failed and messy secular democratic polity. From this perspective, however, the future belongs to ideology whether in an Islamist, multiculturalist or an environmentalist manifestation or in some post-capitalist, post-apocalyptic amalgam. But, before the imminent future transforms the corrupt present, the new world, aching to be born, exists in dualistic tension with the old. To maintain purity the ideologist must have no truck with those who dissent or cavil at the revealed truth of the Koran, the collective wisdom of the IPCC, or Dawkinite atheism.

The new order, therefore, has not lost the need for certitude or salvation. Instead, the narcissistic self-regard of gnostic cults has progressively corrupted and replaced Judeo-Christianity. In this brave new post-Christian spiritual world those who believe in Wicca, Islam or an *Avatar*-style fantasy world have the same faith claim as those who subscribe to the doctrines of the Christian church. Indeed, the decaying Anglican faith, as Phillips nicely demonstrates, embraces a New Age apocalyptic message. Thus, an Anglican celebration of faith and the environment held at Canterbury Cathedral witnessed a performance of an oratorio, *Yanomamo*, based on the beliefs of Amazon rainforest Indians. It is no surprise that Phillips finds the United Kingdom media and intelligentsia at the forefront of promoting the post-Western order, the global laundry for recycling anti-Semitic views, and the 'brand leader' in the assault on Western values.

This is a powerful and original thesis, but how sustainable is Phillips's argument? Clearly there is something culturally deracinating about the intelligentsia's assault upon Western values and Phillips makes a convincing case for its essentially ideological character. However, in mounting the conservative argument in favour of the importance of the Judeo-Christian order, Phillips makes some curious claims about the evolution and political character of that order. Certainly, it is reasonable to propose that this order, and the theological inquiry into the relationship between reason and faith it facilitated, provided the context for the development of the political conditions that made possible the practices of thought that came to define the West. However, from at least the thirteenth century, the universal Catholic Church existed in dynamic tension with an alternative Greco-Roman approach to knowledge, politics and public morality. The politico-theological clash over the limits of religion informed by the reinterrogation of the classical thought of Plato, Aristotle and Cicero during the Renaissance and the Reformation created the conditions for the emergence of the modern state, a new civic humanist public morality and the practice of freedom. Significantly, Aristotle, Cicero and their political and scientific legacy hardly rate a mention. By contrast, the twelfth-century Talmudic thinker Moses Maimonides occupies, in the Phillips view, a central place in defining the Western relationship between faith and reason.

Somewhat differently, to demonstrate the shared authoritarian style of the intelligentsia, Phillips tends to lump thinkers and ideologies together where she should perhaps discriminate between them. The differences between the materialistic atheism of Dawkins and the Koranically-inspired Manicheanism of Qutb are more apparent than the similarities in these styles of thought. Ultimately, despite Phillips's insistence on the centrality of religion to the achievement of Western modernity, an atheist like Christopher Hitchens or Richard Dawkins would have little in common with the habits of thought and practice of either environmentalists, Islamists or multiculturalists.

Analogously, in her somewhat attenuated account of the British and European Enlightenment, thinkers as distinctive as Francis Bacon and G.W.F. Hegel are conflated into a reductionist, materialist and relativist narrative. Bacon, we are told, somewhat anachronistically, was an ideologist, whilst Hegel held that 'nothing was wholly false or wholly true'. Yet in both his *Lectures on the Philosophy of World History* and his *Philosophy of Right* Hegel not only identified a dialectical relationship between the particular and the universal, but he also acknowledged in his theoretical understanding of the Western achievement of reason and freedom, a complex dialectical relationship between classical and Christian ideas.

These limitations notwithstanding, Phillips has written an important and powerful polemic. Its strength resides in its exposure of the manner in which the academic establishment has embraced an ideological style that has corrupted both scholarship and ethics. A cultural revolution has occurred, and Phillips explores it with great skill. As she explains, we now find ourselves in a world where institutions formally committed to learning and scholarship have been reduced to a darkling plain were ignorant armies clash by night.

Soft-totalitarian understandings have, as she convincingly demonstrates, also come to constrain political conduct. They are premised on a cultural relativism where all values are treated equally. The self-regarding intelligentsia has thus come to assume that subscribing absolutely to its new ethnicism is somehow progressive when in many ways it endorses an absolutist retreat into tribalism. As Phillips tellingly concludes:

> the correspondence between Western progressives and Islamists is really quite remarkable. Both are attempting to create utopias in order to redeem past sins; both permit no dissent from the revealed truth; both demonize and seek to suppress their opponents; both project their own bad behaviour onto others; both are consumed by paranoid conspiracy theories... Both have ended up suppressing freedom and imposing a tyranny of the mind.

A work as provocatively conservative as this could not have been produced in an Australian or British university.

Original article published in *Quadrant*, 4th October 2010, by David Martin Jones.

College of fear

Google up 'free-speech crisis on campus' and its 'Machine Learning Fairness' algorithm will serve up a long list of articles from outlets like *The Guardian*, *The Independent* and *Vox*, denying that there is any free-speech crisis. Moreover, if you consider both the written law and the formal statements of the universities on the protection of freedom of expression, one might be forgiven for thinking, where is the problem? Indeed, the declaratory policies around free speech on campus sound very good. But there is a problem, which is that the reality in practice is often very different from the stated good intentions.

In the United States the First Amendment offers formal constitutional protection for freedom of expression. In the United Kingdom, the 1986 Education Act articulates an explicit obligation on universities. 'Lawful free speech', the Act proclaims, 'should never be prevented on campus'.

Fine sounding statements from the university authorities themselves reinforce these legal and constitutional frameworks. The University of Cambridge states that it is 'fully committed to the principle, and to the promotion of freedom of expression'. Oxford University declares that 'Free speech is the lifeblood of a university. It enables the pursuit of knowledge. It helps us approach the truth'.

My own institution, King's College London, declares that it has a 'strong commitment to the values of freedom of expression, freedom of thought, freedom of conscience and religion and freedom of assembly and we want to offer the widest possible opportunity for the free expression of knowledge and ideas...' It also claims to be inspired by the 'Chicago Principles', which are intended to demonstrate a robust commitment to these noble ideals.

The gap between rhetoric and reality
Digging beneath the surface of these proclamations, however, reveals a gap between the rhetorical commitment to the principles of free speech and the operational practice, which far from opening up the space for inquiry often seeks to restrict viewpoint plurality or sometimes even to close down avenues of expression altogether.

Between 2018 and 2019 I ran a speaker series aimed at re-vitalising the discourse around freedom of thought and viewpoint plurality to explore the dimensions of the so-called culture war. Entitled 'Endangered speeches: Debating the culture wars' it was an explicitly academic endeavour. It was initiated, mainly, because many students I spoke to were deeply interested in the subject and wished to discuss these matters overtly. Secondly, I have had an abiding academic interest in the social origins of war, which has formed a principal research interest of mine for some three decades. War as a phenomenon does not emerge out of nothing. It grows out of multiple social origins. War begins in the mind long before it manifests itself as any kind of physical struggle.

To be clear, this speaker series was no freelancing operation. It was carefully planned months in advance by the professional events team within my department of which I was Head at the time. All the organisational formalities, including risk assessments, were complied with. The events were officially advertised for many weeks beforehand on the university's website.

The speaker series ran for two sessions. The events passed off well, with no incidents. The discussions were civil, the debates were calm, often humorous and good-natured on all sides. Those in attendance emerged, one deduced, enlightened and stimulated. What was intriguing, however, was not the events themselves but the university's curious, illogical, reaction.

Two days before the first event a student led petition was raised to get the invited speaker cancelled. The invited guest was a respected academic educationalist who had written an excellent book on conformity in academia. The petition alleged, erroneously, that the speaker had made offensive anti-transgender remarks in their previous writings and should therefore be disinvited.

The petition gathered a meagre 144 signatures (including signees from outside the institution), representing, at most, perhaps no more than 0.2 percent of the university's staff and student body. Regardless of how risibly small it was, the petition startled the university authorities. Apparently, emergency meetings at the highest levels were convened (without my knowledge as the event organiser). Extra security was laid on.

In the end, security was not required. Nothing happened. Everyone enjoyed a perfectly respectful discussion, which was the precise intent of the series. On the surface, then, the university held the line against the insidious forces of 'cancel culture': so far so very good.

Beneath the veneer of academic integrity, a very different story was taking shape. The following day, I was on the receiving end of an incoherent outburst from the faculty executive dean. It was unclear what precisely he was trying to convey apart from some vague accusation that I brought my department into disrepute. Quite why was left unexplained.

The following week I was summoned to a formal meeting with this same faculty dean and my immediate manager, who engaged in another unintelligible harangue. For the sin of holding this speaker series, I was accused of being simultaneously both naïve and disingenuous (if someone can tell me how you can be both at same time, I shall be interested to learn). To this day I haven't a clue as to what precisely was bothering them, other than a feeling that they were incensed that anyone should show any independent initiative.

Following this bizarre set of meetings, there came more measured and polite invitations from the university's senior administrative personnel to discuss the legal and policy frameworks around speaking events. These invitations were issued and then postponed. Emails I sent seeking to re-arrange such meetings went unanswered. No meetings, in the end, were held. Thus, I remained none the wiser as to what the university's overarching position towards speaking events and freedom of speech actually was.

How universities end up privileging the powerful

Why do I recite these somewhat surreal events? Because they caused me to set about analysing why a precept that, to me at least, seems obvious – the idea of the university as a project to advance knowledge and understanding through freedom of expression and viewpoint plurality – was held so equivocally by the very people one might expect would, or should, be its most enthusiastic defenders.

My deliberations led me to conclude that the lofty rhetoric about promoting freedom of thought disguised a paradox at the heart of the free speech debate on campus, namely that ultimately universities end up promoting the very opposite ethos of that which they supposedly exist to uphold. As will be elucidated, the paradox is revealed only when one uncovers the layers of ambiguity that obscure the gap between the rhetoric and practice of free expression. These layers exist at several levels:

Ambiguities in the law

While the United States enjoys constitutional protection for free speech in the form of the First Amendment, various laws in countries like the UK act to delineate a number of legal boundaries. Laws against incitement to violence, racial hatred and threatening and abusive behaviour, function to restrict certain forms of written and spoken thought. Legal rulings and precedents around free speech, which are governed by common law rights, add to the ambivalence. The British legal tradition of free speech rotates around the views of eighteenth-century jurist Sir William Blackstone, and expressed in his *Commentaries on the Laws of England*, which emphasise lack of prior restraint. That is, one does not have to receive permission to speak your mind (from the government, the lord of the manor, your employer, etc.). It does not mean, however, that the individual enjoys protection from the consequences of one's speech from existing legal codes against, say, sedition, defamation and blasphemy. At the outset, then, in defending free speech on campus the absolute right to freedom of expression is circumscribed and forms the wedge via which anti-free speech advocates exploit to hinder discussion of views with which they disagree. In Britain, the Equality Act (2010), for example, allows student groups and university administrators to argue that they have a legal duty to bar speakers who threaten the 'safety' of vulnerable groups.

Ambiguities in statements of universities

Formal legal inhibitions enable university authorities to couch their own regal statements within imprecise terminology. Examining the declarations of universities reveals that worthy sounding rhetoric on free speech is hedged by all manner of qualifications: a word or an expression snuck in here and there that ultimately gives licence to restrict the avenues for open debate.

My own institution, for example, states that it 'cares deeply about how we manage Freedom of Expression'. Those two words 'we' and 'manage' make all the difference. Who is 'we'? And what does 'manage' mean? The answers to those questions will determine whether there is a permissive or a controlled speech environment, especially when university declarations on free speech segue into pronouncements that individuals should also enjoy a 'right to freedom from hate' (King's College London), or that the aim of the university 'is to provide a tolerant and equitable context in which knowledge is acquired' (Sussex University). Laudable sentiments may be, but such caveating introduces wide latitude for interpretation that those who are uninterested in promoting viewpoint plurality can use to 'manage' away any meaningful understanding of free speech.

Risk aversion

The financialisaton of the higher education sector emphasises the search for greater 'surpluses' (i.e. profits), mainly from the exploitation of fee-paying students. The result is that universities come to privilege 'brand' management over loyalty to an academic ethos that extols the virtues of open debate and free expression. The spread of corporatism throughout higher education, obsessed as it is with income and metrics, has produced a managerial elite lacking in sympathy with the idea of the university as a liberal project. Freedom to debate is thus evaluated not as a primary role of the university, something to cherish and be protected, but as a potential source of controversy. Controversy is deemed bad for business – a reputational risk – and thus to be avoided. Risk aversion therefore looms large, making universities scared of anything that might result in negative publicity.

Risk displacement

'Managing' risk presents many opportunities to restrict the freedom of expression. Avoiding the problems that university managers associate with open-handed debate enables controversy to be shifted towards 'health and safety' concerns, and especially those centred on 'security'. Rather than deal with the difficulties related to the intellectual content, university managers can displace the risk into non-substantive matters, which provide easy rationales to frustrate free speech. At a mundane level this may involve form filling and 'risk assessments'. More egregiously, some institutions can impose insurance or security costs on the event organisers or ask for speakers' remarks to be vetted.

While it may seem sensible to have due diligence processes in advance of speaking events such procedures are not only daunting, especially for student societies, but they give off an air of menace, as if seeking to hold normal discussion is somehow dangerous. Accentuating 'risk', moreover, incentivises anti-free speech ideologues to stoke up prior publicity against any speaker of whom they disapprove as 'high risk'. The cumulative effect is to discourage and demotivate those who might wish to engage in the freedom to debate ideas.

Lack of enforcement of disciplinary codes
Many of the barriers to speaking events are instigated by students' unions, which exploit risk factors to get speakers cancelled. Too often university authorities adopt a passive, stand-off, attitude towards what are clearly politically prejudiced attempts to prohibit viewpoints from being heard. Vacillating before vocal and ideologically motivated efforts to revoke speaker invitations stretches into temporising before those who physically disrupt and break-up speaking events or use threatening behaviours to intimidate event organisers. Rarely, if ever, are perpetrators called to account even if they violate university codes on bullying and harassment. Frequently university authorities will cite the intimidation tactics of political activists as constituting their right to protest while allowing those individuals or groups that wish only to engage in debate to swing in the wind. The result is an un-level playing field tilted in favour of those who seek to constrict the discussion of different viewpoints.

Informal sanctioning
Many of the factors mentioned so far culminate in one particularly salutary truth, which is that a sizeable proportion of academics agree with restrictions on free speech. They have little problem curtailing views that they deem to be unacceptable and 'offensive'. This would comport to my understanding in organising the 'Endangered speeches' series where on four occasions in the space of a year I found myself explaining to very senior academic staff what the point of a university was: a forum for, you know, encouraging free and independent thinking, promoting debate on different points of view, and so on. Yet, this notion of a university was unknown to them. The level of obtuseness encountered in trying to relay what to me seemed this most basic of concepts was such that I wondered whether I was intentionally being gaslighted or whether they really were naïve hatchlings: it was like explaining to a two year old that zoos were for exhibiting animals or that airports were places where planes land and take-off.

The degree of ideological alignment with the anti-free speech agenda underlines how many contemporary academics perceive themselves not as facilitators of thought but as curators of 'acceptable' opinion. The origins of this disposition inside the universities are complex but reflects the now well-documented decline of viewpoint plurality among academics who default overwhelmingly to the centre/hard left, and to a consequent quasi-religious belief that they are the embodiment of pure reason. That this temperament corresponds precisely to the policing of thought appears not to bother them.

Whatever the causes, the practical effect is the informal sanctioning of ideas, interpretations and analyses that clash with this 'thought policing' mindset. The lowest level of sanctioning can take the form of bureaucratic obstructionism, for example, university departments refusing to publicise student sponsored speaking events, which they discern as 'problematic'. More seriously it can shade-off into brow beating, social exclusion and – in classic thought police mode – the denunciation of wrong think to higher authority and punitive measures being exacted, ranging from the expulsion of students from their degree programmes or academic members of staff being removed from administrative positions.

The rise of the anti-university and out-of-boundary markers
What much of this boils down to is that institutions of higher learning are imbricated in various levels of fear – fear of upsetting the feelings of students, fear of negative publicity, fear of reputational damage, fear of damaging career progression, fear of loss of prestige, fear of losing income.

It all builds into an ultimate irony: the fear of discussion, the fear of being creative, the fear of taking intellectual risks, the fear of independent ideas... the fear of thinking... the fear of opening one's mouth. That's why I was on the receiving end of such confused and incomprehensible diatribes from university bureaucrats, because they embodied this perfect storm of contradiction

Universities exist, in theory, to extend the boundaries of knowledge and understanding through the freedom to experiment with ideas. In practice, however, the modern, corporately driven higher education sector pushes universities in the very opposite direction of these values. The university is now the anti-university. Trying to articulate a defence of this edifice thus has a deranging effect on the academic managers charged with upholding its contradictory imperatives who are reduced to berating wrong thinking mavericks in the most Kafkaesque of terms (such as being accused of being naïve and disingenuous at the same time).

Fear, then, often lies at the centre of the paradox of the anti-university, because without fear it would not be able to function. Fear is the only way that these contradictions can be obscured and people warned off questioning them. The way this fear is promoted is through a classic authoritarian play of out-of-boundary markers. The free speech boundary is seemingly wide and articulated through a rhetorical commitment to academic freedom. You have the *theoretical* right to speak your mind, but so long as you don't stray outside the boundaries of acceptability prescribed by both by legal constraints and caveats about hate-speech and preserving an atmosphere of 'tolerance'. Yet, and here is the authoritarian trick, the boundaries are never defined in any concrete manner.

Undefined boundary markers leave people uncertain and fearful. Just like all overbearing systems past and present, the authoritarian proclivities of the corporate university maintain control through the promotion of uncertainty and bureaucratisation. Step across an unspecified boundary and you will be informally sanctioned: you will be called in to be rebuked for no clear reason by your managers, your career advancement will be jeopardised, you will be made to feel anxious about keeping your job. Fear is thus a very helpful tool. Thought policing is so much easier to accomplish when you can get people to police themselves.

The paradox of the modern university

We arrive, then, at the position of the modern university as an increasing paradox. Theoretically adhering to the principles of freedom of thought – in the same manner that the former East European communist states theoretically styled themselves as 'democratic' – the universities proceed to controvert the enlightened values that they supposedly exist to encourage. Like those very same totalitarian systems of old, they empower and enrich a risk averse and compliant *nomenklatura* that engages in double-speak and censorship. It is this group that decides what is 'high risk' or a 'safety' issue. They are the ones who interpret terms like 'how we manage freedom of expression' and the 'duty of care to our student community'. Just like the former communist societies of the East, the system nurtures the worst kinds of human conduct that incentivises the denunciation of people for wrongthink while rewarding those who demonstrate ideological conformity to official doctrines, particularly those under the contemporary rubric of 'diversity and inclusion'. In so doing they privilege those who shout the loudest, those who are the most assertive, and the least oppressed. Those, in other words, who are the most powerful.

Exactly like the European communist states of the past, the system marginalises and sanctions those who do not conform, creating a caste of dissidents. They are created in the same manner that Václav Havel described over forty years ago when he observed: 'You do not become a dissident just because you decide one day to take up this most unusual career. You are thrown into it by your personal sense of responsibility, combined with a complex set of external circumstances. You are cast out of the existing structures and placed in a position of conflict with them'. 'It begins', he notes, 'as an attempt to do your work well, and ends with being branded an enemy of society'.

Original article published in *Cieo*, 26th May 2020, by M.L.R. Smith.

The West's Maoist moment

In February 2017, the then Dean of Bristol Cathedral, The Very Reverend David Hoyle, announced his 'openness' to removing the Cathedral's largest stained-glass window because of its links to the prominent seventeenth century Bristol philanthropist, slave trader and deputy governor of the Royal African Company, Edward Colston. In the wake of the violent demonstrations in June 2020 against racism and the toppling of statues like Colston's, the Dean is doubtless even more open to removing his former Cathedral's window.

The demonstrations by Black Lives Matter (BLM), in the wake of the death of George Floyd at the hands of a police officer seeking to restrain him in the Democrat run city of Minneapolis in the United States, supercharged the campaign against Colston's legacy. The Bristol experience is one instalment in a movement originating in the US but with European connections to remove the stigma of slavery, colonialism and racism by taking down statues, renaming buildings on campuses and in public spaces, and 'decolonising' the secondary and tertiary curriculums.

Racism, racism everywhere
The BLM movement, which is a loose and decentralised collection of chapters and affiliates, sees institutional racism everywhere: in the structure of schools, universities, the media, business and across the public and private sectors of the capitalist system. In the United Kingdom it considers Winston Churchill a racist. It demands that Oriel College, Oxford, demolish its statue of the imperialist Cecil Rhodes. It favours the removal of the statue of Thomas Guy from the hospital he founded in London in 1720 with profits he made from investments in the South Sea Company, a company that also engaged in the slave trade. Across the Atlantic, BLM subjects institutions and public statues to similar exhortations and assaults. The prevailing ethical orthodoxy holds that 'opposition to slavery is dead simple. Slavery is wicked and evil'.

BLM ideology considers racism systemic and institutional. In one sense, BLM's advocates are correct, but not for the reasons they assume. Slavery *is* systemically embedded in the deep structure of world history. It is etched into the fabric of human experience. It has been this way since the dawn of civilisation. Slavery, moreover, has not always appeared wicked or evil. From ancient Babylon, Egypt and Rome to the Conquistadores in South America, the Ottoman Empire, Tsarist Russia and eighteenth and nineteenth century North America, slavery was the basis of economic and political development. Slave labour is still prevalent today. In China, its *laogai* (prison camps) enable Chinese enterprises to undercut the prices of its economic competitors, a facet of modernity that the designer clothes wearing, mobile phone carrying members of the BLM and Antifa crowds somewhat conveniently overlook. As some historians still appreciate, conquest, slavery and oppression mark the troubled origins of most empires in the non-Western as well as the Western world.

All human societies, Hannah Arendt wrote, begin in violence. Foundation myths acknowledge the fact: Cain slew Abel and Romulus killed Remus. These myths tell us that 'whatever political organization men have achieved has its origin in crime'. Recognising the fact that the establishment of the modern state order involved war and conquest should be central to any thoughtful, political self-awareness. The anachronistic imposition of a modern sensibility on the past and an impulse to remove its heritage from the present disables the very notion of informed historical inquiry.

Iconoclasm and anti-racism
The passionate fervour that informs BLM's anti-racist rhetoric is deliberately iconoclastic. Iconoclasm is a religious impulse that symbolically rejects and destroys cherished beliefs and images. Indeed, it was the iconoclasm and religious

fanaticism that characterised the seventeenth century English puritan movement that occasioned the installation of Edward Colston's stained glass window in Bristol Cathedral. The opportunity arose precisely because the millenarian enthusiasts of the English Civil War (1642-49) had smashed the original medieval window.

In its later twentieth century European evolution, iconoclasm assumed an ideological and racist idiom rather than a religious one. The Nazi conquest of Poland required the systematic destruction of historic sites associated with a racially inferior Jewish and Slavic culture. And in the twenty-first century, it played a seminal role in Islamic State's explicit policy outlined in its operating manual *The Management of Savagery* (2004) (by Abu Bakr Naji) in Syria and Iraq. In its pursuit of an Islamist utopia, Islamic State rejected any idolatrous (*shirk*) reverence for the past, particularly relics of the pre-Islamic era of *jahiliya* (state of ignorance). Islamic State revealed what this entailed after it captured the ancient Roman city of Palmyra, in March 2015. The very fact that the site featured on a list of United Nations approved World Heritage sites served as the incentive to destroy the artefacts of the pre-Islamic Greco-Roman inspired Palmyrene era.

Paradoxically, the international community denounced as barbaric Islamic State's cultural destruction in Palmyra, when it was a city, like almost all others of the period, built by slave labour. Islamic State, of course, is more violent than the BLM movement, but the strategy of destroying the past to build a purified tomorrow differs only in its utopian goal. Editing the past to meet the standards upheld either by Islamic State, the Third Reich or contemporary campus radicals represents an ideological attempt to kill history, and BLM is no different.

Waging cultural warfare
Ultimately, the recent penchant for image-breaking arising from BLM inspired protests, reflects the neglected impact of Maoism on both Western New Left and Islamist ideology from the late 1960s. Commentators have sometimes referenced the similarities between the statue protests in the West and the period of the Great Proletarian Cultural Revolution in China. Few, however, have dissected the direct and indirect intellectual connections between Mao Zedong's thinking and radical contemporary movements in Europe and North America.

The neglected genealogy of the Cultural Revolution that the BLM movement's, as well as the universities', eagerness to 'decolonise' their curriculums clearly needs recalling. Culture war, after all, represents one of the People's Republic's earliest exports to the West.

Islamic State's manual *The Management of Savagery* acknowledged the importance of Maoism, in a suitably Islamist guise, to its version of permanent revolution. Its advice on cultural warfare also informed the precursors of the Black Lives Matter movement, the student counter-cultural revolutionaries of 1968 who followed Mao's *Little Red Book* (1964) in their denunciation of the 'sugar coated bullets' of the bourgeoisie and the 'paper tiger' of US imperialism.

In the aftermath of the catastrophic failure of Mao's programme of forced industrialisation, the 'Great Leap Forward' between 1958 and 1962 that ended in mass starvation, Mao sought to silence criticism through the institution of a 'Great Proletarian Cultural Revolution'. Launched in the Spring of 1966 to revitalise the socialist spirit and refashion the state structure, the Cultural Revolution required a profound reconstitution of society that would touch the 'people to their very souls'. During the new revolutionary struggle, the masses would spiritually transform themselves and remould their objective social world.

Like its 1960s Western counter-cultural imitators, and its more recent evocation in the BLM movement, it was university and middle school students who first responded to the Maoist call to rebel against established authority. The chaos that subsequently engulfed China began at Beijing University, China's Oxbridge, in May 1966 when a junior philosophy lecturer, Nie Yuanzi, displayed a big character poster on the campus denouncing the university president and calling 'for all revolutionary intellectuals' to go into battle.

Encouraged by a June 1966 party decree postponing university entrance exams, student activists mounted political and eventually physical attacks on their 'reactionary' teachers and the courses they taught. Rallying under slogans like 'it is justified to rebel' and 'destruction before construction' these fanatics marched through cities and towns across the country following the Maoist injunction to destroy 'ghosts and monsters'. Maoist inspired student 'Red Guard' groups targeted 'the four olds' – old ideas, old culture, old customs, and old habits – that had corrupted the masses.

During the summer and autumn of 1966 millions of Red Guards waving copies of the Chairman's *Little Red Book*, ascribed with semi-magical power, campaigned to destroy all symbols of the feudal past and bourgeois influences in the present. Museums and homes were ransacked and old books and works of art destroyed. The students trashed everything from ancient Confucian texts to modern recordings of Beethoven. They gave new revolutionary names to street signs and buildings.

The revolution quickly moved from destroying culture to destroying people. The Red Guards arrested and paraded 'bad elements' through the streets. Forced to wear dunces' caps, these 'cow demons' were often physically as well as psychologically abused at 'struggle sessions' before they confessed their thought crimes at public rallies. Red Guards turned on anyone who had received a Western education and on any intellectual who could be charged with 'feudal' or 'reactionary' thought.

Academics and teachers bore the brunt of the violence. The lucky ones got away with self-criticism and a humiliating process of self-rectification. Those less fortunate, like the Chinese playwright, Lao She, died at the hands of the mob after their houses were pillaged and their books burned.

In *The Search for Modern China* (1990), Jonathan Spence wrote that embedded within this frenzied activism was a political agenda of 'purist egalitarianism'. It involved much more than the confiscation of private property. It required the total transformation of the self to achieve mass revolutionary consciousness. The resulting anarchy was only resolved, ultimately, with the death of Mao and his replacement by the more pragmatic Deng Xiaoping.

Killing history: Mao and cultural revolution in the West
Mao's cultural revolution, however, went down well with the increasingly radical student movements that swept Western university campuses in 1968 protesting against America's imperialist war in Vietnam. Mimicking their Maoist contemporaries the students also denounced 'reactionary' lecturers and organised campus sit-ins to raise consciousness. Mao's *Little Red Book* and a poster of Che Guevara became essential radical artefacts. Some took it beyond a fashion statement. Mao's thinking informed the urban guerrilla tactics of the Red Brigades in Italy, the Baader-Meinhof Gang in West Germany and the Angry Brigade in Britain.

Contemporaneously, in the US, the Black Panthers Party called for Black Power to 'off the pig' (kill the police) and solidarity against 'the [white] man'. They received encouragement from a new generation of Mao-inspired academic enthusiasts like Angela Davis, protégé of Frankfurt School critical theorist Herbert Marcuse, whose unopened copy of *One-Dimensional Man* (1964), the other Little Read Book of the age, could also be found on any self-respecting radical student's bookshelf. One of the Panthers' early leaders, Eldridge Cleaver, considered Mao 'a bad ass motherfucker'. The Afro hairstyle, the clenched fist salute and the cult of violence that Panthers like Huey Newton, H. Rap Brown and Bobby Seale embraced, also made them radically chic adornments at celebrity Upper West Side parties held by the likes of Leonard Bernstein, memorably satirised by Tom Wolfe in his 1970 *New York* magazine article, 'Radical Chic: That party at Lenny's'.

In their own time, unlike the current BLM movement, the counter-culture protests had minimal impact on the West's domestic politics. The urban guerrillas were hunted down ruthlessly by Western democratic governments, whether conservative or social democrat. Members of the Black Panthers, Red Brigades and Red Army Faction ended up in gaol or dead. Yet the memory lingered on, especially in the universities. Mao's *cultural*, as opposed to an economic, approach to revolution influenced the anti-capitalist endeavours of Frankfurt School critical theory and fuelled a generation of French thinkers like Pierre Bourdieu, Michel Foucault and Jean Baudrillard who treated all knowledge as power and found in Maoism the means to deconstruct prevailing power relations and allow the repressed 'subaltern' voice to speak.

The French connection

Deconstructing the epistemic foundations of Western civilisation, the genealogical precursor to its 'decolonisation', reflected radical French academic interest in Mao's philosophy, first outlined in his 1937 tracts *On Contradiction* and *On Practice* as 'a new and novel social and political force in the second half of the twentieth century'. Mao had revealed the 'almost invisible kernel' in Lenin's analysis of imperialism, wrote Philippe Sollers, and developed its implications 'in an entirely original manner'.

The influential radical French philosophical and political journal *Tel Quel* (*As Is*) broke with French Communist Party orthodoxy, which extolled participation in electoral politics, embracing instead Maoist ideas of cultural struggle and permanent revolution in 1971. Under the editorial guidance of Sollers, *Tel Quel* disseminated Maoist thought across Europe. The journal featured the early writings of radical feminists like Julia Kristeva and Hélène Cixous, the semiologist Roland Barthes, and the philosophers Jacques Derrida and Michel Foucault.

The *Tel Quel* group visited China in 1974 and published a special edition celebrating the transformative effects of the Cultural Revolution. According to Sollers, the Chinese revolution had successfully combined 'a living millenarian culture with a revolutionary theory and practice that is rightly passionate'. Julia Kristeva, meanwhile, discovered that Chinese women in their anti-Confucius and Four Olds campaigns had achieved a passionate liberation that far surpassed anything in Western feminism.

Deconstructing the West

Under French influence, after 1968, revolutionary élan moved decisively from the control of the means of production to culture and identity. By the 1980s, given the total economic failure of Soviet and Chinese communism, the Maoist inspired deconstructive turn in thought became a form of radical intellectual self-defence, but it also fitted with a more traditional Marxist imperative to undermine any vestigial admiration for Western civilisation.

The deconstruction of Western culture, a distinctive feature of humanities and social science scholarship at the end of the Cold War, progressively relativised core democratic political understandings, exposing constitutional freedom and the rule of law as modes of control: a tolerant façade concealing a brutal genealogy of Western power. During the post-Cold War period this essentially post-historical, critical, 'reading' became the default position for the academic understanding of Western civilisation.

The long wars in Afghanistan and Iraq, the financial crisis after 2008, identity politics and the rise of so-called populism, provided the cultural theorising practiced on university campuses as well as the mainstream media with material for further cultural struggle. The COVID-19 pandemic, and the frustrating economic and social lockdown that ensued, created an environment ripe for riot and rebellion. George Floyd's death provided the spark for the latest Maoist style protest and its bonfire of Western icons.

Mao's influence is evident in the BLM's UK manifesto guided as it is 'by a commitment to dismantle imperialism, capitalism, white supremacy and the state structures that disproportionately harm black people'. In *On Contradiction*, Mao wrote: 'contradiction and struggle are universal and absolute, but the methods for solving contradictions differ according to the differences in the nature of the contradictions'. The revolutionary must use 'the contradictory aspects in every process'.

According to this formula 'the revolutionary' adjusts practice to contingent social conditions. This might require attacking capitalism at the level of its cultural rather than its economic or material foundations. The formula proved particularly attractive to what philosopher Bernard-Henri Lévy termed the Zombie left, which since 2003 has conducted revolution through culture war whilst dismissing the wealth, tolerance and opportunity afforded by an open democratic market economy.

Operating within this Maoist framework critical race theory, which animates groups like BLM, presents world history as a dialectical struggle between a systemic white racism upholding the capitalist order and an anti-racism that identifies the black race as the universal victim of oppression. Race conflict replaces class conflict in this political melodrama.

The leading contemporary exponent of this melodrama in an anti-racist idiom, Ibram X. Kendi, considers the world divided between racists and anti-racists. In *How To Be An Antiracist* (2019) he explains: 'One either endorses the idea of a racial hierarchy as a racist or racial equality as an antiracist'. Racism is all pervasive. Kendi writes that there are many forms of racism: there is class racism, which conflates blackness with poverty, as well as gender racism, queer racism, and 'space racism', where people associate black neighbourhoods with violence. In the case of education, black students may on average achieve lower scores on standardised tests and drop out of high school at higher rates, but such metrics are themselves institutionally racist, devised to 'degrade' and 'exclude' black students.

In an analogous vein, Robin DiAngelo, the white critical discourse theorist and a leading exponent of 'bias awareness', asserts that white people exercise 'collective social and institutional power and privilege over people of color'. In *White Fragility* (2018) she also reduces humanity to two categories: white and other. Since white people exercise 'institutional power', only people of colour can speak truth to power in this relationship.

From this Manichaean perspective we must necessarily choose a side. Indifference is not an option. Those failing to identify with BLM, whether white or black, are by that fact racist. None of these propositions, it should be stated, are based on the rigorous development of arguments based on evidence, let alone subject to any Popperian principle of falsification.

Creating the land of hatred
The lack of reasoned premises underlying critical race theory partly explains the BLM movement's predilection for melodramatic posturing and monument sacking. Rage rather than reason fuels the latest outbreak of millennial iconoclasm. Indignation is, as the philosopher Alasdair McIntyre remarked, a predominantly modern emotion and protest its distinctive mode of expression: 'a reaction to the alleged invasion of someone's rights in the name of someone else's utility'. The self-assertive shrillness of modern protest conceals behind the 'masks of morality what are in fact the preferences of arbitrary will and desire'. It is not surprising therefore that 'the *utterance* of protest is characteristically addressed to those who already share the protestors' premise'.

To what end, then, is this shrill 'will and desire' directed? If we look at the fanatical image-breaking of the Red Guards in the Cultural Revolution for guidance, we can say that the goal is historical amnesia and the creation of the perfect super-revolutionary persona, one free of all constraints and inhibition, one that has no duty but to the principles of socialist purity. To accomplish this task

Mao sought to shape not just the outward behaviour of the people but to control their inner world as well. The prerequisite for this was cultural erasure. Mao wrote approvingly of the personality as a *tabula rasa* on to which could be inscribed an unadulterated ideological consciousness: 'A blank sheet of paper has no blotches, and so the newest and most beautiful words can be written on it, the newest and most beautiful pictures can be painted on it'.

And what was the ultimate purpose of the sublime revolutionist? Jung Chang in recounting her family's experiences of the Cultural Revolution in *Wild Swans* (1991) best captures the instrumental value of the Red Guards when she wrote: 'Mao had managed to turn the people into the ultimate weapon of dictatorship. That was why under him there was no real equivalent of the KGB in China. There was no need. In bringing out and nourishing the worst in people, Mao had created a moral wasteland and a land of hatred'.

Building visions of the West
This vision, we may presuppose, is what the contemporary Western Maoists have in mind in their attempts to erase history: the creation of a society without any shared civic morality, based on discord and hatred. It does not, as Jung Chang observed, require top-down imposition or secret police. It aims at a self-sustaining politics of struggle and inter-societal loathing: all the better for a revolutionary elite to control and govern according to their own interests.

Where will it all end? If the denouement of the Cultural Revolution in China is anything to go by, it leads to mayhem. Despite the viciousness of the Red Guards, they found that, as they spread out across the countryside, the bulk of the people still preferred holding onto their old ideas, old culture, old customs and old habits. The peasantry resisted. Violence and factional struggles produced chaos resulting in the intervention of the People's Liberation Army to restore order in 1970.

This is the historical pattern that repeats itself wherever social dislocation and political instability present themselves. From Europe to Latin America, when super-revolutionists introduce violence and disorder into the political equation, it inexorably produces a countervailing reaction. A yearning for security rather than permanent revolution is the default position of most people. Authoritarian crackdowns and military governance are almost always the result. Foreshadowing this prospectus, we might contemplate the way universities, the mainstream media and the business sectors have capitulated to the purist assault on capitalism and the 'sordid' history of Western imperialism. To appease the rage, public and private sector PR departments uncritically accept the need to virtue signal their support of a movement that is, in theory, dedicated to their own destruction. Most egregiously, the senior leadership teams and vice-chancelleries of leading Russell group universities unquestioningly accept the need to address their institutional racism and alter their curriculums along BLM approved lines.

Those who resist this latest deconstruction of knowledge will either be silenced or subject to departmental struggle sessions leading no doubt to bias training and self-rectification. China's Great Helmsman detested liberalism, its preoccupation with 'unprincipled peace' and its desire to appease at all costs. He would, nevertheless, be delighted at the success of the latest generation of cultural revolutionaries in forcing a pusillanimous liberal establishment to take a knee.

Original article published in *Cieo*, 8th July 2020, by David Martin Jones and M.L.R. Smith.

Terror in the Western mind: Carnage and culture

As the 20th anniversary of 9/11 passes, we can begin to see how the long war on terror has affected the West's cultural self-understanding. In strategic terms, the forever wars launched after 9/11 spectacularly failed to achieve an outcome better than the *status quo ante*. Little attention, however, has been given to what two decades of media representation of jihadism, asymmetric violence and military intervention have had upon Western popular culture. The genres of film, the novel, art and popular music have all addressed the long war on terror from a variety of perspectives – but the prevailing tone might be summarised as, at best, agnostic, at worst, masochistic and self-loathing.

In the evolving cultural response to the war on terror, few movies or novels have taken a positive view of the US government and its coalition partners' decision to invade Iraq in 2003. Kathryn Bigelow's *The Hurt Locker* (2008) and *Zero Dark Thirty* (2012), as well as Clint Eastwood's *American Sniper* (2014), are perhaps the exceptions. They offer the most conventionally supportive treatment of the US military and intelligence agencies fighting the good fight overseas. So, too, did several country and western singers whose songs might (and occasionally did) serve as a musical accompaniment to the fight 'over there'.

By contrast, the majority of US and European filmmakers and pop icons have adopted a morally ambivalent and increasingly critical posture to the war and the Western democracies' political response to terrorism post-9/11. On the domestic front, films and TV series only dealt tangentially with the home-grown jihadist phenomenon, preferring instead to focus on the evolving surveillance state that manipulated 'the politics of fear' to impose and extend already authoritarian state control. Drama series like *Bodyguard* (2018) and *The Informer* (2018) present government ministers and the shadowy apparatus of the security state manipulating putative Islamist terrorists to promote a covert and fascist political agenda.

The writers of these dramas nonetheless struggled to differentiate their approach to the surveillance state from series like *Homeland* or *The Bureau*, which experienced less difficulty in representing Islamically motivated terrorists. The progressive mainstream press, somewhat predictably, criticised all these series, irrespective of nuance, for 'their cliched description of modern Islamic terrorism'. Depicting terrorists from diasporic Asian backgrounds committed, it seemed, the hate crime of Islamophobia.

Media condemnation notwithstanding, the Western genre of film and television occasionally offered an intelligent dramatic response to the moral and political dilemmas raised by the long war on terror. From *United 93* (2006) to *Homeland* (2011-20), *The Bureau* (2015-20) and *Eye in the Sky* (2015), these films and TV series thoughtfully explored the difficult moral terrain that the long war exposed for the liberal conscience.

The novel, by contrast, has offered only a relativist uncertainty about 9/11 and its aftermath, as is evident in Ian McEwan's *Saturday* (2005) or Claire Messud's *The Emperor's Children* (2005). Meanwhile, those novelists who engaged directly with the jihadi character offered only crude stereotypes like Sheikh Rashid in John Updike's *Terrorist* (2006) or Bassam al Jizani, longing for *shaheed*, in Andre Dubus III's *The Garden of Last Days* (2008). Meanwhile, novelists who found in the war on terror a state conspiracy to spread domestic fear – like Richard Flanagan in *The Unknown Terrorist* (2006), Mohsin Hamid in *The Reluctant Fundamentalist* (2007) and John le Carré in *A Most Wanted Man* (2008) – either considered the jihadist character an invention of the security state or a somewhat complex but sympathetic character, like le Carré's Dr. Abdullah and Hamid's Changez.

If the literary response was equivocal, the popular music response was ephemeral, transitory and again predictable. Patriotic country and western singers supported the war until it seemed futile, whilst protest music post- 9/11 embraced a self-consciously radical pacifist posture. Whilst country and western artist Toby Keith sang 'you'll be sorry you messed with the US of A. / 'Cause we'll put a boot in your ass / It's the American way', the left coast band Green Day condemned the war on terror because 'I don't want to be an American idiot / Don't want a nation under the new media / And can you hear the sound of hysteria?'

Meanwhile, the visual arts, together with academia and the mainstream media, have offered even less insight into jihadist motivation or the rationale for Western intervention in states of concern. The liberal arts establishment sought to adopt a 'balanced' approach to asymmetric violence. The fact that video artists like Theo van Gogh and Ayaan Hirsi Ali or the *Jyllands-Posten* and *Charlie Hebdo* cartoonists might suffer assassination or death threats for satirising Islamist fanaticism failed to trouble this Olympian pursuit of neutrality.

What, however, became evident in the wake of the *Charlie Hebdo* killings in 2015 was that the official, progressive, post-9/11 mindset had difficulty in portraying Islam as anything other than a peaceful religion. This unwillingness to question, interrogate, or criticise reinforced an evolving media, academic and artistic climate of self-censorship. Cross-dressing British artist Grayson Perry was one of the few to admit a baser motive for this posture. In November 2007 Perry acknowledged 'The reason I have not gone all out on attacking Islamism in my art is because I feel the real fear that someone will slit my throat'. A little fear clearly went a long way.

Empathy, Islamophobia and the prehistory of hate speech
In the wake of the *Charlie Hebdo* attacks, the corporate media along with European and US political elites came to endorse, in the name of a fashionable commitment to diversity, a minority practice of religious intolerance. Tolerating intolerance as a response to blasphemy legitimated a growing and widespread condemnation of statements or artistic representations that might cause offence on British, European and North American campuses. Hate speech, 'trigger warnings' and 'no-platforming' campaigns were the ineluctable consequence.

Curating the Imperial War Museum's 2018 *Art in the Age of Terror* exhibition, Sanna Moore told *The New York Times* that the show reflected how the West has changed, and not for the better, through 'mass surveillance... and detentions without trial'. The 'age defining' artwork on display explored not only personal reactions to 9/11 but also the way Western civil liberties had been 'compromised and security and surveillance amplified'.

A visitor to the exhibition would have quickly discerned that the civil liberties at stake were those of Muslim minorities after 9/11, not those of cartoonists or filmmakers assassinated for having an 'Islamophobic' reaction that deviated from the prevailing progressive norm. Wandering through the rooms devoted to 'Art Since 9/11' a spectator would struggle to find any reference to Theo van Gogh, *Jyllands-Posten* or *Charlie Hebdo*'s cartoons or 'the complex issues' they might have raised. Instead, the show addressed four themes: the artists' critical responses to 9/11; the intensified levels of state control after 2001; advancements in weaponry, particularly drone warfare; and the destruction caused by conflict that has 'turned homelands into wastelands'.

Nowhere, however, were the actions or the images of those who perpetrated either the 9/11 or London 7/7 attacks represented. The artwork curated by the Imperial War Museum instead gave simplistic visual support to a radically pacifist, critical terror orthodoxy. This fashionable perspective – which found traction on university campuses after 2005 – held that Western interventions created instability abroad, and jihadism and a surveillance state at home. Its critical tolerance of Islamic intolerance silenced the secular right to blasphemy and cancelled viewpoints on campus or in exhibitions deemed Islamophobic, or, as the 'woke' argot extended its remit after 2016, 'racist and colonialist'.

The visual arts, museum collections and exhibitions – like the university departments of the arts, humanities, and social sciences that promoted this attack on the Western way of war – are, ironically, the most heavily state subsidised institutions of Western cultural life. However, they have adopted and promulgated a 'reflexive' sympathy with the non-Western 'other', in the shape of the jihadist, which contributed over time to a self-lacerating assault on the history and institutional legacy of Western democracy.

Critical theory and its impact on Western self-understanding after 2001 thus offers an important insight into the agnosticism that recurs throughout the novels, music, film, visual arts and academic responses to the war on terror. The radically deconstructive political agenda, which informed French post-modernism and the neo-Marxist Frankfurt School at the end of the Cold War – and which constituted the key ingredient of critical theory – extended a relativism not only towards language but also towards social action. This extreme relativism advocated for an 'ethics of responsibility to the terrorist other', which has since revealed itself to be pure cultural nihilism.

It is only possible to have this empathetic identification with another culture in an open society that questions the values it promotes. The critical theorist's explicit loathing of the very openness that affords him, her and they the opportunity for histrionic grandstanding conveniently ignores this constituting fact.

'Wokeness', terror, and the rise of the revisionist powers

Home-grown Islamists cleverly exploited liberal empathy and used the sanctimonious liberal pursuit of social justice and condemnation of Islamophobia for its own illiberal, politically religious ends. Meanwhile, the progressive media embraced liberal empathy, exploring it in all its 'woke' equivocation in the aftermath of increasingly violent attacks on Western cities between 2011 and 2018. By the second decade of the long war on terror, revisionist regimes of an illiberal or totalitarian hue, observing the confusion that the Western cultural and political response to the war evinced, also sought to exploit it for their own geopolitical ends.

During the Presidency of Donald Trump in the United Stares and following the UK's exit from the European Union, the long wars and terrorism fell into desuetude, but their legacy lingered, mutating and growing into a virulent, critical academic and mainstream media campaign on the West's darkly imperial and colonial past and institutionally racist present.

The incoherence that now besets the progressive establishment manifested itself in the first direct encounter between new US President Joe Biden's foreign policy team and China's top diplomats in March 2021. The Chinese delegation rejected any American attempt to question its human rights record, pointing out, as senior diplomat Yang Jiechi said, that 'I don't think the overwhelming majority of countries in the world would recognize that the universal values advocated by the United States or that the opinion of the United States any longer represents international public opinion'.

From Beijing's perspective, the US no longer exerts either soft power or global influence. Citing the Black Lives Matter movement, Yang observed: 'The challenges facing the United States in human rights are deep-seated'. 'It's important', he advised, 'that we manage our respective affairs well instead of deflecting the blame on somebody else in this world'. A new Democrat administration promoting democracy, a liberal international order, and human rights abroad (whilst selectively denouncing its own racism and social injustice at home) appears both confused and hypocritical. Why, during the war on terror, did America – and, by extension, the West's global influence – become so tarnished? What went wrong?

A culture of queasy agnosticism
In the postscript to his 2010 autobiography, Tony Blair, the key architect of a progressive, Western-led, third way of government and an enthusiastic advocate of the Iraq War, wrote: 'For almost twenty years after 1989 the West set the agenda to which others reacted... the destination to which history appeared to march seemed chosen by us'. He further reflected, 'We thought the ultimate triumph of our way of life was inevitable. Now it is in shadow'.

Obviously, the mixed legacy of globalisation and the financial crisis it unleashed after 2008 has undermined the economic foundations of the progressive project. However, it was the moral and political shortcomings of the long war on terror that played a seminal role in the widespread loss of ideological and idealist faith in a universal liberal institutional order as the culminating moment of world history. In particular, the war on terror, and the ambiguous political response both at home and abroad, have given force to an otherwise academically obscure critical theory that, from the outset, viewed the West and its open societies and civil liberties – but not the jihadists – as the main problem for world emancipation.

This critical theory view that deconstructed the West's commitment to liberalism and democracy became particularly influential on its cultural response to the war on terror, especially after the Iraq invasion. The dark enlightenment of the European and North American left after 2003 fed into popular cultural tropes. Islamophobia had long preoccupied critical theory. It subsequently came to inform films like *Syriana* (2005), *Redacted* (2007) and *Green Zone* (2010), as well as novels like *The Reluctant Fundamentalist* and *The Unknown Terrorist*.

The incoherent Western response to international terrorism – where governments prosecuted a war against Islamism abroad but tolerated its advocates at home – has facilitated a morally ambiguous cultural response to the phenomenon. In film, crime drama, novels and the visual arts the misunderstood or naively misled terrorist was contrasted with the heavy-handed agents, capitalist interests, and agencies that oversaw the Western response. This political and moral ambivalence informs intelligence-led dramas and novels about the war – from *Homeland* and *A Most Wanted Man* to *The Bureau* – as well as the art works on display at the Imperial War Museum.

In the visual arts, the age of terror led to self-censorship, no-platforming, and the repression of imagery deemed sacrilegious or satirical. The response to the *Charlie Hebdo* assassinations and the subsequent silencing of any attempt to discuss or display satirical images of the Prophet and his message demonstrated how the West has now come to accept and comply with the intolerant strictures of Islamist ideology. By the second decade of the 21st century, some version of relativism – or queasy agnosticism – has become the default Western cultural position on international terror. Even for more intelligent attempts to grapple with problems of both *in bello* and *ad bello* conflict – in films like *Eye in the Sky* or Michel Houellebecq's novel *Submission* (2015) – either accept or explore the limitations and failings of Western liberalism.

The popular cultural response to the war on terror peaked midway through the second decade of the 21st century. Thereafter, terror and its threat have functioned as a cultural signifier intimating official stereotyping and as a plot device to expose the mistreated non-Western other. The West's institutions, its police, militaries, judiciary, business interests and political parties are either corrupt, insensitive, morally compromised, or institutionally and individually racist.

Continental philosophers from Jacques Derrida, Gilles Deleuze and Michel Foucault to Theodor Adorno and Jürgen Habermas had from the 1970s exposed the supposedly false consciousness that distorted the West's miserably capitalist self-understanding. The British and American epigone that packaged these writers' reckless ideas for consumption across the Anglosphere came, in the course of the long war on terror, to dominate popular and mainstream media, as well as university humanities departments where the ideology flourished, mimicking and displacing conventional scholarship.

Ironically, the Western media – long held by Herbert Marcuse, the godfather of critical theory, to be the vehicle of a totalising one-dimensional modernity – have translated this histrionic cultural relativism and nihilist deconstruction of secular liberal values into accessible commodities for popular consumption. By 2020, the prevailing popular media depiction of the West, with its inherent propensity to violence and overt and covert racism, placed it on a lower ethical plane than the terrorist whose resistance on behalf of the victimised deserved critical recognition. The two-decades-long encounter with critical theory and the long war deracinated Western cultural self-perceptions, making it impossible for the West to defend its values, let alone promote them, just as Yang Jiechi recognised.

The closing of the Western mind
What does the cultural response tell us about the overall state of the Western mind? Above all, we see the bankruptcy and intellectual exhaustion of progressive thought at the end of history. The dark enlightenment of the left after 2003, like the liberal globalisers of the 1990s they succeeded, assumed that world history was moving towards a socially just, diverse but inclusive utopia. Whereas the Blairite 'third way' leftism had assumed that the West would set this global agenda, the critical-theory inspired 'woke' left saw the West as the problem, with the solution being '*alter*-globalisation' with its transnational networks of NGOs, critical theory academics, radical pacifists, indigenous peoples, sexual minorities, environmental activists, as well as the odd jihadist, promoting universal liberation through the overthrow of the Western capitalist *imperium*.

Such dogmatism is, of course, without any foundation. It is the reckless effort of the critical mind – and of the culture it informs – to escape being stifled by solitude or nihilism, or by a value imposed by those whom the dogma profits, such as those who monetise notions like 'white fragility' or who buy large houses from the financial proceeds of Black Lives Matter donations. As Albert Camus presciently wrote, 'the end of history is not an exemplary or perfectionist value: it is an arbitrary and terroristic principle'.

The problem is that the West, at the end of the Cold War and in the first decade of the long war on terror, had seemed certain of its liberal international purpose – a purpose in which all people could be united. The core lesson of the long war was the failure of this purpose to achieve 'progress toward a society embracing equally all human beings'. This has engendered a moral and political crisis.

The cultural response to the war on terror – the equivocation, relativism, moral ambivalence and self-censorship – defines this crisis of Western progressive faith. It also intimates, if nothing else, the need to return to a more prudent approach that accepts the fact that political society remains what it is and always has been – namely, a society whose primary task is its self-preservation and whose highest calling is its self-improvement. A distracted and confused democratic West needs to thus reclaim its cultural moorings before it again foists its 'universal' values upon the world.

Original article published in the *European Conservative*, 19th September 2021, by David Martin Jones and M.L.R. Smith.

Misreading Mill: On liberty and vaccination

In a comment piece in the *Daily Telegraph* on 22nd December, John Harris makes the moral case for mandatory vaccination in the public interest. Harris might have supported his argument by reference to several political and moral theorists who, like Harris, have endorsed forcing people to do things against their will in the name the greater good. Kant springs to mind. So too does Jean Jacques Rousseau who thought that securing the 'General Will' might require the recalcitrant to be 'forced to be free'.

Curiously, however, Harris co-opts John Stuart Mill's *On Liberty* (1859) to support state mandated COVID vaccines. Harris writes: 'It is difficult, in view of the urgency of the global COVID pandemic and the immense death toll and burden of the disease, not to conclude that, in Mill's famous and uncompromising words, the anti-vaxxers are 'such as to constitute their expression a positive instigation to some mischievous act'.

What Harris seems to mean is that by refusing to get vaccinated, the vaccine refusenik acts in a way to 'do harm to others' and consequently such actions must be controlled 'by the active interference of mankind'. But would Mill have construed a refusal to get vaccinated an action directly harming others?

Clearly not. In the introduction to his essay, from which Harris quotes selectively, Mill warns against the potentially despotic power the people may exercise in a modern democracy. This tyranny of the majority operates 'chiefly through public authorities'. But it can also operate through society collectively acting upon the 'separate individuals who compose it'. 'Society can and does execute its own mandates' and when it does so in areas 'where it ought not to meddle it practises a social tyranny more formidable than many kinds of political oppression'.

The rational and autonomous individual, Mill maintained, needs protection against 'the tyranny of prevailing opinion and feeling; against the tendency of society to impose... its own ideas and practises as rules of conduct on those who dissent from them' to fetter and prevent any 'development not in harmony with its ways'. One could call this the tyranny of the medical-socialist state.

To guard against this evolving modern despotism, Mill proposed one very simple principle to govern the dealings of government and society with the individual 'in the way of compulsion and control'. That simple principle is that the only end for which a government can legitimately interfere 'with the liberty of action of any of their number, is self-protection'.

This, then, is the harm principle that Harris seeks to manipulate for collectivist ends. It in fact recognises that the reasonable individual's own good, either physical or moral, is 'not a sufficient warrant for intervention'. The individual 'cannot rightfully be compelled to do or forbear because it will be better for him to do so' or because 'to do so would be wise, or even right'.

To be sure, such reasons may be good for remonstrating, reasoning, persuading, or entreating with the recalcitrant 'but not for compelling him'. To justify compulsion 'the conduct from which it is desired to deter him must be calculated to produce evil to someone else'. In that part which merely concerns him or herself, the anti-vaxxer's 'independence is, of right, absolute'. On this point Mill insists: 'Over himself, over his own body and mind, the individual is sovereign'. He continues: 'The only freedom which deserves the name, is that of pursuing our own good in our own way... each is the proper guardian of his own health, whether bodily, or mental and spiritual'.

Harris's case for compulsory COVID vaccination rests on a highly questionable interpretation of the harm principle: namely, minimising societal distress by seeking to reduce avoidable death, hospitalisations and excessive pressure on the National Health Service. However, with an infection fatality rate of a little over 0.2 per cent and an average age of death from COVID above the age of 80, the case seems hardly compelling since the social risk does not deviate all that significantly from most winter flu seasons. The fact that vaccinations do not prevent infection or transmission further reduces the force of the argument.

All individuals, when they step out into the world risk bringing unintentional harm – to themselves and others – whether driving a car, going for a walk, or meeting with friends. Everyday life involves all manner of potential hazards. The point is, though, that an individual's engagement in the routines of daily life is in, the vast majority of instances, not 'calculated to produce evil to someone else'.

Thus, enlisting Mill on the side of compulsion because vaccine refusal might indirectly harm others on the grounds it places undue pressure on the NHS, conceptually stretches and ultimately undermines Mill's 'simple principle'. Mill was a utilitarian and a moral consequentialist. He also lived in a *laissez faire* age. There was no NHS in Mill's Day. If there had been, he would quite possibly have argued that if a responsible adult refused the vaccination the NHS offered to prevent an infectious disease, the individual would either forego any right to NHS treatment or be required to pay the cost of his care. Actions, after all, have consequences.

As numerous libertarian commentators on Mill have pointed out, the distinction between self-regarding and other regarding actions is paramount. Simplifying the distinction, Karl Popper, whom Harris quotes, observed 'my freedom to swing my arm stops at your nose'. The point, of course, is that it is *my* arm and I have a sovereign right over whether I choose to have it vaccinated or not. After all: 'Mankind are greater gainers by suffering each other to live as seems good to themselves, than by compelling each to live as seems good to the rest'. To conflate a purely self-regarding act with *another* regarding one is not merely perverse but politically dangerous, as Mill would no doubt have recognised.

Original article published in the *Daily Sceptic*, 28th December 2021, by David Martin Jones and M.L.R. Smith.

We need to talk about trans politics: An oppressed majority

Have you ever felt like you do not meet society's expectations? Are you wondering about your identity? Do you find conforming to social stereotypes oppressive? Do you have 'strange' thoughts about who you might be, causing you to question prior assumptions about yourself?

If the answer to any of these questions is 'yes', then you may well be trans. We're not talking gender here. We're talking politics. The growing ideological fluidity between traditional notions of left and right is leading to political cross-over and convergence. Groups that once had little in common suddenly find they are united.

People who are trans-political, or who identify as politically non-binary, come from both ends of the political spectrum but all now find themselves at odds with the Conservative and Labour parties, as well as the mainstream media narrative of contemporary events. Welcome to the new trans politics.

Here, we have put together a handy guide to help you work out if you too might be trans-political. If you used to describe yourself as a 'classical liberal' and voted Conservative before Brexit was even a thing, but no longer feel at home in Prime Minister Boris Johnson's 'One Nation', the following signs may help you determine if you are, indeed, trans:

1) You once thought Russell Brand a buffoon. You saw his performances on *Question Time* and *Newsnight* (back in the day when you bothered to watch these programmes) and thought he was a braggart spouting new age drivel. You are now an avid follower of his YouTube channel. You find him thoughtful, insightful, often funny, and a perceptive interviewer.
2) You look back and think that while you rarely agreed with Tony Benn's or Michael Foot's political agenda, nevertheless, you admired their commitment to parliamentary democracy, scepticism about power and privilege, and respect for civil political debate. You regret that people like them are nowhere to be found in contemporary politics.
3) You would much rather read or hear the work of a real investigative journalists like Glenn Greenwald than the repetitively predictable opinions of any number of Oxbridge grads who occupy the comment pages of the national newspapers.
4) You find the *Daily Telegraph* boring.
5) You think George Galloway may be self-regarding and idiosyncratic, but he seems more open minded, and certainly far more articulate, than your average university professor.
6) You have a sense that Margaret Thatcher may have been too harsh on the miners.
7) You are increasingly concerned that unfettered capitalism and unregulated big corporations do not necessarily promote the public good.
8) You begin to think there may be such a thing as the 'military-industrial' complex.
9) You would much rather read something from *Left Lockdown Sceptics* or the *Off Guardian* than the mainstream media.
10) You find *Spectator TV* and *Times Radio* unbearably smug.
11) You think a fourth runway should be built at Heathrow, preferably with direct flight paths over Richmond and Putney.

Similarly, if you have always voted Labour because your nan would turn in her grave if you so much as thought of putting a cross elsewhere, but are beginning to feel a bit discombobulated yourself, you might need to consider the possibility that you are actually trans. If you are, here are some questions you might be asking yourself:

1) Why did mainstream left-wing parties across the Anglosphere unreservedly embrace authoritarian lockdowns during the COVID-19 pandemic, which disproportionately harmed the working-class and self-employed tradespeople?

2) Why, during this period, did the mainstream left align with big pharmaceutical interests and a soft totalitarian NHS bureaucracy to erode ideas like bodily autonomy?
3) Why did the NHS state bureaucracy enthusiastically endorse the Chinese model of social organisation?
4) Why does a metropolitan Labour elite appear increasingly to side with smug inner city thirty-somethings, corporate power and big business against the interests of the provincial working-class?
5) Why does Labour value the views of woke, over-privileged citizens of 'anywhere' who wouldn't be able to mark Stoke-on-Trent on a map, let alone deign to visit it, or other similar places in the post-industrial North?
6) Why do they think fobbing people off with benefits and handouts rather than providing decent jobs, will buy them political loyalty?
7) Why does Labour and the left more generally appear to denigrate the United Kingdom, its history, traditions, and people like me? And what's 'decolonising' institutions, like school and university curricula, have to do with left-wing, working-class politics and its history, anyway?
8) Why do prominent female Labour politicians like Stella Creasy think that women should have penises?
9) Why is the *Guardian* so indescribably self-righteous?
10) Why does the left push green politics and the net-zero agenda so eagerly when it only promises to make my life even more difficult and expensive?
11) Why should I keep voting for these people?
12) Why don't they build a fourth runway at Heathrow, preferably running through Richmond or Putney?

If you were 'on the left' when you started asking yourself these questions, but now find that your views are better reflected in the pages of the *Daily Mail* rather than the *Guardian*, then you may be in the first stages of political transition.

The transitioning process
Those who once identified with a conservative disposition often transitioned because of foolish foreign policy decisions and economic and fiscal misconduct. Those coming from the left tended to transition because of culture war and COVID-19. The transitioning process may therefore have taken the following forms:

Foreign policy
The premonitory stirrings of trans politics can often be traced to the second Iraq War. The 9/11 attacks may have found you, initially, on the side of the need to intervene in Afghanistan and even Iraq. Limited expeditions to teach terrorists or terror states a sharp lesson and to deter further attacks seemed logical and just.

What you didn't consider plausible, though, was a delusional programme of democratic 'nation building' that assumed tribal societies, very different from your own, could be transformed through armed social work into secular liberal states. These 'forever wars' merely destabilised regions, inflicted unnecessary suffering on the host society, and wasted both human and material resources whilst eroding the West's international moral standing and soft power.

Perhaps some of those anti-war marchers back in 2003 were more perceptive than you once thought. Maybe they were onto something about how only commercial interests benefitted from such a reckless policy. You find yourself increasingly sceptical concerning mainstream media and political injunctions to intervene in internecine conflicts everywhere from Libya, Yemen, Iraq, Syria, and now Ukraine.

Nothing good seems to come from any intervention by the so-called international community. One thing is for sure, you don't feel more secure, either at home or abroad. Nor is your quality of life enhanced in any way by the increased migration flows of displaced people from conflict zones. Only your taxes and the price of petrol go up.

You wonder if there is a 'liberal' world order at all? Or is it not just a mask for cynical and essentially American interests?

Economics

You once thought that a deregulated economic environment was an unmitigated good. Economies must be free to evolve. Change is not necessarily a bad thing. A competitive economy is usually an efficient and productive one.

What you didn't bargain for, however, was the wholesale globalisation of finance and business that de-industrialised and de-skilled large parts of the country. The offshoring of once reliable manufacturing jobs to countries offering cheap labour was not an unalloyed benefit. Increasingly it appears globalisation and millennial capitalism laid waste to viable industrial towns, transforming once proud working-class communities from Merthyr to Middlesbrough into industrial wastelands. Here a white British hillbilly precariat finds traditional jobs in manufacturing replaced by a gig economy founded on depressed wages, poverty and drug addiction.

You begin to worry about social cohesion: the burgeoning gap between rich and poor as well as the increasingly squeezed middle; the excessive concentration of wealth in a few exclusive financial centres, such as the City of London and Canary Wharf, at the expense of everyone else.

You brood about the loss of community and social solidarity. You become nostalgic for the lost values once embodied by organised labour or in mining and manufacturing communities. Suddenly, not everything about the 1970s seems so bad.

Culture

You favour personal liberties, civil rights, and freedom for people to express themselves in whatever medium. In fact, that's what you once marched for. You endorsed principles of free speech that allowed you to critique positions you disagreed with, especially those that restricted your lifestyle choices.

What you didn't anticipate was that some of your radical confrères would never be satisfied with the attainment of the principles of equality of opportunity for everyone, and that your once libertarian politics would now be used to divide society along racial and ethnic lines. More cynically, you find that those progressives you once marched with, who found free speech useful to promote their views, now occupy the commanding heights of cultural power themselves. You see they are not quite so keen on free speech now, especially if anyone expresses dissent from their fashionably woke orthodoxies.

You begin to suspect that the progressive mind is not quite as open as you once assumed and that cultural conservatives may have a point. In fact, you realise that it is conservatives who are prepared to defend your right to express your opinions rather than your woke comrades, who seem more interested in cancelling you entirely. Indeed, as a left-wing feminist, like Julie Bindel or Suzanne Moore, you find that the *Daily Mail* and *Daily Telegraph* are more willing to offer you a platform than the *Guardian*.

COVID-19

You are a long-time left leaning social democrat, who has always voted Labour. You support the betterment of the education, health and welfare of the working class, yet were dismayed by the response of the mainstream left to the COVID-19 pandemic. The Labour leadership, both in parliament and in its control of the Welsh Assembly, replaced any residual commitment to civil liberty with support and encouragement for a health despotism, encouraging more and harder lockdowns, the economic burden of which fell disproportionately on poorer people.

You observed that the only politicians and commentators prepared to question the disproportionate, anti-science, COVID hysteria were libertarian or sceptic conservatives, who seemed to care more about ideas once cherished by the left, like workers' rights, children's education, equal treatment and civil liberties, than your increasingly soft totalitarian friends on the left.

Mutual recognition

An evolving trans politics, then, rests on a regard for those across the political divide based on mutual respect for the integrity of their views and subsequent recognition of, and tentative agreement on, the standpoint that they each adopt. These might be summarised as follows:

An appreciation of the left's thoughtful and more considered critiques of the machinations of elite power and a recognition of the importance of the thinking of a variety of thinkers from C. Wright Mills and Noam Chomsky to Christopher Lasch and Richard Rorty, who questioned the nature of power elites in modernity, the possibilities and limitations of post-modern bourgeois liberalism, and the difficulties of the minimal self in the narcissistic 'me' decades.

A shared commitment to freedom of thought, speech, and a recognition from some on the traditional left that a classical liberal and conservative disposition is far more willing to uphold the right to dissent. It is traditional conservatives who support cancelled feminists like Julie Bindel, Germaine Greer, Kathleen Stock and J.K. Rowling and defend their right to speak whilst the *Guardian* maintains a stony silence, if not outright hostility.

An acknowledgement that those who do speak out against their former tribe or political identity, whether it's George Galloway, Julie Bindel, Paul Embery or J.K. Rowling, are heterodox dissenters, and their courage deserves to be recognised.

A shared understanding that minorities do often have a hard time and can be victims of prejudice – but not primarily the kind that the woke orthodoxy would like you to believe. Rather, minorities have become the silent victims of a cynical, careerist, managerial class who thrive on keeping classes and minorities downtrodden, divided and dependent. It is daily exemplified in the bigotry of low expectations, or the violence and deprivation of Democrat run cities in the US and Labour run boroughs in the UK.

An evolving consciousness that shared values of history, solidarity and liberty unite elements of the old left and traditional right. Or perhaps more accurately, this equates to a shared understanding of a common fate against impersonal, unaccountable, and self-aggrandising elites.

Transphobia

The emergence of trans politics is uncomfortable for those glued to a traditional binary of left and right. In fact, the crossover or unifying elements of left/right politics, especially its coalescence over certain forms of shared consciousness and cross political solidarity, alarms the elites in politics, business and the media who balk at such apostasy and the dangerous challenge to their power and ideological grip.

This means that if you come out as trans political, you can expect to experience the full spectrum of transphobia. Victimisation and denunciation are the norm for those like J.K. Rowling, Kathleen Stock or Peter Boghossian. For those on the left, ideological deviation will be punished with denunciatory epithets that will deliberately seek to misidentify you as, 'far right', or 'alt right'. Over time, this stretches into lazy ad hominem attacks that see any trans-political deviant labelled as a fascist of indeed, a Nazi.

Conclusion: stunning and brave

Transphobia is merely a symptom of the threat that the trans-political movement poses to existing sources of power and privilege. Keeping people divided along traditional political lines is a means of consolidating power and resources in the hands of increasingly woke elites. If you are truly radical, you will reject political conformity and come out as trans.

Originally article published in *Cieo*, 2nd June 2022, by David Martin Jones and M.L.R. Smith.

6. History re-started: Geopolitics and the revenge of realism

DURING THE NINETEENTH CENTURY, the French characterised their colonialist ambitions as a *mission civilisatrice* – civilising mission – to bring the supposed benefits of superior French culture to their territories overseas. Paradoxically, in an era when the institutions of the liberal West, as the previous chapter noted, were being corroded from within by the advance of a progressivist ideology, liberal idealism was flexing its muscles externally in an enterprise that was, stripped of its progressive verbiage, a new *mission civilisatrice*. The motivation was to act on the world stage to enforce humanitarian norms, promote democracy and uphold the 'rules' of the international order. This moral mission drove Western military interventions after the end of the Cold War.

After the events of 9/11, Western led coalitions were even more determined to campaign on a new civilising cause against an 'axis of evil', comprising terrorist-sponsoring regimes, authoritarian dictators and 'rogue' states. Military interventions were intended to rid countries of religious despots like the Taliban in Afghanistan or tyrants like Saddam Hussein in Iraq, Colonel Muammar Gaddafi in Libya and Bashar al-Assad in Syria. Not only that, but in the cases of Afghanistan and Iraq, the mission was to nation-build, securing central government and instilling these countries with more liberal methods of governance. The ideological basis of Western foreign policy, as the essays in this chapter contend, extended directly from the assumptions contained in the end of history thesis promulgated after 1990 to 'make the world a better place'.

The results of this project have been uniformly disastrous. The human and economic consequences have been catastrophic. In the case of Afghanistan, the result was the abject humiliation of Western power. By acting out of self-professed moral virtue, the nations of the West lost the capacity to think strategically, undertaking ill-considered interventions with little thought given to historical or geopolitical context. The lasting impact of this mission to export liberal values has been to undermine collective Western prestige and rendered the North American and European powers vulnerable to being outfoxed on the world stage by the likes of China and Russia who are only too willing to advance their goals by thinking in hard-edged geo-strategic terms.

Returning to a practical tradition of prudence and statecraft, dispensing with ethicist foreign policies, offers the only hope of escaping the cage of liberal imperialist delusion. Upholding the right of the state to exist as a distinct national entity, and not merely as a servant in a moral crusade in the name of an abstract ideal of an 'international community', should be the primary goal of foreign policy. Western elites assumed that the age of power-politics, and even the modern notion of the state, was passing into history. This placed them at a disadvantage relative to those who do not believe that history has ended and who continue to pursue their national interests with great realist vigour.

The essays that comprise this chapter range over the loss of geopolitical sentience in the West and try to flesh out the contours of what might be a more realistic guide for foreign policy conduct. Some of our speculations, for instance that Russia and France might come together in a new entente, over-estimated the capacity of European states to surpass their idealistic commitment over fixations like ever closer union. Nevertheless, our basic observation that the world will always be one of shifting allegiances that ultimately trump utopian ideas is, we would maintain, fundamentally correct.

Speaking of Trump, the arrival of the 45th President in the White House heralded an interesting turn in US foreign policy. Despite the hysterical reactions to his incumbency by his liberal opponents in the media and academia, Donald Trump's foreign policy record is one of surprising success that intimated a return to a more restrained, careful calibration of the exercise of diplomacy and military power. Our essay on Trump's carrot and stick approach to North Korea, seeking engagement while threatening action if Pyongyang did not restrain its provocative nuclear missile tests, evaluated his 'art of the deal' diplomacy. Not only did Trump's diplomatic etiquette succeed in curtailing North Korea's tests, but his wider foreign policy yielded peace accords that stabilised relations in the Middle East, terminated ISIS as a threat once and for all, curbed Iranian machinations in Iraq, compelled European nations to take their own defence more seriously and put Sino-American relations, especially in trade, on a much surer footing. Overall, Trump's tenure in office was notable for the avoidance of external entanglements. He was the first President since Jimmy Carter (1976-1980) not to begin or extend a war.

The restoration of American authority in the world was put in jeopardy in the post-Trump years. Although mainstream media and academic commentators welcomed the geriatric Joe Biden into office, it was obvious for anyone with eyes to see that the man was suffering from senility and was incapable of offering coherent leadership. The delusions of the commentariat in perceiving the Biden foreign policy team as having the 'adults back in charge' was exposed in all its naïve complacency in the calamitously inept withdrawal from Afghanistan in the summer of 2021, the failure of Western deterrence with Russia's invasion of Ukraine in February 2022, and the Israel-Hamas war of October 2023. All these disasters, and the wider fall-out they have had across the Middle East, Europe and the Pacific, were challenges where the Biden administration was found severely wanting. We shall see where the return of Donald Trump as the 47th President now takes us.

The Russia-Ukraine war marked the unmistakeable return of geopolitics. Of course, geopolitical realities never went away, they had merely been ignored by Western powers for decades. The potential for the war in Ukraine to re-shape world politics along civilisational lines is a theme that several essays in this chapter pursue. The fragmentation of the international system in this way was evident in the football World Cup held in Qatar at the very end of 2022, which David and I turned to, both as a source of light relief and as a valuable illustration of the fault lines that Samuel Huntingdon in *The Clash of Civilizations* – the main counterpunch to Fukuyama's end of history thesis – presciently foresaw. The central themes of this chapter are pulled together in the final essay, which looks at the longer-term impact of the Russia-Ukraine war across the Indo-Pacific and the wider global arena, where we see the emerging recognition among states that they now inhabit a multipolar world, and don't therefore have to defer to the strictures laid down by a US led 'liberal' order. Neither do they have to align with Russia or China. Instead, they are freer than they have ever been to examine the options around them and chart their own path in world affairs. In other words, far from the materialisation of a borderless, post-national end of history, the world order is witnessing the re-awakening of nationalist and civilisational forces.

In fact, the irony is that it has been the very idealism envisaged in the liberal civilising project, its hubristic assumptions, its globalist pretensions, its quasi-imperialist arrogance, its compounding disasters of failed military interventions, which have helped stoke the very forces of resurgent national identity and the recrudescence of the sovereign state that was supposedly in the process of being inexorably superseded.

History doesn't end, but it often has the last laugh.

The return of the Machiavellian moment

Francis Fukuyama's thesis that history ended with the fall of the Berlin Wall in 1989 has exercised a baleful influence upon Western foreign policy. Fukuyama, of course, argued that Western liberal democracy triumphed over communism and fascism and thus constituted the 'final form of human government'.

The imposition of a liberal, democratic, norm-based global order appealed across party political lines and found enthusiastic adherents in the United States and among its key allies. Thus, Democrats like Bill Clinton, Tony Blair's New Labour and John Howard's Liberal Coalition government in Australia also promoted, by various means, global democratic peace, as did their twenty first century Republican, Democratic, Conservative and Labour successors. Some, like Tony Blair and President George W. Bush, adopted a more abrasive neo-conservative stance. Others were inclined to a more emollient 'liberal imperialist' posture that maintained that running the world requires the United States to work closely with allies and international institutions. Regardless, Western political elites and democratic governments subscribed to some version of this project. This progressive cosmopolitan vision prompted interventions, humanitarian or otherwise, in Asia, Africa and the Middle East in support of what was assumed to be a universal normative orientation.

Even though the long wars in Iraq and Afghanistan exposed the limits of imposing the end of history by military means, the values associated with it lingered on in the wake of the assassination of Osama bin Laden, the brief Arab Spring of 2010/11 and overthrow of the Gaddafi regime in 2011, sanctioned as it was by the United Nations.

After a quarter of a century, it is now possible to assess the effectiveness of this liberal project. Its consequences have been ubiquitously calamitous. The United States has been at war for two out of every three years since 1989 and the world is by no means a safer or more integrated place. Given the evolving chaos in the Middle East and its impact on the stability of Europe, is it possible to envisage an alternative, less costly, and more prudent way to conduct international relations?

History re-started

A nineteenth century historicism informed Fukuyama's thesis concerning the end of history. Progress occurred via a dialectic and in Fukuyama's account capitalism had triumphed over rival economic models and alternative ideologies. This teleology also implied the prospect of reforming capitalism's more inegalitarian features. History would witness capitalist democracies transformed through their participation in post-national constellations like the United Nations and the European Union. These state-transcending organisations would over time facilitate human rights, transnational justice and economic re-distribution throughout the international system.

In the aftermath of the wars in Iraq and Afghanistan, however, this teleology has yielded countervailing consequences. Intractable obstacles have appeared. The recrudescence of identity politics everywhere, Russian irredentism in the Caucasus, civil war in Ukraine, China's emergence as a great but authoritarian power on the world stage, together with continued turmoil in the Middle East and consequent refugee flows, intimates not the end of history but the 'revenge of the revisionist powers' and the return of geopolitics. History, after a brief nap, re-awakened, requiring states to reassess how they conduct themselves in an uncertain, anarchical international system where only three verities prevail, namely, diplomacy, alliances, and war.

Faced with this changed reality, Western powers and regional institutions appear distracted and weak in the second decade of the twenty-first century. They are consistently outmanoeuvred on the international stage by Russia and China, states with the will to assert their national interests. Thus, while the European

Union considered the whole notion of geopolitics old-fashioned, geopolitics is happening on its doorstep.

Why have the United States and Europe lost strategic direction, and can a fragmented West recover its sense of purpose?

The twenty-first century world is a complex one, not susceptible to universal panaceas, and this should be the point of departure. The acknowledgement of complexity requires a return to realism in statecraft and balance and order in world politics rather than the promotion of abstract rights and norms. A prudent foreign policy requires the case-by-case analysis of the merits of intervention and a pragmatic assessment of its practical and moral limitations.

What, we might wonder, beyond pragmatic calculation, would such an interest-based and context-driven approach to foreign policy entail? Furthermore, how would it differ from the utopian vision of international lawyers and democratic peace theorists to fashion a world transformed into a morally acceptable, cosmopolitan, and just transnational order?

The reason of states
Contemporary understandings of international law discern that a predetermined set of axioms laid down in Chapter 7 of the UN Charter and developed most recently in the convention on the 'Responsibility to Protect', adopted by the UN General Assembly in 2009, must be fulfilled to justify the use of force. Preoccupied with an abstract, normative model adjudicated by the United Nations and international lawyers, it has lost sight of the particular and the contingent.

Effective state strategy requires a clear political aim that might deviate from axiomatic norms, especially in conditions of war. The failure of contemporary Western statesmen to address this paradox has led to global strategic confusion. In this context, it is necessary to abandon a failed liberal progressivism and return instead to an earlier understanding of statecraft that prudently avoided utopian schemes.

Early modern European political thinkers who defined the modern understanding of sovereignty had much to say about the relationship between the state and force. This statecraft is largely neglected in the contemporary study of international relations, these days largely confined to a dwindling group of so-called realists. Yet, attending more closely to the early modern theory of reason of state sheds an important light on the practical counsel it might provide modern Western democracies in their efforts to maintain their interests in a durably disordered world.

It was in the context of confessional division and internecine strife that the modern European unitary state emerged unsteadily from the disintegrating chrysalis of the medieval Christian realm. With it arose a new scepticism about morality, law and order that came to be termed *raison d'état*, or the 'reason of state'. The thinkers who outlined this political project from Niccoló Machiavelli at the start of the sixteenth century to the Dutch humanist Justus Lipsius at its end were notably wary of abstract moral injunctions when it came to difficult questions of war and governance. Instead, they offered a distinctive counsel of prudence when considering the use of force.

Practical sixteenth century guides to statecraft offered maxims rather than axioms or 'norms' to address difficult cases like war. This understanding afforded practical advice to princes and republics on morality and war. It contrasts dramatically with contemporary international law and its application of a universal moral and legal standard to all cases of the use of force for humanitarian ends.

Machiavelli redux
It was Machiavelli who first drew attention to the gap between an abstract morality and the *virtu* required of a state if it wished to survive in a world of uncertainty.

This dilemma and how to address it has obvious, but invariably overlooked, contemporary relevance.

To preserve the state in a sea of insecurity, rulers need both good counsel and to prepare for war. Significantly, Machiavelli's only political work that was published in his lifetime, *The Art of War* (1521), treated military virtue as a necessary precondition for political or civil virtue. Effective rule, in other words, required close attention be paid to military strategy.

Machiavelli's views on statecraft have proved controversial. Later *étatist* thinkers wrote in a cooler style, recognising that Machiavelli had identified the mystery of statecraft but that it required a more nuanced application to diplomacy. This more restrained style of thought acknowledged the necessity of morally questionable behaviour while simultaneously maintaining the virtue of rule for preserving and advancing the common interest.

By the end of the sixteenth century, it was not Machiavelli but the Dutch humanist Justus Lipsius who did most to clarify this practice through a revised understanding of Roman military and political thought adapted to contemporary political needs. He taught the early modern political elite of Europe how to maintain political order and conduct internal and external war in the context of mounting confessional strife, or what we might term today politically religious or sectarian conflict. What does such counsel involve and how might it apply to contemporary statecraft?

Statecraft and necessity

Early modern realist advice on statecraft reflected the extreme political and religious violence that devastated Europe between 1580 and 1648. This context in some ways resembles those political predicaments facing the major Western nations in the second decade of the twenty-first century.

In this developing idiom of statecraft, political acts were represented in terms more powerfully persuasive than justice – namely, necessity and prudence. These accept the potential for the dissolution of universal moral norms into different and sometimes competing spheres of life.

Because of its pejorative characterisation as a preoccupation entirely with the deliberations of government and its darker arts, this approach to rule is frequently misunderstood because the English phrase 'reason of state' is an inadequate translation of the French *raison* and Italian *ragioni*. This is unfortunate because it obscures the fact that in French and Italian the phrase implies a guiding concern with the actual *right* of the state as the appropriate structure to preserve and sustain the common interest.

The right of the state may be expressed in terms of both the right of the state's survival as well as the conditions for preserving or developing civic and military virtue. Such a realist understanding evinces an acute concern both with the *presentation* of policy that reflects the prevailing conventions of diplomacy, as well as a less obvious concern with the *deliberation* amongst the prince's counsellors directed to the maintenance of the state's 'right' and its capacity to facilitate a condition of civic order and public morality.

Hence, as Lipsius averred, mixed prudence and virtue are the two principal drivers of political life, but prudence is the rudder that guides the virtues. In particular, the notion of mixed prudence offers insight into cases of war or peace and the state's right in such decisions. Here, history and experience, rather than abstract norms, play a central role in determining a prudent course. Indeed, as Lipsius wrote, 'history is the fount from which political and prudential choosing flows'.

Since the end of the Cold War, such a mixed prudential view of international politics has been honoured only in the breach both by US and European governments and their idealist supporters or critics. By contrast, the wise counsellor to early modern monarchs recognised the danger of presenting actions in overly idealistic terms that could lead to a damaging loss of credibility.

To give an example, the EU's and NATO's aspiration to expand its influence up to the border of Russia, undoubtedly fuelled Putin's reclamation of the Crimea and the Ukrainian war. Here, clearly, 'the pretence' of idealism often 'ignites the fires of strife' across Europe. A wise 'prince' in such circumstances would prefer the mixed prudential application of the material of deliberation to the requirements of presentation. With troubling cases like Syria, Crimea and Ukraine, a wise prince would recognise that he 'must do not what is beautiful to say, but what is necessary in practice'.

Conclusion
A sixteenth century realist would be astonished at how little prepared current statesmen in the United States and Europe are for war. Lacking knowledge of military prudence this political class is unlikely to deliberate slowly over the reasons for the use of force or the outcome of using force. Lack of attention to history leads to the problems encountered in Syria and Iraq and a failure to appreciate, for example, either Russia's long-term strategic interest in Eastern Europe and Caucasus or China's in the South China Sea.

Ultimately, an appreciation of the national interest and how it may be maintained is premised on the state's right to self-defence. In the disordered world of states, para-states and failed states, policies based on an abstraction like the 'international community' cannot achieve coherence, let alone order. Inter-state political diplomacy requires the abandonment of a failed utopian moral universalism and the return to a realist appreciation of history, past precedent, and state interest.

Original article published in *War on the Rocks*, 23rd September 2015, by David Martin Jones and M.L.R. Smith.

Are we witnessing a return to *realpolitik*?

In 1998, Anthony Giddens, Third Way enthusiast and Tony Blair's intellectual guru, announced that the era of major inter-state warfare was over. Subsequently, Blairite third wayers, Clinton Democrats and Bush style neo-conservatives all in various ways assumed the global order would be fashioned anew along democratic, cosmopolitan and morally just lines according to international law.

To more idealistic Europeans, the end of inter-state history presaged the progressive transformation of capitalist democracies into peaceful, post-national and regional 'constellations'. The European Union exemplified this brave new world where an internally borderless region pursued policies of economic re-distribution, development aid and human rights

Waving goodbye to realism
The end of the Cold War provided the backdrop for this shift from realism to internationalism, or from power to worldly paradise. Yet, after 9/11, events have increasingly challenged this liberal, post-modern aspiration.

The forces of transnational jihadism, aided and abetted by the long, inconclusive, and costly interventions in Afghanistan and Iraq questioned its validity. Meanwhile, Vladimir Putin's reassertion of Russian irredentism in the Caucasus, China's emergence as a major power in East Asia, and the rise of ISIL across the Middle East revealed it as manifestly implausible.

Nevertheless, governed by an abstract international commitment to universal norms, and preoccupied with 'soft-power', leaders like Putin and Xi Jinping have consistently out manoeuvred the West on the international stage whether in Crimea and the Ukraine or the South China Sea.

Elsewhere, the fallout from the Syrian civil war and the refugee crisis it generated plunged Europe's open border policy into crisis, making Angela Merkel's EU look not unlike a post-modern version of the Holy Roman Empire under Maximillan II (1564-76) before it fell apart under the strain of religious and economic strife after 1600.

War and instability across the Middle East, parts of Asia, Africa and Europe have increasingly rendered ethical foreign policy, peaceful regional and global humanitarian transformation based on transnational institutions like the UN and the EU, redundant.

Instead states or state-like entities such as ISIL that are unaware that history has ended, pursue classic power politics, advancing self-interest through force if necessary, in the vacuum left by a *Europe sans Frontières et sans Armes* and a US leading from behind or, more often, not at all

The return of 'entente' politics?
The recent terrorist attacks in Paris, Istanbul, Moscow and Damascus thus announce not the end of ISIL but a new era of *realpolitik* in Europe and the Mediterranean world. Russia's intervention on the side of the Assad regime in Syria, and the French reaction to the Paris massacre in mid-November reveal its outlines.

President Hollande and Putin's joint announcement in Moscow in late November that France and Russia would make common cause against ISIL, after the Paris attacks that left 138 people dead and following the bombing of a Russian plane full holiday makers by ISIL earlier in the month, alludes to the renaissance of the double entente between the two countries in the era of great power blocs that struggled for mastery in Europe in the decades prior to the First World War.

The Russia-France entente spells the beginning of the end to France's commitment to ever-closer European Union. Russia and France are historically Mediterranean powers and maintain sizable conventional forces including aircraft carriers.

The other major European power, Germany, remains economically powerful but militarily ineffectual, vainly pursuing the increasingly unobtainable goals of closer union and open European borders in Europe. German foreign policy seems to honour more in the breach Frederick the Great's dictum that a state without an army is like an orchestra without instruments.

As a result, Germany seeks to buy off Turkey to sustain its European vision and contain the burgeoning refugee problem. In this, however, Germany only alienates the former Soviet bloc states' commitment to ever-closer union while it also affords Turkish President Recep Tayyip Erdoğan the licence and support to follow his assertive neo-Ottoman foreign policy against Syrian President Assad, Russia's proxy, and against Kurdish and other minorities.

The return of geo-politics
The tangled web of competing interests at work in Europe and the Middle East once again evokes an earlier era in nineteenth century Europe, reprising events that led to the Russo-Turkish war of 1875-78. As US foreign policy calculation in the Mediterranean is notable only by its absence, national interest and the forgotten charms of European *realpolitik* inexorably reassert themselves. Geo-politics is back in fashion. It is in this realist context that Britain's Parliament has voted to intervene in Syria (reversing an earlier 2013 vote against intervention). Seemingly, ethical foreign policies are out, prudent assessments of the doctrine of the lesser evil are back in.

The question whether to join in military strikes on Syria is thus as much diplomatic as military. Few analysts believe air strikes, let alone greater British involvement, will destroy ISIL in Syria. However, Prime Minister David Cameron's advocacy of the right to deploy force on international legal grounds is less about law and ethics and more about Britain's regional power status, and its resolve to play a role in the resolution of the Middle East. In that respect, joining France and Russia raises the interesting prospect of the formation of a new triple entente.

The only permanent international institutions
History of course does not repeat itself, but it may as Mark Twain observed, 'rhyme'. Thus, although it is unlikely that any informal Franco-Russo-British cooperation will herald another world confrontation on the scale of the First World War, it does intimate an emerging European balance where the entente powers curtail the assertive idealism of Germany, which under Merkel pursues a Mittel European fantasy with an Ottoman connection, a fantasy that first emerged in the years prior to 1914.

Whatever else it is, a structural fact about world politics is that, contra Lord Giddens, there will always be a world of enemies, competitors and adversaries. In that respect, the nation state has no permanent friends and no permanent enemies, only permanent interests. These verities always reaffirm themselves when utopian ideals and grand transformative schemes like the European Union or institutions like the United Nations end in moral humbug and political chaos. To echo an under-appreciated British theorist of international politics, Martin Wight, recent events demonstrate, yet again, that ultimately there are only three permanent institutions in the international system: diplomacy, alliances, and war.

Original article published the *Daily Telegraph*, 3rd December 2015, by David Martin Jones and M.L.R. Smith.

Apocalypse soon?

'I shall return', announced General Douglas MacArthur in March 1942 following the fall of the Philippines to the Japanese in the Second World War. MacArthur did indeed return, reconquering the Philippines and leading the Allies to victory in the Pacific in 1945.

MacArthur went on to lead the United Nations forces in Korea following the North's invasion of the South in June 1950, halting the communist advance with the audacious amphibious assault at Inchon. This notwithstanding, President Harry Truman sacked MacArthur the following year for insubordination after he advocated invading northern China, which had sent the People's Liberation Army to the aid of North Korea. MacArthur's plan included atomic attacks against China, making the prospect all the more disquieting.

Currently, the spectre of General MacArthur haunts the peninsula because the strategic conundrum the Americans face today remains eerily similar to 1951: namely, how to curtail a recalcitrant North Korea without recourse to outright war and nuclear escalation?

Missile etiquette

During his presidential campaign and after his inauguration, Donald Trump asserted that he would deal more forcefully with the Kim dynasty that has ruled North Korea since 1948. The policy seemed somewhat clearer when National Security Adviser, HR McMaster, stated that Pyongyang's pattern of threatening and provocative behaviour 'just can't continue'.

The 'provocative' behaviour is the North Korean nuclear missile threat. Its nuclear programme gained momentum after the end of the Cold War when communist states were becoming an endangered species. A nuclear capability was perceived as a deterrent to possible invasion from Western imperialist powers.

In the following years, the North has increasingly flaunted its potential nuclear delivery capability. Beginning in 2005 with its short-range Rodong missile the North Koreans have on a regular basis conducted live missile-firing tests into the Sea of Japan. The later generation Taepodong-2 missile platforms have an estimated range of more than 6,000 kilometres, enough to bring the United States' Western seaboard within Pyongyang's nuclear range.

The difficulties of trying to deal with the North prompted the administration of President Barack Obama to adopt a posture of 'strategic patience'.

Such a posture, however, represented the triumph of the hope that North Korea might voluntarily de-nuclearise or spontaneously implode, over the actual experience of the regime's rapidly growing nuclear confidence. The US Secretary of State, Rex Tillerson, rang down the curtain on this era of passivity on 17th March 2017, stating at a news conference in Seoul: 'Let me be very clear: the policy of strategic patience has ended. We are exploring a new range of security and diplomatic measures. All options are on the table'.

The Trump doctrine?

Starting in April 2017, with the cruise missile strike against a Syrian airfield, Trump's apparent readiness to use military force to reinforce red lines has underscored this changed diplomatic calculus. But what does this mean for the complex security balance in East Asia? What outcome, short of a pre-emptive war, would suit the current administration and how might it differ from Obama's now seemingly forgotten 'pivot' to Asia?

In other words, there might be a new international policeman on the block, but this is a hood that tough-minded cops like Truman and Eisenhower found particularly troublesome. The current security dilemma reflects, in fact, the conclusion to the forgotten war in the Asia-Pacific that left in its wake a divided Korea. The fallout from the atomic denouement to the Second World War saw a

Soviet-backed Leninist regime in the North led by Kim Jong-un's grandfather, Kim Il-Sung, and a US-backed government in the South.

The unexpected loss of China to communism in 1949 followed by Kim Il-Sung's invasion of South Korea in 1950 meant that the Truman Doctrine, initially intended to contain Soviet-style communism in Europe, was rapidly rolled out to Asia, in the process embracing the Korean Peninsula, the 'dagger' pointed at Japan's heart.

Frozen conflict
The Korean War never ended. It was frozen in time with an armistice in 1953 along the 38th parallel that fixed the current borders between North and South. It also drew the US into a structure of alliances in East and Southeast Asia, dating from the US-Japan Mutual Defence Treaty of 1952 that remains the cornerstone of US regional policy.

Meanwhile, the *Juche* or 'national self-reliance' regime of Kim Il-Sung and his grandson Kim Jong-un became increasingly dependent on China. Mao Zedong and successive Chinese leaders viewed the Kimocracy as 'close as lips and teeth', and a buffer against the threat of a united peninsula under US influence. The informal China-North Korea alliance however has a downside. The North Korean regime signed the Nuclear Non-Proliferation Treaty, or NPT, in 1985 but continued to develop bomb-usable plutonium from its heavy water reactor at Yongbyon, while China turned a blind eye.

The Clinton administration contemplated a preventative war to enforce the non-proliferation regime as early as 1994, but instead negotiated an Agreed Framework where North Korea would abandon its nuclear aspirations in return for US aid and recognition.

The framework broke down in the aftermath of 11th September 2001, when the Bush administration identified North Korea as a rogue state and Kim Jong-il, Kim Jong-un's father, fearing a fate similar to Saddam Hussein, withdrew from the NPT and accelerated the regime's nuclear and ballistic missile programmes.

In an effort to resolve this cycle of provocation and punishment a multilateral framework involving China, South Korea, Russia and Japan, as well as North Korea and the US, began meeting in 2003.

These six-party talks led to a 2005 pact where Pyongyang agreed, again, to abandon its nuclear programme and re-join the NPT in exchange for food and energy assistance. The accord paved the way for Pyongyang to normalise relations with both the United States and Japan and negotiate a peace agreement for the Korean Peninsula.

The talks, however, broke down in 2009. North Korea left them and conducted multiple missile tests followed by a nuclear test in May 2009. After he assumed supreme leadership in 2011, Kim Jong-un expanded the missile and nuclear bomb programme, while China exercised minimal restraint on its alliance partner's provocative actions against South Korea and Japan. By September 2016, North Korea had conducted five nuclear and innumerable ballistic missile tests, prompting the US to announce its intent to deploy its Terminal High-Altitude Area Defence (THAAD) anti-missile system in South Korea. Beijing considers the deployment a direct threat to its security interests because of the radar's ability to monitor military activities deep inside China.

Changed narrative with the art of the deal
However, Trump's announcement in April of an 'armada' heading for North Korea, along with the prospect of a US-Chinese 'grand bargain' and the intransigence of Kim Jong-un, evidently prompted a rethink in Beijing. There is some evidence to suggest that China might now be pressing North Korea to curb its enthusiasm for a long-distance nuclear attack capacity.

At the presidential summit in Florida in April, Chinese leaders indicated their readiness to push Pyongyang more heavily in return for an American abandonment of plans for a trade war. Several factors have now emerged that might lead Beijing to reappraise the 'close as lips and teeth' relationship between China and North Korea. China is particularly concerned that if the US acts successfully in Korea, then Washington will regain the regional ascendancy it lost during the Obama administration's somewhat vacuous pivot to Asia.

Trump's recent rhetoric, which he may be prepared to reinforce with military deeds and the odd bluff, serves to remind China that North Korea's ballistic antics may imperil China's commercial interests or lead to a nuclear Japan. Trump is acting unpredictably and forcefully against Pyongyang on the assumption that, without war, he can achieve containment.

The general aim, then, is to remind China and its proxy of US strength and that the new president is willing to use it. Even so, China remains constrained by its desire to avoid regime implosion and so lose its buffer with US forces in South Korea. In the meantime, although Japan remains committed to the US, South Korea has a newly elected president, Moon Jae-In, who favours accommodation rather than confrontation with Pyongyang.

Pyongyang has displayed considerable skill over its 70-year history in playing off its neighbours against each other, and while relations with China may have cooled, its links to Russia have warmed. Moreover, Vladimir Putin is not in as giving a mood as he once might have been when it comes to Trump's avowed intention to stop North Korea 'doing the wrong thing'.

Back to the future?
Ultimately, Trump either requires a Chinese-mediated return to the complete verifiable and immediate dismantlement of North Korea's weapon programme, which was the basis for the six-party agreement in 2005, or it could break the current Mexican standoff with 'a sea of fire'.

In this aim, Trump and his generals seek to correct the misapprehension that the US is in decline rather than re-emerging from a self-imposed period of patience. Once the US has reasserted its capacity for deterrence then it will be able to talk to Russia and China from a position of strength to address areas of mutual concern from world trade to nuclear proliferation and radical Islam.

The second option, and the clear downside of this post-Cold War form of brinkmanship, would certainly alter regional geometry and, ironically, reverts to the nuclear solution that General MacArthur proposed in 1951 shortly before Truman sacked him while Secretary of State Dean Acheson opted for containment and regional stalemate. The MacArthur solution, which in 1950, while of course risky, might have been feasible, in 2017 looks more like Apocalypse Soon.

Original article published in *The World Today*, June-July 2017, by David Martin Jones and M.L.R. Smith.

Putin's geopolitics: Making sense of the war in Ukraine

Geopolitics is often used to describe the self-interested realism that shapes the international political strategies employed by states like China and Russia. In this context, geopolitics nods to a desire to revise the liberal international rules-based order that evolved since the end of the Cold War. It becomes a synonym for having scant regard for international law.

But this use of geopolitics can cover up a failure to understand the evolution of the self-interested international realism employed by China and Russia and what such strategies imply for the contemporary conduct of the revisionist powers on the Eurasian landmass

A brief history of geopolitics

It was Rudolf Kjellén, a Swedish conservative geographer and political scientist, who first coined the term geopolitics. In his *Lectures on Swedish Geography* (1900) he applied geopolitics to the problems and conditions within a state that arise from its geographic features and their impact upon how modern states flourish and then decay. After 1914 and the collapse of the balance of power that had maintained the world order that dominated much of the nineteenth century, Kjellén's idea of the 'state as a life-form' (*Staten Sum Lifs Form*, 1916) powerfully influenced inter-war German thinking. In particular, the German general Karl Haushofer maintained that a lack of geographical knowledge accounted for Germany's defeat in World War I. Haushofer developed the concept of *lebensraum* and his journal *Zeit Schrift für Geopolitik* (Journal of Geopolitics) influenced the Reich's strategic thinking. At the Nuremberg Trials, Sidney Alderman described Haushofer as 'Hitler's intellectual Godfather'.

But ideas on the importance of geography to international politics did not flourish just in Nazi Germany. In conservative and realist circles across Europe in the first decades of the twentieth century, geopolitics offered an alternative to the balance of power thinking that broke down so catastrophically in 1914. After 1918, when Europe 'ceased to be the centre of the world', and instead became 'merely the European question', a new generation of realist thinkers conceived world politics in geographical terms.

It was, in fact, the English political geographer Halford Mackinder's 1904 essay on 'the geographical pivot of history' that particularly influenced strategic thinking from 1918 to 1945. Although the understanding that geography and climate affect political organisation had occurred to Aristotle, and later to Machiavelli and Montesquieu, this view assumed increasing relevance in terms of the impact of new industrial technologies, modes of communication and military organisation during the nineteenth century. Mackinder argued that a 'heartland power' could come to dominate Euro-Asia, the name he gave for the 'world continent' that stretched from Amsterdam to Shanghai. Mackinder speculated that the replacement of the balance of power in Europe would 'favour' a 'pivot state' whose expansion over the marginal lands of Euro-Asia, from the Baltics to Mongolia, would 'permit the use of vast continental resources' and 'the empire of the world would then be in sight'.

A world island

Mackinder further observed that Russia held the 'central strategical position' on the world continent, although he also considered Germany and even China well placed for global dominance. As he subsequently wrote in his prescient work *Democratic Ideals and Reality* (1919), 'the heartland is as real a physical fact as the world island'. Moreover, 'whoever rules East Europe, commands the heartland, who commands the heartland commands the world island, who rules the world island rules the world'.

In 1894, the US naval strategist Alfred Thayer Mahan emphasised the importance of sea power in shaping global politics, an argument that seemed to fit global developments since the seventeenth century and the rise of the British empire in the nineteenth century. Mackinder likewise assumed that sea power would continue to play the dominant role in world politics. However, his geopolitical thinking implied that land power could ultimately trump sea power, the foundation of the British empire in the nineteenth century and United States' hegemony in the twentieth.

Meanwhile, in Germany, Haushofer and the Reich jurist Carl Schmitt maintained that war and technological change announced a new era of world politics dominated by territorial units of increased size. Haushofer termed this evolution *lebensraum*; for Schmitt it meant the *Grossraum* or the great space. In this process of transformation weaker states would disappear and, in their place, larger pan-regions or 'extended spaces' (*Grossraum*) would arrange themselves as friends or enemies. Haushofer posited four world regions: pan-Europe (which included Africa) dominated by Germany; pan-Asia dominated by Japan; pan-America; and pan-Russia directed by the Soviet Union. Control of the Berlin-Moscow, Berlin-Tehran and Berlin-Tokyo geographic axes would determine German dominance of the world continent.

Schmitt additionally maintained there would be a new understanding of world order that reflected 'the highest, unchangeable and concrete qualities of order' that reflected the ethnic homogeneity or shared values that inform the institutions of these enlarged spaces and guarantee the status quo between different *Grossraum*. This new *nomos*, as Schmitt termed it, would replace what he saw as the problem of the unstable international law or rules-based order that the Treaty of Versailles and the League of Nations bequeathed.

The age of liberal international law
This twentieth century liberal order had overturned the nineteenth century *nomos* of European order, the *Jus Europaeum Publicum* (European Public Law), the inter-state system that had determined the global balance of power between 1815 and 1914, ending with its collapse in 1918. It was superseded by liberal international law that lacked any spatial reference. The pursuit of liberal international law replaced the more concrete order of European public law, or *völkerrecht*. This meant that only a shadow of the old European order remained in the international legal regimes after 1918. The Versailles Treaty had dethroned Europe and international law distorted the nineteenth century understanding of European public law that had evolved with the Westphalian system of European state sovereignty after the collapse of the *res publica Christiana* in the sixteenth century.

After 1918, the Wilsonian universalist view of international law sought to subjugate all inter-state or revolutionary conflict to abstract liberal norms, assessed according to a criterion of justness and adjudicated by international courts. Schmitt considered this normative universalism to be unstable and illegitimate. Both the League of Nations and the 'Europe' that emerged after Versailles were new and ambiguous formations that ultimately benefited a liberal imperialism. The new universalism implied a world order subject to a liberal code ultimately enforced by the US, itself a continent-wide extended space. Ultimately, the US *Grossraum*, which sat outside the world continent, asserted its view of liberalism as a form of world governance.

Meanwhile, the British empire, the superpower of the nineteenth century, was ill-suited to the heartland-based environment of Eurasian politics that contested the liberal Versailles regime in the 1930s and would, as Haushofer foresaw, disintegrate. After the defeat of Nazi Germany, the US and Russia emerged as the two geopolitical units best situated by size and location to define the post-1945 era.

Geopoliticians vigorously disagreed, however, about the character, number and location of the entities that would prove most viable. In this context, the American geopolitical thinker Nicholas J. Spykman contended that it was, in fact, the rimland region of the world island, which stretches in a crescent from Europe to East Asia, which had the geopolitical potential to unite in the hands of one state. Contra Haushofer and Mackinder, Spykman considered that the country that controlled the rimland, controlled Eurasia and would control the destiny of the world or would at least be able to contain the heartland.

The popularity of geopolitical theory declined after World War II because of its association with Nazi aggression. Nevertheless, geopolitics continued to influence US Cold War thinking. George Kennan's promotion of the doctrine of containment and deterrence reflected the influence of Spykman's *Geography of the Peace* (1944). It served as the US template to limit the expansion of the Soviet Union during the Cold War.

The return of the heartland after 1990
Despite the decline of geopolitical theorising in the 1950s, Schmitt continued to outline his criticism of the unstable secular, liberal project of world governance. In *Nomos Der Erde* (The Nomos of the Earth) (1960) Schmitt argued that the development of the new world order after 1945 continued to confront its antithesis, namely distinct and separate extended land spaces like the Soviet Union and China. Moreover, while liberal universalism suited what Schmitt termed the maritime based 'thalassocratic' powers, firstly the United Kingdom and, after 1945, the US, this liberal order was inimical to land based or telluric power. Summating his thinking in his panoptic overview of geopolitics, Schmitt showed, at least to his own satisfaction, that an international order reflecting maritime power could never suit land based great spaces or 'tellurocracies' physically grounded in the world island. The telluric state retained a more intimate connection with *blut und boden* (blood and earth) in a way that thalassocrat liberal internationalism could not.

Schmitt further argued that, reflecting its maritime character, liberal universalism was inherently unstable. It licensed transnational bureaucrats to reduce international affairs to regulations and procedures that gave international law courts a central role in the creation and maintenance of a normative regime antithetical to the concrete order of a telluric world island *Grossraum*. Tellurocracy thus offered a concrete order opposed to universalist liberal rules. In the *Law of the Sea* (1942) Schmitt presented this conflict in Manichean and Old Testament terms as an irreconcilable conflict between the land-based Behemoth and the maritime Leviathan.

This myth, Heinrich Meier argues, reflected Schmitt's thinking on the 'fundamental jurisdiction of political theology' in international and domestic politics. It is from his eschatological view of history that Schmitt developed the idea of the *katechon*, a biblical concept that is developed into a political philosophy. In his *Second Letter to the Thessalonians*, St Paul wrote that a *katechon* would be necessary to 'restrain' the 'lawless one', namely the Antichrist, during the last days prior to Christ's Second Coming when the eschaton would be immanentised. Schmitt's pluralistic ideal of multiple *Grossraum*, therefore, was not only geopolitical but also apocalyptic. He believed that multipolarity was necessary to restrain the more destructive features of liberal universalism through the mutual recognition of friends and enemies against the Antichrist of world unity.

From Schmitt's political theological perspective, the malady that beset Europe after 1918 was the disintegration of Western faith in both Christianity and Enlightenment rationalism that had made possible the only sustainable *nomos* of the earth, the *Jus Europaeum Publicum* of the nineteenth century. No longer the centre of world politics, Western Europe had also lost its geopolitical grounding. Because of the ubiquitous liberal critique of the European Age of Discovery, 'everything European is on the defensive' and so also was Western civilisation.

Europe as a peninsula of greater Eurasia
Apocalypse and Europe's inexorable decline notwithstanding, it was the US rimland version of geopolitical strategy that ultimately triumphed during the Cold War. George Kennan's policy of 'firm and vigilant containment' eventually brought about the internal collapse of the Soviet totalitarian model over the course of the 1990s. The Russian Commonwealth of Independent States that replaced it after 1993 was a profoundly unstable affair. The loss of former Russian territories like Georgia and the Ukraine with their predominantly Slavic populations provoked a sense of growing unease about Western liberal designs on the Russian Commonwealth. Significantly, George Kennan the architect of the containment doctrine warned against the West's eastward expansion. NATO and EU expansion would, Kenan wrote, 'inflame the nationalistic, anti-Western and militaristic tendencies in Russian opinion' and have an 'adverse effect on the development of Russian democracy' ultimately impelling 'Russian foreign policy in directions decidedly not to our liking'.

This is indeed what happened. Wounded pride, a sense of grievance and resentment toward US backed liberal democratic universalism, shaped the emergence of a new irredentist, pan-Russian nationalism. Vladimir Putin's Presidency and the United

Russia party that legitimates his authority cemented national revival at the core of domestic and foreign policy at the millennium. Geopolitical considerations became central to Russian strategic thinking as its wealth and internal resilience recovered under Putin's autocratic guidance in the second decade of the twenty-first century. Whilst the European Union dismissed geopolitics after the Cold War, it now happened on its doorstep with the Russian seizure of the Crimea in 2014. What then is the geopolitical vision animating Putinism?

It is, not surprisingly, a potent and promiscuous mixture of Schmitt, Haushofer and Mackinder's analysis of the political geography of the world island that currently informs both Putin's vision of a Russian led enlarged space of Eurasia and the Chinese Communist Party's (CCP) thinking on global domination of the world island. Schmitt is widely read in Chinese policy circles.

Putin's geopolitical brain

In Moscow, however, it is Alexander Dugin, Russia's most influential exponent and interpreter of Schmitt, who has, in several books and essays, adapted Schmitt's conservative geopolitical eschatology to the current dilemmas of Eastern Europe. Dugin's adaptation of Schmitt to post-Soviet Russia has given intellectual and strategic depth to Putin and his core advisers' thinking on rectifying the trauma left by the dismemberment of the Soviet Union between 1990 and 1996. Since 1997, Dugin's *Foundations of Geopolitics* has been a prescribed text at the Russian Military Academy. What, we might then wonder, is Dugin's understanding of multipolarity, and 'the last war of the world island'?

Dugin is a Russian ultranationalist philosopher and mystic. His writings on philosophy and geopolitics contemplate the unification of all Russian speaking peoples within a single enlarged space, by force if necessary. He considers the revival of a Eurasian heartland to offer the concrete basis for building a new Russian Tsardom. To achieve this, he argues, Russia must 'defeat the maritime world exemplified by the United States'.

Dugin's most widely known work, *The Fourth Political Theory* (2012) offers a 'conservative revolutionary' ideology for a post-liberal age. His new political theory transcends the failed dogmas of communism, liberalism and, somewhat less certainly, fascism, and offers instead an ethnically based, Neo-Eurasian, alternative.

Neo-Eurasianism may be characterised as the latest non-liberal response to the inevitable conflict Schmitt first identified between tellurocracies (land powers) and thalassocracies (sea powers). In Dugin's version, Russia replaces Germany as the Reich (Empire) and Eurasia is its *Grossraum*, acting as the pivotal hegemon within an enlarged territorial space. The Russian imperial duty is both to promulgate the 'political idea' necessary to unify the *Grossraum* and decide upon its external relations with other *Grossraum*.

Dugin considers the great spaces on the world continent as 'a unification' between themselves as geographical units and '*the Narodni*' (people or ethnos), an imperial condition 'built on historical kinship' and a 'common fate'. Indeed, for Dugin, the political ideal of a Great Space is the homogeneity of its *narod*. Thus, Neo-Eurasianism promotes a positive attitude toward the native population. By contrast 'liberalism... is entirely incompatible' with nativism and ethnocentrism.

Geographical determinism

Dugin's *Fourth Political Theory* thus revives a German nationalist rhetoric of *Blut und Boden* in a Eurasian guise. It maintains that the sea based or maritime order that emerged with the British and US empires is inherently unstable because it lacks the geographical fixity necessary for a healthy civilisation's 'ethnic sphere'. Geographical determinism means that civilisations rooted in the structural fixity of land 'generate conservatism', whereas those founded on the sea generate instability, hostility and isolation as they are 'constantly subject to change'.

Dugin's Eurasianism, as opposed to the 'Westernism' that oversaw the dismemberment of the Soviet Union, is reflected in his book *The Last War of the World Island* (2015) as 'the constants of Russian history'. After 2011, Dugin welcomed the fact that Putin spoke increasingly of the need for a Eurasian union founded on a pan-Slavic ethnos. He considered Putin to have effectively embraced the Eurasian model, 'a new supranational organization built on civilisational commonality'.

A revived Eurasia would, moreover, form a pole in a multipolar world order that Dugin, following Schmitt, argues would contest the unipolar liberal order that America and its allies seek to impose globally. The unipolar order seeks legally to transform itself into a universal world government through the 'depoliticisation' and 'de-sovereignisation' of nation states.

By contrast, multipolarity and Eurasianism would offer a 'model of the world based on the paradigm of unique civilisations and Great Spaces'. Consequently, Dugin argued that if Putin secures Russia's sovereignty and instantiates a successful policy for building a multipolar world, re-establishing Russia's strategic role in the global context, 'we can state that Russia has not yet passed the point of no return'. Dugin concludes his account of the last war of the world island with the observation that the geopolitical cycle Putin began in 1999 remains unfinished. The historical fate of the government and 'the civilization of... the heartland Russia-Eurasia remains open'.

The interchangeable use of multipolarity and Eurasianism reflects the important role that Schmitt's concept of the *katechon* also plays in Dugin's, and by extension, in Putin's geopolitical thought and its eschatological justification for the invasion of Ukraine. Dugin's 1997 article, 'Katechon and Revolution' first introduced Schmitt's notion to a Russian audience. Given that it evoked a long-standing tradition of invoking the *katechon* in Russian Orthodox theology, it received a receptive audience.

Why Ukraine?

Dugin's Neo-Eurasian dream thus revives Russia's divine purpose in world history, combined with the historic spatial understanding of Russia as *Grossraum*, unified by the Russian Orthodox faith. The main Neo-Eurasian government backed think-tank is aptly named *Katechon* and subtitled 'Geopolitics and tradition'. Its mission is to 'defend the principle of a multipolar world' with distinct 'civilisational spheres', and it frequently features articles by Dugin himself. Significantly Dugin concludes his *Last War* with a quote from Curzio Malaparte: 'nothing is lost until all is lost'. His suggestion is that there remains the capacity to create this great continental Eurasian future for Russia 'with our own hands'.

Putin's conversion to Neo-Eurasianism enables him to depict Russia, in the world-historical role of *katechon*, confronting the unipolar American Empire – the Antichrist. Yet as with the Third Reich in 1942, the Russian attempt to establish its civilisational great space has foundered disastrously in the borderland of Central Europe that is Ukraine.

It is crucial that Western diplomacy and military support for Ukraine considers this millenarian background to the Russian invasion. At some point the West will have to decide how best to confront a nuclear armed power informed by a messianic determination to fight the world island's last war.

Original article published in *Cieo*, 24th March 2022, by David Martin Jones.

How does this end? Europe after Ukraine

Since 2022, there has been a heightened strategic and diplomatic interest in the countries of Central and Eastern Europe. This is hardly surprising since the war in Ukraine borders seven of them – namely: Belarus, Hungary, Moldova, Poland, Romania, Slovakia, and of course Russia. But there are other reasons too. President Joe Biden's visit to Kyiv, his speech in Warsaw, and his meeting with the 'Bucharest Nine' to discuss strengthening NATO's Eastern flank, have all aroused curiosity about a shift of policy on the war.

One reason for this speculation is the contrast in tone between Biden's Warsaw speech in February and President Putin's sombre address on the progress of his special military operation the day before. Putin was uncompromising, but downbeat: the war had not gone as expected but Russia would press on until it gained its objectives in Ukraine. Biden, on the other hand, was positively euphoric about the anticipated victory of freedom over autocracy.

The contrasting rhetoric conceals a series of clashing national and regional impulses on financial, economic, and energy sanctions on Russia and on how to end the war. How quickly and by what strategy? Those differences have been held in check by the diplomatic desire of almost all the NATO allies and EU partners to maintain a united front and by giving opt-outs from sanctions to countries like Slovakia and Hungary whose economies would be massively damaged by them. But the longer the war lasts, and the heavier the economic costs become, the more European governments will be tempted to breach Western unity to prevent the conflict stabilising into a frozen forever war.

Broadly speaking, Europe is divided into two camps on the question of how to end the war. One camp believes that there should be an early cease-fire followed by negotiations on a final 'peace settlement' that might not actually be agreed for several years. The most vocal advocate of this view is Hungary's Prime Minister, Viktor Orbán. But it would be delusory to think that Hungary is either alone or the most influential in promulgating this view. As Germany's actions indicate and, as the occasional hints of a new diplomatic initiative from the *Quai d'Orsay* suggest, 'core Europe' (Germany, France, and the Benelux countries) is also uncomfortable with a policy of living with a long war. The EU does not want Russia to win, but they have no appetite for wanting it to lose completely either. Europe pre-24 February 2022 suited the European status quo very well.

The alternative view envisages a defeat for Russia so unmistakable that it would both render any future Russian irredentism impossible and persuade Russia's political establishment to relinquish any neo-imperial ambitions in Central Europe. Not surprisingly, this policy has the support of Russia's near neighbours such as Poland and the Baltic States which have frequently been invaded and occupied by both Czars and Commissars as well as by Prussians. It is supported, moreover, by the US and the UK (what the French persist in terming 'Les Anglo-Saxons'), which have provided Ukraine with the training, the arms and the bulk of diplomatic and political support that has enabled the Ukrainian struggle led by President Volodymyr Zelenskyy to be prosecuted to a potentially successful conclusion.

It is important to realise that neither of these two perspectives on the war will change substantially. And this long-term reality is dawning on both sides. Biden's trip to meet the Bucharest Nine is, therefore, portentous. The Bucharest Nine consists of the following countries on NATO's Eastern flank: Bulgaria, the Czech Republic, Estonia, Hungary, Latvia, Lithuania, Poland, Romania and Slovakia. Finland and Sweden would be in this group if allowed to join NATO, as seems likely. Four of its members are in the group of countries bordering Ukraine. In effect the Bucharest Nine brings together countries in northern and eastern Europe which between them have an unavoidable connection to Ukraine and a strong collective suspicion of Russian power, as well as a historic memory of German eastward expansionism across *Mitteleuropa* in the nineteenth and twentieth centuries. If you were a US president anxious to preserve an anti-Russian European coalition in the face of the doubts and hesitations of core Europe, why wouldn't you be interested in an expanding Bucharest Nine?

Others, in Central Europe and beyond have expressed similar ideas. They revive, in new forms, federal models that date back to the nineteenth century (Lajos Kossuth's

Danube Confederation (1848), Aurel Popovici's *United States of Greater Austria* (1906) and Józef Piłsudski's *Intermarium* proposed after 1918, spring to mind). In this context, the Visegrád Group, consisting of the Czech Republic, Hungary, Poland and Slovakia, was formed in 1991. The Three Seas Initiative, comprising Austria, Bulgaria, Croatia, the Czech Republic, Estonia, Hungary, Latvia, Lithuania, Poland, Romania, Slovakia and Slovenia, took shape in 2016. It gave Ukraine the status of a partner-participant in 2022. The Lublin Triangle of Lithuania, Poland and Ukraine formed in 2020. In Scandinavia, the Nordic Council represents a similar regional organisation. In a similar vein, the cooperation among the UK, Scandinavia and much of Eastern Europe reflects increasing trends towards cooperation on the part of these countries that have existed for decades.

In November 2021 the UK's Defence Secretary, Ben Wallace, signed a defence cooperation agreement with Poland and Ukraine (complete with plans and business contracts for force modernisation.) By then, the UK had already been the lead nation in the Joint Expeditionary Force, formed in 2015. It now includes nine other northern European nations – Denmark, Estonia, Finland, Iceland, Latvia, Lithuania, the Netherlands, Norway and Sweden – and it has been a 'dynamic' element in the West's military support for the Baltic states as well as Ukraine. According to a report in *Corriere Della Sera* in May 2022, then Prime Minister Boris Johnson privately floated the idea of a 'European Commonwealth' that would unite countries in Scandinavia, the Baltics and Eastern Europe that wanted to maintain a stronger position than 'Core Europe' on Ukraine. It would, alleged *Corriere*, offer a potential alternative to the European Union.

Somewhat differently, French President Emmanuel Macron is himself floating ideas of a new, looser, European structure (though one built around the Franco-German core leadership). The Russian invasion of Ukraine has unsettled European politics in general, opening a space for new ideas; and it is far from impossible that under the stress of war, new alliances could take solid, larger and practical forms that divide Northern and Central Europe from core Europe.

The US already provides most of the money and materiel for the defence of Ukraine. The US also has a track record of supporting regional agreements in Central Europe. In 2018, President Donald Trump backed Poland's Three Seas Initiative on infrastructure, energy and the economy – all now given greater salience by Russia's actions in the war. In the light of these earlier commitments, Biden's convening of the Bucharest Nine seems to suggest that Washington could take a more direct role in shaping whatever grouping of Central and Eastern Europe would be helpful in dealing with the next stage of the Ukraine crisis, if necessary, without Germany and France. What might that entail?

We have a reasonable idea of what Russia hoped to secure from a victory in Ukraine – namely, the restoration of a security alliance comprising Russia, Ukraine, Belarus and Kazakhstan – because *Ria Novosztyi*, the Russian information agency, prematurely leaked Putin's war aims in the first days of the invasion. A limited version of this might still be achieved if Russia reverses Kyiv's recent advances, but how much would survive?

Examining the balance of forces (including economic strength and population) between this Russian alliance and different potential European coalitions in the event of Ukrainian success are thought-provoking. Thus, Russian victory achieving a version of *Ria Novosztyi*'s vision would see, according to the analysis by Csaba Barnabás Horváth:

> The combined population of such a conglomeration would be roughly 220 million people. By contrast, the combined population of the member states of the Three Seas Initiative, the broadest regional bloc proposed in Central and Eastern Europe, is, without Ukraine, only 110 million – half the population of a potential greater Russian grouping.

By contrast in the event of Ukrainian success:

> Russia would be reduced to the Union State of Russia and Belarus. The two countries have a combined population of 154 million. On the side of the Three Seas Initiative, if we add Ukraine to it as well, its population also amounts to

about 154 million people. With a two-to-one population ratio in the case of a Russian victory, as opposed to a one-to-one ratio in the case of a Ukrainian victory, the geopolitical picture is pretty clear.

And that geopolitical picture? It is hard to imagine Ukraine as a useful future security partner to Moscow and still harder to imagine Russia without Ukraine as a major Eurasian power. As Zbigniew Brzezinski famously wrote, after the Cold War, 'without Ukraine, Russia ceases to be a Eurasian empire'.

Central Europeans, the US and the UK can see the strategic utility of putting together a reliably friendly coalition to prepare for whatever advantages or setbacks the military facts on the ground in Ukraine subsequently reveal. It is also evident that core Europe and even Hungary have doubts about a Central European confederation. Whatever else, the war in Ukraine, following hard upon the end of the COVID lockdown, announced a new era in European politics. Structures that had emerged during the Cold and post-Cold War eras now seem increasingly otiose. Instead, a new *Struggle for Mastery in Europe* might return.

In the context of European war and its aftermath new forms of cooperation and conflict are inevitable. As the Governor of the Central Bank of Hungary, György Matolcsy writes, 'the 2020s seem to be the initial decades of a new institutional/political cycle – just like the 1940s were eighty years ago'. The new dispensation is one marked by European land war, inflation, anxiety and de-globalisation. This stands in marked dialectical contrast to the era that preceded it. The new cycle will see new and perhaps old forms emerging or reconstituting themselves, especially in Central Europe. The structure of European politics and the new balance of powers within it will be profoundly affected by the way the war in Ukraine ends.

Original article published in *Cieo*, 9th March 2023, by David Martin Jones.

At the Baal Game:
The World Cup and the clash of civilisations

Baal was one of the more important gods in the ancient pantheon, a pre-Christian deity worshipped across the Middle East. As a Semitic common noun, *Baal* (Hebrew *Ba'al*) meant 'owner or lord'. In some ancient civilisations like Carthage, Baal was worshipped as the supreme being associated with everything from the weather to fertility. The modern incarnation of such worship of a pagan supreme lord might be said to be Footbaal.

In the ancient setting of the Qatari desert in December 2022, Footbaal enjoyed its regular quadrennial celebration, with its High Priest, FIFA President Gianni Infantino declaring the 2022 World Cup 'the greatest ever'. Like most creeds, Footbaal evokes a universalist totalising vision. FIFA's official commandment asserted 'Football unites the world'. The slogan subliminally echoed a secular Western preoccupation with an open, borderless, post-Cold War world promoted relentlessly ever since Francis Fukuyama announced the end of history in 1989.

The problem, however, is that this integrated world order is not dawning. And football, far from uniting the world, instead reflects its transformation into something very different, namely a growing clash of civilisational identities. If the analogy holds, in a curious way the month-long event in the uber-wealthy Gulf sheikhdom merely intimated the schismatic nature of this new secular faith. It reflected and magnified the state of the post-Western world disorder and what the American political scientist Samuel Huntington presciently described in 1996 as an inexorable clash of civilisations. Huntington observed that as the West weakened economically, demographically and territorially compared with 'challenger' cultures like China, the Muslim world, Latin America, India and Eurasia, so too would its hard and soft power.

Huntingdon's paradox: cohesion versus disintegration
In the post-Cold War world, according to Huntington, civilisational identities would inform an evolving 'pattern of cohesion, disintegration and conflict'. Inhabiting 'a mirage of immortality', a purblind West would fail to see that this brave new world was multi-civilisational. As they acquired Western technologies and wealth, while also securing their energy and manufacturing base, different civilisations came to resent the drive to 'Westernise' their societies. Democratisation was the euphemistic term for this form of Westernisation. It sought to persuade non-Western civilisations to accept a universal progressive agenda, where supposedly shared liberal moral values of human rights and social justice prevail. Failure to align with this progressive institutional order was to be consigned to the outer darkness of impoverished pariahdom, like Afghanistan, Iraq, Cuba, Iran and North Korea.

Despite the homogenising pretentions inherent in a universal moral order, the clash between the West and the Rest was immediately evident in Doha. Western commentators drew attention to Qatar's abysmal human rights record. The country's *kalafa* system that reduces migrant workers to little more than indentured labour, resulted in the cavalier sacrifice of an estimated 6,500 workers, mainly from Egypt, Pakistan, Philippines and Nepal, to construct Qatar's cavernous temples to footbaal. Meanwhile, woke Western football pundits questioned the Arab kleptocracy's treatment of women and the LGBTQ+ community, although only after the cheque for their commentating services had cleared the account of the Qatari sports channels

Burnishing their progressive credentials, the England team and seven other Western nations committed to wearing the 'one love' rainbow arm band. The commitment did not even survive the official kick off. FIFA's stipulation that the display of political statements like wearing the armband would incur an automatic yellow card quickly saw off that principled commitment. The German team's crass gesture of covering their mouths in protest at being prevented from wearing the 'one love' arm band received relentless mockery in the Qatari media. Commentators on the Alkass sports channel placed their hands over their mouths, barely concealing their mirth, while waving goodbye to Germany following the country's humiliating exit at the group stage.

Meanwhile, the England team's 'taking the knee' against racism looked even more vacuous, especially when they performed it against the United States, where the gesture originated but whose football team now studiously avoided it. Moral principles were notable only for their mutability in the post-modern Muslim paradise.

As the BBC commentary team achieved new heights of moral sententiousness, Infantino righteously denounced the West for 'its staggering hypocrisy and racism'. For their past crimes against humanity, Europeans should be 'apologizing for the next 3,000 years before starting to give lessons to people'. Yet on the eve of the opening ceremony, Infantino, engaged in a further round of weirdly contradictory pronouncements, declaring that he felt Qatari (possibly because he has a large second home there), Arabic, gay, disabled and like a migrant worker because he had been bullied at school for being 'a foreigner'. The World Cup was about 'pleasure and joy'. Fans only wanted to watch 'ninety minutes without thinking about anything', the FIFA president declared.

Indeed, FIFA claimed it went to great lengths to keep political messaging out of the tournament. It even denied Volodymyr Zelenskyy's request to share a message of world peace on the eve of the cup final, while Qatar, of course, maintained that it defended human rights 'in its own way'.

Sport is politics

Politics is, however, never far away from sport. And political messaging was subliminally on display everywhere. It took the shape of largely non-Western crowds fanatically disporting their national allegiances. Japanese fans chanted *Nippon* and *Banzai* as their team reached the last sixteen, South Koreans passionately declaimed *Dae Han Min Guk*, a homage to the Republic of Korea, whilst Argentine fans and their football team predictably chanted *Muchachos*, an anthem denouncing 'the fucking English' and the Falklands War 'don't forget'.

As fancied European teams fell by the wayside and England predictably choked, the Rest rose in the shape of Argentina, Japan (who defeated the once mighty Germans 2–1) and, of course, plucky little Morocco. Morocco, in fact, served as a proxy for the Muslim world in general and Qatar in particular. The North African kingdom and the desert sheikdom share close cultural and business ties. Every Moroccan game was a home tie, with its fans screaming and whistling incessantly to unsettle their opponents, rather successfully as their unlikely victory over Portugal demonstrated. Less widely acknowledged was the widespread display of the Palestinian flag at Moroccan games. Whilst the Western media chose to ignore such obvious political statements, Qatar's state-owned international broadcaster *Al Jazeera* regularly hosted broadcasts from the Gaza Strip where Hamas supporters celebrated every Moroccan goal.

As Huntington noted in *The Clash of Civilizations*, civilisational affiliations are not eroded by globalising and cosmopolitan forces but are instead exacerbated by them. In the borderless post-Cold War world, large migrant communities increasingly identify with different civilisations. In such conflicted cultural circumstances, previously coherent nation-states become 'cleft', as minority populations and their host country find that 'the forces of repulsion drive them apart and they gravitate toward civilisational magnets in other societies'. As a result of uncontrolled migration flows such cleavages have become a familiar demographic feature of European and American states.

The cleft state

During the World Cup the 'cleft' character of Western Europe became all too apparent. After much fancied Belgium lost to Morocco, Brussels experienced several nights of rioting in the city that hosts a population of 40 per cent Muslim migrants. Riots also broke out in Antwerp and Rotterdam. After France defeated Morocco in the semi-final several days later, rioting again broke out in Brussels, as well as in Paris and Montpellier, where an angry mob assaulted a car disporting a French flag and at least one person died. Yet, somewhat ironically, as the cup final whistle blew at the end of 120 minutes, the French team consisted of only one native European, the ageing goalkeeper Hugo Lloris. The rest of his teammates on the field hailed from Francophone Africa or were sons of migrant families from the Parisian *banlieues*, home also to many migrant rioters.

In these circumstances of burgeoning greater civilisational identities, all too evident in Qatar, Huntington wrote that states may become 'torn'. A *torn* state once possessed a single predominant culture placing it in one civilisation, but its leaders want 'to shift to another'. In such societies an elite chooses an identity contrary to the inclinations and attachments of the masses. This is evidently not true of the Arab world or of China, but it has become an all too apparent feature of Western civilisation and was very much in evidence in the Qatar heat where its punditry's embrace of woke multicultural values clashed with the instincts and beliefs of its masses huddled in their homes, bars, cafés and public houses. Political elites have at various times attempted to disavow their cultural heritage and shift the identity of their country from one civilisation to another. In no case to date have they succeeded. Instead, they have created schizophrenic, torn countries. In an era of civilisational clashes, woke multiculturalism endeavours to create a country of many civilisations, which is to say a country not belonging to any civilisation and lacking a cultural core.

Multiculturalism at home threatens the United States and the West', Huntington observed. At the same time, 'universalism abroad threatens the West and the world'. Both deny the uniqueness of Western culture. 'The global monoculturalists want to make the world like America. The domestic multiculturalists want to make America like the world'.

In the deepening clash of civilisations, Europe and America would hang together or hang separately. The World Cup in Qatar was where England but not the United States took the knee, and where multimillionaire soccer pundit Gary Neville compared the treatment of striking nurses, railwaymen and postal workers in the UK to that of migrant workers in Qatar, whilst also receiving a nice little earner from beIN, Qatar's state-owned sports channels. Meanwhile, Belgian police investigate progressive socialist European MEPs concealing suitcases stuffed with euros courtesy of Qatar for supporting its global sporting endeavours. Such cumulative dissonance intimates a West collapsing under the weight of its own hypocrisy and performative contradictions.

Latter day bread and circuses

Yet perhaps, ultimately, to adapt what the Italian semiologist Umberto Eco wrote of an earlier World Cup, there really is no need to ask ourselves why the devotional spectacle in the desert has so morbidly captured the attention of the global public and the devotion of the mass media. From the famous story of how a comedy by Terence played to an empty house because there was a trained bear show elsewhere, and the acute observation of Roman emperors about the usefulness of circuses, to the shrewd use that dictatorships have always made of great competitive events, it is clear that the masses prefer soccer to strikes or the latest rise in the price of everything.

Sports debate is a useful substitute for political debate. Instead of judging the inept and vanishing Prime Minister Rishi Sunak you discuss the job done by Gareth Southgate or Didier Deschamps. Instead of criticising the record of the Conservative Party or President Emmanuel Macron you assess the record of the players. Instead of worrying about energy prices and the war in Ukraine, you ask if the final game will be decided by chance, athletic prowess, or by bribery, corruption and diplomatic alchemy. Talk about soccer does not oblige you to intervene personally because you are talking about something outside the area of the speaker's power. For the male and female fan, Eco sagely noted, 'it's like little girls playing ladies: a pedagogical game, which teaches you how to occupy your proper place'.

Finally, in political circumstances like these, considering the current state of government and opposition, populations in the West are increasingly traumatised and depressed. Faced with this situation, those who expose the World Cup in all its fake grandeur should perhaps be careful not to mar the pleasure taken in this quasi-sacred mystery play. This World Cup arrived like Santa Claus, and we are now left with the aftermath of energy crisis, war and famine. No wonder Qatar, FIFA and its EU dependents want to expand the number of teams and hold the event every three years.

Original article published in *Hungarian Conservative*, Vol. 3, No. 1, 2023, by David Martin Jones and M.L.R. Smith.

The return of grand strategy in the Indo-Pacific

In a seminal article published in mid-2014, Walter Russell Mead proclaimed the 'Return of Geopolitics'. Mead's contention was that Russia's seizure of Crimea earlier in the year, along with China's assertive claims in the South China Sea and Iran's political manoeuvring in the Middle East, heralded the 'Revenge of the Revisionist Powers'. Moreover, he argued, the United States and European states had, since the end of the Cold War, distracted themselves from 'old fashioned power plays' by an idealistic agenda that emphasised trade liberalisation, universal human rights, nuclear non-proliferation and climate change. Believing that the 'rules of the game' had changed, Western nations felt they could 'move past geopolitical questions of territory and military power' and towards issues of 'world order and global governance'.

Ignoring the old rules of international politics, however, meant Western powers were vulnerable to being taken by surprise. 'To be dragged back into old-school contests such as that in Ukraine', Mead noted, did not just divert time and energy away from the West's idealistic preoccupations 'but it also changes the character of international politics'. Mead's point, of course, was that the fundamental realities of international relations had not changed, only that Western nations had merely misread the realities, mistaking the 'ideological triumph of liberal capitalist democracy over communism' for the 'obsolescence of hard power'.

After 2014, the dawning realisation that the West was being led into a new era of 'great-power competition' by the revisionist powers resulted in a renewed interest in geopolitics and especially in the notion of 'grand strategy'. Grand strategy represents a commitment to a national vision where the key elements of power – economic, military and social – are coordinated to sustain the values and commitments that uphold the vision over the long term. Adherence to a coherent and well-formulated grand strategy on the part of powers like China and Russia placed the West at a disadvantage. From the 2010s onward, books, articles and centres of study sprouted, seeking to rehabilitate the idea of grand strategy as a way of reviving Western understandings of the realities of geopolitics.

Russia's invasion of Ukraine in February 2022 heightened the sense that Western nations required an effective plan that would unify political and military efforts to counter Russian irredentism. In the words of Anthony Cordesman, 'optimistic rhetoric is no substitute for grand strategic realism'. Western powers, according to Cordesman, 'need to determine what grand strategy they should pursue to shape the longer-term course of the war and its lasting outcome'.

The felt need for a grand strategic endeavour to unite the West and return it to geopolitical sentience was necessary not only to take on Russia but also Russia's chief ally, China, whose hegemonic ambitions were also of increasing concern, especially in the region known as the Indo-Pacific – the broad expanse of Eurasia extending eastward from Russia towards China and the Pacific littoral in North and Southeast Asia. The course of this essay, then, seeks to dissect the question of how the war in Ukraine has affected the return of grand strategy in the Indo-Pacific. The key contention is, echoing Mead, that grand strategy and geopolitics never really went away in the region. The Russia-Ukraine War has, however, brought pre-existing geopolitical tensions to the surface and re-presented them in sharper and more aggravated forms in ways that presage serious fault lines in the regional and global order.

The West's grand strategic plan

If it is true to claim that geopolitics departed the scene after the end of the Cold War, it is only to the extent that a *realistic* understanding of geopolitics went away. After 1990, global idealists – a strange collocation of neo-conservatives, neo-liberals, international ethicists and post-national cosmopolitans – captured the commanding heights of US and Western foreign policymaking. Viewing the world as it ought to be, it was they who believed that the world was embarked on a liberal-democratic end of history.

Idealistic though this vision was, in many respects it has represented the 'grand strategy' of the West for some three decades. This grand strategic vision holds that Western forces should intervene – militarily if necessary – in countries to re-mould regions towards a 'rules-based' liberal international order that, coincidentally or not, broadly aligns with US economic and security interests. We can see this grand strategy manifesting all the way from the Gulf War of 1990-1991 to eject Iraq from Kuwait, various humanitarian interventions, notably in the Balkans in the 1990s, through to the interventions in Afghanistan, Iraq, Libya and Syria.

Arguably, this grand strategy has also been realised with NATO's eastward expansion since the end of the Cold War. This reached its crescendo – or its denouement – with Russia's invasion of Ukraine, which several scholars plausibly maintain was provoked by NATO's eastward enlargement, something that even NATO officials now admit. We can debate whether this policy has been prudent or wise, but the pursuit of a liberal international order undoubtedly exemplifies a 'grand strategic' enterprise on the part of the West.

Axis of autocracy vs. axis of democracy
So, the question this article seeks to address is, after the invasion of Ukraine, what has been the geopolitical fallout for countries on the periphery of this conflict in the Indo-Pacific? To state the obvious, the consequence of the Russia-Ukraine War is that it has forced a great power dividing line between the overt supporters of Russia, and its main backer, China, and the supporters of Ukraine, behind which stands the US and the West more generally.

The reaction of the US to Russia's invasion has been that states need to choose between freedom and tyranny. Either back Ukraine or be condemned. This stance was expressed in President Joe Biden's Warsaw speech on 26th March 2022, when he declared that 'democracies must unite in a fight against autocracy'. In other words, it was time to pick a side: were you with Putin and China or with the people of Ukraine and the struggle for democracy and national sovereignty?

Such appeals play out in the Indo-Pacific largely as a proxy for China's great power aspirations, in particular the degree to which China might wish to forcibly reclaim Taiwan in the way that Russia has attempted to assert itself over Ukraine, and the broader extent to which China is seeking to strong-arm its way to regional dominance by quashing democracy in Hong Kong, oppressing its minority populations, forcefully pressing its claims in the South China Sea, and extending its quasi-imperial reach through the Belt and Road Initiative. The fact that China supports Russia in the conflict suggests – if we are to employ Biden's ideological lens – that the world is confronted by an 'axis of autocracy' comprising Russia, China and its supporters on the one hand, and an 'axis of democracy' represented by the US and its various allies, most notably in the Indo-Pacific, Japan and Australia, on the other.

Existing in geopolitical ambiguity
For powers that are not formally allied to, or affiliated with, either of these axes, the geopolitical challenges are complex. What we see in the Indo-Pacific arena are degrees of alignment, where countries exist in a condition of geopolitical ambiguity. Nations either lean towards or away from these axes, depending largely on their geostrategic position, but also on political traditions, history and perceived national interests. Those Indo-Pacific nations that are not necessarily connected by formal arrangements with either axis tend to associate by degrees with one side or the other. The countries of Central Asia most obviously lean towards the 'axis of autocracy' and away from the axis led by the US and NATO. These states, Kazakhstan, Kyrgyzstan, Uzbekistan, Tajikistan and Turkmenistan are caught between the competing geopolitical interests of Russia and China. Regardless of what people in these countries think of Russia's invasion of Ukraine, their governments are predisposed not to be critical of Russia's actions, dependent as they are on Russian economic support, energy supplies and working opportunities for their nationals in Russia. Also, these one-party dominant states rely on Russia as a security guarantor. In early 2022, for example, the intervention of Russian security forces ensured the continuing rule of the regime in Kazakhstan in the face of anti-government protests.

Equally, the Central Asian states are deferential to Chinese interests and the economic pull of China's Belt and Road investments. All these countries, except for

Turkmenistan, function within the Shanghai Cooperation Organisation (SCO), which is the world's largest economic and security cooperation group both by geographical size and population, covering 60 per cent of the Eurasian land mass and 40 per cent of the world's population. The SCO expanded to include India and Pakistan in 2017, and Iran in 2023. It also maintains dialogue partners from across the rest of Asia and the Middle East, including Saudi Arabia, Türkiye, Egypt and the UAE. This is a major developmental, defence and security arrangement through which many countries now orbit both China and Russia.

In contrast, the states of the Asia-Pacific littoral – Japan, South Korea, and much of Southeast Asia (excluding Cambodia and Myanmar) – are primarily concerned with the implications of the spread of Chinese power and influence in the region, and so naturally tilt towards the Western line, and a so-called 'axis of democracy'. The Russia-Ukraine War merely sharpens the sense of insecurity in relation to the more assertive line that Xi Jinping's regime promotes to restore China to a position of global pre-eminence.

The main Indo-Pacific players in the 'axis of democracy' therefore wish to offset China's influence via institutions such as the Quadrilateral Security Dialogue (QUAD). The QUAD comprises Australia, Japan, the US and India. This diplomatic network seeks to reaffirm – according to its Joint Statement of March 2022 – its commitment to an 'Indo-Pacific, in which the sovereignty and territorial integrity of all states is respected, and countries are free from military, economic, and political coercion'. All of which can be taken as loosely aimed in the direction of China. Such sentiments broadly accord with the security outlook of most member states of the Association of Southeast Asian Nations (ASEAN), which by degrees of hedging and strategic ambiguity bend toward the West.

India and the third diplomatic dimension
India is a member of the QUAD and has historically had a fractious relationship with the People's Republic of China, including several ongoing border disputes that have resulted in armed clashes over the decades. Nevertheless, when it comes to the impact of the Russia-Ukraine War on its foreign policy, India provides some interesting pointers in terms of which way the diplomatic wind might be blowing.

India represents a 'third diplomatic dimension', as a major regional power. India's foreign policy is, moreover, heir to a historical tradition of non-alignment between the superpowers. During the Cold War India leant towards the USSR, especially in military procurements, seeking to counter-balance both US and Chinese power. Consequently, India does not feel any compulsion to align itself over the Russia-Ukraine War, instead preserving the latitude to lean towards or away from these axes as befits its national interests. This trend has been sharpened in the post-Cold War era in which India increasingly regards itself as a major player in the international system.

As a force to be reckoned with, India wishes to chart its own path in world affairs. Over the war in Ukraine, India's non-aligned approach has led to tensions with the US and Europe. As India sees it, the West demands that it should take sides against Russia. The pushback from India is most forcefully expressed by the country's minister for External Affairs, Dr Subrahmanyam Jaishankar, who makes the point that India should not be made to feel that Europe's problems are its problems. This is especially so when India's perception is that the West helped create the conditions that led to the Ukraine crisis through its policy of NATO expansion. India, and other states, both within and beyond the Indo-Pacific, argue they should not be asked to choose sides, and resent it when they are prevailed upon to do so.

The multiple geopolitical dynamics in the Indo-Pacific
Thus, what we are witnessing in the Indo-Pacific in the light of the Russia-Ukraine conflict is a set of complex dynamics, both obvious and less obvious. Firstly, and most perceptibly, the Russia-Ukraine War has forced a dividing line among states in the region, causing some states to align with one or other of these geopolitical axes. Beyond those states that are formally allied with – or obviously bound closely to – one or other of the axes (in the West's case Australia, Japan and South Korea, or the Central Asian powers with respect to Russia and China), the responses of other states have been more ambiguous.

Much of this ambiguity reflects diplomatic traditions of hedging and non-alignment that one sees across the Indo-Pacific, especially in Southeast Asia. However, some of the ambiguity also speaks to a loss of status, prestige and economic clout that the collective West has suffered because of the imprudence and hubris embedded within the Western grand strategic project. This has resulted in a grudging, and sometimes not-so grudging, respect for both Russia and China for standing up for their national interests and civilisational codes against what is perceived to be a 'liberal imperialist' crusade that has seen the West meddle in the internal affairs of countries or intervene directly with military force. The well-known recent examples are of course Afghanistan, Iraq, Libya and Syria, but now includes Ukraine, which for decades has been the object of interest for Western policymakers, principally as a tool to intrude upon Russian geopolitical sensibilities.

Several factors are in play here that are acting to weaken the gravitational pull of the West: notably the blow to Western prestige wrought by the chaotic withdrawal from Afghanistan in the summer of 2021 following two decades of futile nation building. Other factors include the de-industrialisation and economic waning of the West over thirty years caused by neo-liberal economics and the outsourcing of manufacturing capacity to cheaper labour markets elsewhere, and the follies of net-zero and the undermining of energy self-sufficiency. Along with the failure of Western financial sanctions against Russia, these factors combine to make the West look weak in contrast to the rising and economically and culturally resilient powers of China and Russia. These factors cause nations to look around and entertain options other than to defer to Western/US interests, as they might have felt compelled to do in the past.

Axis of democracy or axis of hypocrisy?
It is, moreover, the sense of Western double standards that multiplies this alienating effect. The Russian invasion of Ukraine strikes many in the West as an obvious case of aggression. It gets Western governments up in arms about violations of sovereignty and democracy. Yet, claim other countries, where were the calls for UN condemnation, sanctions, military intervention and war crimes trials when it was Western countries that were doing the invading, knocking over regimes, de-stabilising regions, and inflicting humanitarian suffering on host populations?

It is this enduring perception of Western inconsistency embedded in notions of the 'liberal international order' that cause nations to doubt the sincerity of Western commitments to freedom and democracy. Along with the sense that liberal imperialism embodies the promotion of individualistic and self-indulgent lifestyles, the character of contending grand-strategic visions begins to intimate a clash of civilisations. As a result, this putative clash of cultural worldviews causes states to lean towards the axis of autocracy because they do not necessarily see the other side as an axis of democracy, but as an axis of hypocrisy.

You do not have to be a strategic genius
In this respect, Western grand strategy in its liberal crusading posture is deeply flawed in conception and execution. Western policy has, consequently, pursued a particularly inept diplomatic path, especially under the current US administration, because it produces outcomes that are seemingly contradictory to prudential calculations of Western geopolitical interests. For example, one reason why China's leaders support Russia and will not allow it to be defeated in Ukraine is the fear that if Russia is routed and the regime in Moscow is overthrown that they will be the next target. This is not delusional thinking on the part of Beijing. It is a goal that has been canvassed openly in circles close to the Washington foreign policy establishment even before Russia's invasion of Ukraine. Therefore, it does not take a strategic genius to work out that such a policy is guaranteed to drive Russia and China – despite their geopolitical differences – to back each other to the hilt. A smarter Western foreign policy, as was exercised under the previous Trump administration, would be to remain firm but also to actively engage in dialogue with these regimes, which – if Russia had proceeded to invade Ukraine or if China made moves against Taiwan – could well have offered possibilities to play off China against Russia, or vice versa.

As it is, the West's 'for us or against us' attitude tends to alienate far more than it attracts, and not just in the Indo-Pacific. Important regional players like Saudi Arabia and Brazil, along with many parts of Africa and the Middle East, are increasingly estranged from what they perceive as Western stridency. Furthermore, China has to some extent played a calm diplomatic game. Its appeals for negotiations and a settlement in Ukraine, in comparison to the West's advocacy of escalation and open-ended war, strikes many developing countries as far more reasonable.

Not only does this sound more reasonable, but Russia and China are not threatening regime change or sanctions or providing economic investment and developmental aid with all sorts of strings attached. Trade, investment and non-interference look very attractive in contrast to an ideologically fixated, hectoring West – a West, moreover, that appears increasingly internally divided between its neo-liberal globalist elites and its own citizenry.

Conclusion: The Rest terminating the West
In consequence, the Russia-Ukraine War clearly intimates an emerging multipolar order. States, and not just those in the Indo-Pacific, look around the world and discern that they have options. It is not necessarily the case that they wish to align themselves overtly with China and Russia. The point is that they do not feel the need to choose sides anymore. We are truly in a New World Order. Just not the one that its 'end of history' architects originally envisaged.

The overarching intent behind Western grand strategy to bend the world towards a so-called liberal international order reached its high point between 1991 and 2001. However, its ideological fixation upon an end of history teleology has, in the manner that Walter Russell Mead lamented, ultimately rendered Western leaders' incapable of making smart, prudential, geopolitical calculations. Their obsessions have ended up dissipating the West's economic and military resources and undermined Western prestige and soft power. An evolving international system where a liberal, some might say 'woke West' (or at least the West's woke elites), are ranged against more traditional societies of the East and the developing worlds, has profound implications for the global order. One of which is the uncomfortable realisation that in the aftermath of the Russia-Ukraine War, it may well be that the world is isolating the West rather than isolating Russia.

Original article published in the *Hungarian Conservative*, Vol. 4, No. 1 (2024), by M.L.R. Smith.

7. The right state of the union: Democracy and dystopia

THE RHETORIC OF SILENCE was the term David and I used to describe the pre-woke mechanism of exclusion and marginalisation before being 'cancelled' became a thing in public discourse. Mainly, it operated at the mundane level of being ignored and not invited to participate in academic events. Much of it, we suspect, arose unconsciously, the instinctive reflexes of those who recoiled from being around people whose views were seen as edgy and dangerously heterodox.

At the same time, the effort could be conscious and directed. While we became immune to the silencing process, accepting it – even anticipating it – as the price of retaining one's self-respect. Nevertheless, its effects could be palpable. On occasions they could even be poignant. The saddest manifestation of the rhetoric of silence might be when a promising young co-writer suddenly dropped out of contact, or when colleagues and associates with whom we had been on cordial terms began distancing themselves, sometimes ghosting us entirely. Or it might be when a former writing partner conspicuously erased the publications, they had co-written with us on their biographies. These were the techniques of silencing and isolation.

We knew how this process worked. By the late 1990s we had already queered our pitch amongst the cognoscenti within the field of international relations. We were known disruptors who did not conform to a variety of 'tick box' issues that put one at the 'cutting-edge' of fashionable thinking and, of course, on the front rank for academic grants and promotions. We expressed scepticism that the nation state was facing a slow extinction in the face of inexorable globalising forces. We remained unconvinced that the world was being transformed into peaceful, cooperative regions, presided over by benign multilateral institutions like the European Union, ASEAN and the United Nations. These were all signs of dissent that got you noticed in the small world of academia. We were marked out as irredeemable realists and sovereigntists.

In the early 2000s we submitted an article to a journal specialising in diplomacy and statecraft. The article critiqued the contemporary academic orthodoxy of Australian international history, which extolled the Labor Prime Minister of Gough Whitlam (1972-1975). For years Whitlam had been elevated to secular sainthood by the scholarocracy, who – so the hagiography went – broke the mould of Australian politics. He had freed Australia from dependency on great and powerful friends like the US and Britain and set the country on an independent course in world affairs.

Going back over the historical record, our assessment begged to differ. Whitlam's record in office, in foreign affairs and much else, was characterised by missteps, controversy and fiascos. He kowtowed to communist China, thus alienating just about all of Australia's neighbours in Southeast Asia. He cosied up to the Soviet Union, recognising the *de jure* incorporation of the Baltic states into the USSR (the only Western democracy to do so). He acquiesced to the Indonesian invasion of East Timor in 1975, with all the tragic consequences that followed. It was a shameful legacy. One that should, at the very least, be interrogated rather than unquestioningly fêted.

But the questioning of fashionable myths is not permitted. We had co-written this article with a talented young historian from the University of New South Wales who contacted us a few weeks later to say that he had received a message from a senior politics professor, well known in the field, who suggested that he withdraw his name from our submission because it was purportedly of poor historical quality. It would damage his reputation if he did not do so.

The journal review process is meant to be completely anonymous. Reviewers are not supposed to know who the authors of submissions are, and vice versa. The intervention from this self-appointed guardian of the orthodoxy broke every ethical principle of academic conduct. Our young writing colleague was worried, but deeply affronted. Heated letters to the editor of the journal went unanswered. We never, in fact, heard from the journal again about our submission, which told us all we needed to know about its editorial standards. But, more than that, it lifted the veil on the sordid practices that underpinned the rhetoric of silence.

Therefore, whenever we had a writing collaborator who suddenly disappeared on us, or a colleague who went strangely quiet, or an invitation to participate at an event mysteriously withdrawn for unspecified reasons, we knew the likely routine. Someone had had a 'word' with the relevant individual: 'Nice career you have there. Shame if something happened to it'. Here, in all its ignoble sleaziness, the true face of academic life revealed itself. 'Academafia' was the word we coined for it.

What is the point of this vignette? Really, it is the fact that we had come to expect, and indeed predict, this kind of treatment from the international relations fraternity in Britain and Australia. Despite its name, the discipline of international relations in these countries has always been parochial. Our low expectations were rarely confounded. In contrast, we found the United States much more receptive to our work and ideas. The sheer size of its academic community, its greater scope for pluralism, and a more genuine interest in the freedom to test new ideas, and critique fashionable thought, provided a more welcoming atmosphere. Or so we thought.

As the 2000s progressed, David and I began to write for web-based platforms, then still in their infancy. In 2012, one of the best of these new online publications, *War on the Rocks*, was founded by a very smart former graduate student of mine. The idea for a security affairs website dedicated to intelligent, deep dive, assessments was a terrific idea. We were there at the beginning, encouraging its formation, making some connections to get it off the ground. I was listed as one of its contributing editors and even paid up $100 to be immortalised on its website as one of the illustrious entrants of its 'founder members club'.

The website quickly gained a reputation for being one of the most lively, thoughtful and authoritative online publications within the Washington DC 'Beltway', notable for its consistently high-quality war studies and international relations think pieces. It proved a congenial home for several of the articles that appear in this volume. To us, it represented the very best of everything we admired of the open-handed nature of US academic debate.

Forward to October 2017, and I found myself in DC at the fifth-year anniversary celebrations of the founding of *War on the Rocks*. The mood, however, was far from celebratory. Donald Trump was in the White House, and it was fourteen months on from Britain's referendum to exit the EU. As anniversary celebrants we endured a dirge of downbeat assessments from former four-star admirals and professors of strategic studies from Johns Hopkins University. Trump, we were told, was a giant know-nothing. His administration was chaotic. Brexit Britain was now very disappointing for all the key foreign policy masterminds in Europe like Angela Merkel. Dark mutterings of Russian influence and infiltration were in the air. The nadir took place on the final morning, when everyone was bussed out to the Army and Navy Club to sit at the feet of John Brennan, former CIA Director, and incorrigible Trump-abominator. It felt like an audience with the Pope, as people listened enrapt to the meanderings of this transparently sinister blowhard.

Back in the bars of our DC hotel, I tried to make sense of these surreal events. 'Why the animus against Trump?' I inquired of some of my co-participants. 'Is he really so heinous compared to some of the other crooked, scandal-ridden chancers, airheads and monsters who have occupied the office of the president (Warren Harding, Lyndon Johnson, Richard Nixon, Bill Clinton, George W. Bush... to name a few of the many)?' 'How do you explain his election, then?' 'Is he not, at least, the symptom of something rather than the cause?' 'Discontent with the existing political establishment, perhaps?'

Not being an American citizen, I had no dog in the fight. I was simply curious, that's all. I was trying to be open to different explanations. Yet, I should have known better. The motto of *War on the Rocks* is: 'National security. For insiders. By insiders'. And if there was one thing that David and I were not, it was 'insiders'. You see, as 'insiders', you already know the truth. You don't need to ask questions. You are the self-anointed experts. Being anti-Trump is an article of faith among the Beltway congregants. It is not something up for discussion. You shouldn't ask questions. That's the first step towards heresy.

Expressing scepticism toward the received narrative gets you noticed. Evidently, the *word* went out. We never appeared in *War on the Rocks* again. My name and photo were disappeared from the 'Contributing editors' page and sadly I never secured my place in the Pantheon of great foreign policy and security studies geniuses as a gold club founding member.

I don't wish to be too hard on *War on the Rocks*. It is still an excellent publication, and my recommended go-to place for informed, insightful, commentary on geopolitical events. Ultimately, the publication must respond to and function within the social and intellectual milieu in which it finds itself. That is its honest rationale, and one cannot criticise it for that. It is, in the end, as it says, 'for insiders'.

So, what is the moral of the story? It is that, in the end, self-proclaimed 'insiders' are the same everywhere. In Britain, Europe, Australia and regrettably the US too, one comes across the same 'insider' arrogance. The lack of humility. The assumed moral superiority. The blanket absence of any felt need to be accountable. The unwillingness to examine motives or assumptions. The inability to show even a flicker of self-awareness that they might be wrong about anything. The same disdain for 'outsiders' who dare ask questions.

The essays in this chapter speak to this growing disillusionment with what might be called the American *imperium*. This is not disillusion with the American populace, but with its self-satisfied elites and untouchable bureaucracies, and their British, European and Australasian appendages. The current American political class, as David's first essay on 'Democracy and dystopia' relays, clearly knows little of the country's founding principles as a constitutional republic, which was explicitly intended by its founders to balance power centres to prevent unaccountable bureaucratic and political interests entrenching themselves.

These elites, moreover, have charted a downward path. Their neo-liberal faith in the virtues of borderless millennial capital have facilitated the downfall of manufacturing in the West, and the rise of an exploitative and controlling big-tech, which seeks to monopolise minds as much as the market. The collapse of once stable industries, and the thriving communities they sustained, along with widening wealth and income disparities, are the fruits of this ideology. Political elites might go on about Trump being a threat to 'democracy', but as the essays in this chapter submit, it is the fatal conjunction of these baleful elite-driven political and economic interests that pose the real threat, and which are already conspiring – as the title of David's essay presciently sensed – to make America miserable again.

The final essays in this chapter exemplify the more pensive mood that David and I entered as we both moved into the autumn of our lives, as we contemplated the dimming prospects for Western liberalism through several social, cultural and historical lenses. The penultimate essay, which peers into the world of UFOlogy, represents the enduring admiration we had for the spirit of free inquiry that symbolises the best of America. Yet, it is a spirit that is under attack, may be as all free inquiry ultimately is, by the forces of orthodox belief that behave like religious authorities, which will always work to dismiss challenges to their worldview and their worldly power. In the current era these forces present us with labels that are constructed to suppress dissenting viewpoints, such as disinformation, misinformation and conspiracy theory. This, after all, is an old story, repeated and re-told in different ways throughout time.

The last essay in the chapter is an extended disquisition on my own intellectual journey, where I came to dwell on the question whether the US and the West more generally really can be said to be on the side of 'democracy'? It has been a question that has gnawed away at me for years but was heightened by my brushes with the outer echelons of the American national security bureaucracy of the kind that I encountered at this strange anniversary event in Washington in 2017.

I doubt that my fretting can provide readers with any great revelations, except that only in recent years did I arrive at a likely explanation of the utility of the 'rhetoric of silence' for its practitioners, beyond simply an elementary tribal need to drive away outsiders. After a lifetime in academia functioning within the exotic spheres of 'war studies', 'international relations', 'security studies' and 'world politics', one realises that much of the effort in these disciplines is not about advancing knowledge, let alone trying to 'make the world a better place'. It is about intelligent people suppressing their natural inquisitiveness, and closing down others in the process, in order to be near power.

This is the purpose that the rhetoric of silence serves. It is a system where clever, knowledgeable, well-qualified people are prepared to trade away their intellect, their credentials, their capacity to question, even a piece of their soul, for the frisson of being adjacent to power. All this in exchange for a reptilian ego boost? Is this what the game is all about? If so, what are the costs of the game?

Being shut out from some online publication and being excluded and marginalised in the halls of the academy is one thing. Ultimately, this feature of 'the game' is trivial and, in the broader scheme of things, relatively inconsequential. Out in the real world, however, real people suffer and die to satisfy the quest of a few self-possessed egomaniacs to claim that they are 'in the room' with the power brokers.

In fact, this status game is not even about being in the same room. It is about being in the anteroom, or a few doors down the corridor, even in a separate building entirely, kneeling at the feet of some has-been national security 'insider' droning on about their war stories and handing down *ex cathedra* statements on political events. What informs this peculiar desire? What intellectual value does it possess beyond a desperate voyeurism?

'Are we just ghouls?' asked one of the most principled and thoughtful people I know, not so long ago. We reflected upon our three-decade careers spent in the Department of War Studies, at King's College London. We managed to come up with some justifications that rationalised our endeavours. But the older I get the more I wonder whether the truthful answer is, 'yes'.

Making America miserable again

The election of Joe Biden as the forty sixth president of the United States will see a reversion to Washington's default liberal, progressive values in foreign policy, a revival of the Wilsonian, rules-based international order that the Obama, Bush and Clinton presidencies embraced, and the liberal academic establishment advanced during the Trump interregnum.

Shortly after the election, Biden declared that 'America is back' and will reassume its seat at 'the head of the international table'. Linda Thomas-Greenfield, Biden's nominee for Ambassador to the United Nations, asserted that not only was America back but so too was multilateralism. Henceforth no problem would be 'irresolvable' with America once more 'leading the way'.

Whatever else the new administration may do in its first hundred days, Biden, a former chair of the Senate Committee on Foreign Relations, plans to reverse Trump's America First approach to foreign policy that eschewed international institutions that no longer served American interests. Shortly after Trump's electoral defeat, Harvard's foreign policy eminence grise, Joseph Nye, called for the new administration to 'rediscover the importance of international organisations' and revive its fading 'soft power of attraction'.

Shortly after, Biden announced that America would re-enter the Paris climate change agreement that Trump had only recently left. The symbolism was clear. America would re-engage with the international organisations it had largely created during the 1990s, pursuing, as influential ivy league professor John Ikenberry prognosticated, 'institution building' that locks states into 'desired policy orientations'. In making *A World Safe for Democracy*, Ikenberry sees America leading a resuscitated rules-based order through multilateral cooperation. What might this mean for reviving US prestige as the indispensable global power?

Across the Atlantic, Biden will reverse Trump's dismissive treatment of NATO and contemptuous view of the EU, especially those he and his nominee for Secretary of State, the Paris-educated Tony Blinken, most admire, Angela Merkel and Emmanuel Macron. Liberal institutionalists still see the EU as central to a progressive, post-national, European regional order. Paradoxically, they ignore its democratic deficit and the EU's comprehensive investment agreement with China that gives the People's Republic unfettered access to the European market, endorsing its indifference to a rules-based international order.

By contrast, it views Brexit as a disturbing form of populism and considers Boris Johnson a racist 'shape-shifting creep'. The Democrats will adopt a punitive line if Brexit sees the UK government pursuing policies that abrogate treaty protocols with the EU covering the Irish border. Revived US commitment to international treaties and institutions, together with Biden's Irish Catholic ancestry, will see Sinn Féin assuming a higher Washington profile than English Conservatives with their imperial baggage. The UK might quickly discover that its special relationship is special only in the sense of an intellectually challenged child and the relationship an essentially disciplinary one. The Slovaks, Poles and Hungarians can expect similar reprimands for their enthusiasm for conservative politicians who adopt unacceptably populist attitudes to immigration and diversity.

Moving East, Biden's team will follow a hard line on Russia and Syria, but will also have little time for Recep Tayyip Erdoğan's Ottoman Sunni expansionism. This policy reset might exacerbate tensions in an area Trump largely ignored. A revival of the Iran nuclear deal, the abandonment of which Biden considers 'a profound mistake', will give much needed oxygen to Iran's regional proxies in Palestine, Lebanon and Syria, further destabilising an already volatile region, as well as reviving a theocratic regime that, as a result of Trump's sanctions, was on the verge of collapse.

It is, however, in reviving Obama's multilateral pivot to Asia that the new dispensation will face the most profound challenge. Trump dumped Obama's Trans-Pacific Partnership which envisaged a multilateral trade deal with a variety of Asian and South American partners. Trumpian realism directly challenged China's growing regional hegemony and its manipulation and corruption of international institutions like the UN, the WHO and WTO. It preferred bilateral to multilateral agreements, forged closer ties with Japan, Australia and India, courted regimes with questionable human rights records and illiberal governments in the Philippines, Thailand and Vietnam, ignored regional arrangements like ASEAN and APEC and challenged China's hegemonic ambitions. As Xi Jinping acted with growing impunity in the South China Sea and across the McMahon line in Northeast India, as well as sanctioning Australia for questioning its conduct, Trump's secretary of state, Mike Pompeo, proposed an alliance of littoral states stretching across the Indo-Pacific to contain China's burgeoning hard power.

The new Biden administration will also build alliances in the Indo-Pacific but ones with a democratic bias which might further alienate Southeast Asian states that have always found US democracy promotion an unwarranted interference in their internal affairs. Even India, Asia's largest democracy might find that Kamala Harris is not quite the supportive 'chitty' the Hindu nationalist government in Delhi assumes. Meanwhile, the Xi regime will relish the knowledge that Biden wants 'to work with China' on areas of common interest like climate change.

A renewed commitment to universal liberal values and resuming America's place at the head of an unstable multilateral table fails to recognise how the world's revisionist powers – China, Russia and Iran – dismiss such values as naive and easy to manipulate. Treating the world as it ought to be rather than as it is, offers the worrying prospect of a re-run of Obama's sanctimonious foreign policy that did so much to encourage the rise of Russia, Iran and an increasingly irridentist China in the first place.

Behind its tired, gerontocratic leadership, sits a more radical Democrat caucus eager to transform the international order along far more progressive lines. The woke wing of the party seeks to slash US military spending, disavow the US militarism responsible for wars in Afghanistan and Iraq and promote an emancipated utopia of social justice and human rights. It would open borders to immigration and seek the decolonisation of the West. It will be unsparingly critical, not of China, Iran and Russia, but of the UK and other European nations for their dark colonial pasts. It will cherish the oppressed victims of capitalism everywhere and expose the myth of the US as a promised land as a perverse distortion of its unseemly beginnings in slavery and the conquest of native peoples.

The progressive orthodoxy in its various forms is back, enhanced by Trump's impeachment and a Democrat majority in both houses. As Talleyrand observed of the restored Bourbon monarchy, it has learned nothing and forgotten nothing. Its virtuous, multilateral, social justice signalling might very quickly make America miserable again.

Original article published *Spectator Australia*, 23rd January 2020, by David Martin Jones.

Democracy in the USA: Clarifying acts of violence

The sacking of the Capitol building on the 6th January 2020 embarrassed the US in the eyes of the world and did little to advance a liberal universalism that has long held that representative democratic institutions best answer the needs of pluralist, ethnically diverse populations in a complex, interconnected, but by no means integrated world.

But was it, as Harvard Kennedy School professors maintain, 'the most dangerous threat to American democracy in our history', trampling over its norms and exposing its fragility? Was the 'insurrection' the premonitory snuffling of an impending *Kristallnacht* or merely the action of a 'stagnant crowd' anticipating its own 'immediate death'?

Rather than taking a pessimistic view of the future and an anachronistic view of the past, it might be worth considering what more prudent observers of republican and democratic practice, in its historical context from Machiavelli to Hannah Arendt, considered necessary for an enduring political order.

Observing the past and applying its prudential reasoning to the present, Machiavelli found that, in virtuous republics, conflict 'between the populace and the Senate' may be looked on 'as an inconvenience', which it was necessary to endure 'in order to arrive at greatness'. Machiavelli was the first to point out that political conflict may be functional for class-based democracies like those of the West. Significantly, the American Founding Fathers closely attended to Machiavelli and the classical republican model in framing a revolutionary constitution for a *novus ordo saeclorum* (a new order of centuries). More precisely, according to Hannah Arendt, they were, 'if anything more learned in the ways of ancient and modern prudence than their colleagues in the old world'.

The conformity of democracy theory
Yet interest in these principles dried up almost immediately after the task had been achieved. What was lost through this failure of thought and remembrance were the revolutionary ideals of 'public freedom, public happiness and public spirit' that began something both new and enduring. This has been the chief reason the American revolution, unlike the French, has remained largely neglected in world politics.

As Arendt explained, the American aversion to conceptual thought meant that the interpretation of American history, ever since Tocqueville, succumbed 'to theories whose roots of experience lay elsewhere'. Consequently, the US, its mainstream media and professoriate, have shown 'a deplorable tendency to magnify almost every fad and humbug which the disintegration... of the European political and social fabric... has brought into intellectual prominence'.

In the context of the current democratic malaise, this American inattention to its own revolutionary constitutional particularity reflects a broader mood swing in comparative political science from liberal optimism to Spenglerian pessimism about democracy's future. The reasons for this loss of faith, however, reveal a crisis not so much in democratic institutions themselves, but in the limited and abstract democratic theory the media and social scientists employ to compare systems of government and promote a rationalistic rather than a historically informed account of how they should function.

Casting our minds back to the end of history, we might recall that in the 1990s, both conservative and liberal political scientists from Samuel Huntington to Seymour Martin Lipset, Larry Diamond and Robert Dahl identified a 'third wave' of democracy sweeping the globe. Dahl wrote that an unprecedented political change had occurred. 'All of the main alternatives to democracy had either disappeared, turned into eccentric survivals or retreated from the field to hunker down in their last strongholds'. Yet what democratic theorists understood by democracy proved curiously mutable over time.

During the Cold War, the inchoate American discipline of comparative political science opted for a parsimonious definition. Following Joseph Schumpeter's work on *Capitalism, Socialism and Democracy* (1943) political scientists considered 'the democratic method' as that 'institutional arrangement for arriving at political decisions... by means of a competitive struggle for the people's vote'. Dahl spelt out its minimal procedural requirements: elected officials, free, fair and frequent elections, freedom of expression, alternative sources of information, associational autonomy and inclusive citizenship. It also eschewed unelected 'tutelary' authorities like monarchs, militaries and priesthoods.

Samuel Huntington added that this realist democratic model involved two dimensions: contestation and participation. From this perspective, Seymour Martin Lipset identified the economic preconditions that determined the processes of liberalisation and democratisation in developing as well as developed states. Subsequently, his student, Larry Diamond, in *In Search of Democracy* (2016), found that although it has many causes, a common thread linked regime effectiveness to democratic accountability.

Political science and academic verbicide
Even authoritarian regimes that survived this inexorable global movement felt, it seemed, constrained to offer some form of electoral competition, however specious. Yet as 1990s style electoral democracy became 'the only game in town', the concept itself also stretched to include something more virtuous than mere procedure. The democratic package increasingly came with the additional norms of good governance, accountability, transparency, the rule of law and respect for civil liberties alongside equitable economic growth. As the Third Wave peaked, Dahl regretted 'that every actual democracy has always fallen short' of the requisite criteria he and his fellow liberal academicians increasingly demanded. Democracy extended elastically to embrace both an ideal as well as 'a procedural actuality that is only a partial attainment of the goal'.

Introducing progressive values into what is an empirically measurable procedure is a recipe for confusion, and the fact that those defining the values were partisans of this idealist agenda did not help. Diamond, who launched the *Journal of Democracy* in 1990 in order to decode, advance and promote the democratic model, found that 'democracies in trouble were virtually all illiberal'. To avoid illiberal breakdowns, he averred, states must achieve 'democratic consolidation'. This required 'horizontal accountability', different means of 'checking and restraining the abuse of power' and 'truly free, accountable, honest, just, inclusive and responsive government'. Daniel Levitsky and Steven Ziblatt stretched the concept further, 'precising' – to use their preferred participle – democracy with an additional attribute, 'the existence of a reasonably level playing field between incumbents and opposition'. Without such morally accountable and socially just governance, democracy was vulnerable to breakdown. Consequently, many democracies were, by 2016, in 'recession', 'degraded by the actions of their own democratically elected executives'.

This diagnosis eschewed the fact, however, that in its first American 'wave' democracy assumed something rather different: namely, a state where impersonal law regulated personal freedom. It implied that governments were responsive to the desires and opinions of the governed and accountable to them. A government regulated by law and responsible to the body politic was a constitutional government, and constitutionalism or republicanism, is therefore perhaps a more adequate appellation for this form of government than democracy. Indeed, in the careless hands of political scientists, the term 'democracy' has suffered a form of verbicide.

This becomes evident when the political science departments of most Anglo-American universities attribute the current democratic crisis to 'authoritarianism'. Curiously, according to this way of thinking, it is only Republicans that cultivate this intolerant, politically polarising disposition. Black Lives Matter protesters, Democrats, or unelected tutelary bodies like the universities themselves, have, we are told, 'not been the principal drivers' of 'deeper polarisation'.

Instead, democracy in the US is said to be 'dying from within' slowly eviscerated by conservatives with a penchant for something only recently added to the political science vocabulary, namely, authoritarianism. 'Authoritarian', and its cognate terms, 'authoritarianism' and 'the authoritarian personality', do a lot of work in this vocabulary of democratic decline but what do they actually mean? Their origins may be traced to the Frankfurt School of Theodor Adorno and Max Horkheimer who first detected authoritarianism corrupting European politics between the wars. Somewhat predictably, democracy theorists find similarities between contemporary US politics, and the collapse of the Weimar Republic in 1933. The rise of fascism in Italy and Germany, it is alleged, 'highlight the type of fateful alliance that often elevates authoritarians to power'.

The 'authoritarian personality' and academic gerrymandering
However, to reduce contemporary political outcomes to an 'authoritarian personality' disorder requires a certain amount of academic gerrymandering. The term is an ideological construction, not a political theory. Fleeing Germany for a more tolerant America in 1938, Adorno subsequently floated the concept as a device for smoking out concealed fascism everywhere and especially in the false consciousness of successful post-war liberal, consumer capitalism of the United States.

Such theoretical fads crossing the Atlantic, Arendt observed presciently, lost their basis in reality and with it all limitations of common sense. As a result, democratic theory increasingly came to accept almost anything critical and abstract while its foremost task, the comprehensive understanding of reality and the coming to terms with it, is in danger of being fatally compromised.

For as Montesquieu and the authors of *The Federalist Papers* recognised, democracy's virtues of liberty and equality require limits, not progressive extensions. The preoccupation with permanence and stability, not abstract norms, or authoritarian predispositions, runs like a red thread through the American constitutional debates, which were conducted in terms of the ancient notion of a mixed form of government which combined the monarchic, aristocratic and the democratic elements in the same body politic, thereby 'arresting the cycle of sempiternal change'.

When John Adams, following Montesquieu's understanding of democracy, wrote: 'Power must be opposed to power, force to force, strength to strength, interest to interest, as well as reason to reason, eloquence to eloquence, and passion to passion', he obviously believed he had found in this very opposition an instrument to generate more power, more strength, more reason, and not to abolish them. In practice, this required proportion and the balancing of power. Montesquieu's reasoning suggests that once invested with power, even liberals are apt to abuse it and will carry authority as far as it will go. Virtue, and especially virtue signalling, also requires constitutional restraint.

Sustaining this balance in a complex, modern, and increasingly polarised society requires concerned democrats to recall the 'prudent diffidence' of classical scepticism that informed the thinking of the Founding Fathers. This will be crucial to offsetting the growing predilection for an apolitical, rationalist, managerial omnicompetence. Before embarking on new schemes of progressive perfection, the new administration should perhaps recall the advice of the authors of *The Federalist Papers*. They were profoundly aware that government had to perform its office of preserving order and balance 'relevant to the current conditions of society'. This requires both 'a balance of attention' and a recognition of the need for an internal 'balance of power'.

Original article published in *Cieo* 25th January 2021, by David Martin Jones.

Democracy and dystopia: Part one – the intangible economy

At the end of the Cold War, Western democracies emerged as the wealthiest and most powerful states the world had ever seen. Four decades later, in the wake of a global pandemic, they were hugely indebted, self-loathing states, riddled by fears of migration and disease and beset by identity crisis. What went wrong?

One answer might be hubris. In 1989, a triumphant West assumed the globe was *en route* to a secular, liberal democratic, international order. Tony Blair, one of the more enthusiastic proponents of this triumphalism, observed in 2010 that 'for almost twenty years... the West set the agenda'.

Following the collapse of Soviet-style communism, it was all too easy to believe that the West's model of liberal democracy and free-market capitalism, supported by a clear set of US-sponsored international rules, would spread to the four corners of the earth. Ultimately, however, this proved to be nonsense. How did the triumph of the Western model unravel? And what remains of it in the wake of both financial meltdown and the massive debt which democracies accumulated when they opted to lock down once-open societies in response to the COVID-19 pandemic?

The globalisation dilemma

At the turn of the millennium, the Washington consensus held that the democratisation of technology, finance and information would drive international integration. Globalisation created a new global power source – the 'electronic herd'. The herd comprised 'the faceless stock, bond and currency traders' pioneering exciting new financial products, like derivatives. It rewarded, with investment capital, countries that put on a so-called 'golden straightjacket' of deregulation.

Western capital went in search of cheap, emerging-market labour and found the most efficient low-cost producers, mainly in Asia. The best way to achieve rapid increases in living standards was to follow the market. States either got on board the global highway to a borderless, liberal democratic future, or found themselves consigned to failed statehood, where only crime and terror flourished.

The consequences were staggering, but not quite what the borderless world enthusiasts anticipated. The lazy assumption that, with the Cold War over, the rest of the world would embrace supposedly universal truths associated with liberal democracy proved an illusion. By the second decade of the twenty-first century, many countries, notably China and Russia, had done no such thing. The geopolitical consequences of the US sub-prime crisis of 2008–2010, followed by the fiscal attrition of the eurozone crisis between 2010 and 2018, indicated that history had far from ended. Globalisation revealed its uncomfortable dark side.

The rise and fall of millennial capital

The politico-economic structure at the millennium was distinguished by overlapping jurisdictions and cross-cutting allegiances where the transnational character of global exchanges undermined the traditional territoriality and allegiances of the nation state, de-concentrating loyalty as it deracinated identities. At the same time, millennial capital, driven by increasingly global financial markets, undermined state based, or regionally focused, capitalism. Globalisation shattered the post-1945, Ford-era contract between capital and the nation state. It recast socio-economic relations and political conduct. The global division of labour sounded the death knell of the blue-collar working class, replacing it with an insecure new 'precariat', a growing section of the populace suffering wage depression and job insecurity.

The political impact of millennial capital had already diminished assumptions about the equitable, wealth-enhancing character of globalised currency and trade flows. The financial crisis of 2008 and its aftermath dramatically intensified the inegalitarian, anomic character of the global marketplace. Western democracies reacted with a range of responses that have come into focus since the financial crisis and the panicked return of big state regulation during the global pandemic of 2020.

The collapse of the liberal market order, 2008-2018

The 2008 crash was a credit crisis, where liquidity dried up and banks with low deposit bases, dependent for lending upon the international money market, went bust (as was the case with Northern Rock, the UK lender, and small, open economies, like Iceland and Ireland).

Cheap interest rates, kept low by the US Federal Reserve after 9/11, had fuelled a consumption-driven asset price boom. Investment banks like Merrill Lynch, Lehman Brothers and Bear Sterns became mortgage-based money machines vending leverage and securitisation. In 2008, there was an estimated US$684 trillion in debt-related, credit-backed, derivatives in the global market – some twelve times the size of total global gross domestic product. When the money machine went bust, the cumulative actions of the Federal Bank and the Bush and Obama administrations succeeded in stabilising the financial system and recapitalising megabanks deemed 'too big to fail'.

If the ultimate test of the policy of stabilisation was the health of the banks, then the result was impressive. However, saving that system came at a price. The crisis revealed that national economic policy was ultimately subordinated to the needs of the financial system. To save it, national taxpayers paid to bail out global institutions. With much higher levels of government debt because of the financial crisis, and now the costs of lockdown, they will be paying for many years to come.

Fragmenting Europe 2010-2020

The eurozone crisis evolved somewhat differently from the US sub-prime crash, with consequences that were far more politically damaging for the EU's project of closer political union. Millennial Wall Street was a North Atlantic, as well as a North American system. The City of London hosted 250 foreign banks prior to the crisis. RBS, Deutsche Bank and BNP were the three largest banks in the world by assets. In 2007, the balance sheet of each came close to matching the GDP of its home country.

The fact that the eurozone was a work in progress exacerbated the European crisis. The dominance of the German economy within the European Union dictated its course. A German penchant for fiscal rigidity and a reluctance, prior to 2015, to let the European Central Bank's President, Mario Draghi, 'do whatever it takes' deepened the crisis. Europe's economies diverged, intensifying a North-South divide. Germany's export surpluses grew, while the PIGS (Portugal, Ireland, Greece and Spain) endured recession and mass unemployment. Europe's largest economies, France and Germany, did not suffer the extreme inegalitarian distributional effects of the US sub-prime crash. Instead, they off-loaded the problem onto the weaker states of Southern Europe.

The Eurocratic approach to crisis management, particularly its treatment of Greece, exposed the democratic deficit at the heart of Europe. Post-crisis Europe, rather than being a regional model, became instead, in the words of Adam Tooze, 'the object of other people's corporatist capitalism'.

Debt and democracy

Notwithstanding Europe's fiscal incoherence, the magical monetary medicine of quantitative easing facilitated a bull run on equities between 2009 and 2020, disproportionately rewarding the top 10 per cent of households that owned 90 per cent of the total value of financial assets. Liberal progressive ideology, committed to social justice and the idea that all social ills were amenable to state-engineered technocratic remedies, had unintentionally achieved this inegalitarian outcome. The contrast between Wall Street and Main Street could not have been starker. American crisis management nevertheless worked. After 2012, the US economy started to recover, but inequality was institutionalised.

The spirit of inequality, Montesquieu observed, corrupts democracy. It 'arises when citizens no longer identify their interests with the interests of their country, and therefore seek both to advance their own private interests… and to acquire political power over them'. This corruption of the democratic spirit began in Silicon Valley and spread, as if by an invisible hand.

AI and the great disruption

After 2008, American capitalism recast itself in a monopolistic mould. Information technology companies, with their global footprint, were the major beneficiaries. In the process they built a new economic model. The emergence of the GAFA (Google, Amazon, Facebook and Apple) tetrarchy that escaped anti-trust, data protection and tax investigation distorted the free market, corrupted the understanding of free speech and fractured, perhaps irreparably, the relationship between individualism, property rights and political democracy. As recent scandals involving Facebook, Twitter and Google demonstrate, the new media now surpasses traditional mainstream media in influencing voter behaviour and acting as an arbiter of political speech.

In practical terms, the new technology companies have achieved immense financial power. Amazon, PayPal and Google (restructured as Alphabet in 2015) launched after 1994, Gmail first appeared in 2004, as did Facebook. Twitter began tweeting in 2006, Airbnb renting rooms in 2008, Tesla making driverless cars in 2003, and Uber ride hailing in 2009. Silicon Valley hosts the corporate headquarters of Apple, Google, Facebook, Twitter, Uber, PayPal and Airbnb. The Valley engineers the future, and the future is algorithmic.

By 2017, eight of the world's most highly valued companies were technology businesses. Of these companies, five (Apple, Alphabet, Microsoft, Amazon and Facebook) are based in the US, two (Ali Baba and Tencent) in China and one (Samsung) in South Korea. European companies are notable only by their absence.

A progressive, anti-establishment worldview informed Silicon Valley's mutation from counter-culture to cyber-culture. The Siliconians assume they are 'the solution, not the problem'. They want 'one global community', but to build it, they 'disrupt' the old. Libertarian in their origins, the engineers of the virtual world conceived it as an anarchy. Yet, big-tech behaviour quickly eschewed its roots. The economic strategy of the new media leviathans encourages creative monopoly, not competition. Facebook, Google and Twitter are media platforms that mine data and generate profits through advertising. In 2017, Google and Facebook received 63 per cent of all US digital advertising revenue. In the process they created a distinctly intangible economy.

The intangible economy

Developed economies now invest in design, branding, R&D and software, rather than in tangible assets, such as physical plants and machinery. Intangibility has determined the key economic changes of the last decade, from economic inequality to stagnating productivity.

This intangible economy is fundamentally different from the pre-tech one, as the shuttered retail outlets on UK high streets since lockdown eloquently testify. Its characteristics involve 'scalability' of product design, spillovers into other products in the same domain, and synergies where design and development create dynamic hubs, whilst generating greater inequalities in wealth across the wider society. As intangibility flourishes, the old economy dies.

Intangibility has also intensified the rise of super-dominant companies, removed from political or fiscal oversight. The oligopolist character of the new economy means that since the 2008 financial crisis, the Gini coefficient has widened in all developed economies, fracturing a crucial link between capitalism and democracy.

The new media platforms gather data to produce information that influences decision-making, disrupting the political relationship between the individual citizen, the constitutional order and the market. Paradoxically, the anarchic space of virtual freedom offers the most valuable weapon for political control, manipulation and the dissemination of non-information. Social media companies already offer platforms to target voter preferences and facilitate extremist ideologies that render democratic processes open to manipulation by alien powers.

After 2012, a semi-detached, transnational, big tech and investment banking elite promoted intangible capitalism, divorced from the concerns and values of their tangible democratic nation state containers. 'Woke' capitalism has pursued an increasingly disruptive, emancipatory, green, virtual, but still progressive, global vision. It favours an 'iron law of oligarchy' in a twenty-first century networked form.

Whilst the intangible economy enabled the emergence of a transnational progressive class detached from the concerns of the nation state across the Anglosphere, things developed differently but equally oligarchically in Europe. The European project, once envisaged as the harbinger of a more enlightened, socially just regional order, found – through conventional fiscal means – a route to inegalitarian outcomes that divorced its cosmopolitan elites from their dissatisfied masses. Ironically, the desire of former German Chancellor, Angela Merkel, Europe's most powerful head of state, to keep the eurozone together whatever the cost, achieved the populist backlash that ever closer union sought to avoid.

Original article published in *Cieo*, 3rd March 2022, by David Martin Jones.

Democracy dystopia: Part two – the revenge of politics

In part one of this essay, we looked at how the financial crisis created the economic conditions for an increasingly illiberal form of politics. Here, we discuss the populist reaction to transnational progressivism after 2016 and the political challenges Western democracy now confronts.

In Greece, the UK, across Western Europe, and in the US, an unanticipated and inchoate popular reaction to the financial crisis questioned the progressive assumptions that had informed the end of history project. To the astonishment of the transnational elites in politics, academia, finance and the mainstream media, the second decade of the twenty-first century witnessed a resurgence of nationalism and populism on both the left and right of the political spectrum and on both sides of the Atlantic.

The financial crisis of 2008 and the decade of bank bailouts and austerity that followed, created a mounting sense of unease about the governance of Western Europe and the United States. It fed a loss of confidence in established political parties. In 2016, the Brexit referendum, the election of Donald Trump to the US presidency, and the rise of nativist and radical socialist political movements everywhere, announced a wave of angry populism crashing on the rapidly eroding shore of Western progressive orthodoxy. Trump and Brexit signalled a revolt of the masses against a progressive antipathy to borders. The pandemic lockdowns of 2020 further reinforced a growing predilection for national solidarity.

Across Europe, parties have either emerged from nowhere or chased electability from the political fringes. Populism finds the new social media particularly congenial for transmitting its message, bypassing established party systems that acted as filters to limit their appeal. Social media enabled the electoral success of previously fringe movements, such as Syriza in Greece or the Five Star Movement in Italy, as well as the hijacking of mainstream parties. Donald Trump secured the Republican nomination for the 2016 US presidential election against the wishes of the party establishment, whilst Jeremy Corbyn's Labour Party leadership victory in 2015 lit a bonfire under Tony Blair's progressive 'third way' vanities.

The revolt of the masses and the decline of the West

Since 2020, Brexit, the election of Donald Trump, the *gilets jaune* (yellow vest) protesters in France, and the growing protests against lockdown restrictions, have all exposed a divide between two 'value blocs' across the modern West. As J.D. Vance, author of *Hillbilly Elegy* (and later junior US Senator for Ohio and Donald Trump's Vice Presidential running mate in the 2024 election) explained in an interview with *The Times*, Silicon Valley represents,

> a dystopian view of what middle America sees in the future. Two fundamental subsets of the population... completely separated by culture and wealth... [who] don't really interact with each other or feel any kinship.

David Goodhart in his influential 2017 book, *The Road to Somewhere,* termed these subsets 'anywhere' and 'somewhere'. Meanwhile, in France, a Parisian, urban, bobo elite dominates media, business and finance and inhabits a different world from those who live in 'lower France' on the *périphérie*.

The economic and cultural gulf between these worlds and worldviews accounts for the rise of Western populism. Vance considers himself a rare 'cultural migrant' who discovers that 'the wealthy and powerful are not just wealthy and powerful, they follow a different set of norms'. These norms are the antithesis of the hillbilly, redneck culture of the Midwest, lower France or Northern England. Vance's memoir, *Hillbilly Elegy*, captures a white, working-class culture disintegrating, as manufacturing jobs that once supported stable family life disappear overseas. Meanwhile in France the *gilets jaunes*, like their hillbilly equivalents, watch powerless, according to Christophe Guilluy, 'as the implacable law of global markets asserts its authority everywhere'. Within a few decades

France became 'an American society... inegalitarian and multicultural... polarised and seething with tension'.

The road to nowhere

In the *The Road to Somewhere*, Goodhart estimates that in the UK metropolitan elites represent 20-25 per cent of the population, while the periphery constitutes more than half the population. By wealth and education, they correspond to a similar divide across the US and Western Europe. The peripherals are, according to Goodhart, socially conservative, political 'outsiders', uncomfortable with mass immigration, and 'an achievement society in which they struggle to achieve'. Forty years ago their values prevailed across the West. Brexit in the UK, Trump in the US, the *Lega Nord* in Italy, Éric Zemmour in France and the *Alternative für Deutschland* (AfD) in Germany represent an instinctive response to the failure of the progressive agenda.

By contrast, the progressive worldview of the transnational class is pro-globalisation but 'combined with state enforcement of greater racial and gender equality'. Its worldview places a high value on mobility and novelty and a much lower value on national social contracts, tradition or group identity, always excepting abstract minorities. It is comfortable with mass migration, European integration and universal human rights, all of which dilute national citizenship. Although meritocracy is the official creed, this new, and increasingly non-domiciled class are, says Goodhart, 'almost always born into the wealthy or professional classes'. Education at elite universities and inter-marriage reinforce their shared values. Before Brexit and Trump their viewpoint prevailed in the media and set the agenda of mainstream political parties across the West.

In the nineteenth century, Karl Marx assumed the affluent bourgeoisie would be more nationalist than the proletariat because they formed the 'executive committee' of the modern state. Marx was wrong. The global economy transformed the nineteenth century *haute bourgeoisie* into an intangible *internationale*. This transnational class now 'have more in common with each other – regardless of their respective national, racial or religious identities – than they have with everybody else'. The universal values of social justice and minority entitlements that the new oligarchy embrace provide an ideological alternative to national identity. The abstract equality of all is taken to mean that partiality for fellow nationals is racist.

In Europe, the political class's minority and migration fixation made three interlinked assumptions. Firstly, that mass migration was an economic boon rather than a cost to overstretched European welfare states. Secondly, that an ageing European population needed replacement by culturally very different people. And thirdly, that this new population would integrate and contribute much-needed diversity to stale and pale Europe in urgent need of rejuvenation.

Nations divided

These assumptions proved mistaken. The ideological endeavour to forge a multiculturalism that accorded special group rights to minorities fragmented national identity. Without any incentive to integrate, these very different cultures developed separately, sometimes exhibiting violently illiberal enthusiasms. Failed interventions in Libya, internecine conflict in Syria, and the Islamic State's attacks on European cities only exacerbated the West's identity crisis.

The baleful consequences of this agenda are all too evident. Britain in the mid-1990s was a multi-racial society with a settled minority migrant population of around 4 million or 7 per cent. By 2016, 18 percent of the UK's working age population was born overseas and Britain's official immigrant population had tripled. This was not inevitable but official EU and mainstream political party dogma.

The primary losers from mass migration are poorer people in rich countries. Thus, in the working-class towns of Northeast England, young white males aged between eighteen and twenty-four, without education or training, enter a twilight world of low-status jobs. Significantly, Northeast England, like once industrial South Wales, voted Brexit in 2016. Similar constituencies in the US, Germany, Italy, Spain and France support, *inter alia*, Trump, the AfD, the *Lega Nord*, *Vox* and *Rassemblement National*.

By contrast, London, which dominates the UK economy, has evolved into an economically global, ethnically polarised, megalopolis where a largely migrant, menial class services a free-spending transnational oligarchy. Across Europe the move to ever closer union and the free movement of labour erected a social gulf between bobo cosmopolites in London or Paris and the peripheral precariat that mainstream political parties ignored. Even after the disastrous failure to manage the 2015 refugee crisis, European Commission President Jean-Claude Juncker insouciantly maintained 'that borders are the worst invention ever made by politicians'.

The failure of the progressive project
Thomas Hobbes, observing the internecine strife of the English Civil War in 1650, argued that a social contract establishing an abstract, sovereign state, must afford its members peace and protection, otherwise 'solitary, poor, nasty [and] brutish' conditions will prevail. Hobbes would have foreseen Europe's open borders incubating well-meaning doom. The failure of the progressive project between 2010 and 2019, and the lockdowns of 2020, saw former nation states across Europe scrabbling to reclaim their borders, undermining one of the four 'essential' freedoms on which the project precariously rested.

Liberal democratic trading states, led by the US, built the international architecture that governed globalisation: the UN, the IMF and the World Trade Organisation. However, the unintended consequence of the huge increase in cross-border capital flows from the early 1980s rendered these institutions increasingly impotent. This shift, together with the financial crisis it generated and the intangible economy it facilitated, undermined the democratic legitimacy of globalisation as well as its claims to advance shared universal norms. In the US it has fomented deepening divisions on ethnic and class lines that threaten its constitutional foundations. Meanwhile, the once 'turbulent and mighty continent' of Europe, looks 'exhausted'. History did not end. New geopolitics extracts its revenge on the hubristic assumptions of the progressive West. Internally it assumes the form of a haemorrhaging Western body politic, externally it takes the shape of rising revisionist powers.

Originally published in *Cieo*, 10th March 2022, by David Martin Jones.

Contemplating phenomenology: UFO's, religion and technology

For the first time in over fifty years, in May 2022, a United States House subcommittee opened a congressional hearing to receive testimony on 'unidentified aerial phenomena', or 'the phenomenon', as initiates term it. Although the committee did not draw any inferences, it examined the growing body of photographic and video evidence, much of it accumulated by the US Navy and Air Force, of aeriform objects which appeared to defy the known physics of gravity, speed and movement. These phenomena could not, moreover, be rationalised with reference to alternative explanations, such as the secret testing of advanced military technology, drones, the operations of hostile states, optical illusions or hoaxes.

Unidentified Flying Objects (UFOs) or Unidentified Aerial Vehicles (UAVs) are, of course, the stuff of myth, legend, science fiction and much else in popular culture from films and TV series in the mould of *Star Wars* and *ET*, to the *X-Files*. No doubt a great deal of hokum surrounds the subject, and UFO enthusiasts are still routinely stereotyped as fantasists prone to outlandish conspiracy theories. Yet, the congressional hearings for the first time in decades acknowledged that there was a legitimate discussion to be had about some of the most intriguing questions of all time: what may be 'out there', and are we alone in the universe?

Indeed, that Congress was prepared to consider the implications of 'The Phenomenon' in an evidential, dispassionate, manner was itself testament to a growing body of scholarly endeavour that has sought to bring a degree of intellectual rigour to the study of 'Ufology'. *American Cosmic: UFOs, Religion, Technology* by D.W. Pasulka is one of the most engaging of these recent works because it is premised on two central ideas. The first is that UFOs do not appear only to 'cranks and wierdos' but to highly intelligent and successful people. Not only does Pasulka converse with high achieving 'believers' throughout the book, but she points out that pioneering figures of Soviet and US rocketry such as Konstantin Tsiolkovsky and Jack Parsons, respectively, believed in ethereal beings and non-human intelligence. Others, like the psychoanalyst, Carl Jung, felt that the UFO phenomenon should not be dismissed but studied seriously.

The second underlying premise is that the way people understand UFOs can provide insight into how technology and religion often intersect. British science fiction writer Arthur C. Clarke was acutely aware that the dimensions of the 'the phenomenon' represent a 'fusion of magic, or the supernatural, and the technological'. As the co-writer of the screenplay for Stanley Kubrick's epic *2001: A Space Odyssey* (1968), he remarked: 'MGM is making the first ten-million-dollar religious movie, only they don't know it yet'.

Quasi-religious practices
American Cosmic digs into the ways in which social and technological infrastructures shape quasi-religious practices. UFO phenomena are considered by 'believers' to be advanced technology/intelligence that allows humans to connect with other minds, both human and extra-terrestrial, and to places outside current scientific understandings of time and space. Pasulka draws attention to the existence of an 'invisible' college of scientists and academics who study UFOs but who do not make their work public and receive no wider scholarly recognition, either because they are associated with classified government programmes, or because they fear ridicule for touching the subject, let alone suggesting that UFOs might comprise real phenomena under intelligent control.

Within this invisible college, according to Pasulka, there exists two main schools. The first emphasises the study of material evidence (namely, the object and empirical effects of 'The Phenomenon', such as UFO sightings, radar traces and radiation burns), while the second school addresses the subjective and spiritual implications, with a focus on the 'experiencers' and 'contactees', that is, of those who claim to have interfaced in some way with 'The Phenomenon'.

As the author argues, the two schools are sometimes antagonistic, with the former endeavouring to bring the methods of scientific inquiry to UFO occurrences. This school usually stresses the 'debunking' of fakes and the ruling out of alternative explanations in pursuit of the truth. In that respect, this 'nuts and bolts' school rests on the disavowal of the 'weird' and the psychic dimensions of 'The Phenomenon'. Even though this school remains hidden and marginalised, the hope is, nonetheless, that mainstream science will one day embrace its findings.

The second school, however, embraces the psychic and extra-sensory facets associated with 'The Phenomenon'. Pasulka demonstrates how this approach possesses profound religious parallels because 'experiencers' invariably interpret UFO events in a spiritual context, causing a fracturing or reinterpreting of prior belief, or non-belief. For most experiencers, she observes, UFO events do not begin as UFO events. They become UFO events via a process of interpretation. No experiencer she has met, Pasulka states, has automatically felt that a UAV was a UFO. No-one wants to be known as a crank, so they look first for the obvious explanations. When the obvious cannot account for the event, this starts the interpretive process that sees the experiencer coming to terms with an epistemic shock to their fundamental understandings of the world and the universe.

First contact, then, is usually not experienced as a religious event and a UAV is not interpreted as a UFO event: they become so through a process that shapes and solidifies experiences as a religious or a UFO event. In turn, these craft cultural and/or media representations that both create and nurture belief. The parallels between UFO and religious experience are significant because the history of religion is frequently a record of perceived contact with supernatural beings, which descend from the heavens in a 'miraculous way'. The remembered effects of these experiences are absorbed by social processes and fashioned into elaborate myths and rituals that we call religions. Religions arise because adherents believe in their truth without overt evidence. Religious truth therefore exists independently of belief or disbelief and sustains the notion that the truth postponed does not, of itself, make the religious proposition false.

Pasulka argues that a great deal of Christian thinking encompasses many of the interpretative and evaluative aspects that characterise the evidence-based approach of the first school of Ufology. In Catholicism, for example, any hierophany – the technical term for a manifestation of the sacred where a non-human entity, say, in the form of an angelic host, descends from the sky – is subject to scrutiny from the Church to determine whether there is sufficient confirmation from other sources to warrant recognition as a general revelation of the divine, which can be publicly venerated, or a matter of 'private revelation' that cannot be validated beyond the experience of an individual receiver of a heavenly message. Assessing the credibility of witnesses, sifting the evidence of revelation, is broadly similar in both cases. Where the evidence of revelation is widely accepted by a community of believers as a manifestation of the sacred/The Phenomenon, a place can become a religious/quasi-religious site. Roswell in New Mexico functions like this, complete with gift shops and alien themed restaurants. Lourdes is similar, Pasulka wryly notes: 'Where hierophanies appear, consumerism often follows'.

Ufology
The spinning of the UFO phenomenon by those wanting to commodify it, wrapping it in elaborate stories or hoaxes, and selling it to a popular audience for publicity or profit is anathema to the protagonists of Pasulka's study, who wish to scrutinise unusual events carefully, applying scientific principles to rule out contending theories and to reject advocating hypothesis that cannot demonstrate proof of non-human activity. This leaves evidence that may support the existence of the 'The Phenomenon' but which cannot be explained. Still, according to 'James' and 'Tyler', two of the scrupulously scientifically minded interviewees in Pasulka's research, it is possible to study the effects of 'The Phenomenon' on human experiencers and the modes of interaction, namely, contact manifestations that register as anomalous, such as telepathy, random sightings, abnormal cognition, etc. These manifestations cannot be rationalised within the precepts of currently accepted scientific understanding, but they open spaces for exploration particularly in the fields of quantum theory.

Ufologists like James and Tyler are comfortable operating in a world of grey areas, not knowing how to account for anomalous events, and this, Pasulka explains, prevents them from being dogmatic: 'They are wise because they do not know and are trying to find out'. This forms the central insight of the book. During her study, Pasulka realises that her task is not to seek, let alone reach, a conclusion about the reality of 'The Phenomenon'. Instead, it is to recognise the integrity of the process of intellectual exploration that motivates serious-minded individuals to grapple with some of the most mystifying, yet important, questions that humankind can pose.

For this reason, some readers might be frustrated that Pasulka offers no firm viewpoint on the existence of 'The Phenomenon', either declaring it all bunkum or asserting sensationalist claims that 'something must be out there'. Instead, she focuses on the ways that the relationships between UFOs, advanced technology and religious thinking can be revealed. The study of the spiritual and scientific nexus around UFOs is, thereby, capable of producing surprising emotional responses. In the case of Tyler, it leads to his embrace of religion and conversion to Catholicism. In my case, I found reading this volume highly resonant as it caused me to reflect upon the legacy of my late father.

Reflections on a 'born again' atheist: An orbit around my father

Jim, my father, was an inveterate hobbyist. He had more pastimes over his life than you could shake a stick at. Most would be temporary enthusiasms that would subside after a few months but one of his most enduring was astronomy. Jim was fascinated by the planets and stars. He tracked them, studied them, and made notes on them. He bought refracting and reflecting telescopes. He even built a small observatory down the bottom of the garden. The imposing structure, complete with classic white dome, was sufficiently distinctive as a local landmark that it became a visual reference point for pilots at the nearby Elstree aerodrome. Sadly, the observatory was blown away during the Great Storm of 1987, the dome last being sighted at 200 feet over southern Hertfordshire.

Jim's continuing passion for astronomy survived the Great Storm and lasted well into later life. He gave regular talks to the local astronomy club and gradually rebuilt another observatory. He would take up residence on any clear night, staying up until the early hours, sitting in a deckchair with his binoculars or telescopes, gazing at the night sky above.

Born into an impoverished background in Clapton, East London, in 1934, Jim's parents were inspired by the 'cockney dream'... to live in Essex. Slowly, his family migrated from one cramped basement tenement to another, moving northward through Hackney and the Kingsland Road, eventually ending up in Enfield Lock, where their home counties dream finally died a few hundred yards from the Hertfordshire border. You'll know if you have ever been to Enfield Lock.

Afflicted by the pitifully low expectations of his background, which are still a feature of this country's social landscape, Jim finally got a leg up, courtesy of the 11+ and secured a place at Enfield Grammar School, where he was able to reach educational heights unknown to his family: O levels. Despite not progressing further, his grammar school education provided a discipline and structure to his natural curiosity that marked him for the rest of his life. Enlisting for four years in the Royal Air Force as a radio technician, and then at his local college, he went on to complete his formal training as an electrical engineer.

Stable employment for such a restless mind was never my father's priority. He was a prototype for today's gig economy, changing jobs at frequent intervals throughout his career. His business model was not therefore conducive to wealth accumulation and growing up there was never much money around. Only much later in life did I apprehend how much my father and mother (a part-time dinner lady and medical receptionist) must have struggled to provide my sister and I with even the basics.

Financial difficulties aside, the household was, nevertheless, always one of healthy intellectual curiosity. That was, as I look back now, my parents' gift to their children. Money might have been tight: expensive presents a rarity; exotic foreign holidays occasional-to-non-existent; a car for your 21st birthday, out of the question. But an atmosphere where you were encouraged to think for yourself and explore the world around you existed in abundance. My father set the example: try out new things; experiment with ideas; question received wisdom, were his guiding principles.

Consequently, and unsurprisingly, Jim despised virtually all forms of authority. Doctors and vicars were his particular *bête noir*. Local trade union busy bodies of the National and Local Government Officers' Association (NALGO), who wanted to tell him what to do and think, also riled him. Organised religion he had no time for whatsoever. He rejected his admittedly tepid Church of England upbringing. At best he saw the churches, and all organised religion, as a deceit. At worst, he regarded them as mind controlling. He was the epitome of the scientific rationalist and discounted the existence of God based on a lack of empirical evidence. He joked that he was a born-again atheist.

Even so, the point of my father was that he was capable of metaphysical reflection, particularly on the mysteries of the universe, which his interest in astronomy undoubtedly gave him. He was a sceptic, an anti-authoritarian, an atheist, but he was endlessly curious and, like Tyler and James in Pasulka's study, was willing to acknowledge what he did not know and that some questions, for now, existed beyond scientific explanation.

The family bookshelf mirrored this disposition. As well as being packed with volumes that reflected his hobby interests (*inter alia*, wood turning, boat building, beer making and amateur 'ham' radio – his other lifelong obsession), it was replete with many other miscellaneous offerings. It was genuinely 'multidisciplinary'. There were books on electronics, physics and maths. But there was also literature: Shakespeare's works and Paul Scott's *Raj Quartet*. Quite impressive for a working-class boy from Enfield Lock.

As well as all manner of books on astronomy, there were works on cosmology. Growing up in the 1970s, I remember volumes by Carl Sagan and Erich von Däniken also populating the shelves, along with science fiction novels, including Arthur C. Clarke's *Rendezvous with Rama*.

And that was the crucial thing, I now realise, about my father. He was a genuine freethinker. While he could be impetuous and contrarian, sometimes willing to argue his point into oblivion, ultimately, he accepted that his view was only ever provisional and could be contested with new or countervailing evidence. He was headstrong. He was a robust debater. But he was self-critical and self-aware. Although he did have his preoccupations, he was open to new ways of thinking. You just had to be sure of your ground. He was, too, in that sense, wise.

Jim was, in other words, admirably innovative. He was, like the figures in Pasulka's book, prepared to consider alternative explanations, examine the evidence, explore novel interpretations, and work out his own conclusions free from peer pressure, social expectation and intellectual faddism. Although his numerous hobbies and interests often led nowhere, others did not, and in the process, he acquired a remarkable breadth of knowledge and became highly accomplished in several fields. Jim was acutely interested in the future of advanced technology. In the early 1970s he taught himself computer programming, and became one of the UK's earliest software engineers, even going onto work on Britain's Advanced Early Warning (AEW) defence system with GEC-Marconi.

In these respects, he was surprisingly 'modern', even ahead of his time. His fascination for astronomy and cosmology nourished from the late 1960s an acute interest in themes such as climatology and energy policy, long before either was considered a 'thing' in public discourse. Over dinner conversations in the 1970s and 1980s he held forth on these subjects. He argued, for instance, that in the absence of any feasible means to harness nuclear fusion, there could be no such thing as 'green' energy. All energy generation involves an exchange of action/reaction forces as the basic laws of physics suggest. Only nuclear fission generated power in his view, possibly along with hydro-electricity, offered a cost-effective way of producing relatively clean energy. Looking back, his thinking on the subject seems prophetic.

Likewise, his knowledge, in fact his expertise, of atmospherics and astronomy meant that he recognised that the earth's climate and surface temperature varied naturally. However, he was scathing of alarmist claims of a 'new Ice-Age', and end-of-the world catastrophising, which early on he thought were merely new forms of ideology rather than scientific statements. He regarded Prince Charles's pontifications on the environment as ignorant. He couldn't stand the Royals anyway. He took the side of Princess Diana when the royal couple's marital problems started making the news. When the climate debate got going from the 1990s, he enjoyed baiting the doomsters. If global warming results in the melting of the polar ice fields, what should happen, he asked? Water expands when it freezes. Since ice displaces its mass, then when it melts, technically, sea levels should fall. It's a law of thermodynamics. Amusingly, to this day, when I have posited my father's query to green ideologues, I have never received anything but a babblingly incoherent response.

Having knowledge of science, astronomy, engineering and physics, and possessing an appreciation of the vastness of the universe, and the infinitesimal role that humanity plays in it, rendered my father susceptible to the theoretical possibility of the existence of intelligent life beyond our solar system. He was a sceptic but he never, as far as I recall, dismissed those with an interest in the UFO phenomenon as cranks and weirdos. 'After all', I remember him once saying, 'we possess the technological capacity to explore the limits of our solar system with satellites and rovers. Who is to say there are no other intelligent beings out there who can do the same, and more?'

Reflections upon the 'inconvenient mind'

Meditating upon *American Cosmic's* analysis of UFOs and its connections with technology and religion, and the disquisition about my father, which it involuntarily stimulated, leads to several general observations that may, perhaps, have some bearing on our current predicaments.

The first is to reiterate Pasulka's reflection that to be wise is not to be dogmatic, and to admit that you sometimes do not know. Just because you have an interest in something, but do not yet comprehend how to explain it, does not make you weird, it makes you inquisitive. If you are intrigued by the mysteries of the universe, the implications of advanced technology, future science, time and space, the possibility of the existence of non-human intelligence and worlds yet to be discovered, well, good for you.

A second observation is that the inquisitive mind is often an inconvenient mind, especially for those in power, be they Church or government. Authorities and elites do hide and cover up things. Preserving the arcana of power is a technique of rule. The active suppression of information derived from free thought is a path well-trodden by religions and governments. The Catholic Church, we know, persecuted the astronomer Galileo for refusing to disavow the principles of Copernican heliocentrism, lest it threaten the removal of humanity from the centrality of God's plan. The possibility of UFOs, and the existence of non-human intelligence, similarly poses potential threats to religious and temporal authority.

We should therefore, thirdly, be wary of those in society, in the mainstream media and academia, who seek to do the bidding of those in power to close-down the inquiring mind. Invariably this is accomplished through the employment of delegitimising labels, such as cranks and weirdos but also in the current argot through the rhetorical devices of accusing others of being conspiracy theorists or peddlers of 'misinformation' or 'disinformation'. Those who seek to pronounce, *ex cathedra*, upon what constitutes truthful information and what is falsehood, are themselves acting as religious authorities, and should be regarded as such. The proximity between political and religious modes of thought can be closely intertwined.

Indeed, a fourth observation is that perhaps we should question the existence of the notion of 'conspiracy theory' in its entirety. Conspiracies – to secretly plan something unlawful or harmful – occur all the time. However, a 'theory' in conventional science is simply a proposition that can be investigated through testable hypotheses. A good theory withstands rigorous testing. A bad one does not. Therefore, there can only be 'good' or 'bad' theories, rather than conspiracy theories.

A fifth observation, then, is that a condition of proper scientific scepticism should be the default position of anyone who aspires to a dispassionate assessment of any proposition. The tendency, especially of those in power, to treat one's version of the truth as unfalsifiable, beyond the reach of the inquiring mind to question and scrutinise, constructs an implicit religious realm. The practice of scepticism is the antithesis to the growth of new political religions.

We are but stardust
For me at least, a final, and hopefully fitting, observation upon *American Cosmic* is contained in a comment my father made towards the end of his life. His words are inscribed onto the memorial plaque honouring his life that resides below a tree in a quiet corner of Dorset. In his final years, Jim was very ill. As he contemplated his condition, and the inevitable outcome it foretold, he drew upon his understanding of the cosmos to reach a consoling, philosophical, and maybe even spiritual, reflection upon life. Whatever one's conscious problems, worries or concerns, he noted, we should appreciate that we as humans, within the enormity of the universe, are ultimately nothing but stardust.

Original article published in *Cieo*, 18th August 2022, by M.L.R. Smith.

From axis of democracy to axis of hypocrisy

The older I get, the more I find value in books that stir memories of times past. I am not about to go all Marcel Proust on you; my reflections are not that deep or contemplative, let alone complex or literary. But works that spark a moment of recollection are likely to resonate with those who have reached a point where they look back on life with a mix of conflicting emotions and hope of finding some reconciliation with the past. A book about spies and the early years of the Cold War may not seem the most obvious candidate to provoke this reaction but let me recount the memory it kindled and the way it helped resolve a puzzle that for years had been needling the back of my mind.

A Friday afternoon in Singapore
Friday afternoons in Singapore are particularly languorous. The mixture of tropical heat and humidity, along with the prospect of the end of the working week, induce a distinctive kind of lethargy. The late 1990s found me working in the city-state, helping to set up a Master's programme at the Nanyang Technological University. Sometimes on these sluggish afternoons, one of my colleagues and I would wander over to a small outside café located on the nearby campus of the Singapore Armed Forces Training Institute (SAFTI). We would sip iced tea and embrace our end-of-week indolence by musing over the latest office gossip.

Typically, the café at SAFTI was deserted on these torpid afternoons – the Singapore armed forces adhering to the universal Friday ethic of military institutions the world over of 'POETS' Day (P**s Off Early Tomorrow's Saturday). My friend and I would enjoy the solitude but one Friday afternoon, we saw two other people sitting there. Even now, I recall the slight feeling of annoyance at the sight of their presence. I knew we would be compelled to talk to them, distracting my colleague and I from our ritual chinwag.

Their presence also signalled something unusual. Not only had we not seen them before, but they were clearly not Singaporeans. The two men sitting there were Caucasians; both similar in age – late forties or so – well dressed in colourful short sleeved shirts and with neatly trimmed beards. We began conversing. Who were they? What were they doing? How did they end up here?

The two men were Americans. Quiet, softly spoken, Americans. They had been in Singapore for over two decades, since the early 1970s, working as English language teachers at SAFTI. Plainly, they led steady, settled lives. Predictably, our banter ranged over what they thought of life in modern Singapore. But at this point they became decidedly unforthcoming. Why, I wondered? I made some cutting remarks about Singapore being an illiberal polity with little room for dissenting opinions that transgressed the orthodoxy of the ruling party. Anyone from outside Singapore with a liberal sense of ethics was likely, eventually, to find working in the place a challenge. After all, the government persecutes political opponents.

My colleague – an Australian of Singapore-Chinese origin – and I sat back and waited for the anticipated response. We had motioned in the right direction: we believed in tolerance, pluralism and the innate superiority of Western values. We expected our discussants to reciprocate with a corresponding rhetorical gesture of liberal solidarity.

None came. Instead, one of the men responded: 'This place persecutes political opponents and is intolerant of dissent you say? It sounds like it is no different from the United States'. The other, visibly assented. This was surprising. It was not the reaction that either my friend or I were envisaging… or perhaps wanting to hear.

A few more minutes of conversation revealed that they had been part of the anti-Vietnam War movement back in the 1960s, organising protests and marches. They said they had been tailed by the FBI, and in other respects had been subject to surveillance and intimidation. The experience had scarred them. Their alienation was complete. Soon after, they finished up their drinks and returned to whatever remained of their day, slightly relieved – I suspected – to end the dialogue with two tiresome expats. This was a discussion that they had almost certainly had on more than one occasion.

We never saw them again. Yet, the memory of this otherwise innocuous conversation stayed with me. There was something disconcerting about these quiet

Americans. How had they become so estranged from their homeland? Despite its faults, surely, the US remained a far freer society than almost anywhere else on earth, with avenues open to pursue reform and to right injustices. And, even if they had bad experiences during the tumult of the late 1960s, why swap a life in an imperfect democracy for the overt authoritarianism of a place like Singapore? There might be many other more agreeable countries to have fled to.

The unipolar years

This chance conversation clearly touched a nerve with me. Reflecting on my own caste of mind back then, I confess that I was probably a different kind of person, one that harboured views that I look upon now with some regret. To a greater or lesser extent, I had absorbed elements of the contemporary *zeitgeist* of the 1990s. These were my 'unipolar' years. I never overtly subscribed to the end of history thesis, but I reflected some of its early traits, with a disposition towards believing in the innate desirability of Western hegemony.

By the mid/late 1990s, young adults like me had been moulded by multiple events, not least epic ideological struggle of the Cold War, culminating in the collapse of the Soviet Union in 1990/91 and the 'victory' of the West. Furthermore, the prospect of a more liberal 'New World Order', presaged by the successful reversal of Iraq's aggression against Kuwait in 1991, held out the promise of collective action against obvious wrongdoing. Elsewhere, the Balkan wars of the mid-1990s and the Rwandan genocide of 1994, demanded a moral imperative to act in the face of monstrous crimes against humanity. I vividly recall also how the brave struggles of Hong Kong's fledgling democrats to preserve a modest set of freedoms in the face of China's authoritarian gaze during the lead up to the territory's handover in 1997 had an especially strong impact upon me. The morally principled position was to stand against belligerence, atrocious crimes of ethnic cleansing, and totalitarian duress wherever their ugly features appeared.

Had a combination of these factors, though, caused me to imbibe certain facets of Western self-satisfaction and hubris that I sensed had irritated the two quiet Americans all those years before? Later, 9/11 and the invasion of Iraq in 2003 would cause me to re-evaluate my assumptions. But I was left still with unanswered questions. How had these Americans come to repudiate the land of their birth and all its best political traditions? And, if they were really exercised about political freedom, why settle in Singapore, a country not known for courting left-wing peaceniks (indeed, it had largely backed US intervention in Vietnam)?

From moral mission to moral cynicism

Scott Anderson's compelling book, *The Quiet Americans: Four CIA Spies at the Dawn of the Cold War – A Tragedy in Three Acts*, helped provide some answers to these questions. The book's premise is that between 1944 and 1956 the moral arc of the United States underwent a transformation. In 1944, the US stood tall as an industrial and moral colossus. It was the arsenal of democracy, the powerhouse that defeated the tyranny of the Axis powers in World War II. Fundamentally, this democratic beacon-on-the-hill held out the promise of carrying on that moral mission, envisioning an end to the obsolete, and widely despised, European empires.

Yet, in the space of twelve years, far from dismantling those empires, the US was paying for their maintenance, and instead of fostering democracy was busily undermining freely elected governments. Not only did these foreign policy missteps come back to haunt US policymakers, the Vietnam War being the most obvious, but the wages of sin that accompanied the American crusade against communism succeeded in destroying much of the US's moral standing in the eyes of many nations, leaving a legacy of deep suspicion over US motives no matter how neatly dressed up in the language of 'freedom' and 'democracy'.

Equally damaging, the author points out, was the impact of this era upon American society in general, which endured the slow-motion hysteria of state sanctioned anti-communist witch-hunts, largely engineered by the manipulative head of the FBI, J. Edgar Hoover. Hoover's primary motivation, so it seems, was less to expunge communists from the US domestic polity, than to outwit his bureaucratic opponents, not least those in the fledgling CIA, who were perceived to be a threat to his institutional power. Cumulatively, these years, according to Anderson, fuelled a 'cynicism and distrust of governments from which the United States has never truly recovered'. At last, I was perhaps beginning to apprehend the mentality that afflicted my two American interlocutors all those years ago back in Singapore.

The anti-communist conundrum

The conundrum that Anderson presents us with is that, given its appalling historical record, anyone in their right mind *should* be anti-communist. However, the cause of anti-communism came to be tarnished over the course of the later twentieth century. The author himself admits being troubled by the question from his childhood in Taiwan, where he came to see that much of the regime's anti-communist rhetoric was merely political theatre to justify authoritarian rule. Years later, as a journalist, he bore witness to a political assassination carried out by the US backed regime in El Salvador. How did it come to all this? How did the noble vision of America at the end of World War II end up legitimising the direct opposite of its ideals?

Anderson answers these questions through the personal journeys, stories and experiences of four notable American intelligence officers at the dawn of the Cold War – the eponymous quiet Americans: Michael Burke, Edward Lansdale, Peter Sichel and Frank Wisner. All four were present at the creation of the US intelligence apparatus in the later years of the Second World War with the Office of Strategic Services, which was later to evolve into the Central Intelligence Agency. Wisner, Burke and Sichel were initiated into the world of espionage in World War II, undertaking covert operations in Eastern and Western Europe. Landsdale, perhaps the most renown of the group, was the late bloomer who was to make his mark shortly after the end of the war in Southeast Asia, first in the Philippines and later in South Vietnam.

The book charts the highs and lows of the careers of each of these 'Quiet Americans', but also conveys the progressive disillusionment each suffered partly because of the moral compromises involved in living in the secret world but also as they gradually realised the impact of the corrupted idealism that they had conspired to create. Their doubts coalesce in questions about what their missions were meant to accomplish, and whether it was worth the costs, both human and moral.

These doubts became acute for those like Michael Burke and Frank Wisner, who were responsible for running early infiltration operations into communist Eastern Europe. The known failures of these missions, be it parachuting anti-communist commandos into Albania, landing agents by sea into the Baltics, running partisan teams in Poland or the Ukraine, were such that no-one to this day can be sure that any of these missions yielded anything worthwhile. Burke himself estimated that over half the commandos he had dispatched into Albania ended up dead or captured. Those that survived were more than likely to have been compromised and 'played back', so adept was the Soviet KGB, and its East European appendages, at trapping and turning agents.

Despite the failures, Wisner attested to the 'mindless momentum' that often saw such fruitless operations continue even though the likely odds were known. The CIA's freewheeling approach meant that a junior officer with a pet project could work their way around more seasoned, and cautious, supervisors. Sichel recalls the sheer bureaucratic complexity and amateurishness that prevailed. Shutting down poorly performing or clearly compromised operations was inordinately difficult. With so many agents on the payroll, it became difficult to drop them for fear they would defect and betray everyone else. Far easier to let dead-end missions limp on.

The futility of it all seemed increasingly obvious. Anderson suggests we should forget the idea of a secret agent sneaking through the forests to spy on some hidden Soviet missile base. The entire Soviet bloc was battened down by systems of internal passports and travel permits, while security perimeters often began dozens, sometimes hundreds, of miles from the installations themselves. No Western intelligence-gathering agent was ever going to get anywhere near them. So, what were the operations for? No one really knew.

Such questions were even more sharp-edged with respect to those who were infiltrated to stir up rebellion against communist rule in Eastern Europe: what would happen if these underground movements were successful? What support from the West would be forthcoming? The answer had been delivered with the popular uprisings in East Germany in 1953 and Hungary in 1956: none whatsoever. For the Eisenhower administration, the uprisings merely validated the belief that the Soviet empire was crumbling, which justified even more (useless) covert operations.

Bureaucratic pyromania
Often the four protagonists consoled themselves that they were merely foot-soldiers in a great moral contest, and that there were better minds in Washington working out how all these events would play-out on the geostrategic chessboard. But, ultimately, each came to realise that there was no synchronisation of operations and no thought-through planning. They came to believe that operations were haphazard at best and, at worst, an exercise in cynical opportunism. Those in the American foreign policy bureaucracy, like the Secretary of State John Foster Dulles, didn't care about moral principles. They were happy to trade lives for propaganda points and wished only to create more situations where this happened. According to veteran CIA officer Miles Copeland, the Agency was the equivalent of an arsonist-fireman that would seek fires to put out, 'even if we had to light them ourselves'.

Through bureaucratic self-perpetuation, the US became addicted to covert operations and interfering in the affairs of other states. Furthermore, during this era, US administrations learnt the pleasing lesson that in contrast to the 'dreary stasis' in Eastern Europe displacing uncongenial regimes in Latin America, the Middle East and Asia was far easier. Working through proxy forces, the intelligence services could bolster regimes it regarded as allies and get rid of those it did not. Facilitating the overthrow of the Mossadegh government in Iran in 1953 and installing the monarchical rule of the Shah provided the initial proof of concept. Sponsoring the coup against Guatemalan President Jacobo Árbenz in 1954 was rated another 'success', as was Landsdale's manoeuvring to install Ngo Dinh Diem as the premier of South Vietnam.

Few, if any, of these regime-change operations forestalled communist take-overs. The governments in Iran and Guatemala were not Soviet stooges, or in danger of falling into the communist orbit. They were democratically elected administrations that were inconvenient to US/Western commercial interests. In the ideologically charged atmosphere of the Cold War, however, there was no room for ambiguity. Non-aligned countries were seen as dupes of the Soviet Union in the ultimate clash between good and evil. The overall result, Anderson observes, was the erosion of the US's moral standing and 'the extinguishing of whatever claim to a higher degree of honor or altruism it still enjoyed. It was the final laying bare of the myth of America as the herald of freedom'.

Anderson's damning verdict is that the US had no one to blame but itself. It had chosen dictatorships over democracy. It had supported France in quelling anti-colonial resistance in Southeast Asia. It had compiled hit lists of awkward foreign leaders to be removed, sometimes assassinated. It promoted the rhetoric of freeing the 'enslaved peoples' in Eastern Europe while doing nothing to support them on the few occasions that they were courageous enough to rise-up. It missed opportunities to lower the temperature of superpower confrontation, especially in the wake of Nikita Khrushchev's efforts to de-Stalinise the USSR. It had institutionalised a system that was to lead to countless other proxy wars, coups, death-squads and tragedies. All the while, at home, it instantiated a bureaucracy that was willing to spy on its own population.

The long journey back to Singapore
All of which brings us back to the two very different quiet Americans I chanced upon in Singapore. Having read Anderson's impressive account, I now wondered whether these former anti-war activists had not found their own form of peace there for one simple reason: *honesty*. Singapore's political system may not be very democratic, but it was at least honest. The authorities made little secret of their disdain for Western democracy and their lack of tolerance for political dissent. Combined with a record of competent government, Singapore autocrats could sustain their claim to rule. Competence and

honesty present themselves as attractive alternatives to the hypocrisy of twisted idealism as recounted in this book.

Was this the line of reasoning that inspired the life choices of these Americans? I'll never know. Did this answer the question that had been bothering me for all these years? I'm not sure. This reflection did, though, prompt another reminiscence. In 2000, while attending a seminar, I ran into the Head of Operations of the Internal Security Department (ISD), Singapore's 'secret police'. Benny was his first name. He looked disconcertingly young and was very self-assured. But he spoke quite openly about the kind of work his organisation undertook – namely, keeping tabs on those with undesirable, dangerously liberal, points of view. As far as Benny was concerned, politics was a game of winner takes-all. Those in power had done a good job, so they have a right, if not a duty, to ensure that the system remains stable and does not allow disruptive elements anywhere near power. 'That's the set up here', he said. An unpleasant perspective, I remember thinking. But in its own way, it did possess the integrity of being scrupulously candid.

All the flaws and hypocrisies aside, I am thankful that I live in a society that, for the moment, preserves most of the freedoms and benefits of liberalism. The most salutary aspect for me in reading Anderson's work, however, was that it underlined how far I had travelled in my personal and political journey, away from the presuppositions of the unipolar years to a position which finds itself more in sympathy with the book's core arguments than once might have been the case.

Red-scare, red states
The importance of Anderson's analysis is that it makes clear the moral costs that are incurred when democratic nations fall below their stated ideals. He points especially to the harm inflicted upon the American body-politic by an excess of anti-communist zeal, which he believes accounts for the current dividing line in the contemporary US between red and blue states. Those who embraced the Red Scare, believing that America was under siege from within, went down one path, while those who believed it was all a 'cynical myth' went down another. So antithetical are these perspectives that they lack even a modicum of empathy for each other. Knowing where someone stood on the Red Scare, Anderson maintains, is a reliable predictor of where their views, and often their offspring's views, reside on all manner of foreign policy issues, be it support for or against the Vietnam War, the Star Wars programme in the 1980s, or the Iraq War after 2003.

Anderson claims, 'There is very little sign that this divide, rooted in the Cold War passions of seventy years ago, will narrow any time soon'. Here, the critical reader might take issue with this contention, as the evidence is that it is blue-state Democrats rather than red-state Republicans who increasingly present themselves as the modern heirs of McCarthy and Hoover. The election of Donald Trump to the Presidency in 2016 highlighted a convergence among elements of the left and right in American politics with once solidly Democrat constituencies switching allegiance to a Republican candidate who advocated an end to foreign policy adventurism and an America-First emphasis that sought to fix problems at home rather than engage in endless meddling abroad.

By contrast, ever since President Bill Clinton's policy of triangulation in the 1990s, the modern Democrat Party's movement towards, if not outright capture by, commercial-donor interests, including large arms corporations, has facilitated a political role reversal. It is the Democrat establishment that now appears all too willing to pursue confrontation, regime-change and reckless military intervention externally, while directing the efforts of the intelligence agencies and the wider bureaucracy internally against domestic political adversaries, who are now deemed to be subversive rather than simply oppositional as one would expect in any functioning democracy.

Plus, ça change?
The irony is that much of the turbulence in US domestic politics in recent years rotates around a variant of the Red-Scare with routine allegations that domestic opponents are in league with Russia, leading to confected conspiracies of Russian collusion – often endorsed by former senior intelligence officers. These have proved every bit as pernicious and damaging to the democratic fabric than anything McCarthy or Hoover dreamt up. I

discern that Anderson's political inclinations reside on the Democrat-leaning centre-left of US politics. I hope he would agree that the contemporary Russia-scare is as equally fallacious as the Red-scare of the early Cold War years, especially when these concoctions are used to bend the domestic political apparatus towards suppressing dissent and the persecution of political opponents. It was wrong then and it is wrong now.

Meanwhile, I do wonder which side of the political fence the two quiet Americans in Singapore would now find themselves.

Original article published in *Cieo*, 3rd August 2023, by M.L.R. Smith.

8. The endnote of history: Britain's terminal decline?

THE MOUNTAINS OF THE BRINDABELLA RANGE, located on the border of the Australian Capital Territory and New South Wales, unfold beyond my window where I am writing the final instalment of this book. I am lucky to live here. The beauty and serenity of the surroundings nurture an atmosphere conducive to calm reflection. It is about as far removed from any turbulent frontline of history as one can imagine. The backdrop radiates permanence, continuity and detachment. It provides the space to bring perspective to the ideas that appear in this volume, as well as to the life and work of my friend, David.

At this point, I should tell you that David killed himself. The words are difficult to write and hard to read because such an act speaks of a different kind of terror from the kind that we often wrote about, one that is personal and profoundly distressing. Reflecting upon our long association, it is true to say that in contrast to David I was more of a 'happy warrior'. Some maladapted gene meant that I was less affected by our sometimes-gloomy prognostications for Western civilisation or by the difficulties we periodically encountered with the ideologues who inhabit modern universities. David was more mournful and downbeat. In contrast, I was slightly more optimistic that Western culture could rehabilitate itself: not easily or quickly, but the recuperation of a strong sense of national place and purpose, and of a Western mythos more generally, is a hope that I cultivated, and still do. For David, this wasn't the case. David's obituary in *The Times* quoted him as saying: 'After COVID the West is far weaker politically and economically. I'm frankly quite depressed about its prospects'.

It may sound strange, but despite his pessimism David was a gregarious personality and a much more convivial lunch or dinner companion. His natural eloquence and gentle charm won people over far more easily than I was ever able. His gloomy, usually very accurate, assessments of the prevailing political and cultural malaise would invariably be couched within a great deal of affable, self-deprecating humour, or faux, but very droll, world weariness. Outwardly, it was if he was performing a role, acting out the character of a melancholic, disillusioned, romantic. At a more private level, though, may be this was his reality.

This is the mystery David left us with. It causes me much soul-searching still, examining whether I could have offered him wiser counsel over the years, and been, in that respect, a better friend. I came to ponder whether the marginalisation, professional rejection and the rhetoric of silence that we had encountered over the decades, which was undoubtedly part of our reality, played a part in the choices that came to haunt him at the end? Whereas I was content to blow it all off and be comfortable in a 'club of one' – or two – David found the experience more hurtful.

Marginalisation is a battle in a war that cannot be won. A person of David's sociable, passionate nature may be disillusioned by it, but nonetheless he continuously out-performed his academic peers in terms of the quality and extent of his writings, and much else, and was consistently ahead of the game, sometimes by decades. In contrast to the fashionable conformity to which most of his contemporaries adhered, his astute observations proved far-sighted and accurate. David's work relentlessly exposed the dangers of the cult of radical progressivism. He perceived the damaging impact this new political religion was having upon politics and public life, and how it was manifesting in national and cultural nihilism, the misidentification of threats at home, disastrous military adventurism abroad, the failures of multiculturalism, as well as elite arrogance and incompetence.

Saying these things in the current era is not necessarily controversial, when they are clearly observable all around us; saying such things in the 1990s and early 2000s, decidedly was. For most of his career his foresight was not rewarded with honours, public recognition or chairs in political philosophy at prestigious universities but more often with cold-shouldering and career blight. Late in his career, David took up the position of Research Director of the Danube Institute, which put him at the heart of a movement helping to shape new political understandings in line with his own thinking. It was a role, moreover, that he took to with enthusiasm and rigour. At the end, he was increasingly held in wide regard as a significant and prophetic voice in conservative circles, as the many obituaries, including those in *The Times* and the *Telegraph*, attested. He had every reason to live. Paradoxically, in that that sense also it could be said that his life came to a fitting conclusion. His death however embodies the complexities that informed his writing, a reminder perhaps that outcomes rarely conform to our wishes or desires.

* * *

The splendour of my surroundings outside Canberra also reminds me that despite our sharply differing personalities we shared many affinities, one of which was a curious reverse symmetry in that we both accidentally became Anglo-Australians. David was born in Britain, worked in Australia for most of his career and returned to the UK in later life. Although I was born in Britain, much of my childhood was spent in Perth, Western Australia. My parents came back to Britain in the early 1970s. While I experienced interludes in Luxembourg, Singapore and the US, my working life was chiefly based in London. Yet, in my own advancing years, I find myself living beneath the stars of the Southern Cross once again.

The Anglo-Australian persona is one that, if nothing else, offers a dual sense of loyalty to, yet detachment from, both countries. The land of our birth, and especially the idea of Britain as an independent sovereign nation with its unique character and historical traditions, was something to which David and I were steadfast in our fidelity. However, the physical separation by vast distance from Britain, which we underwent throughout our lives, afforded us a degree of emotional disinterestedness. Rarely did we find ourselves over-committing to one political cause or feel too aggrieved if events did not work out the way we might have liked. Primarily, we sought to be observers from afar. It is this disposition that governs most of the content in this final chapter, where we seek to cast a weary eye over the fate of our native land.

By returning to Australia late in my career, I suppose that I am following Peter Hitchens' injunction to Britons, which is that they should emigrate. David and I admired Hitchens and often felt in tune with his curmudgeonly outlook. His book, *The Abolition of Britain*, first published in 1999, was a forecasting masterclass in predicting all the long-term effects on the British constitution and way of life soon to be inflicted upon the country by the Blairite revolution.

Sympathetic though we were, for all his perceptive brilliance we never entirely shared Hitchens' relentless negativity and message of hopelessness, which seemed strangely dissonant. If your view is that Britain is doomed and there is no way back, then why should anyone listen only to a litany of dejection? If you are not prepared to do anything purposeful to try to rectify things, then you might as well abandon yourself to the apocalypse. Hitchens' nihilism, moreover, redounded to the benefit of the progressive ideologues he so despised because it steered those with more conservative inclinations into a condition of despair. Worse, the logical advice that really extended from Hitchens' position was not emigration, but that young people should simply throw in their lot with the cultural revolution in the West, if only as a means of self-preservation.

For my part, by returning to my childhood roots down under, I was not fleeing Britain as such. I had the good fortune to be offered a new job here. Sure, I was running away from the dreadful British university system, but I wasn't running from Britain per se. From the late twenty-teens onward there wasn't much sense of a pluralistic community of scholars left to cherish in Britain. Our academic careers in the UK finally expired at King's College London, where I had been a full-time member of staff in the Department of War Studies, and where David also saw out his time as a Visiting Professor following the end of his Australian sojourn. By the early 2020s, even this department, once an outpost of sanity and genuine heterogeneity, had fallen victim to the forces of progressive ideology, leaving David to lament, in his own immaculate turn of phrase, 'how War Studies went Woke Studies'.

The essays in this chapter are, indeed, laments of a sort. They reflect, however, not a loss of faith in Britain or its people but rather our sorrow for the country's prospects under its chronically inept political class, who seem determined to reduce Britain to an endnote of history.

Chapter one examines the evolving tensions between the people and the 'ineptocracy' that rules over Britain. Seemingly incapable of escaping the Stockholm Syndrome of an EU inspired desire to abolish national tribes, the political classes are willing to destroy centuries of settled tradition in favour of a self-serving vision of a post-democratic future. It is for this reason that in foreign policy terms a lazy and incompetent 'elite', as the second chapter explains, has been unable to think realistically about ways to advance the welfare of the country that don't involve either Euro-appeasement or mindlessly coat-trailing the Americans into an endless series of wars or security commitments that are peripheral to the national interest.

Unsurprisingly, the economic mismanagement of Britain, particularly following the blunders over the COVID-19 pandemic, induce degrees of nostalgia in those of us who can remember more interesting, and in some respects pleasanter, times. Even we were surprised to look back on the 1970s, the theme of the third essay, as a lost world of cultural creativity and national solidarity. As we point out, the dead hand of neo-liberal economics, with its predatory, extractive, homogenising, instincts has expunged much of the creative vitality in British life. It was this vitality that provided the engine for the country's recovery from the hardships of the seventies and its rejuvenation in the two decades that followed. Today, the relative absence of such cultural resources is symbolic of a vanished kingdom.

The next essay, 'The suicide and conquest of Britain revisited' argues that decline at the hands of a decadent and corrupt ruling class is a recurring feature of British history. The collapse of Roman civilisation in Britain, stimulated partly by the effects of migration, reveals some uncanny parallels with our present situation. The parallels remind us especially that the undermining of prosperous, thriving societies is largely the product of a selfish choice by the elites to preserve their waning power and prestige. History doesn't end, but it does echo down the millennia.

The final two essays contain David's poignant reflections on the re-writing of history, both local and global, to conform to an anachronistic set of woke moral narratives. In the case of Abergynolwyn, the Welsh village of David's childhood memories, the ideological enforcers of Gwynedd Council wish not to celebrate the beauty and particularity of this unique place, but to shrink its rich history down to a story about the sins of slavery, about which Abergynolwyn has all but the most tenuous of associations. Woke conformity also negates any proper scholarly accounting of the moral failures and achievements of the British Empire, the subject of the last essay. In fact, it erodes all standards of scholarship. In the cases of Abergynolwyn and the Empire, one detects the neo-Maoist attempt at historical and cultural annihilation that seeks to deprive people of any connection to their past, tendentiously reducing fascinating and complex stories to melodrama in pursuit of an empty, soulless ideological agenda of endless denunciation and moral rectification.

If all this sounds like a discouraging note upon which to bring this book to a conclusion, that is not the intention. If David and I were fortunate to enjoy a front row seat at the end of history and to have had the immense privilege of being able to ruminate on the contours of the post-Cold War era, we witnessed enough to know that nothing in our condition, either as individuals or as nations and peoples, is ever predestined. As the Czech playwright and dissident Václav Havel observed in the struggles against communist totalitarianism in Eastern Europe, a fundamental element of the human spirit is a striving to live in truth. So long as that spirit survives, the possibilities for human salvation and regeneration, both personal and collective, will always remain. And, were he still with us in this life, I am certain David would have told us that the pursuit of truth, and the responsibility for seeking salvation, ultimately resides within ourselves and not in the vacuous lie of the end of history.

A Union without Faith or Law:
Part one – The post-Brexit game of thrones

Whoever yet a Union saw
Of Kingdoms without Faith or Law?
(Jonathan Swift, 1707)

The concept of the national interest is straightforward. In democratic societies like the United Kingdom, government exists to represent the interests of those who elected it to power, reflecting and promoting the values, traditions and aspirations of the wider population. The nation's foreign policy should therefore serve these interests by engaging with the world in a manner that seeks to safeguard and maximise the well-being of its people.

After Brexit, government policy making was supposed to focus on securing the national interest. 'Taking back control' was the guiding principle of those who supported leaving the European Union (EU). The expectation was that the United Kingdom government would resume control of its territorial borders, reassert parliamentary sovereignty and return Britain to its historic role as an independent sovereign state with a commitment to a rule-governed international trading order.

At first, the government of Prime Minister Boris Johnson seemed to be moving in this direction. It sought to re-establish the UK's economic and political links with the world beyond Western Europe. It forged 'bespoke' free trade agreements with Australia, New Zealand and Japan, and has applied for membership of the Comprehensive and Progressive Agreement for Trans-Pacific Partnership (CPTPP).

As a naval power, Britain has also shown a willingness to promote maritime freedom across the Indo-Pacific. The signing of the AUKUS (Australia, United Kingdom, United States) security pact in September 2021, evinced a welcome desire to form new and strategically relevant global alliances. The UK has also adopted, with some equivocation, a more critical stance toward China's geopolitical ambitions.

From the perspective of 'taking back control' these are constructive achievements. Yet since Boris Johnson's resounding election victory in December 2019, the much-anticipated global Britain project of a state at ease with itself and with the world remains, at best, a work in progress. More disconcertingly, there are also signs that the government is diverging from its vision of reasserting national independence and accepting instead the self-harming policies promoted by a still anti-Brexit establishment.

The paradoxes of the pandemic
Obviously, the COVID-19 pandemic upset the new government's plans to release the nation's animal spirits after their long hibernation, shackled by decades of stifling EU regulation. The pandemic, of course, had a traumatic impact upon all the Western democracies. In this regard the UK government at least performed no worse than its European counterparts. Indeed, in some areas it performed much better. It achieved a faster roll out of its vaccination programme and a swifter exit from COVID inspired health restrictions, thus showing that, liberated from European controls, the government could engage in effective decision making.

Nevertheless, in common with most EU countries, Australasia, and many US state legislatures, the British parliament and the devolved assemblies in Scotland, Wales and Northern Ireland, developed a dangerous penchant for lockdowns and quarantines at the slightest rise in cases or at the latest mutation of the virus.

Health bureaucracies and vested interest groups from media corporations to trade unions and the pharmaceutical industry, became addicted to catastrophic projections. The scientifically questionable attempt to hold back the spread of a virus through lockdowns, social distancing rules, mask mandates and school closures incurred huge economic and social costs. The great health disruption undermined the normal functions of democratic governance and the wider open trading order.

Pandemic consequences
In the UK this dangerously valetudinarian policy response has created the deepest recession since the union's formation three centuries ago. At the same time, the funding of COVID support programmes raised national indebtedness to levels only previously achieved in times of war and existential threat to the state's survival. The lockdown induced recession and the uncertain economic recovery since September 2021 has seen supply chain disruption, labour and energy shortages, rising inflation, rising interest rates and the prospect of economic stagflation.

Whilst the UK shared its big state pandemic management strategy with most developed nations, it also revealed distinctive features that do not portend well for the once optimistic vision of a global Britain promoted by think tanks like the Policy Exchange report, *Making Global Britain Work* and elaborated in the government's report, *Global Britain in a Competitive Age: The Integrated Review of Security, Defence, Development and Foreign Policy* in 2020, which was intended to chart the course for Britain's foreign policy in the new era. Emerging from the pandemic starkly exposes the challenges to re-establishing a coherent view of the British national interest after forty years of submission to the demands of European supranationalism and the fallout from two-decades of constitutional rationalisation.

Evolving disunion
The immediate challenge evident after the referendum on European membership in June 2016 was that a metropolitan elite, which dominates the mainstream media, politics, business and the civil service, remained committed to the European Union, despite the democratic vote to leave it. Unwilling to abandon a cosmopolitan faith in ever closer European union, these elites shared a worldview with their European and North American confrères that sought to question, undermine, and ultimately reverse, Britain's process of withdrawal from the European institutions. Between 2017 and 2019 the Conservative government of Theresa May failed to negotiate a withdrawal agreement that would satisfy a largely Remainer parliament or her own Leaver backbenchers. Immured in a constitutional deadlock of her own devising, May's administration lost authority, momentum and purpose.

Brussels, with the complicity of leading civil servants, tried to force the UK into a new referendum or a new treaty that afforded the worst of all possible outcomes for national self-determination. Only after Boris Johnson became leader of the Conservative Party in October 2019 was a dissolution of parliament achieved. Johnson's overwhelming electoral victory in December 2019 based on a campaign to get Brexit done, gave the new Conservative government the legitimacy to negotiate a treaty that separated the UK from Europe whilst still maintaining a trading relationship.

Even so, the new treaty, rather than a clean break with European institutions left unresolved questions vital to parliamentary sovereignty. The UK-EU Trade and Cooperation Agreement left an unsustainable customs border in the Irish Sea between the province of Northern Ireland and the UK mainland. This together with disputes with the EU over the UK's maritime boundaries created an increasingly fraught relationship that, without resolution, undermines the prospect of an economically integrated state.

In November 2021, Britain's most effective Brexit negotiator, Lord David Frost, resigned citing his difficulties with the 'direction of travel' the government had taken during the pandemic. Liz Truss, the new foreign secretary took responsibility for the border issue in 2022. Like Frost, she threatened to invoke Article 16 of the Northern Ireland Protocol governing the UK and Brussels' post-Brexit relationship with Ireland. However, the issue remains unresolved, and the EU's intransigence has revealed that Brussels remains profoundly hostile to a unified and independent Britain. Moreover, in this they receive overt and covert support from leading UK civil servants, business, academe and the mainstream media.

The inability of the Johnson government to address these burgeoning divisions between the United Kingdom's elites and the revolting masses has hamstrung coherent foreign and domestic policy planning. This became increasingly manifest over the course of the pandemic that greeted the new government in its first months. Its viral response –

composed of lockdowns, furloughs and quarantines – not only damaged the economy and created the conditions for inflation and the impoverishment of the least well off, it also unintentionally gave credence to the demands for independence in the devolved administrations of Wales and Scotland.

The Celtic Costa Bureaucratica
The Scottish National Party (SNP) in Scotland and the Labour Party in alliance with *Plaid Cymru* in Wales have used the pandemic to implement notably tougher measures governing their respective peoples than those applied in England. Nicola Sturgeon, Scotland's First Minister and Mark Drakeford, her Welsh equivalent (*Prif Wienidog Cymru*), deliberately distanced themselves from the English government's attempts to limit lockdown and quarantine measures. Entering Wales from across the Severn Bridge motorists were constantly reminded that different and stricter measures applied to those under the jurisdiction of the Welsh Assembly. Similarly in Scotland, the SNP enforced more draconian policing measures than those in operation across the border.

Somewhat surprisingly, Sturgeon and Drakeford drew plaudits from the media for their tough stance. Indeed, Drakeford, despite unnecessarily reverting to much stricter measures that included fining people for going to work in December 2021, continued to receive far higher approval ratings than Boris Johnson who followed a more economically sensible approach to lockdown.

Similarly in Scotland, the SNP still enjoys majority support for its strict virus policy. Both Wales and Scotland benefit from higher government funding than England and have little in the way of a private sector. The public sector dominates the political economy in both devolved regions. This is particularly the case in Wales, which is a Costa Geriatrica in the North and a Costa Bureaucratica in the South. Consequently, outside tourism and hospitality, public sector workers have not been penalised by the lockdown. In fact, the dependent populations of Wales and Scotland have become more servile and more responsive to the politics of fear promoted by the devolved authorities in Cardiff and Edinburgh. The different pandemic responses in Wales and Scotland have given these devolved governments an increasing appetite for independence by stealth.

This was not meant to happen. Westminster's indifference to this growing appetite for self-governance without economic responsibility has reduced the United Kingdom to an implicit federation, the precursor to inevitable demands for full autonomy. Instead of taking advantage of getting Brexit done to reassert sovereignty and a common rule of law overseen by its highest court of parliament sitting in Westminster, the pandemic response strengthened those forces on the Celtic fringe working for the dissolution of the union. Whilst there is disunion in Downing Street as the Prime Minister struggles to explain his cavalier attitude to lockdown rules that his government made and enforced, the *de facto* federation appears increasingly rudderless. The directional problem Lord Frost identified is not only a product of a critical mainstream media and a civil service, some of whose senior figures have much greater sympathy for a European union rather than a British one. It is also a product of the government's propensity for self-induced harm.

Whilst the pandemic response destabilised the union, the Johnson government's idealistic environmental agenda, which seeks to reduce the UK's carbon emissions to net zero within a decade, courts the approval of the green lobby, woke capitalists and investment funds, but imposes destructive economic costs. Driven by an apocalyptic vision of manmade climate catastrophe, this policy has increased energy prices to British manufacturing and domestic consumers at a time of rising inflation, whilst at the same time destabilising Britain's energy security and rendering the UK dependent on supplies from potentially hostile powers, notably Russia.

Eco-idealism has undermined the potential for national resilience and renders rebuilding the UK as a manufacturing base potentially unaffordable. With oil prices anticipated to reach $100 a barrel, the UK government and the Scottish Assembly regulate and restrict the extraction of North Sea oil and natural gas, as well as gas fracking, which would achieve the energy security the country urgently needs. A government sympathetic to an elite lobby of climate ideologists could ironically extinguish the United Kingdom as a sustainable body politic within a decade. As Clint Eastwood memorably put it, in a somewhat different context, 'that's a helluva price to pay for being stylish'.

The assault on history

If such a self-destructive energy policy were not bad enough, the elite's pathological reaction to Brexit has also accelerated a wider ideological assault in academe and the mainstream media on the origins of the United Kingdom, its involvement in colonialism and slavery and the structural legacy it manifests in Britain's institutions. It was no accident that in the aftermath of Brexit the universities, the corporate media and even business elites, supported an increasingly negative view of the nation state and its successful development into a modern multicultural democratic polity.

The history of the development of the United Kingdom became the subject of an iconoclastic ideological assault both in the United States and in the UK in the wake of the death of George Floyd in the American city of Minneapolis in May 2020. Despite occurring over 3,000 miles away and in an entirely different historical and political context, this event catalysed the woke campus left to expose the systemic racism that the democratic, constitutional, and legal rights enjoyed by all citizens irrespective of creed, colour or sex had allegedly concealed. The Black Lives Matter movement exploited the pandemic to advance an anti-racist agenda that reversed the values and self-understanding of most citizens evidently lost in false consciousness.

For the woke ideologists who analysed this condition, the fact that most people imagined they inhabited a law governed and politically accountable democratic polity merely evinced their misguided and distorted perception of reality. The antidote to this condition of ignorance required not only the transvaluation of political values that recognise and cherish the presumed victimhood endured by the UK's minority populations, but the correction of the UK's modern history to reveal its roots in colonialism and slavery. This further required the demolition and erasure of iconic imagery and heritage sites associated with the eighteenth-century slave trade, which according to this ultimately Maoist understanding, was not only the material, but the formal, efficient and final cause of the UK's imperial success in the nineteenth century.

This progressive rhetoric of collective moral guilt required atonement. It entails not only the rewriting of the recent past but the demolition of statues celebrating the false memory of imperial glory. The progressive sensibility and its distinctive grammar of self-vilification deemed statues like those erected at the high-water mark of Victorian imperialism to Edward Colston in the city of Bristol, the seventeenth century British philanthropist and director of the Royal African Company who developed the Atlantic slave trade, particularly egregious.

The ideology of collective guilt

Black Lives Matter supercharged the campaign against the Colston legacy and justified the tearing down of his statue, the mere existence of which its perpetrators regarded as a 'hate crime'. The Bristol experience is but one instalment of an essentially American movement with UK and Australian connections to remove the stigma of slavery, colonialism and racism by taking down statues, renaming buildings on campuses and in public spaces and 'decolonising' the secondary and tertiary curriculums.

This anachronistic, misleading and guilt inducing interpretation of the history of the union since 1707 gained political traction in 2020 because it gave credence to the elite belief in a rationalist project of European integration that dissolved national pasts into a collective post-national constellation leading eventually to a borderless world and the end of history.

Such a cosmopolitan, anti-state and anti-democratic worldview, aligned to a progressive and increasingly woke ideology, generated a rhetoric that now dominates public life and the terms in which moral, historical and contemporary social issues are discussed. It generates a vision of modern Britain as a tangle of inherited injustices that demand both rectification and compensation. As Thomas Sowell, a long time sceptic of the politics of collective guilt explains, 'political decisions about the future are made as if they were moral decisions about the past'.

In this regard, the particularly virulent response to Brexit and the assault on the UK's past, which anti-racists contend continued into the present, reflected how the cosmopolitan elites saw in the utopian prospect of ever closer European union a source of relief from the moral treadmill of atonement, reparation and confession. The post-national constellation and norms of social justice that European rules offered intimated the prospect of release from the apparent burden of Europe's past and a way to by-pass the menace of parochial populism: a project rudely interrupted by Brexit, which erroneously permitted the majority to have a say in the future being prepared for them.

The dashing of the hoped-for release from the UK's guilty nationalist and colonialist past thus added to the division of the increasingly divided kingdom and fuelled its further retribalisation into minorities according to their ethnic, gender, religious, lesbian, gay and transgender identities. Notwithstanding the pandemic, the government has done little to redress the harm inflicted upon the union by its dissolution into tribal affinities whether Scots, Welsh, Irish, gay, feminist, transgender, or Muslim.

Why has the Johnson government behaved so ineptly and what does it mean for the idea of 'global Britain'? It is to this question that we shall address in part two.

Original article published in *Cieo*, 17th February 2022, by David Martin Jones and M.L.R. Smith.

A Union without Faith or Law:
Part two – global Britain or vanishing kingdom?

As we showed in part one of our exploration of the post-Brexit world, the Conservative government has failed to make the domestic case for the union since its beginnings in 1707 or for its future as a coherent and stable framework for a sovereign parliamentary democracy. By 2022, Johnson's chaotic optimism and his inability to exercise control over his office and advisory staff, undermined his authority and divided his party. The divisions in government and its civil service reflected a wider anxiety concerning the economic prospects and future stability of the realm. The incoherence at the heart of the government's domestic agenda served to expose the constitutive dissonances in its post-Brexit foreign policy.

Since 2016, proponents of Brexit had envisaged Britain once more playing a global role in promoting free trade and a liberal, rules based, multilateral, international order. In an early attempt at appraising Britain's options in a paper entitled, *Making Sense of British Foreign Policy After Brexit*, the historian John Bew, now a key figure in the Downing Street Policy Unit, observed that the 'the greatest challenge to the new government was to identify some guiding principles for a new global strategy' and take measures 'to transform current uncertainty into opportunity'.

Taking Bew's paper as its cue, in December 2020, the Johnson government advertised its intention to undertake the 'largest review of Britain's security, defence and foreign policy since the end of the Cold War'. It would evaluate 'Global Britain's foreign policy, British alliances and diplomacy, shifts of power and wealth to Asia, how to use the UK's huge expenditure on international development and the role of technology'. The fruits of this strategic review were eventually published in March 2021.

Whilst *Global Britain in a Competitive Age: The Integrated Review of Security, Defence, Development and Foreign Policy* clarified important aspects of Britain's future military posture, it left several hostages to fortune: concerning Europe; the liberal international order it seeks to promote; the rising totalitarian power of China; and Russian revanchism. Events since the installation of Joe Biden as the new American President, who has shown little inclination to pursue a free trade agreement or facilitate closer ties with the UK, merely added to a list of unresolved policy issues.

The European dilemma

The guiding principles for a new global strategy not only remain unfinished business, they also now seem both over-ambitious and worryingly unrealistic. The review envisaged that 'future prosperity will be enhanced by deepening our economic connections with dynamic parts of the world such as the Indo-Pacific, Africa and the Gulf, as well as trade with Europe'. One of the issues to be confronted is that while the UK may be out of the EU, it remains crucial to the maintenance of Europe's security architecture, ironically, perhaps, more than almost any other state in the EU.

Because of the continuing commitment to European stability, collaborative alliances in terms of security and economic partnerships need to be maintained. This applies most notably in the strengthening of the UK's ties with the Baltic and the Central European states and its bilateral relations with those countries that empathised with Britain's decision to leave the EU.

Thus, paradoxically, whilst Europe remained of enduring relevance, the UK's relationship with the European Union, particularly with its leading players Germany and France, has become increasingly contentious. Given the uncertainties of current treaty arrangements with the EU, the government's *Integrated Review* foresaw that 'in the decade ahead', the UK would deepen its 'engagement in the Indo-Pacific, establishing a greater and more persistent presence than any other European country'. Consequently, the UK rapidly ratified trade agreements with several Indo-Pacific states and applied to join the multilateral Comprehensive and Progressive Agreement for Trans-Pacific Partnership (CPTPP).

The China paradox

At the same time, the *Integrated Review* was notably ambivalent about the rising power of China. China is central to the UK's economic security, the *Review* stated, but also an 'increasingly important partner' in tackling global challenges. Yet, China's growing global reach means that 'Easternisation' not only has implications for investment and development in the UK, but it also raises issues of national and international security.

As a maritime power committed to maintaining the freedom of navigation and the *status quo* in the Indo-Pacific, the UK was drawn not only into closer trading ties with Japan and Australia but also into security ties. In September the AUKUS agreement evinced this direction with the UK bolstering cooperation with Australia and the US in maintaining the maritime freedom of the Asia-Pacific. It is also in the process of concluding a reciprocal access agreement with Japan.

Yet, whilst the UK reconfigures its foreign policy increasingly towards the Indo-Pacific, it still maintains its commitment to NATO and its post-1996 expansion into Eastern Europe. Russia, as the successor state to the Soviet Union, has always interpreted this eastward expansion, at a time of political and economic weakness, as both gratuitously humiliating and a strategic threat to its traditional sphere of influence.

The Russian impasse

Significantly, the government's *Integrated Review* assumed a far less nuanced tone towards a revisionist Russia than it adopted towards a rising and more internationally powerful China. The UK would, the *Review* announced, 'actively deter and defend against the full spectrum of threats emanating from Russia'. Moreover, through NATO, the UK would 'ensure a united Western response, combining our military, diplomatic and intelligence assets in support of collective security'.

Consequently, when Russia built up its military force and conducted manoeuvres on its contested border with Ukraine in January 2022, demanding that NATO never allow Ukraine to become a member, the British Foreign Secretary, Liz Truss, along with the US Secretary of State, Antony Blinken, dismissed Russian demands. In this, they differed markedly from the far more ambivalent French and German diplomatic posture. The new German coalition government prevented Estonia from shipping weaponry across German territory to aid Ukraine. As the former Inspector General of the German Navy, Vice-Admiral Kay-Achim Schönbach observed, the Russian President Vladimir 'Putin really wants respect. Giving someone respect is low cost, even no cost.' The Admiral also observed that Russia was an old, important and Christian state.

Tom Tugendhat MP, the Chairman of the Foreign Affairs Committee, noted that the EU has maintained 'a deafening silence' towards Russia's provocative behaviour. Europe and its most powerful state Germany have proved incapable of deciding a response to Putin and have tried to keep the Ukraine problem on the diplomatic back burner since the last time Russian forces moved into the largely Russian populated area of Eastern Ukraine and seized the Crimea in 2014. Whilst the US and the UK offered military support and threatened economic sanctions against any further Russian aggression, French President Emmanuel Macron, and the German Chancellor Olaf Scholz, looked to de-escalate tensions and refused to sanction Russian energy exports or the Nord Stream 2 pipeline upon which Germany's energy future depends.

The end of the liberal international order

Whatever else Putin's manoeuvring achieves, it has already exposed the fragmentation of the West and altered the US perception of the European Union as an arrangement to be supported as a necessary democratic bulwark. At the same time, it is unclear what exactly the UK gains from its special relationship with the United States except being treated as a reliable but somewhat servile dependent that, unlike Australia, does not even deserve the benefit of a free trade agreement.

Despite the Anglo-American clamour for the defence of a liberal rules-based order, which demands strong and united response to defend Ukraine's freedom, there is evidently little appetite for conflict in Berlin, Paris or Brussels. More sceptical Europeans, unlike their British and American counterparts, recognise that Russia is reasserting its geopolitical presence in its traditional sphere of influence. It is reviving a role that it has played since the eighteenth century when Catherine the Great along with Prussia and Austria-Hungary embarked on the partition of the kingdom of Poland (the southern borderland, which was known as Ukraine 'or the borderland').

The Ukraine problem ultimately reflects the hubris of US liberal end of history foreign policy thinking. The impotent posturing of Blinken and Truss represent its last hurrah. Realist conservative observers of the implosion of the Soviet Union in the 1990s, like Robert Conquest and Owen Harries, warned against the expansion of NATO eastward at a time of Russian weakness. The 1994 expansion now looks like post-Cold War liberal overstretch or as Michael Clarke and Michael MccGwire argued in 2008 'a historical error of the first importance'.

A Prime Minister and his key foreign policy adviser familiar with the nineteenth century struggle for political mastery in Europe should perhaps be more sympathetic to the recent outbreak of appeasement in the major European capitals. They should recognise, as realists from Thucydides to Bismarck would, that Putin is merely doing what great powers, with a historic grievance of NATO's own devising do when confronting a weak state propped up by indecisive and divided opponents.

In this context, the idea that the UK would send troops to the Ukraine when it cannot police its own borders, prevent boatloads of illegal migrants crossing the English Channel, or reverse a protocol dividing Northern Ireland from the mainland, would strike any nineteenth century practitioner of *realpolitik* from Lord Palmerston to Benjamin Disraeli as either idealist delusion or insanity. Moreover, given that the UK, like the US, is riven by guilt about the racism and slavery that disfigures its past and disturbs its present view of itself and the world, it is somewhat odd that these troubled democracies want to export such an ethnically and religiously divisive model to Eastern Europe and across the Indo-Pacific.

Asleep at the wheel
The cumulative effects of the uncertainty and loss of faith in its own democratic identity also lead to further unnecessary diplomatic gaffes. The progressive propensity to excoriate the UK for its past misdeeds has justified foreign policy indifference to reviving a potentially fruitful relationship with its former colonies. Driven by the woke assumption that the Commonwealth countries must abhor their colonial legacy (as the Director of the Institute for Commonwealth Studies avers), the Foreign Office has given little credence to the scale and potential power of Britain's Anglosphere and the Commonwealth assets that might be mobilised. Instead, the Foreign Secretary makes grandiose statements about issues peripheral to the national interest like defending the integrity of Ukraine or sending aircraft carriers to the Taiwan Straits, whilst overlooking a historic resource of enduring strategic value. Significantly, it is the Indian and Australian Prime Ministers who show more enthusiasm for reinvigorating the Commonwealth than any recent British Prime Minister.

The recent decision by Barbados to remove the Queen as its head of state and declare itself a republic without a referendum in November 2021 vividly demonstrates how a woke foreign policy establishment and its academic apologists undermine rather than promote the UK's national interest. Attending the Bajan independence celebrations, the Prince of Wales felt constrained to apologise for the 'darkest days of our past and the appalling atrocity of slavery, which forever stains our history'. He, like his Foreign Office handlers, failed to observe that it was in fact the People's Republic of China that had actively encouraged the BLM movement in Barbados to campaign to remove the monarchy and helped foster its membership of China's Belt and Road Initiative. Facilitated by Chinese soft power aid and investment, Bajan independence could set off a domino effect across the West Indies of far more geopolitical consequence to UK and US interests than events in Eastern Ukraine or the Taiwan Straits.

Conclusion
In its current condition of disunion, the United Kingdom looks more like a failed state than a global Britain. Brexit and the COVID-19 pandemic did not cause this situation. Rather,

these two events have exposed the fault lines within the British state, which have been exacerbated by elite mismanagement since the end of the Cold War. If there is a positive outlook to be gained, it is that facing uncomfortable truths might be the beginning of wisdom.

There are benefits that can legitimately be expected to be reaped from regaining national sovereignty after forty years of unhappy engagement with pan-Europeanism. To accomplish this, however, all realist political thinking should begin with an appreciation of the national interest and the importance of parliamentary sovereignty to British constitutional self-understanding. Before a UK polity can think globally it must reassert the integrity of the union and roll back devolution. Scotland and Wales now look and act like quasi-states that undermine the prospects of a coherent presence on the international stage.

National integrity requires national resilience. A prudent administration must develop policies to reverse the self-harm inflicted by identity politics and the Maoist assault on the nation's history, heritage and institutions. The economic impoverishment that green utopianism imposes through unsustainably expensive energy further undermines any potential to revitalise the UK's manufacturing base or exploit its offshore resources. zero carbon, like zero COVID, is a recipe for economic disaster.

As the European Union fragments, a realistic UK foreign policy should recognise and prudently adapt to the evolving balance of power that is reshaping Central and Southern Europe. This would suggest that Britain should recognise that Brussels is more of a threat than a partner and instead promote bilateral relations with those states, most notably in Eastern Europe, with which it is most aligned and shares common values. In an economic climate of great post-pandemic uncertainty, the idea of the UK punching above its weight in either Europe or the Indo-Pacific looks increasingly fanciful. When global Britain cannot even secure its own borders or exercise sovereignty throughout the union, the view that it must defend the integrity of Ukraine or Taiwan seems, and indeed is, preposterous.

The UK's relationships with both the EU and the US must be recalibrated along more pragmatic lines. The Royal Navy should not be dragged into an East Asian conflict at the behest of a United States that exploits, rather than values, its special relationship. The UK should be in the Indo-Pacific for one purpose only: mutually beneficial free-trade. Trade deals with Japan and Australia and the CPTPP offer clear benefits. Collaborating with like-minded states to ensure maritime freedom also makes economic as well as strategic sense. The defence of Taiwan or South Korea does not. Equally, Britain has no interest in conflict with Russia, which is at best a middle economic power but one that deserves respect. Russia may not be a friend, but it does not have to be an enemy.

The UK should instead devote more attention to the Anglosphere, cultivating the Commonwealth rather than ridding itself of what an elite views as an inconvenient past. Absent close ties with Australia and potentially India, the Commonwealth faces the prospect of imminent dissolution. Worryingly, the Foreign Office is either asleep at the wheel, or actively undermining the prospect of a re-booted United Kingdom project. It requires root and branch reform.

Ultimately, a prudentially realist foreign policy has no permanent friends, only permanent interests. The UK should avoid, as it did under Prime Minister Benjamin Disraeli in the nineteenth century, all sanctimonious and costly liberal interventions in pursuit of norms that are demonstrably no longer universal.

Originally published in *Cieo*, 24th February 2022, by David Martin Jones and M.L.R. Smith.

The 1970s weren't all bad

Tube strikes, rail strikes, uncollected rubbish, energy crisis, rampant inflation, recession, and burgeoning national debt. We seem to have been here before. For those of us over a certain age, the current experience of rising interest rates, rising prices, strikes or 'industrial unrest', as it used to be called when we still had industries, is eerily reminiscent of the 1970s. Those who experienced it, were glad to see the noisome decade of three-day weeks, power-cuts, flared trousers, the Bay City Rollers, Red Diamond beer, Angel Delight and SpudUlike consigned to history's dustbin.

Economists and cartoonists, however, have recently taken to comparing our current financial and political malaise to that of the 1970s. Of course, there are significant differences between then and now. The structure of the economy and the composition of the population have altered dramatically, but for those of us who still just about have the capacity to remember, those unsettled times seem to be returning. The portents aren't good.

At the same time, those who lived through that difficult decade may also dimly recall that a stuttering economy was not, by itself, indicative of complete social and cultural collapse. Unsettling as those strange days were, they also possessed some redeeming features worth recalling. Not only do we face hard times analogous to the 1970s, but we do so with few of the cultural and political resources that made life bearable then, and which may be required again to extricate ourselves from our current predicament. While in economic terms we might be hurtling back towards the 1970s, we are doing it without the style, wit and cultural innovativeness that defined that decade.

What, we might wonder, was attractive about British society and cultural life in the 1970s, but which is notably lacking today?

First, the mass media has been revolutionised, but not for the better. Television, both the BBC and ITV, was worth watching in the 1970s. This was before the era of satellite TV, multiple channels and on-demand programming, but few would contend that the relative lack of choice denoted a lack of quality. From documentaries and drama series to children's programming, British television was innovative and iconic. Intelligent drama spanned the decade from the social commentary of *Play for Today* to the brilliance of *Tinker, Taylor, Soldier, Spy*. News and current affairs programmes were remarkably impartial, whilst investigative series like *Panorama* and *World in Action* demonstrated fine research coupled with fair-mindedness. Popular entertainment from *Match of the Day* to *The Generation Game* and *That's Life*, would keep families glued to the set on Saturday and Sunday evenings, unintentionally reinforcing a sense of national cohesion.

The comedy was funny. Classic comedy in the 1970s was often a function of the commitment to innovative commissioning by the national broadcaster. But TV comedy is worth singling out because it typified not only the nation's humour in hard times, but also its touching modesty, self-deprecation and sometimes its willingness to mock its own pretensions mercilessly. Okay, one might not wish to watch repeats of *George and Mildred* or *Mind Your Language*, but the classics remain: *Steptoe and Son, Morecambe and Wise, Monty Python, Fawlty Towers, Porridge, Rising Damp* and *Whatever Happened to the Likely Lads*?

And what do we have now? *Miranda* and *Mrs Brown's Boy's*, if you're lucky. *Live at the Apollo* and Nish Kumar if you're not. Indeed, a banal predictability characterises contemporary British television. From dating shows like *Naked Attraction* and *Love Island*, to reality TV like *Big Brother*, and poorly scripted dramas intent only on pushing a woke agenda, quality programming is not a term one associates with current British television output.

Elsewhere, the decline in the standard and reputation of news and current affairs coverage is a more disturbing political change in the role of the media since the seventies. Back then, this domain was the preserve of intrepid, dispassionate journalism. Nowadays, it is characterised by overpaid, grandstanding presenters, who use their positions to push sanctimonious metro-elite values. In the 1970s you had Robin Day and Brian Walden. Today we have Emily Maitlis and Gary Lineker.

Private Eye was a brilliant satirical magazine in the 1970s. That must come as a surprise to anyone born in the twenty first century, but in its prime under the editorship of Richard Ingrams and the likes of Peter Cook, Willie Rushton and Christopher Booker, as well as its resident 'commo' Paul Foot, the magazine was irreverent, rebellious and relentlessly anti-establishment, as opposed to the sad mouthpiece of Remoaner orthodoxy that it is today.

The broader cultural scene, most notably in music and drama, was one of continuous evolution and radical innovation. At the start of the decade the Rolling Stones, the Beatles and Led Zeppelin were at their zenith, while newer artists from Roxy Music to Elton John were receiving recognition for their creative genius. The social tumults of the era, however, were also stirring genuinely insurgent cultural forces that were to burst forth towards the end of the 1970s in punk, perhaps the only good thing you can say to emerge from the 1970s comprehensive school system. What constitutes the leading edge of the *zeitgeist* now? Harry Styles pretending to be gay.

Turning to party politics, despite the oil shock of 1973-74, membership of the Common Market and the breakdown of industrial bargaining, 1970s politicians often demonstrated principled commitments and authentic accomplishment. In the 1970s the public shared a perception that those in political life, with some notable exceptions (Jeremy Thorpe springs to mind), had a sincere commitment to public service. They came from a variety of backgrounds – business, trade unions, teaching, the merchant navy, mining and the factory floor. Many had served with distinction in World War II. The likes of James Callaghan, Harold Wilson, Denis Healey, Barbara Castle, Merlyn Rees, Roy Mason and Peter Shore evinced a genuine concern for the political health of the country. Tony Benn gave up his peerage to pursue a political vocation. Michael Foot was an outstanding political journalist and parliamentarian. The Conservative Party boasted Margaret Thatcher, a trained chemist, as well as Geoffrey Howe and Keith Joseph, both accomplished lawyers and ex-Army officers. Even a political disaster like Ted Heath was a talented musician and yachtsman.

Once more it is hard to resist the comparison. In contrast to the 1970s, the current ruling class come from similar backgrounds – middle-class, university educated, with little prior career experience outside the law, journalism, or politics itself. Parliamentarians increasingly sound alike, think alike and act alike. Of course, the politicians of the 1970s made mistakes, but their decisions, whether right or wrong, were not driven by spin and the learned helplessness and groupthink that typifies the current ineptocracy. The vacuous posturing over Brexit and its aftermath has led to national calamities on a grand scale – most obviously the fiscal disaster of COVID lockdowns and two decades of net zero greenoid fantasy. In other words, the kind of policies that are leading us back down the rabbit hole that leads to 1970s style 'industrial' unrest.

The wider point perhaps is that political debate generally in the 1970s seemed to be over sober matters of policy, coloured by different political perspectives concerning the role of the state, social class and financial rectitude, rather than pronouns, rainbow-coloured crossings, going 'carbon neutral' or whether nursing mothers should be referred to as 'chest feeders'. Politics in the 1970s was a serious business; today it seems trivial and deluded.

Traversing the social landscape, we would find in the seventies the police still trying to prevent and solve crime. Back then, the police acted more like the Sweeney (the classic cop drama of the era) and less like the paramilitary wing of the *Guardian*. Today they twerk and tweet, preferring to police thought and language. In the 1970s much of the public thought the police did a decent job in difficult circumstances. Now they don't.

In the 1970s you could usually get a doctor's appointment within 24 hours. You could even see an actual doctor in person. They even made house calls! Future generations are likely to look back and wonder how this was even possible.

Universities were still worth going to in the 1970s. They were institutions where pluralism and free thought flourished. Today they are repositories of ideological conformity and student debt.

Significantly, Britons made things in the 1970s. They built ships, cars and aircraft. The UK had leading electronics companies and was home to the world's largest chemical conglomerate. Britons pioneered early computing technology. Britain also had its own large-scale car industry. Yes, managerial failure and the militant unionism of Red Robbo undermined British Leyland, but this overlooks the fact that Britain still produced marques like MG, Jaguar and Land Rover. It's easy to mock the Morris Maxi and Marina, but the Rover 3500 SD1 series or the Mini-Metro were pioneering projects that influenced car design the world over.

Where did it go? Sold off. Broken up. Shipped abroad. It wasn't the case that Britain just wasn't very good at making things anymore. We were. Neither was it true that manufacturing necessarily thrived under foreign ownership. All this was a product of political and economic choices. It did not need to happen.

In the 1970s Britain mined coal, drilled for oil, and was on the verge of energy self-sufficiency. Power cuts and energy rationing did occur in the early 1970s, but these were the result of industrial strife, rather than a self-sabotaging policy of net-zero. Britain was still home to manufacturing and industrial centres that sustained stable and vibrant communities in South Wales, the North and across the Midlands. The offshoring of industrial capacity and the corresponding decline of these once thriving communities has resulted in a burgeoning national divide, both geographic and social, where wealth and capital are concentrated in a select few financial hubs like the City of London at the expense of everywhere else. In the 1970s an ordinary hard-working citizen stood a reasonable chance of getting on the housing ladder, raising a family on a single income, and retiring on a decent pension. These once common expectations are now beyond the reach of most millennials who do not have access to a trust fund or the bank of mum and dad.

Britons once shared a feeling of social solidarity, regardless of their political differences. These days, as the gap between rich and poor widens by the day, there is a palpable sense of antagonism between an out-of-touch cosmopolitan 'elite' and the alienated 'populist' masses.

Are we looking back to the 1970s through a rose-tinted haze? Of course, there's an element of nostalgia for a bygone era. There are things about the seventies that no one would miss: monastic Sundays, racial prejudice, trade union militancy and brutalist architecture. Still less would one wish to re-visit the horrors of the Northern Ireland conflict in the 70s (for those interested, this is the place where a culture war inevitably ends).

The 1970s was a time of turmoil. But it was also a time of cultural dynamism, free thought, serious political debate, semi-decent public services and thriving communities with strong civic attachments. Above all, a brief trip down memory lane shows that many attributes of the seventies that we have noted here also set the pre-conditions for the national renewal that succeeded it in the decade that followed. Pre-conditions which seem disconcertingly absent in the current era.

As we contemplate our leaner, meaner and greener futures, we can look back with the one thing which has not yet been criminalised – irony. In the words of the theme song to *Whatever Happened to the Likely Lads?*: 'Tomorrow's almost over, today went by so fast / It's the only thing to look forward to – the past'.

Original article published in the *Daily Sceptic*, 31st August 2022, by David Martin Jones and M.L.R. Smith.

The suicide and conquest of Britain revisited

What, wretched man... is it given to you... to keep the charge committed to you against such a series of inveterate crimes which has spread far and wide, without interruption, for so many years?

The mid-sixth century Welsh monk, Gildas Sapiens (Saint Gildas the Wise), asked himself this question, as he observed the Saxon invasion and subsequent descent of Roman Britain into barbarism. Gildas wrote *De Excidio et Conquestu Brittaniae* (The Suicide and Conquest of Britain) as both a warning to posterity and an explanation of how a wealthy, civilised, Roman province declined into what historians once referred to as the Dark Ages.

Given the current divided and depressed state of Britain, Gildas's commentary on how and why Roman Britain disintegrated is perhaps worth recalling. The problem Gildas identified in the mid-sixth century, which also besets the UK today, was the growing separation of the isles into divided 'nations' and the threat to its integrity posed by unlimited migration from Europe. Over a period of half a century, Gildas argued, migration turned into an invasion that fundamentally transformed the British Isles, and not for the better.

If Gildas returned today he would no doubt be alarmed, but not entirely surprised, to learn that official figures show that more than 10 million people living in the UK were born overseas. In the year 2022 alone, the UK attracted more than half a million migrants, more than twice the number entering the country the previous year. In the same year, some 40,000 migrants from Albania and Afghanistan arrived from France, often on boats organised by criminal gangs. Somewhat predictably, the *Financial Times* deemed the problem insoluble. Interestingly, this was the same conclusion Gildas' more complacent contemporaries reached fifteen hundred years earlier in response to the 'godless hordes' entering the country from the southeast.

Unlike in the sixth century, a solution to the crisis has been proposed – sending migrants to Rwanda for their claims to be heard – but for setting this plan in motion then Home Secretary Suella Braverman incurred the wrath of the *Financial Times*, Human Rights lawyers, NGOs and the European Court of Human Rights. Braverman further invoked progressive opprobrium for describing the number of arrivals as an 'invasion of our southern coast'. The Archbishop of Canterbury declared such rhetoric to be 'shrill', 'immoral' and 'disgraceful'. He argued that treating migrants as 'invaders' to be deterred denied them both 'dignity' and 'value' as fellow human beings.

However, given that millions of migrants have descended upon these shores in the space of a decade, 'invasion' might indeed be the noun that best captures the current reality. Welby's sixth century Celtic church predecessor would certainly have thought so. Yet for Welby, the mainstream media, and academic and business elites, this invasion has been welcomed as a positive contribution to a declining population, not a cause of existential concern.

It is daily more evident that current levels of migration place unwarranted pressure on already stressed health and social services, housing and education as well as what were once seen as traditional British values. In other words, *contra* Archbishop Welby and the progressive establishment, we should perhaps be far less indifferent to the profound change two decades of open borders have had upon a British way of life and self-understanding. Once large-scale migration begins it becomes a self-reinforcing process.

'If there is a single law in migration', Myron Weiner wrote in *The Global Migration Crisis*, 'it is that a migration flow, once begun, induces its own flow. Migrants enable their friends and relatives back home to migrate by providing them with information about how to migrate, resources to facilitate movement, and assistance in finding jobs and housing'. As Samuel Huntington observed in his prescient *The Clash of Civilizations and the Remaking of World Order* (1996), Europe and the UK experienced an evolving post-Cold War migration crisis partly because of these unregulated flows, but also because not all migrants from different cultures fully integrate into society.

The challenge is both demographic and cultural. Sustained immigration can produce divided communities. Moreover, as culture assumes increasing salience in an identity obsessed post-Cold War disorder, formerly monocultural European societies have become 'cleft'. In a cleft country, Huntington tells us, minority groups and their host country find that 'the forces of repulsion drive them apart and they gravitate toward civilisational magnets in other societies'.

Unlike mainland Europe, the UK has not had to cope with either unregulated migration or an 'invasion' until the last decade of the twentieth century. Ironically, Brexit has only exacerbated the problem. Whilst European countries endured a history of internal and external war, invasion and conquest, the United Kingdom, as an island once preserved by a silver sea which, as Shakespeare had it, 'serves it in the office as a wall, or as in a moat defensive to a house' had always controlled its borders. Its defensive moat repelled foreign invaders from the Spanish Armada in the sixteenth century, to Napoleon in the nineteenth and the Third Reich in the twentieth. All found the island fortress and its naval defences impregnable. The last successful conquest of Britain was undertaken in 1066.

The Barbarian invasion problem revisited

It was a very different and much earlier invasion that most resembles the UK's current migration chaos. As fifth-century Rome endured sustained assaults from barbarian tribes – Huns, Goths and Visigoths – its legions retreated from the British Isles to shore up the West's crumbling European frontiers. Left to their own devices the Romanised, or more precisely, civilised, Britons failed to maintain their internal defences. Instead, they endured growing incursions from the Scots and Pictish tribes from across the Irish Sea and beyond Hadrian's Wall, which the Romans had built 'to repel' these uncivilised 'foes'. The Britons, 'with no head to guide them' and the legions gone, Gildas wrote, impotently witnessed:

> the Picts and Scots, like worms which in the heat of the mid-day come forth from their holes... differing one from another in manners, but inspired with the same avidity for blood, and all more eager to shroud their villainous faces in bushy hair than to cover with decent clothing those parts of their body which required it, having heard of the departure of our [Roman] friends, and their resolution never to return, they seized with greater boldness than before on all the country towards the extreme north.

The Romanised Britons ignored the northern threat and continued to revel in the 'extraordinary plenty' that the cultivated towns and cities of England still enjoyed. Wealth licensed 'every kind of luxury and licentiousness'.

This is a pattern all too reminiscent of a woke generation working from home and accustomed to sanctimonious virtue signalling. As Gildas wrote:

> It grew with so firm a root, that one might truly say of it, 'Such fornication is heard of among you, as never was known the like among the Gentiles'. But besides this vice, there arose also every other, to which human nature is liable and, in particular, that hatred of truth... which still at present destroys everything good in the island...

...and, we might add, still does.

Eventually, in order to protect their comfortable lifestyle, the Britons called a council 'to settle what was best and most expedient to be done, in order to repel such frequent and fatal irruptions and plundering that civilised Britain continued to suffer at the hands of the Scots and Irish 'nations'.

The solution arrived at was again an all too familiar one. 'All the councillors', together with 'Gurthrigern' [Vortigern], the British king:

> were so blinded, that, as a protection to their country, they sealed its doom by inviting in among them (like wolves into the sheep-fold), the fierce and impious Saxons, a race hateful both to God and men, to repel the invasions of the

northern nations. Nothing was ever so pernicious to our country; nothing was ever so unlucky. What palpable darkness must have enveloped their minds- darkness, desperate and cruel! Those very people whom, when absent, they dreaded more than death itself, were invited to reside, as one may say, under the self-same roof. Foolish are the princes, as it is said, of Thafneos, giving counsel to unwise Pharaoh. A multitude of whelps came forth from the lair of this barbaric lioness.

The new migrants,

> being thus introduced… into the island, to encounter, as they falsely said, any dangers in defence of their hospitable entertainers, obtain an allowance of provisions, which, for some time being plentifully bestowed, stopped their doggish mouths. Yet they complain that their monthly supplies are not furnished in sufficient abundance, and they industriously aggravate each occasion of quarrel, saying that unless more liberality is shown to them, they will break the treaty and plunder the whole island. In a short time, they follow up their threats with deeds.

Evidently, the migrant arrivals today are far less brutal. Yet there remain uncanny resemblances. While they may not be 'hateful to God and man', they often form sufficiently culturally distinct and increasingly welfare dependent communities that can undermine the traditional structures and institutions the United Kingdom once enjoyed. Significantly, under pressure from the Saxon invasion, 'the miserable remnant' of sixth century Britons took to the mountains or constrained by famine, came, and yielded themselves to be slaves forever to their foes. Some, under the influence of Ambrosius Aurelianus, the prototype of the legendary Arthur, mounted a resistance to 'their cruel' migrant 'conquerors', but were increasingly confined to the country. As Gildas concludes his account of Britain's ruin:

> And yet neither to this day are the cities of our country inhabited as before, but being forsaken and overthrown, still lie desolate; our foreign wars having ceased, but our civil troubles still remaining, as well the remembrance of such terrible desolation of the island.

Roman Britain never recovered from its earlier migrant invasion, although its Celtic church maintained itself uncertainly in West Wales and Cornwall. Gildas' account, like more recent studies of civilisational decline, illustrates how decline starts from within before it is defeated on the battlefield. What happens within a civilisation is crucial to containing internal sources of decay. This was the deracinating danger Huntington thought multiculturalism, together with unrestricted migration flows, posed to the survival of the West. The multicultural ideology that dominated UK and US political discourse from the end of the Cold War envisages a country of no civilisation without a cultural core. 'Multiculturalism at home', Huntington wrote, 'threatens the US and the West, whilst universalism abroad threatens the West and the world'. Of course, the twenty-first century United Kingdom is not dark age Britain, but there are some uncanny resemblances between the civilisational collapse of late Roman Britain and today's decline in general and that of the UK in particular. As in Britain on the brink of the dark age, an out of touch elite, preoccupied with multicultural virtue signalling, considers mass migration by culturally distinct peoples no threat to the cultural integrity of the United Kingdom. Indeed, its more woke multicultural enthusiasts, like the Archbishop of Canterbury, consider its civilisation an oppressive weight worth trashing. History does not repeat itself but, as Mark Twain reputedly observed, it does rhyme.

Original article published in *Cieo*, 19th January 2023, by David Martin Jones.

Woke Wales: From death to character assassination

You've probably never heard of Abergynolwyn. This small village in the Dysynni valley in Merioneth, sits at the southern end of Lake Talyllyn, in the foothills of the Snowdon massif and beneath Wales' second largest peak, Cadair Idris. Now home to just 400 people, Abergynolwyn was established in the nineteenth century to house workers at the nearby Bryneglwys slate quarry situated near the narrow-gauge Talyllyn Railway, which served both the quarry and the village in the distinctive slate landscape of Northwest Wales – a region designated a World Heritage Site by the United Nations Educational, Scientific and Cultural Organisation (UNESCO) in 2021.

Abergynolwyn falls within the jurisdiction of Gwynedd Council, or Cyngor Gwynedd as it is known in Welsh, and the council manages 'the slate landscape' on behalf of UNESCO. In April, Gwynedd Council announced that this tiny village must publicly acknowledge its relationship to the slave trade. As part of what the Welsh nationalist party, *Plaid Cymru* council leader Dyfrig Siencyn describes as his party's 'broader mission' to expose the North Wales slate industry's association with slavery, a plaque advertising the somewhat tenuous link will henceforth adorn the village hall. 'Slavery and colonisation form part of the slate story', a council spokesperson explained.

This news will no doubt come as a surprise to the small number of local inhabitants of the village. It also came as a surprise to me. As a child I spent summer holidays with my father's relatives who formed a kin network of small tenant farmers across Meirionnydd (aka Merioneth). This news would also have shocked my grandmother, Ellen Pugh, who lived in Abergynolwyn. Ellen married my grandfather, Daffyd Jones, in 1917 at the Horeb congregationalist chapel, Dolgellau. They farmed a remote sheep farm near Dinas Mawddwy until Daffyd died in 1952 and Ellen retired to 6 Heol Llanegryn, Abergynolwyn (a council cottage, originally built by the Abergynolwyn Slate Company which was established in 1864 to house workers). This is where she died, a century later, in 1964. Ellen profited little from whatever connections the village had to the slave trade. In her will, she left only a Welsh dresser and, as a devoted member of the congregation of the Cwrt chapel, a Welsh bible, *Y Beibl*, which I still have among my possessions.

So, what exactly is the association between this small industrial village and slavery? Significantly, in its application for World Heritage Status, Gwynedd Council and the Snowdonia National Park Authority made no mention of any slavery links. Instead, in 2017 they commissioned the historian and urban archaeologist, Richard Hayman, to write an 'urban character study of Abergynolwyn' which was submitted to UNESCO 'in support of the Wales Slate World Heritage Nomination'. In this well-researched analysis, Hayman finds that 'Abergynolwyn retains a strong and distinctive nineteenth-century character based on its unique combination of topography, economic and social history, and the local natural resources with which its buildings were constructed'. 'Historic character', Hayman continues, 'confers identity, creates a sense of belonging and contributes to the quality of the places where we live, work and visit. It can also be an asset for economic vitality and regeneration.'

Hayman discloses that John Pugh, a native of the area, initially took a fifty-year lease for quarrying at Bryn Eglwys in 1844. However, 'the scale of early operations was inhibited by the problem of transportation'. It was only in 1864, when William McConnel (1809-1902) and his brother Thomas bought the quarry, that the landscape was transformed into its current state. Over the course of two generations, the McConnels had established themselves in Lancashire cloth manufacturing as owners of a cotton-spinning mill in Ancoats, Manchester. The American Civil War (1861-1865) disrupted their supplies of raw cotton and so to offset these losses, the brothers shrewdly diversified their business holdings. They bought the Bryn Eglwys quarry in 1864, established the Abergynolwyn Slate Company, and formed The Talyllyn Railway Company in 1865 to transport the slate for export. The line to the quarry passed above Abergynolwyn village, which was built from the coast at Tywyn and opened in 1866. It was the first of the slate railways in North Wales specifically designed for steam locomotives and from December 1866 was the first of the narrow-gauge railways in North Wales to run passenger services.

William McConnel built the village at Abergynolwyn to house his workers. He employed the Manchester architect James Stevens, who drew up plans in 1864. The attractive details, which characterise the buildings include wedge lintels and overhanging eaves, can still be seen in houses throughout the village. The first houses to be built by the company, between 1865 and 1868, were two terraces of single-storey houses on Heol Llanegryn, where my grandmother later lived.

William McConnel was an outstanding example of the principled Victorian entrepreneurs who forged modern Britain. He developed slate quarrying on an industrial scale to the benefit of both his family, his employees and the nation as a whole, or as Hayman puts it, he demonstrated 'how the influence of capitalist owners extended from the workplace to the home in the nineteenth century'.

Gwynedd Council's proposal to UNESCO promoted Abergynolwyn as 'a well-preserved nineteenth-century industrial village with a unique history and strong regional character of special architectural and historical interest'. It was on these grounds that UNESCO accorded the landscape World Heritage Status. Indeed, UNESCO is even more generous in its praise for the landscape than Hayman was in his report. UNESCO considers the site 'internationally significant not only for the export of slates but also for the export of technology and skilled workers. It 'constituted a model for other slate quarries in different parts of the world', offering a remarkable example of the 'interchange of materials, technology and human values'.

By the late nineteenth century, the area around Abergynolwyn produced about a third of the world output of roofing slates and architectural slabs. Its use in terraced houses, factories, warehouses and architecture contributed to rapid global urbanisation. It influenced building styles: 'Technologies that were innovated, adopted and adapted in the quarries included the ingenious application of waterpower and the first known application of the circular saw for cutting stone'. These were diffused by specialists and by the emigration of skilled Welsh quarrymen to the developing slate industries of the United States, continental Europe and Ireland. Narrow-gauge railway systems like the Talyllyn railway McConnel designed gained global influence and were adopted from Asia and America to Africa and Australasia. It was McConnel's achievements in pioneering the modern slate industry while preserving the natural beauty of the local landscape that earned the area its World Heritage Status. How then does an industry that used local materials and local labour come to be associated with slavery? Here we have to explore the perverse reasoning, economic illiteracy, historically challenged and duplicitous behaviour of Cyngor Gwynedd. In its behaviour it crystalises all the cultural self-loathing that now pervades both the Welsh Labour Party and *Plaid Cymru*.

McConnel was English and a capitalist to boot. Such a background is anathema to the cultural Maoists who currently run Wales and micro-manage the Welsh version of the cultural revolution. From this perspective, McConnel's achievements must be re-defined to fit an ideology that reduces history to melodrama, where brutal and rapacious English capitalists despoil the Welsh landscape and immiserate its people.

McConnel invested in the slate industry during the American Civil War and the cotton famine that caused the temporary closure of many cloth manufacturing factories across Lancashire. Like all Lancastrian mill owners, McConnel used raw cotton from the plantations of the American South to weave his cloth. The McConnel family owned no slaves, and – as good liberals – supported the struggle for emancipation. Like other manufacturers, he did not attempt to break the naval blockade preventing the export of cotton from the American South and suffered financially as a consequence. According to Cyngor Gwynedd, the mere fact that the major source of the raw material that fed into McConnel's mills derived from this tainted source (before the empire developed India and Australia as alternative sources of raw cotton) makes McConnel, the Welsh slate industry, and the industrial revolution more generally, guilty by association.

This, of course, is tendentious and a deliberate distortion of the historical record. This is not history but ideological posturing that does a disservice to Abergynolwyn and its fascinating past which needs to be understood in its own terms and not through some anachronistic ideological projection. Whilst such distortion is now firmly entrenched in the Welsh political and educational establishment, the Abergynolwyn case stands out for the thinness of its connection to slavery and the fact that Gwynedd Council made no mention of it in its application to UNESCO. It made the application on the grounds that McConnel's endeavours transformed the locality positively, but after the iconic status had been granted proceeded to rewrite history to suit its own questionable agenda. This is self-serving and mendacious, but sadly such mendacity is now meat and drink to the cultural enforcers of woke Wales.

Original article published in *Cieo*, 11th May 2023, by David Martin Jones.

Was the British Empire evil?

The British Empire went through numerous permutations between 1600 and 1960 yet the conventional view, dominant in universities and the mainstream media, is that it was a morally deplorable exercise in colonialism, racism, brutal exploitation and violence. This view of the empire is not merely an act of historical revisionism, it also legitimates a progressive assault on British institutions in the present. It has been disseminated to Anglosphere states like Australia, New Zealand and Canada where it demands the re-education of the former empire's deluded white subjects who are *ipso facto* permeated by both conscious and unconscious racism as a consequence of their benighted imperial past.

As Nigel Biggar argues in his latest book, *Colonialism: A Moral Reckoning*, if the arguments made in the name of a decolonising, anti-colonialist project have a valid basis in historical fact then a moral reckoning is long overdue. But is the now dominant view of colonialism based on fact or fiction?

Biggar considers the history of the empire through careful examination of hard moral cases in order to answer serious accusations made against the 'colonial project'. These are that the empire was:

- driven by greed and the lust to dominate
- 'equivalent to slavery' (even after parliament abolished slavery in 1807)
- essentially racist
- pervasively violent, addicted to state terror and guilty of genocide
- economically exploitative, based on the theft of land
- undemocratic and therefore illegitimate.

Biggar deals with each of these charges in a measured way that makes a notable contrast to the shrill rhetoric of the post-colonial discourse theorists he has to address. In particular, he scrupulously examines cases of historical abuse and arrives at informed judgements about what actually happened, the context of the claim and the outcome.

Biggar recognises Britain's role in the Atlantic slave trade to be 'morally repugnant' and that, at its height in the eighteenth century, it furnished a degree of dubious wealth for the evolving colonial power's industrialising economy. Yet, as Biggar argues and as recent studies of Britain's industrial take off after 1760 demonstrate, the ill-gotten gains of the slave trade played comparatively little role in Britain's industrialisation. Other factors, like the emergence of a stock market, country banks and the development of canals, together with a political climate that facilitated an entrepreneurial spirit, played a far more significant role in forging modernity. Moreover, the UK not only abolished the slave trade in 1807 but, under the pressure of moral argument, it also devoted its powerful naval resources to abolishing the trade in Africa and the Mediterranean over the course of the nineteenth century.

Biggar also contends that British rule in India, initially under the auspices of the East India Company from the 1750s and direct colonial rule after 1857, was far from the rapacious affair that Whigs at the time (Burke springs to mind) or later historians, like William Dalrymple assert. East Indian Company officials like Ernest 'Oriental' Jones and Warren Hastings showed a profound interest in Hindu culture and went to great lengths to accommodate Indian custom to utilitarian understandings of law and property. Biggar suggests that Edward Said, the author of the 1978 book *Orientalism* which spawned post-colonial discourse theory and decolonisation campaigns in education, distorted the character of European and British interests in both India and China. Biggar shows that despite several conspicuous failings, the general intention of the British in developing colonies in Canada after 1785, Australia and New Zealand a decade or two later, and Africa from the 1870s, was to recognise native title rather than support the actions of migrant settlers in depriving natives of their customary lands. Indeed, the Conservative ministry of Lord North in the early 1770s tried to prevent the thirteen North American colonies from pushing inexorably westwards across the Appalachians and triggering the struggle for an independent United States.

In this context, Biggar also examines cases of alleged genocide, like that of the Tasmanian Aboriginals, and shows that the record is far more nuanced than has become accepted as Australian academic orthodoxy. Much of the reduction in native populations in Van Diemen's Land and elsewhere owed far more to disease, a historical fact the *Annales* school historian Emmanuel Le Roy Ladurie convincingly established in the 1980s, than to European agency. Indeed, colonial governors like George Arthur in Van Diemen's Land, and later in Upper Canada, and Lachlan Macquarie in New South Wales, worked tirelessly to constrain settler rapacity and ill-treatment of native populations.

Against the tendency to present the empire as a unitary colonial behemoth run by a ruthless centralised political and business oligarchy, Biggar shows that, in fact, the colonial office in London was politically weak and limited in its authority. Before the invention and development of the telegraph, it took weeks for a letter to reach Sydney from Westminster. Ultimately, colonial rule in Australia and Canada relied on the support of English, Scottish, Irish and Welsh migrants and in both India and Africa it was dependent on the consent of native populations. Without that consent the diffuse imperial arrangement would have broken down long before it did. The eventual end of the empire came about less because of imperial resistance and more because of the massive expense funding two world wars imposed upon the UK treasury. In 1941 the British Eighth Army was the most ethnically varied force to assemble in modern history. Ironically, the Second World War witnessed a coordinated British-led global effort 'the like of which will never be seen again'.

This view contrasts rather dramatically with the assumption that colonial peoples were living with a deluded and false imperial consciousness, or desperate to remove the British boot-heel weighing upon their collective necks. In order to take seriously claims not only of genocide and persistent imperial violence, Biggar further examines in detail *inter alia* the Opium War (1842), the Irish Famine (1846-49), the famine on the great plains of Canada (1879-83 – a 'genocide' that resulted in the loss of 45 lives), the Benin Expedition (1897), the Second Boer War (1899-1902), the Amritsar Massacre (1919) and the Mau Mau insurgency in Kenya between 1952 and 1956. In all these cases, Biggar shows that mistakes were made by the colonial powers as well as the military authorities on the ground. However, in none of these cases is there any evidence of a systematic attempt to commit genocide, destroy local culture or conduct a state licensed reign of terror. The Opium War, which saw the Qing dynasty cede Hong Kong to the UK, alone stands out as an example of an unjust war.

In fact, the empire in its most enlightened late nineteenth century manifestation demanded that its officials were committed, as Lord Cromer put it, to the 'granite code' of Christian values. Significantly, an earlier and more nuanced generation of historians of the post-war period, like Margery Perham, recognised that during the Victorian era 'Christian humanitarianism, a commitment to public service and a liberal vision of public life' supplemented the desire to maintain trade and the empire's global strategic advantage. By the late nineteenth century, the public service mindset developed the particular character type of the devoted District Commissioner who worked tirelessly and with a notable lack of corruption that earned native affection – a fact that Graham Greene, no great friend of empire, depicted in the character of Scobie in *The Heart of the Matter* (1948). As a native schoolboy informed his white school teacher in 1970 when asked whether Rhodesia should have home rule, replied: 'No Sir... because the tribes will all kill themselves'. In other words, the trauma of contemporary Africa is not the result of empire but the rise of ethno-nationalism.

The rise and fall of the British Empire occurred over 300-years. It was neither unchanging nor monolithic; it was a different thing in Ireland from what it was in Australia, New Zealand, or Africa to say nothing of India or Southeast Asia, which, surprisingly receives very little attention. There are no campaigns to pull down the statue of Sir Stamford Raffles on Clarke Quay in Singapore or to erase the memory of Frank Swettenham in contemporary Malaysia. Biggar comprehensively dispels the myth that Britain was a brutal genocidal dictatorship. So how has this destructive and distorted interpretation of British and Commonwealth history gained such political and academic traction?

Biggar suggests several reasons. Intellectual fashion in the final decades of the last century, encapsulated in the work of Edward Said, sired a dramatic revision of Western civilisation generally and British imperialism in particular. No academic today could receive a large research grant for extolling the virtues of empire. Certainly, as Biggar asserts, 'anti-colonialists cannot be blamed for condemning racism'. However, 'they can be blamed for letting their condemnation run ahead of the data' in order to arrive at a predetermined moral judgement. A consistent feature of post-colonial discourse is its exaggeration of the sins of British colonialism. A notable exemplar of this distorted mode of inquiry is Dan Hicks, Oxford professor of contemporary archaeology and curator of the Pitt River Museum, who develops a form of 'ethical schizophrenia' in his analysis of the British seizure of Benin in 1897. The British intervention sought to remove the slave owning and slave trading rule of the Edo people, a regime addicted to human sacrifice. These historical facts notwithstanding, Hicks finds the Edo casual victims of 'extractive capitalism', 'militarism', 'racism' and 'proto fascism'. Somewhat incoherently, this post-colonial method is 'morally neutral and infinitely indulgent with regard' to native practices but applies moral absolutism to British values.

What propels this mindset, beyond scholarly fashion, is a 'dogmatic revolutionary authoritarianism' that dismisses contradictory evidence and reasons as mere reactionary rationalisation. A Maoist cultural revolution thus pervades what passes for analysis. Three of the essential keywords of historical inquiry: 'evidence', 'context' and 'explanation' are disconcertingly absent from such critical studies.

Biggar, following Pascal Bruckner, finds that contemporary European propensity to self-loathing reinforces this denunciation of a decaying West. Such corrosive self-hatred really has no place for the non-Western other. It is a form of narcissism in which the African, Indian, or aboriginal merely serve as a convenient prop. 'The evil white colonialist fills the centre stage, entirely obscuring black agency'. Meanwhile, 'the white post-colonialist gets to play champion of the oppressed'.

One might add a further factor to this genre of specious, academic melodrama. As Kenneth Minogue wrote in his neglected 1985 study *Alien Powers: The Pure Theory of Ideology*, the revolutionary left has always had a fascination with intellectual validation. Instead of historical inquiry proper, which assumes an understanding of a past that has been completed and needs to be understood in its own terms before any judgement, Marxist critical mimesis instead requires a simplistic melodrama cloaked in the apparatus of scholarship. The more recent Maoist dialectic further reveals a thesis, namely a brutally evil, white, racist supremacism, masking a seemingly liberal imperial humanitarian project. Its antithesis, meanwhile, sees the oppressed throw off their chains, leading to a synthesis where true consciousness, endless re-education and emancipation prevail. In its long march through the institutions, this pseudo-scholarship has captured all the apparatus of academic inquiry across the Anglosphere. It relishes academic promotions, celebrates large grants and conferences, legitimates questionable sources and obscure methodologies, establishes specialist journals with impact ratings and controls university presses. But it is an essentially imitative endeavour riven with envy and subsumed with what Roger Scruton referred to as 'a culture of repudiation'.

Biggar's seminal study exposes the depths to which this perverse culture has sunk. It should be a required text on all introductory university modern history and social science courses. Instead, Biggar had difficulty finding a publisher and *Colonialism: A Moral Reckoning* receives captious and denunciatory reviews in once reputable scholarly periodicals. As Cicero remarked in an analogous age of corruption and confusion, 'O tempora, O mores'.

Original article published in *Cieo*, 20th June 2023, by David Martin Jones.

Epilogue

A ballad of disenchanted modernity – Reading *Woke* in Son Kul

'There's no electricity or internet there, you know?' Lola, my wife, called out to me as we packed our things for a short trip into the hinterlands of Kyrgyzstan. 'Oh... in that case I might actually need to bring my NOB', I replied. I could sense Lola's scepticism. Ah, my NOB: my much travelled but Never Opened Book, which I habitually, but always idealistically, pack every time I venture abroad.

For each long journey away from home my NOB is a choice volume selected to accompany me across hundreds if not thousands of miles but destined to remain wholly unread. I convince myself that I'll have the luxury of relaxing, kicking back, and becoming engrossed in its pages. It never happens. Variously, I find myself too tired, too lazy, too jet-lagged, too distracted... too drunk.

The unfortunate candidate for this year's NOB was Joanna Williams's *How Woke Won*. For good measure, the book cover had already been mauled by Ponchik (Russian for doughnut), our adopted ginger kitten. While returning from an earlier excursion we found him abandoned at a wayside café, covered in dirt and fleas. We couldn't help but take pity.

Ponchik's handiwork made the book appear suitably well thumbed and careworn. Nothing could have been further from the truth. But into the luggage it went, ordained once more to bear witness to our exotic travels without ever being caressed.

Our destination this time was Son Kul, a remote lake high in the mountains to the south of the Kyrgyz capital, Bishkek. The place is accessible only at certain times of the year through twisting mountain passes and rutted dirt tracks. Getting there is a feat in itself: a long taxi ride to the nearest large town, Kochkor. Then haggling frantically outside the local bus station for another ride in a ramshackle 4 x 4 to take us the next fifty miles up into the mountains. Four, dusty, bone-rattling hours later, we finally arrive in pitch-darkness at our campsite on the lake.

In the light of day, Son Kul is overpowering in its splendour and simplicity. It's easy to overdo the 'unspoilt by tourism' schtick. The moment any tourist sets foot on a beauty spot they subtly, if unintentionally, disrupt a natural eco-system and any absolute authenticity is lost. Throughout the summer months Son Kul attracts its share of foreign visitors willing to wander off the beaten track to experience its charms. They stay in yurt camps of varying sizes and amenities dotted along the shoreline. Around the larger camps you don't have to stroll far before encountering the human debris of discarded beer cans and vodka bottles scattered along the periphery.

Constructing clichés
Nevertheless, the relatively unsullied environment is striking. There are no fixed structures. No boats or jet skis on the lake. No cafés, restaurants, museums or gift shops. No telegraph poles or phone masts. The majestic quiet, the spectacular mountain backdrop and the perfect blue of the lake are impeccable. The clarity of the night-time sky is a wonder to behold. To do justice to the magical panorama in words is to feel oneself slipping into a cliched travelogue.

Here you are, 10,000 feet high, at the edge of hypoxia, truly separated from the busy world beyond, amongst communities of nomadic herdsmen tending their cattle and horses that roam free across the mountain valleys. At dusk, the packs of horses quietly make their way down to the waterline. It's a ghostly, almost dreamlike, sight.

At last, in this primordial setting and freed from all the electronic impedimenta, one found the time and space to do something unique: contemplate my NOB. Settled in a deck chair, with cirrus cloud formations high above, the sunlight gently refracting off the ripples of the flawless lake (there, told you it was cliché), tentatively I turn the pages.

Joanna Williams's book has been justly praised for its dissection of the contemporary movement in the West that, in the words of the subtitle, 'threatens democracy, tolerance and reason'. But as I proceeded further into Joanna's analysis, I was struck by a particular thought that I have never considered before: namely, that *where* you read a book may matter as much as its content. Reading *Woke* in Son Kul provoked several – I hesitate to say, profound – observations.

In the first instance, assimilating the contours of woke in such evocative surroundings sharpens the dislocation between the fixations of the contemporary social justice movement that dominates the mentality in Western cityscapes on the one hand, and the wider – more traditional – world beyond on the other. It is not simply that in the vastness of a remote mountain plateau that woke obsessions seem trivial, narcissistic and deluded, it underlines that they *are* objectively disconnected from the way that most people choose to live their lives.

Constructing communities

Among the Western travel cognoscenti Kyrgyzstan has gained a certain cachet. A few months previously in London, a near neighbour, a slightly batty, extremely left-wing, former social worker who spends her retirement travelling the world without a great deal of concern for her carbon footprint, lectured me non-stop for fifteen minutes on the bus about discovering the scenic joys of this little-known country. Clearly, a secret gem known only to a few inductees. I didn't have the chance to inform her that my spouse is Kyrgyz before she alighted at her stop. A few months ago, too – if I heard correctly – journalist and broadcaster Benjamin Butterworth, the token woke member of GB News's 'superstar panel' on the Dan Wootton Tonight show, had recently been on vacation horse-riding in the Kyrgyz mountains.

Back in Son Kul, in our small complex of six yurts, our near neighbours were a young German couple, and an American man and his daughter. All were travelling through Central Asia, and like most Westerners who ended up there, were attracted by the peace, tranquillity, and the glowing reviews on travel websites.

Let me state at the outset that both the Germans and Americans were charming holiday companions. They were friendly, gracious and possessed an invincible spirit of adventure (to reiterate, just getting to Son Kul under their own steam was an accomplishment). The next stop for both parties was Uzbekistan. Another challenging destination. I had the benefit of a Kyrgyz wife to facilitate my every move, be it in Kyrgyz or Russian. They had to navigate the place without the advantage of a native speaker in a region where English is still not spoken widely. Their independent traveller status was estimable. I liked and admired them.

The American dad turned out to be a veteran New York based war reporter and history writer of some distinction (I subsequently read two of his books, and they were both outstanding). As it happened, being of similar age and disposition, we discovered that both of us had been present in Northern Ireland at the same time in the 1980s, as observers of the province's 'Troubles'. Picture the scene: on a far-flung mountainside in Central Asia, in a yurt, a war reporter and a professor of war studies recount the follies of yesteryear, rattling off a host of familiar, but now far-off, names and places.

His fifteen-year-old daughter was equally delightful: articulate, curious about the world, and without a hint of pretension. The German couple were more solicitous, but equally amiable. She was a special needs teacher. He was a scientist who worked in the agricultural industry and had spent part of his university education studying in China.

The woke spectrum

I wouldn't place any of these acquaintances on the outer reaches of woke, but their political inclinations were very different from mine. Not that this mattered. I appreciate the company of others with different perspectives from my own, and who might – at their own risk – seek to challenge my preconceptions. In fact, they never came to know my views. It was not necessary. I enjoyed interrogating theirs instead. The American dad self-identified as 'Democrat central' and a Hillary supporter in 2016. Both he and his daughter expressed a visceral dislike for Donald Trump, for reasons of manners rather than policies as far as I could tell.

I probed them: 'love him or hate him, was Trump not a symptom of something important?' Having seen for myself the de-industrialised towns in the mid-West, could they not understand the disillusionment of these communities, which had previously voted for Obama? Was this why they turned towards a political maverick? A desperate cry for help?

Yes, they could understand, in theory.

'What might win them back?'

The manufacturing jobs were gone for good, the father said. The situation was bad but there was no solution for their plight.

A counsel of despair, I suggested, was not a convincing policy platform. The father agreed. He was, I discerned, genuinely perturbed at the hopelessness of his own analysis.

The German couple were less vocal in their political views. We talked about the man's job. He was confident that the ban on the export of farming machinery would have an impact on Russian agriculture. Food production would be affected... eventually: a morally just punishment for Russia's misguided 'special military operation' in the Ukraine. His own company had been impacted by the sanctions.

'What about the failure of the financial sanctions on Russia?', I asked, 'and the cravenly short-sighted green energy policies that had rendered Germany dangerously dependent on Russian oil and gas?' A slightly awkward silence ensued. It transpired that in recent years he had moved from supporting the SDP to the Greens.

He was jetting off to China as soon as he returned from holiday to cultivate new customers for agricultural equipment to replace losses in the Russian market. Ah... the People's Republic of China, a place not at all like Russia, well known for its high labour standards, political freedoms, regional good citizenship and respect for the treatment of ethnic minorities.

Anywhere, except everywhere else

Regardless of where my yurt neighbours stood on the woke spectrum, they were undoubtedly part of the community of 'Anywhere', the professional-managerial class, which Joanna Williams identifies as a sub-elite. This grouping functions as the supporting counsellors to the governing class and enables woke to flourish in so many domains: the media, civil service, publishing, academia, business and the arts.

Technically, I too am an 'Anywhere'. A classic of the genre: an over-privileged, highly mobile, university doyen whose peripatetic lifestyle has taken them from Australia, to Britain, to Luxembourg, to Singapore, to the US, and back to Australia.

Of course, being an 'Anywhere' doesn't mean you'll fit in anywhere, let alone be happy living anywhere. Being a member of this sub-elite, and benefitting from its many prerequisites, means inhabiting the prosperous environs and gated communities of London, New York and Sydney mainly, perhaps with a few other national capitals and university towns thrown in. It doesn't mean Lagos, Manila and Huddersfield, or a million places in between. It really means, 'anywhere' except everywhere else.

Even so, I am a traitor to my Anywhere tribe. Something in my background has engendered a natural resistance to conformity. Why this is so I can only speculate. A combination of the influence of my free-thinking father and my Methodist mother might have something to do with it: that and being miseducated at the local comprehensive school in the 1970s, rather than inculcated into the norms of the upper strata as I might have been at private school. Such an upbringing has afflicted me with an inability to transcend my lower middle-class roots. Lola still complains. She would like me to behave, and certainly dress, like a proper English gentleman. Such lost causes aside, there is no doubt that I am guilty of any number of crimes against good taste and fashionable orthodoxy.

Many of my Anywhere academic confrères would probably secretly wish for ideological deviationists like me to be exiled from polite society and quite possibly, if their utopian dreams come true, to see woke trials and incarceration for non-conforming miscreants, purveyors of 'misinformation' and counter-orthodox narratives. Nonetheless, one's destiny as a dissenting Anywhere is to be possessed of a facility to rub along with the members of this sub-elite, while rejecting many of its prejudices, particularly towards the working class and other lesser mortals (Brexit voters, lockdown sceptics, *Daily Mail* readers, lab-leak advocates, etc.).

So, how, I wondered, might Anywheres view their surroundings in Son Kul? I don't mean the American father and daughter or the German couple specifically, but how would the woke disposition potentially engage with, say, the indigenous communities who populate the grasslands and valleys near the lake? Most obviously, the lives of the nomadic herdsman functioned in a realm where patriarchy and traditional gender roles were unmistakably visible to the outsider. The men and boys, with their weather-beaten faces, rode the horses and minded the cattle. The women folk stayed put supervising the household. Not only had these customary ways of living persisted for millennia, but it was clear that they were never going to change.

Woke versus tradition

What would the woke view be? How might the woke – or proto-woke Anywhere – mindset regard the scene? Would it disdain the lifestyle of these communities? Are they custom-ridden, backward societies, enveloped in poverty and lost in misery and patriarchy? Are they to be pitied, condemned and reformed? If this is the case, then the progressive Western traveller is certainly not deterred from visiting such places of immiseration and partaking in the traditional ways of rural living, riding horses and pursuing the simple life in the confines of a yurt encampment.

Or are these societies to be esteemed, precisely because they are spotless examples of authenticity, untarnished by the evils of colonialism, racism and slavery, which the brilliance of the contemporary education system has convinced a generation of Western students are exclusively European and North American historical sins? Are traditional societies therefore absolved from woke rules that would otherwise seek to denounce and destroy tradition in the name of advancing towards a one-size fits-all progressivist utopia?

The contradictions in the progressive worldview and its tendency to degenerate into a facile reverence for the non-Western other was something the late anthropologist, Roger Sandall, interrogated in his study *The Culture Cult: Designer Tribalism and Other Essays*. The notion of a woke consciousness was unknown at the time of the book's publication in 2001, but the cognitive dissonance in the disposition that was to evolve into woke was something Sandall fully recognised. It is a condition that on the one hand would extol Son Kul for its pristine beauty, yet on the other would see it as a great place to be plastered with wind turbines and solar panels.

A world re-enchanted?

Maybe, though, we should be charitable to our culturally sensitive, putatively woke, tourist who arrives in Son Kul and finds in its solitude something consoling, away from the disenchanted condition of secular modernity? To experience the wonders of Son Kul – its uncorrupted natural beauty and the pre-modern communities that surround it – may be one can discover possibilities for a better way of living in harmony with nature?

Or is this being too sympathetic? Or too jaundiced? In the end, would any of us Westerners, woke or not woke, wish to stay in a place like Son Kul for long without the accoutrements of modern life: our mobile phones, our laptops, our televisions, our sofas, comfy chairs, coffee shops and fast-food outlets? Perhaps a stay in Son Kul, for all its peace and calm, merely reminds us of what we miss and take for granted back in the world of easy living?

Returning from Son Kul to Bishkek, the bustling capital, burgeoning with markets, restaurants, shopping malls, and all the other facets of modern life, we meet with our friend, Nurika. Nurika is a highly qualified medical doctor. She works in a research laboratory in Kazakhstan specialising in the study of HIV. Over dinner, we touch on the growing impact of the 'woke world' in the West. Nurika is curious. She has heard of the preoccupations with gender fluidity, identity politics, race-essentialism and the penchant for dividing people into victims and oppressors.

General bemusement and incredulity are her principal reactions. Yet, at another level, both she and Lola discern in the woke agenda themes that remind them of their earlier lives in the Soviet Union, notably the concern for the policing of language, the willingness to compromise principles of objective science for the sake of officially approved doctrines, and the formal and informal sanctioning of those who don't conform.

In other off-the-cuff conversations with family and friends in Bishkek – a dentist, a college teacher, people in finance and business – similar replies were received whenever the subject occasionally reared its head. Unsystematic though my *vox populi* might have been, here, amongst members of the educated, socially conscious, Kyrgyz 'sub-elite', one detected a series of cluster responses: mild amusement and ridicule at best, thinly disguised derision at worst: a contempt for this latest incarnation of 'Western values' and for a decadent and decaying civilisation. What a contrast, I thought, with the feedback one would obtain in the fake liberal heartlands of London, like Islington or Brockley?

What these casual observations underscored yet again was that outside the narrow circumference of the West, in both the urban centres and rural hinterlands, woke has no purchase whatsoever. The wider world beyond is not woke and will never become woke. Quite possibly, the more radical woke protagonists don't care about any of this. Theirs is a minority avocation. They are a revolutionary vanguard, and the masses are to be led, browbeaten or dragged to their progressive destiny whether they like it or not. Then again...

Ways of escape
A further subversive notion enters my head – surely another thought crime. Could there actually be a substantial portion of people along the woke spectrum who *are* aware that their cause is disbelieved and derided by the vast majority, and who at some intuitive level doubt their own woke attachments? Somewhere, in the recesses of their soul, perhaps they have the uneasy feeling that all their social justice politicking is merely a form of displacement activity that seeks to fill the vacuous heart of their post-religious lives?

Maybe they sense the void, the Nietzschean abyss beginning to stare back at them? All the endless politics of everyday life – the rainbow lanyards, the multicoloured pedestrian crossings, the taking of the knee, the cheap radicalism of social media, announcing one's pronouns, the mind your language self-censorship, the endless moral messaging in films and television. In the end, what does it all mean? Along with all the other relentless virtue-signalling and moral posturing, woke is exhausting.

Reading *Woke* in Son Kul, then, elicits a final revelation: is the retreat to the sanctuaries of the pre-modern world primarily a means of seeking refuge? Is Son Kul a haven where even deracinated progressives can flee the grotesque world they are seeking to create and seeking to impose on everyone else? Not only an escape from disenchanted modernity but, ultimately, an escape from themselves?

Original article published in *Cieo*, 14th December 2022, by M.L.R. Smith.

Notes on Authors

David Martin Jones was a political scientist, writer and commentator. He was born in Essex and raised in Cardiff. He graduated in History from the University of Reading in 1971 and earned an MA in History at McMaster University in Canada. Returning to Britain, he became a school teacher, teaching in some of the toughest neighbourhoods in the London Borough of Brent, during which time he wrote his doctoral thesis on seventeenth-century political thought at the London School of Economics, under the supervision of conservative philosopher, Kenneth Minogue. He gained his first academic teaching post in the Department of Political Science at the National University of Singapore, where he met M.L.R. Smith, before moving first to the University of Tasmania and then to the University of Queensland in Australia. He was a Visiting Professor in the Department of War Studies at King's College London and at the University of Buckingham. Between 2022 and 2024 he was Director of Research at the Danube Institute in Budapest. He was the author of numerous books, academic articles and essays. His sole authored works include *Political Development in Pacific Asia* (1998), *Conscience and Allegiance in Seventeenth Century England* (1999), *The Image of China in Western Social and Political Thought* (2001) and *History's Fool's: The Pursuit of Idealism and the Revenge of Politics* (2020). He died in April 2024.

M.L.R. Smith was Professor of Strategic Theory at King's College London, working in the Department of War Studies between 1997 and 2023, and rose to become Head of the Department between 2016 and 2019. He was born in England but raised in Perth, Western Australia. He earned his BScEcon in International Politics and Strategic Studies from the University College of Wales, Aberystwyth in 1985 and went on to gain his MA in 1987 and PhD in 1991 from King's College, University of London. Beginning his career in the Department of History at the National University of Singapore, he went on to hold positions at the Royal Naval College, Greenwich, Nanyang Technological University, Singapore, and the Defence Studies Department, Joint Services Staff and Command College. He is author/co-author of many books, articles, essays and periodicals, including *Fighting for Ireland: The Military Strategy of the Irish Republican Movement* (1995), *Australian Foreign and Defence Policy at the Millennium* (2000), *ASEAN and East Asian International Relations* (2006); *The Strategy of Terrorism: How it Works and Why it Fails* (2007), *Asian Security and the Rise of China* (2013), *Sacred Violence: Political Religion in a Secular Age* (2014), *The Political Impossibility of Modern Counterinsurgency* (2015); *Terror in the Western Mind: Cultural Responses to 9/11* (2021) and *The Strategy of Maoism in the West: Rage and the Radical Left* (2022). He lives and works in Australia.

Proceeds from this volume will be donated to the Bad Law Project in memory of David Martin Jones. Should you wish to donate independently please use the following reference:
RECLAIM THE MEDIA LTD
Bank: Nat West, Sort Code: 51-61-35, Account number: 83072748
BIC: NWBKGB2L
IBAN: GB07NWBK51613583072748
Please use the subject heading: JONES BAD LAW PROJECT when you make the transfer. All funds in this account are ring-fenced and released on instruction from the Bad Law Project.

Index

7/7 bombings 88-90, 110, 167
9/11 attacks 11, 27, 29, 32, 42, 44, 52, 57, 63-64, 67, 71-72, 74, 76-78, 91-92, 103, 106, 110, 115-116, 148, 165-166, 173, 176, 182, 214, 227

Abergynolwyn United Nations Educational, Scientific and Cultural Organisation (UNESCO) world heritage site 251-253
Abu Bakr Naji 63-64, 66, 72, 106, 107
Abu Musab al Zarqawi 64, 66
Abu Musab al-Suri 63-64, 106, 110
Abu Sangkar in Johor 41
Abu Sayyaf 23-24, 29, 30, 41-42, 48, 50
Adams, John 212
Addison, Joseph 112-113
Adorno, Theodor 168, 211, 212
al Ghozi, Fathur Rahman 30, 34
Al Jazeera 196
Al-Assad, Bashar (Syrian president) 176
Al-Awlaki Anwar 64, 107, 110
Al-Bagdadi, Abu Bakr 101
Albert, Camus 169
Ali, Ayaan Hirsi 166
al-Kasasbeh, Lieutenant Moaz (Jordanian pilot) 62-63, 106
Alkass sports channel (Qatar) 19
Al-Ma'unah 24-25, 48
Al-Muhajiroun (The Migrants) 89, 92, 96, 104
al-Qaeda 11, 24, 27-33, 41, 45, 49, 51, 64, 65, 72, 81, 84, 92, 96, 99, 102-103, 105, 115
Alternative für Deutschland (AfD) 218
American Sniper 74, 165
Amnesty International 20
Amritsar Massacre (1919) 255
Anderson, John (philosopher) 82
Anderson, Scott 229-231
Angry Brigade 161
Annan, Kofi 55, 85
Apocalyptic millenarian Caliphism 63
APT (ASEAN Plus Three comprising China, South Korea and Japan) 35, 36
Árbenz, Jacobo (President of Guatamala) 229
Arendt, Hannah 97, 100-101, 150, 151, 159, 210, 212

ARF workshops 39
Aristotle 3, 100-101, 143, 153, 187
Arnold, Matthew 27
Arthur, George (colonial governor) 255
Article 50 (of the European Union) 125
ASEAN summit (27th) 38
Asian Infrastructure Investment Bank (AIIB) 127
Association of Southeast Asian Nations (ASEAN) 17, 22-43, 50, 77, 127, 140, 201, 204, 209
AUKUS - Australia, UK and US nuclear technology agreement 138-141, 236, 242
Aurelianus, Ambrosius 250
Ayman al-Zawahiri 65, 91, 103
Aziz, Abdul (Imam Samudra) 32

Baader-Meinhof Gang 161
Bacharuddin Jusuf Habibie (President of Indonesia) 20, 21, 25
Bacon, Francis 153
Bahrun Naim (coordinator of Islamic State in Southeast Asia) 41
Bali bombing 32, 34, 41-42, 44, 51
Barroso, Jorge Manuel 120
Barthes, Roland, 162
Bashir, Abu Bakr ('emir' of Jemmah Islamiyah) 29, 32-34, 41, 49, 51
Baudrillard, Jean 163
Begg, Moazzam (former Guantanamo internee) 115-116
Behavioural Science of Terrorism and Political Aggression (journal) 111
Belt and Road Initiative 127, 139, 200, 243
Benin expedition (1897) 255-257
Benjamin, Daniel 24
Benjamin, Walter 148
Benn, Tony 172, 246
Bennett, James C. (originator of the term Canzuk) 127
Bentham, Jeremy 108, 112
Bernstein, Leonard 161
Bew, Professor John (historian) 241
Biden, Joe (US President) 138, 140, 167, 177, 192, 193, 200, 208, 241
Bigelow, Kathryn (director of The Hurt Locker (2008) and Zero Dark Thirty (2012)) 165
Biggar, Nigel 254-256

Bilahari Kausikan (Singaporean senior foreign ministry official) 139
Bin Laden, Osama 7, 24, 27, 30, 47, 48, 65, 84-85, 94, 178
Bin Nurhasyim, Amrozi 32-34
Bindel, Julie 174-175
Bishop, Julie (Australian Foreign Minister) 38
Bismarck, Otto von 243
Black Lives Matter (BLM) 148, 159, 160-164, 243
Blackstone, Sir William 155
Blair, Tony 12, 27, 44, 53-54, 88, 95-96, 106, 168, 169, 178, 182, 213, 217, 233
Blinken, Tony 208, 243-244
Board, Douglas 129-131
Boghossian, Peter 175
Booker, Christopher 246
Booth, Ken 80-86
Boston Legal 87
Bourdieu, Pierre 162
Boyes, Roger 62, 106
Brand, Russell 172
Braverman, Suella 248
Brecht, Berthold 148
Brennan, John (former CIA director) 205
Brexlit 118, 129, 130-137
Bronte, Emily 136
Brown, H. Rap 161
Bruckner, Pascal 256
Brzezinski, Zbigniew 194
Bucharest Nine (Bulgaria, the Czech Republic, Estonia, Hungary, Latvia, Lithuania, Poland, Romania, and Slovakia) 192, 194
Burke, Anthony 80-86
Burke, Michael 228
Bush, George W. (US President), 15, 32, 35, 44, 52, 178, 182, 185, 205, 208, 214
Butterworth, Benjamin 258
Byers, Sam 129, 131-132, 135

Caldwell, Malcolm 88, 90, 94
Callaghan, James (UK Prime Minister) 246
Cameron, David (UK Prime Minister) 95-96, 119, 129, 133, 183
Camp Abubakar 30,32
Canadian plains famine (1879-83) 255
Canberra based Centre for International Economics 126
Carlyle, Thomas 136

Carter, Ashton (US Defense Secretary) 40, 127
Castle, Barbara 246
Ceaușescu, Nicolae 15
Central Committee of the Chinese Communist Party (CCP) 138-141, 190
Centre of Strategic and International Studies (CSIS) 50-51
Chamberlain, Joseph 128
Charles, Prince (later King 223
Charlie Hebdo magazine 106, 108, 133, 166, 168
Chartism 136
Chee Soon Juan 28
Cheng, Curtis 111
Chicago Principles' 154
Chomsky, Noam 175
Churchill, Sir Winston 120, 159
Cicero 153, 256
Cixous, Hélène 162
Clarke, Arthur C. 220, 223
Clarke, Michael 243
Clarke, Peter (former head of the counter-terrorism command at the Metropolitan Police) 59
Clausewitz, Carl von 52, 55, 60, 63, 64, 69
Cleaver, Eldridge 161
Clinton, Bill 22, 178, 182, 185, 205, 208
Coe, Jonathan 129, 131-132
COIN 56-61, 67-69
Colston, Edward 159-160, 239
Commonwealth, The 126-127, 141, 243-244, 256
Confucius Institutes 139
Conquest, Robert 13, 243
Cook, Joana 65
Cook, Peter 246
Cooper, Barry 83, 98
Cope, Abiezer (Ranter) 112
Copeland, Miles (CIA officer) 229
Counterinsurgency Field Manual (US Army and Marines) 56, 67
COVID-19 11, 138, 140, 162, 172-174, 213, 236, 234, 236, 243
Creasy, Stella 173
Crick, Bernard 100
Critical Studies on Terrorism (journal) 79, 87
Critical theory 77-78, 82-85, 87, 91, 103, 115-116, 148, 151, 162, 167-169
Cromer, Lord 255
Cultural Revolution (Chinese), 148-149, 160-164, 256
Cusk, Rachel 129-131, 135

Dabiq (Islamic State official journal) 101, 105, 116
Dahl, Robert, 210-211
Dalrymple, William 254
Dar-al-Islam (sphere of faith) 27
Darul Islam movement 41-42, 48, 71
Daulah Islamiyah Nusantara 30
Davies, Norman (historian) 142-143
Davis, Angela 161
Davis, David (UK Brexit minister) 128
Dawkins, Richard 150, 153
Day, Robin 245
Deleuze, Gilles 82, 168
Delors, Jacques 120
Deng Xiaoping 162
Derrida, Jacques 82, 162, 168
Deschamps, Didier 197
Diamond, Larry 210-211
DiAngelo, Robin (author of White Fragility (2018)) 163
Dickens, Charles 129, 136-137
Disraeli, Benjamin 243-244
Docherty, Professor Thomas 129
Douglass, William A. 80-81, 84
Draghi, Mario (Director of the European Central Bank) 214
Drakeford, Mark (Welsh first minister) 238
Dubus, Andre III (author of The Garden of Last Days (2008)) 165
Dugin, Alexander 190-191
Dulles, John Foster (US Secretary of State 229
Durkheim, Émile 113
Dusenbury, D.L 10, 13
Dutton, Peter (Australian Defence Minister) 140
Dwifungsi (dual function) 25

Eaglestone, Robert (professor of contemporary literature at the University of London) 129
East Anglia, University of (Climatic Research Unit) 150
Eastwood, Clint 165, 239
Eco, Umberto 63, 105-106, 197
Ed Husain (former member of Hizb-ut Tahrir) 96, 115
Embery, Paul 175
English Civil War (1642-49) 143, 160, 219
Equality Act (2010) 157
Erdoğan, Recep Tayyip (Turkish president) 183, 208
EU referendum, 117, 127

European Central Bank 214
Eye in the Sky (2015)) 74-76, 165, 168
Exclusive Economic Zones (EEZ) 38-39

Farr, Charles (UK's director of the Office for Security and Counterterrorism) 108
Fateha (The opening) group 28
Ferguson, Niall 142
Financial crisis (global downturn) of 2008 168, 213-215, 217, 219
Five Eyes intelligence nations (US, UK Australia, Canada, and New Zealand) 141
Flanagan, Richard (author The Unknown Terrorist (2006)) 165
Floyd, George 159, 162, 239
Foot, Michael 172, 246
Foot, Paul 246
Foucault, Michel 82, 148, 163, 168,
Frankfurt School 82, 115, 148, 161-162, 167, 211
Franklin, Benjamin 121
Frederick the Great 142, 183
Free Aceh Movement (Gerakanan Aceh Merdeka - GAM) 25
Free Papua Movement (Organisasi Papua Merdeka) 25
Freud, Sigmund 113
Front Pembela Islam (Islamic Defenders Front) 49
Frost, Lord David (chief Brexit negotiator) 237-238
Frost, Robert 121
Frydenberg, Josh (Australian Treasurer) 140
Fukuyama, Francis 11, 15, 177-178, 195

Gaddafi, Colonel Muammar 91, 102, 176, 178,
GAFA (Google, Amazon, Facebook and Apple) tetrarchy 215
Galloway, George 172, 175
Gardiner, Professor Michael 129
Gaskell, Elizabeth 136
Ghalib Robot Andang 24
Giddens, Anthony 182-183
Gildas Sapiens (Saint Gildas the Wise) 248-250
Gilets jaunes (yellow shirts) 217
Global Call for Inspire 64, 107
Global Call to Islamic Resistance 64, 106, 110
Global insurgency 56-60

Gomez, James 28
Goodhart, David (author of The Road to Somewhere) 2117-218
Graham, James (author of The Uncivil War) 129
Gramsci, Antonio 115
Green Zone (2010) 168
Greene, Graham 52, 255
Greenham Common 53
Greenwald, Glenn 172
Greer, Germaine 175
Guattari, Felix 82
Guelke, Adrian 80-81, 86
Guevara, Che 47, 58, 161
Gulf War (1990-1) 27, 200
Gurthrigern (Vortigern) 249

Habermas, Jürgen 84, 168
Hagel, Chuck (US Defence Secretary) 38, 40
Hamid, Mohsin (author of The Reluctant Fundamentalist) 165
Hamzah Haz 50
Harding, Warren 205
Harries, Owen 13, 245
Harris, John, 170-171
Harris, Kamala 209
Harvard University's Center for International Development 20
Hastings, Warren 254
Haushofer Karl 187-188, 190
Havel, Václav 158, 235
Havelock, Sir Henry (Brig Gen of Lucknow) 97
Healey, Denis 246
Heath, Edward 246
Hegel, G.W.F. 153
Heidegger, Martin 82
Hezbollah 46
Hicks, Dan (Oxford professor of contemporary archaeology and curator of the Pitt River Museum) 256
Hitchens, Christopher 153
Hitchens, Peter 233
Hizb-ut Tahrir (Party of Liberation) 49, 50, 71-72, 89, 96-98, 104, 111
Hobbes, Thomas 100, 143, 219
Hollande (French president) 182
Homeland (TV drama) 74, 82, 165, 168
Hoover, J. Edgar 227, 230
Horodlo, Act of (1413) 143
Horváth, Csaba Barnabás 193
Houellebecq, Michel (author of Submission) 168
House of Cards (TV drama) (2015) 74
Howard, John (Prime Minister of Australia) 36, 51, 178
Howe, Geoffrey 246
Hoyle, David (Very Reverend) 159
Huawei 139-140
Human Rights Watch 51
Hume, David 112
Huntington, Samuel (US political scientist) 3, 177, 195-197, 210-211, 248-250
Hussein, Saddam 15, 52-54, 102, 151-152, 176, 185

Ibrahim, Anwar 19, 22
Ikenberry, Professor John 208
Ilyin, Ivan (1883-1954) 123
Indonesia Raya (greater Indonesia) 30
Infantino, Gianni (FIFA president) 195-196
Infocus Computers 29
Ingrams, Richard 246
Integrated Review 138-139, 237, 241-242
International Affairs (Chatham House journal) 88-89
International Monetary Fund (IMF) 18-21, 35, 219
International Panel on Climate Change (IPCC) 150
Iraq War (2003) 52, 168, 173, 230
Irish famine (1846-49) 255
ISD Internal Security Department (Singapore) 10, 230
ISIS: Inside an Army of Terror by Michael Weiss and Hassan Hassan 64
Islamic Defender's Front 30
Islamic State of Iraq and the Levant (ISIL) 41-43, 62-65, 71-72, 106, 108, 109, 182-183
Islamophobia 61-62, 89, 165-168

Jabhar, Farhad 111
Jackson, Richard 79, 80-81, 90
Jahiliya (condition of pagan ignorance) 66, 71, 103, 160
Jaishankar, Dr Subrahmanyam (Indian minister of external affairs) 201
Jakarta bomb attack 32, 34, 41
Jemaah Islamiyah (Islamic Congregation) 28, 32-34, 41-42, 49, 50, 81

Johnson, Boris (UK Prime Minister) 62, 129, 133, 172, 193, 208, 236-238, 240-241
Johnson, Lyndon B 205
Jones, Ernest 'Oriental' 254
Jones, Sidney (International Crisis Group) 33
Jonson, Ben (author of Bartholomew Fair) 112
Joseph, Keith 246
Juncker, Jean-Claude (European Commission president) 124, 219
Jung Chang (author of Wild Swans) 164
Jung, Carl 220
Jus Europaeum Publicum (European Public Law) 188-189

Kant, Immanuel 170
Katibah Nusantara (Katibah Archipelago) 42
Keating, Paul (Australian premier) 27, 50
Keelty, Mick, (Australian federal police commissioner) 33
Keith, Toby (country and western singer) 166
Kendi, Ibram X. (author of How To Be An Antiracist), 163
Khalifa, Mohammad 29
khalifah [caliphate] system 98
Khrushchev, Nikita 229
Kilcullen, David 56, 58, 115
Kim Dae Jung (President of Korea) 21
Kim Il-Sung (North Korean leader) 185
Kim Jong-un (North Korean leader) 185
Kirbiantoro, Slamet (Major General) 25
Kissinger, Henry 115
Kjellén, Rudolf (Swedish geographer and political scientist) 187
KMM (Kumpulan Militan Malaysia) 29-30, 32
Kojève, Alexander 120
Komando Jihad (Jihad Commando) 29, 51
Kossuth, Lajos (Danube Confederation (1848) 192-193
Kristeva, Julia 162
Krugman, Paul 18-19
Kubrick, Stanley 222
Kulturkampf (cultural struggle) 148
Kumar, Nish 245

Kumpulan Mujahideen Malaysia 29, 32, 41, 50
Kuta bombing (2002) 49-50

Ladurie, Emmanuel Le Roy (historian) 255
Laing, Olivia 129-131, 135
Landsdale, Edward 228-229
Lao She (Chinese playwright) 161
Lasch, Christopher 113, 175
Laskar Jihad (Warriors of Jihad) 25, 30, 49, 51
Lawrence, T.E. 56
le Carré, John 52 165
Leaderless resistance 63-64, 106-107, 110
Lebedev Igor (deputy chairman of the Russian football federation and deputy chairman of the Duma) 122
Lee Hsien Loong (Prime Minister of Singapore) 38, 43
Lee Kuan Yew 16, 28, 30
Lega Nord 134, 218
Levitsky, Daniel 211
Liberal modernity 16
Lineker, Gary 245
Lingle, Christopher 10
Lipset, Seymour Martin 210-211
Lipsius, Justus (Dutch Humanist) 3, 179-180
Lisbon Treaty (2007) 143
Little Red Book, Mao's (1964) 160-161
Lloris, Hugo (French goalkeeper) 197
Locke, John 143
London rally of Islamist radicals (August 2002) 97
Lormel, Dennis (FBI section chief) 33
Lukács, György 148
Luxor tourist massacre (1997) 47
Lysenko, Trofim (Lysencoism) 151

Maastricht Treaty (1991) 120
MacArthur, General Douglas 184, 186
Machiavelli, Niccoló 3, 9, 52, 69, 101, 178-180, 187, 210
Mackay, Charles 125
Mackie, J.L. 82
Mackinder, Halford 187-188, 190
Mackinlay, John 56
Macquarie, Lachlan 255
Macron, Emmanuel (French President) 193, 197, 208, 242
Madrid train bombings 105-106

Mahan, Alfred Thayer (US naval strategist) 187
Mahbubani, Kishore 35
Maher, Dr Shiraz 94, 115
Maitlis, Emily 245
Majelis Mujahideen Indonesia (Islamist Mujahidin Council of Indonesia) (MMI), 25, 29, 49
Malaparte Curzio 191
Malayan Emergency 56, 58, 67
Man Haron Monis 63
Management of Savagery (Islamic State manual) 64-66, 72, 105, 107, 160
Mandate of Heaven 141, 147
Mantiqi (Jemmah Islamiya regional spheres of operation) 42
Mao Zedong 36, 47, 64, 148, 160, 185
Marcuse, Herbert 113, 161, 169
Markaz (Jemmah Islamiya governing council) 42
Markin, Vladimir 122
Marriott Hotel, Jakarta, 32, 34
Mason, Roy 246
Matolcsy, György (governor of the Central Bank of Hungary) 194
Mau Mau insurgency, Kenya (1952 and 1956) 67, 255
Maule, George (treasury solicitor to the attorney-general) 135
Maximillan II (1564-76) 182
May, Theresa 71, 118, 128, 237
McCarthy/McCarthyism 89, 230
McGwire, Michael 245
McMaster, HR (national security advisor 184
Mead, Walter Russell 199, 203
Megawati Sukarnoputri (president of Indonesia) 32
Meibion Glyndŵr (Sons of Glyndŵr) 81
Meier, Heinrich 189
Merkel, Angela 108, 135, 182-183, 205 208, 216
Messud, Claire (author of The Emperor's Children (2005)) 165
Milestones by Sayyid Qutb (1903-66) 71, 84
Mill, James 108, 112
Mill, John Stuart 108, 170-171
Millenarianism (Islamic and Christian) 24, 63, 92, 106, 112-114, 151-152, 160, 160
Mills, C. Wright 175
Minogue, Kenneth 100, 256
Mirren, Helen 74

Mischief Reef (Chinse occupation 1995) 39
mission civilisatrice (civilising mission) 176
Mohamad, Mahathir (Prime Minister of Malaysia) 16, 18-22, 27, 30, 35
Mohammad, Feiz 110
Molodoi, Alex 122
Monnet, Jean 120
Montesquieu, Charles Louis de Secondat 189, 212, 214
Moon Jae-In (South Korean president) 186
Moore, Sanna (curator of the Imperial War Museum's 2018 Art in the Age of Terror exhibition) 167
Moore, Suzanne 174
Moro Islamic Liberation Front (MILF) 24, 29, 30
Moro National Liberation Front (MNLF) 24, 30
Moussaoui, Zacarias (9/11 Pentagon bomber) 29, 32
Multiculturalism 45, 59, 73, 78, 88-90, 95-96, 111. 123, 152, 197, 218, 232, 250
Murad, Abdul Hakim 27
Mutko, Vitaly (Russian Sports Minister) 122

Nahdlatul Ulama (Revival of the Ulama by Abdurrhaman Wahid) 30
Napier, Sir Charles (Maj Gen, governor of Sindh and CinC India) 97
Napoleon (Bonaparte) 52, 249
NATO 56, 92, 95, 103, 119, 142, 181, 189, 192, 200-201, 208, 242-243
Nelson, Admiral Horatio 97
Net zero 238, 246
Neville, Garry 197
New Order (President Suharto's) 25, 29, 30, 41
New World Order 15-16, 44, 102, 189, 203, 227
Newton, Huey 161
Ngo Dinh Diem (premier of South Vietnam) 229
Nie Yuanzi (junior philosophy lecturer, Beijing University) 160
Nietzsche, Friedrich 113, 261
Nixon, Richard 2
Nizam al kufir 65, 107
North, Frederick Lord 254
Nurjuman Riduan (aka Hambali) 29, 32-33, 41

Nye, Joseph (Harvard University) 119, 208

O'Toole, Fintan 129
Oakeshott, Michael (philosopher) 144-145
Obama, Barack 62, 66, 85, 102, 108, 110, 119, 121, 121, 127, 130, 184, 186, 208-209 214, 259
On Contradiction (1937), Mao Zedong, 162-163
On Practice (1937) Mao Zedong, 162
Opium War (1842) 255
Orbán, Viktor (Prime Minister of Hungary) 192
Orwell, George 13, 108, 129, 135
Osborne, George (UK Chancellor) 125-6

Pacific Century 15-16, 18, 23, 25, 35, 44, 50, 77, 125
Palestine and the Palestinian conflict/peace process 47, 49, 58, 64, 72, 90, 96, 151, 196, 208
Palmerston, Lord 65, 243
Paris attacks (13th November 2015) 41, 62-63, 71-72, 106, 108-111, 115, 133, 182
Parris, Matthew 119
Parti Islam Se-Malaysia (PAS) 24, 30, 41
Pasulka, D.W. (author of American Cosmic: UFOs, Religion, Technology) 220-224
Pearson, Geoff 122
People's Action Party (PAP) 28
Perry, Grayson (artist) 166
Pesantren (Islamic religious schools) 42
Phillips, Melanie 150-153
Phillips, Thomas Jones (mayor of Newport) 135
Piłsudski, Józef (Intermarium) 193
Plaid Cymru 238, 251-252
PLAN (modernisation of the force projection capacity of the People's Liberation Army Navy) 39
Plato 92, 143, 153
Pol Pot 47, 88
Policy Exchange (UK think tank) 237
Pompeo, Mike (US secretary of state) 209
Pope, Alexander 112
Popovic, Aurel (United States of Greater Austria (1906)) 193
Popper, Karl 73, 163, 171

Powell, Anthony 135
Powell, Colin 135
Powell, Enoch 130
Powell, Jonathan, 106
Pozzo, Vittorio (manager of the Italian national football team) 123
Prakash, Neil (rapper, aka Abu Khalid al Cambodi) 110-111
Prevent (British counter-terrorism policy) 110-111
Proust, Marcel 226
Putin, Vladimir 120, 123-124, 142, 181-182 186-187, 189-193, 200, 242-243

Qing dynasty 37, 255
QUAD (Quadrilateral Security Dialogue) 139-140, 201
Quiet Americans: Michael Burke, Edward Landsdale, Peter Sichel and Frank Wisner (as featured by Scott Anderson in his book of the same name) 226-231
Qutb, Sayeed 42, 49, 71-72, 84, 98, 113, 151, 153

Raffles, Sir Stamford 255
Rahmat Hassan 49
Rais, Amien - speaker in the People's Consultative Assembly (Majelis Permusyawaratan Rakyat) and leader of Muhammadiyah 25, 50
RAND-St Andrews chronology of International Terrorism 46
Rassemblement National 218
Raznotovic, Zeljko (aka Arkan) 123
Real Irish Republican Army 46
Recession 18-21, 125, 136, 211, 214, 237, 245
Red Robbo 247
Redacted (2007) 74, 169
Rees, Merlyn 246
Rees-Mogg, Jacob 130
Regional Comprehensive Economic Partnership (RCEP) 127
Regis Debray 47
Renzi, Matteo (Italian president) 124
Ria Novosztyi (Russian information agency) 193
Riduan Isamuddin 41
Rorty, Richard 175
Roswell (New Mexico) 221
Rousseau, Jean Jacques 170
Rowling, J.K. 175
Roy, Olivier 24
Rushton, Willie 246

Said, Edward 151, 254, 256
Salaf al saleh 71
Sandall, Roger (author of The Culture Cult: Designer Tribalism and Other Essays) 260
Sarkozy, Nikolas 124
Saya Teroris? Sebuah Pleidoi (Am I a Terrorist? A Plea) by Fauzan al-Anshari 49
Schengen Agreement (1985) 120
Schmitt, Carl (reich jurist) 188-191
Scholz, Olaf (German Chancellor) 242
Schönbach, Vice-Admiral Kay-Achim 242
Schumpeter, Joseph 210
Seale, Bobby 161
Second Boer War (1899-1902) 255
Segal, Gerry 37
Shanghai Cooperation Organisation (SCO) 139, 201
Shinawatra, Thaksin (prime minister of Thailand 33
Shinzo Abe 40
Shore, Peter 246
Short, Clare (international development secretary) 52
Shultz, George 46
Sichel, Peter 228
Shorter Oxford Dictionary 81
Silat (martial art) 48
Siliconians (tech company founders of Silicon Valley) 215
Simon, Steven 24
Sipadan and Jol (islands) 23
Slave trade, Atlantic 159-160, 239, 251, 254, 256
Smith, 'Jim' 222-225
Smith, Adam 3, 121
Smith, Ali (author of Autumn) 129
Sogoshosha 21
Sollers, Philippe 162
Soros, George 18, 121
Southgate, Gareth 197
Spence, Jonathan (author of The Search for Modern China) 161
Spengler, Oswald 142, 210
Spratly Islands, 36, 38-40, 140 38
Spykman, Nicholas J. 188
St Paul (Second Letter to the Thessalonians) 189
Stages theory - of revolution 64
State University of Islamic Studies 50
Stewart, Rory 69
Stock, Kathleen 175

Stohl, Michael 80-81, 86
Stonebridge, Professor Lyndsey 129, 133
Strauss, Leo 84, 97, 99-100
Studies in Conflict and Terrorism (journal) 79, 81
Sturgeon, Nicola (Scottish First Minister) 238
Sub-prime crisis, US (2008–2010) 213-214
Sufaat, Yazid 29
Suharto, President of Indonesia 18, 25, 29, 49
Sukarno, President of Indonesia 30
Sunak, Rishi (UK Prime Minister) 197
Swift, Jonathan 112, 236
Syriana (2005) 74, 168

TAC - Treaty of Amity and Cooperation (ASEAN) 31, 36
Taiwan 19, 37-38, 138, 140, 200,202, 228, 243-244
Talbott, Strobe (US Deputy Secretary of State) 119
Talleyrand, Charles Maurice de 209
Taqiuddin al-Nabhani (founder of Hizb-ut Tahrir in 1952) 71, 98
Team America: World Police (2004) 74
Tel Quel, 162
Tenet, George 32
Thatcher, Margaret 134, 172, 246
Third generation jihadism 63-64, 72, 106
Threat-based versus risk-based intelligence 53
Three Seas initiative 193
Thucydides 3, 243
Tocqueville, Alexis de 210
Tooze, Adam 214
Trans-Atlantic Trade and Investment Partnership 127
Trans-Pacific Partnership (CPTPP) 127, 209, 236, 241, 244
Treaty of Amity and Cooperation (1976) 31, 36
Truman Doctrine, 185
Truman, Harry 184, 186
Trump, Donald (US President) 131, 142, 167, 176-177, 184-186, 193, 202, 205-206, 208-209, 217-218, 230, 258-259
Truss, Liz 237, 242-243
Tugendhat, Tom (UK MP) 242
Turnbull, Malcolm (Australian Prime Minister) 71, 111

Twain, Mark, 183, 250

UFOlogy 206, 220-221
UMNO (United Malays National Organisation) 20, 30, 41-42
United 93 (2006)74, 165
United Malay National Organisation (UMNO) 20, 30, 41-42
United Nations (UN) 93, 150, 160, 178-179, 183-184, 204, 208
UNESCO (United Nations Educational, Scientific and Cultural Organisation),
Updike, John (author of The Terrorist) 165
US-Japan Mutual Defence Treaty (1952) 185

Vaccination, COVID-19 171-172, 236
van Gogh, Theo 166
Versailles, Treaty of 188
Violent peace 97
Voegelin, Eric 83, 97-99, 101

Walden, Brian 245
Wallace, Ben (UK Defence Secretary) 193
Wang Yi (Chinese foreign minister) 40
Waugh, Evelyn 135
Weber, Max 75, 101, 113
Weiner, Myron (author of The Global Migration Crisis) 248
Whitlam, Gough (Australian Prime Minister) 204
Wight, Martin 183
Williams, Joanna (author of How Woke Won) 257, 259
Wilson, Harold (UK Prime Minister) 246
Wilson, Woodrow (US President) 83, 188, 208
WingTech (electronics company) 139
Wirayuda, Hasan (Indonesian foreign minister) 33
Wisner, Frank 228
Wolfe, Tom 113, 161,
Wootton, Dan 258
World Bank 19, 27
World Health Organisation (WHO) 209
World Trade Center 27, 41, 44, 47, 49
World Trade Organisation (WTO) 17, 140, 209, 219

Xia dynasty 39
Xi Jinping 39, 138-140, 182, 201, 209
Yang Jiechi (Chinese diplomat) 167, 169

Yassir Morsi 63
Yes-Minister (speak) 53
Young, Baroness, of Hornsey 129
Yousef, Ramzi 27

Zelenskyy, Volodymyr (President of Ukraine) 192, 196
Zemmour, Éric 218
Zero Dark Thirty (2012)
Zhou Enlai (premier PRC) 36
Ziblatt, Steven 211
Zulaika, Joseba 80-81, 84
Zulfikar Mohamad (Fateha leader) 28
Zweig, Stefan (novelist) 144-145

THE BRUGES GROUP

The Bruges Group is an independent all-party think tank. Set up in 1989, its founding purpose was to resist the encroachments of the European Union on our democratic self-government. The Bruges Group spearheaded the intellectual battle to win a vote to leave the European Union and against the emergence of a centralised EU state. With personal freedom at its core, its formation was inspired by the speech of Margaret Thatcher in Bruges in September 1988 where the Prime Minister stated, "We have not successfully rolled back the frontiers of the State in Britain only to see them re-imposed at a European level."

We now face a more insidious and profound challenge to our liberties – the rising tide of intolerance. The Bruges Group challenges false and damaging orthodoxies that suppress debate and incite enmity. It will continue to direct Britain's role in the world, act as a voice for the Union, and promote our historic liberty, democracy, transparency, and rights. It spearheads the resistance to attacks on free speech and provides a voice for those who value our freedoms and way of life.

WHO WE ARE

Founder President:
The Rt Hon. The Baroness Thatcher of Kesteven LG, OM, FRS

Chairman:
Barry Legg

Director:
Robert Oulds MA, FRSA

Washington D.C. Representative:
John O'Sullivan CBE

Founder Chairman:
Lord Harris of High Cross

Former Chairmen:
Dr Brian Hindley, Dr Martin Holmes & Professor Kenneth Minogue

Academic Advisory Council:
Professor Tim Congdon
Dr Richard Howarth
Professor Patrick Minford
Andrew Roberts
Martin Howe, KC
John O'Sullivan, CBE

Sponsors and Patrons:
E P Gardner Dryden
Gilling-Smith
Lord Kalms
David Caldow
Andrew Cook
Lord Howard
Brian Kingham
Lord Pearson of Rannoch
Eddie Addison
Ian Butler
Thomas Griffin
Lord Young of Graffham
Michael Fisher
Oliver Marriott
Hon. Sir Rocco Forte
Michael Freeman
Richard E.L. Smith

MEETINGS

The Bruges Group holds regular high-profile public meetings, seminars, debates, and conferences. These enable influential speakers to contribute to the European debate. Speakers are selected purely by the contribution they can make to enhance the debate.

For further information about the Bruges Group, to attend our meetings, or join and receive our publications, please see the membership form at the end of this paper. Alternatively, you can visit our website www.brugesgroup.com or contact us at info@brugesgroup.com.

Contact us
For more information about the Bruges Group please contact:
Robert Oulds, Director
The Bruges Group, 246 Linen Hall, 162-168 Regent Street, London W1B 5TB
Tel: +44 (0)20 7287 4414 Email: info@brugesgroup.com

www.brugesgroup.com

www.ingramcontent.com/pod-product-compliance
Lightning Source LLC
Chambersburg PA
CBHW031144020426
42333CB00013B/507